THE COURTROOM AS A SPACE OF RESISTANCE

This timely and powerful volume presents the court not as a neutral instrument of justice but as a site of contestation and critique, where the normative and performative clash, and where discourses of domination encounter practices of resistance. The chapters are challenging in the best sense of the word – they contest accepted views and interrogate received orthodoxies.

Lawrence Douglas, Amherst College, USA

A welcome collection of intelligently crafted and often inspirational analyses that look back to the Rivonia Trial, a legendary and dramatic event in the struggle against Apartheid. At its heart, of course, is the bold and gracious figure of Nelson Mandela, the accused, engaging the rapt court with his momentous speech: a supreme act of resistance, articulated through the sincere admiration of Law, which served to expose the absurdities and betrayals of apartheid's perversion of Justice. The contributors explore the trial from their many complementary perspectives, showing how Mandela's vision for what seemed then like an impossible post-apartheid South Africa was a gift to which, still, we cannot stop giving time.

Vikki Bell, Goldsmiths College, University of London, UK

The Edinburgh/Glasgow Law and Society Series

Series Editors: Professor Emilios A. Christodoulidis and Dr Sharon Cowan

Titles in the Series

Polity and Crisis
Reflections on the European Odyssey
Edited by Massimo Fichera, Sakari Hänninen and Kaarlo Tuori

The Anxiety of the Jurist
Legality, Exchange and Judgement
Edited by Maksymilian Del Mar and Claudio Michelon

'Integration through Law' Revisited
The Making of the European Polity
Edited by Daniel Augenstein

The Public in Law
Representations of the Political in Legal Discourse
Edited by Claudio Michelon, Gregor Clunie,
Christopher McCorkindale and Haris Psarras

The Many Constitutions of Europe
Edited by Kaarlo Tuori and Suvi Sankari

Law as Institutional Normative Order
Edited by Maksymilian Del Mar and Zenon Bańkowski

Law and Agonistic Politics
Edited by Andrew Schaap

Public Law and Politics
The Scope and Limits of Constitutionalism
Edited by Emilios Christodoulidis and Stephen Tierney

Transformations of Policing
Edited by Alistair Henry and David J. Smith

The Universal and the Particular in Legal Reasoning
Edited by Zenon Bańkowski and James MacLean

The Courtroom as a Space of Resistance

Reflections on the Legacy of the Rivonia Trial

Edited by

AWOL ALLO
London School of Economics and Political Science, UK

Routledge
Taylor & Francis Group

LONDON AND NEW YORK

First published 2015 by Ashgate Publishing

2 Park Square, Milton Park, Abingdon, Oxon OX14 4RN
711 Third Avenue, New York, NY 10017, USA

Routledge is an imprint of the Taylor & Francis Group, an informa business

First issued in paperback 2017

British Library Cataloguing in Publication Data
A catalogue record for this book is available from the British Library

The Library of Congress has cataloged the printed edition as follows:
The courtroom as a space of resistance : reflections on the legacy of the Rivonia trial / by Awol Allo.
    pages cm. -- (Edinburgh/Glasgow law and society series)
 Includes bibliographical references and index.
 ISBN 978-1-4724-4460-8 (hardback)
1. Rivonia Trial, Pretoria, South Africa, 1964--Social aspects. 2. Trials (Political crimes and offenses)--South Africa--Social aspects. 3. Mandela, Nelson, 1918-2013--Influence. 4. Apartheid--South Africa 5. South Africa--Social conditions--1961-1994. I. Allo, Awol Kassim, author.
 KTL42.R58C68 2015
 345.68'0231--dc23

2015000870

ISBN 978-1-4724-4460-8 (hbk)
ISBN 978-1-138-29596-4 (pbk)

Contents

Notes on Contributors

Catherine Albertyn is Professor of Law at the University of the Witwatersrand, Johannesburg, where she teaches undergraduate and postgraduate courses on Constitutional Law and Human Rights. Prior to joining the Wits School of Law, she was the Director of the Centre for Applied Legal Studies (2001–7) and headed its Gender Research Programme for 10 years (1992–2001). Cathi has a BA, LLB from the University of Cape Town and an MPhil, PhD from Cambridge University, where she wrote a thesis on South African political trials. She is an attorney of the High Court of South Africa (non-practising roll). Cathi's research interests include equality, gender studies, human rights and constitutional law. She has published extensively on equality and gender, most recently a chapter on 'Judicial Diversity' in C. Hoexter and M. Olivier, *The South African Judiciary* (2014). Cathi is an editor of the *South African Journal on Human Rights*, and was a Commissioner at the South African Law Reform Commission from 2007 to 2011.

Awol Allo is Fellow at the Centre for the Study of Human Rights, the London School of Economics and Political Science. Prior to joining LSE, Allo held the position of senior lecturer in law at St Mary's University College, Ethiopia; and was the Lord Kelvin/Adam Smith Scholar at the University of Glasgow, UK. His research interest is in the areas of critical legal theory, law and performativity, and the sociology of human rights.

Jaco Barnard-Naudé is Professor of Private Law at the University of Cape Town (UCT). He is a recipient of the UCT Fellows' Award and a National Research Foundation rated researcher. His research interests include post-structural legal theory, queer legal theory, law and literature and post-apartheid jurisprudence. He has spent time on research fellowships at the Max Planck Institute for Private International Law in Hamburg and as Honorary Research Fellow at the Birkbeck Institute for the Humanities, University of London. He is a director at the Institute for Justice and Reconciliation and at Triangle Project in Cape Town.

Catherine M. Cole is Professor and Chair of Theater, Dance and Performance Studies at the University of California, Berkeley. She is the author of *Performing South Africa's Truth Commission: Stages of Transition* (2010) and *Ghana's Concert Party Theatre* (2001). She served as editor of *Theatre Survey*, and co-edited the book *Africa After Gender?* (2007), a special issue of *Theatre Survey* on African and Afro-Caribbean Performance, and a special issue of *TDR: The Drama Review* entitled 'Routes of Blackface'. Her dance theatre piece *Five Foot*

Feat, created in collaboration with Christopher Pilafian, toured North America in 2002–5. Cole has published articles in *Africa, Critical Inquiry, Disability Studies Quarterly, International Journal of Transitional Justice, Research in African Literatures, Theatre, Theatre Journal* and *TDR*, as well as numerous chapters in edited volumes.

Chloé S. Georas is an associate professor at the University of Puerto Rico Law School where she combines her formation in law (JD from New York University Law School and LLM from University of Ottawa) and cultural studies/art history (MA up to ABD from State University of New York, Binghamton) to examine the complex intersections of technology with gender, colonial/racial histories, cultural memory and art. In her creative endeavours, she combines her multi-lingual literary writings with visual works. She has published and presented her creative work in Puerto Rico and abroad. She is the author of the book *rediviva: lost in trance. lations* (Editorial Isla Negra, 2006; Libros Nómadas, 2001), which was distinguished by the Puerto Rico Pen Club.

Derek Hook is an associate professor of psychology at Duquesne University, an occasional lecturer at the London School of Economics, and an extraordinary professor in psychology at the University of Pretoria. He is the author of *Biko: Voice of Liberation* (2014), *Post-Apartheid Conditions* (2013) and *A Critical Psychology of the Postcolonial* (2011). He is also a psychoanalytic practitioner.

Ted Laros studied Dutch and comparative literature in Utrecht (Netherlands), Los Angeles and Oldenburg (Germany). From 2010 to mid 2014 he worked as a research associate and lecturer at the Department of Dutch Studies of the University of Oldenburg. In August 2014 he took up an assistant professorship in modern Dutch literature at the Radboud University Nijmegen (Netherlands).

Peter Leman is an assistant professor of English at Brigham Young University. His research and teaching areas include Anglophone African literature, contemporary British and Irish literature, literature and human rights, and law and literature. Peter's scholarly work has appeared in *Research in African Literatures, Law and Literature, Interventions: International Journal of Postcolonial Studies* and *ARIEL: A Review of International English Literature*. He is currently completing a book titled *Vocal Jurisprudence: Literature, Law, and Oral Cultures in Eastern Africa*, which examines works of colonial and postcolonial literature in Eastern Africa in the context of both colonial legal history and African oral law.

Joel M. Modiri is a lecturer in the School of Law at the University of the Witwatersrand. He teaches courses in criminal law, research methodology, and jurisprudence. His research broadly explores the relation between law, justice and politicised identity and he is currently engaged in a study on the jurisprudential thought of Steve Biko. He has published extensively on themes relating to critical race theory, black and post-structural feminism, African philosophy and critical legal pedagogy.

Alison Phipps is Professor of Languages and Intercultural Studies at the University of Glasgow where she is also co-convener of Glasgow Refugee, Asylum and Migration Network (GRAMNet).

Kanika Sharma is a PhD candidate and sessional lecturer at the School of Law, Birkbeck College, University of London. Using theories of psychoanalytic jurisprudence she analyses images and trials to understand how the legal subject is created in India.

Mia Swart coordinates and teaches the LLM programme in international law at the University of Johannesburg. She obtained an LLM from Humboldt University in 1999. She previously worked as Research Fellow at the Bingham Centre for the Rule of Law in London and as assistant professor of Public International law and Global Justice at Leiden University, from which she earned her PhD in 2006. She also holds the title of Honorary Associate Professor at the University of the Witwatersrand in Johannesburg, where she previously worked as Associate Professor. Published in the areas of transitional justice, international criminal law, and comparative constitutional law, Mia currently focuses her research on reparations in international criminal law.

Isolde de Villiers grew up in the economic capital of South Africa, completed her LLB in the administrative capital, struggled through articles of clerkship in the legislative capital and returned to the city of Church Square and the Union Buildings to take up a lecturer position in the department of jurisprudence at the University of Pretoria. She is currently busy with her LLD on law and spatiality, with specific reference to the Tshwane urban space.

Johan van der Walt is Professor of Philosophy of Law at the University of Luxembourg since 2011 and Professor Extraordinarius of the University of Pretoria. Before moving to Luxembourg he held chairs in law and legal theory at the University of Glasgow (2007–11) and the University of Johannesburg (1997–2006).

Acknowledgements

The idea for the book grew out of my doctoral project and a conversation with participants of the 2012 Brown International Advanced Research Institute (BIARI). That conversation paved the way for a collaborative conference I co-organized with Professor Emilios Christodoulidis and Professor Karin van Marle at Pretoria University, Pretoria, South Africa, from 18–19 June 2013. These occasions provided a collegial space for a productive intellectual exchange and I am extremely indebted to all those who made both occasions possible. I owe a special debt of gratitude to Brown University's BIARI Alum Seed Grant scheme, Glasgow University's Kelvin Smith Scholarship scheme, and Pretoria University for their financial support. My heartfelt thanks to all the authors who contributed to the volume for their great patience and enthusiasm throughout the project.

I am specifically grateful to Professor Emilios Christodoulidis and Alison Phipps for the excellent guidance and mentorship they provided throughout my PhD and during this project. I would like to extend my deepest thanks to Professor Karin van Marle for her unwavering support of the project, and to Hilary Stauffer for her insightful comment and critique of the introduction. Aimée Feenan, Senior Editor at Ashgate, did as much as anyone to see the manuscript to completion. I thank her for her patience and understanding during the birth of my wonderful daughter, the wee Amal Awol. Finally, I would like to thank my wife, Munira Husen, for her selfless and exemplary generosity.

Chapter 1

The Courtroom as a Space of Resistance: Reflections on the Legacy of the Rivonia Trial

Awol Allo

Introduction

I have lain in the soil and criticized the worm.[1]

Just as none of us are beyond geography, none of us is completely free from the struggle over geography. That struggle is complex and interesting because it is not only about soldiers and cannons but also about ideas, about forms, about images and imaginings.[2]

I was the symbol of justice in the court of the oppressor, the representative of the great ideals of freedom, fairness and democracy in a society that dishonoured those virtues. I realized then and there that I could carry on the fight even within the fortress of the enemy ... I would use my trial as a showcase for the ANC's moral opposition to racism. I would not attempt to defend myself so much as put the state itself on trial.[3]

On 11 July 1963, South African police raided Liliesleaf Farm in Rivonia, Johannesburg, and arrested seven core members of the African National Congress (ANC), in what was to become 'the most celebrated arrests in South African history'. The arrest attracted extensive media coverage and begat explosive and triumphant headlines. The jubilant spokesmen of the government described the arrest as 'a major breakthrough in the elimination of subversive organizations' and promised the end of all subversive activities. The state presented its zealous crusade against the liberation struggle as a battle against subversive forces and raised the spectre of communism over and over again to submerge and subjugate the audibility and visibility of the accused. After 90 days of detention without

---

1 T.S. Eliot, *Murder in the Cathedral* (London: Faber & Faber, 1935), 65.
2 Edward Said, *Culture and Imperialism* (London: Vintage, 1993), 7.
3 Nelson Mandela, *Long Walk to Freedom* (London: Little, Brown & Company, 1994), 317.

charges, the accused were charged with sabotage and conspiracy, enabling the judicial apparatus to sit in judgment over one of the most insoluble conflicts between mankind and its laws.

Over the next year, South Africa staged one of the most destabilizing and gripping trials of the twentieth century and one that will define the contours of South African history. On 12 June 1964, Justice Quartus de Wet handed down the most anticipated verdicts of his career, sentencing Nelson Mandela and seven other leading members of the ANC to life imprisonment. But the verdict of history was radically at odds with the verdict of the court. In the verdict of history, the accused were freedom fighters, and the trial, a trial of conscience. Instead of ushering in a society cleansed of subversive elements, Rivonia become a constitutive historical event that catapulted South Africa's struggle for freedom and justice onto the international stage, redefining and reinvigorating subversive activities. The trial assumed a symbolic meaning and value far greater than that imagined by the ANC and acquired a life of its own; becoming a cultural artefact of global renown. It became the crucible and the fulcrum for the liberation struggle, an expression of conscience that provided its values, sense of identity and mission, and supplied the energy and passion that eventually led to the disintegration of Apartheid. Whatever the setback represented by the life sentence in the short term, it is here, in this trial, that the anti-Apartheid movement developed the myth of the struggle and planted the seed of the post-Apartheid society.

Mandela used the law as a sword and shield. In his encounters with Apartheid's courts, we witness a strategic engagement with law and an unrelenting confrontation with the state. As a man before the law, he appropriates his speaking position as a defendant to filter stories of oppression and indignation into the court of public opinion; stories capable of reworking and destabilizing sovereignty's myths of oppression. In re-telling these stories in which law often legitimizes and stabilizes itself, Mandela spatializes the moment of origin to reinterpret it; to move within, beyond and in-between existing geographies; to go beyond stories of law and right and to get behind the discourse of right; and slip into its interstices to re-signify its discourses and symbols from within.

Mandela re-territorializes the space of the trial to return to fundamental questions of foundation and inaugural dispossession. Using the very spaces and speaking positions made available by the system, he returns to the moment of origin to re-politicize the trial and expand the horizon of the legally permissible and imaginable. Mandela used his knowledge of the law to reveal the agonizing contradictions at the heart of Apartheid's order of representation. By re-setting the margins of what could be thought, said and done, by causing fissure in the system's order of representation, his appeal exposed the juridical conditions which made Apartheid possible – law's self-reference, its normative closures and epistemic violence.

The Rivonia story was a tale of foundations and of aporetic dispossession. It was a trial that disclosed the insufferable indignation of black people to the world and the role of law and legal institutions in preserving, legitimizing and consolidating a racist and oppressive state. Fifty years on, the places on the map of the Rivonia Trial have become sites in history while the accused become prominent figures that changed the course of history. Liliesleaf Farm, where the accused were arrested, is now one of 'South Africa's foremost, award winning heritage sites, where the journey to democracy in South Africa is honored'. Robben Island, where Nelson Mandela and other political prisoners were held, is now a national monument and a UNESCO World Heritage site remembered as 'a symbol of the triumph of the human spirit over adversity'. Rivonia's Accused No. 1, the late Nelson Mandela, is widely regarded as 'the single most vital symbol not only of liberation from the tyranny of Apartheid, but of a new way of life in South Africa'.[4] The name 'Mandela' has ceased to function as a mere name and become a pure symbol that represent ideas of freedom, justice, hope, reconciliation and resistance. As Derek Hook's contribution to this volume demonstrates, the Mandela brand represents 'an emblem of integrity' and 'a touchstone of moral capital'. In Hook's terms, Mandela is a 'master signifier' that 'makes a type of subjectivity' and 'a version of society' possible. In short, Rivonia entered the historical record and the global public consciousness as a map of resistance, spatializing South African identity and history.

The Spatiality of Resistance

Resistance, whatever its form, genre, strategy and end, is a counter-conduct against modalities of power that constitute and regulate the subject. Resistance may orient itself towards constitutive norms and discourses that colonize the inner psychic space of the subject or may be directed against regulative conditions that define, categorize, and govern the subject. In both instances, resistance is counter-conduct that *takes place* on or *through* specific geographies: in the mind, in public squares, on streets, before parliaments, palaces, army bases, embassies, inside courts, parks, prisons and on cyberspace. Whatever the specific nature of the action – a march, a sit-in, strike, graffiti, hunger strike or other visible or invisible expressions or gestures of struggle – resistance always involves spatialities of location and discourse. It always *takes place* and involves the spatialization of discourse and action.

Regardless of where it takes place, within the fortress of sovereignty or away from its centres of gravity, resistance is a profoundly spatial undertaking whose condition of possibility, significance and meaning cannot be adequately explained in isolation from the place in which it *takes place*. As Michel Foucault pointed out, 'It is somewhat arbitrary to try to dissociate the effective practice of freedom by people, the practice of social relations, and the spatial distributions in which they

---

4   Nelson Mandela, *The Struggle is My Life* (London: Pathfinder Press, 1990), 13.

find themselves. If they are separated, they become impossible to understand.'[5] While space makes resistance possible, resistance in turn defines space as space of resistance. From Beijing's Tiananmen Square to Tehran's Azadi Square; from Santiago's Alameda to Athens's Syntagma; from Madrid's Plaza del Sol to New York's Zuccotti Park; from Kiev's Independence Square to Cairo's Tahrir or Istanbul's Gezi, we observe the mutually-constitutive relations between space and acts and gestures of resistance. Space prefigures acts of resistance and informs their meaning and significance.

To speak of geographies of resistance suggests that resistance has its own distinct spatialities. However, resistance cannot be fully uncoupled from domination and does not have an independent and autonomous spatiality of its own. Resistance often occupies and deploys spatialities defined and made available by the very power and discourse it resists. This entanglement of geographies of domination and resistances raises several questions: how does resistance take up its space? If space is the ground that defines the nature, meaning and significance of acts and gestures of resistance, how do subjects of resistance distinguish between spaces of resistance and domination? And finally, what is the generative potential of the spatial paradigm for thinking, speaking and performing acts of resistance in the courtroom? To address these questions and provide an overall conceptual framework for the volume, let me offer a brief summary of contemporary conceptions of space and the spatial paradigm.

The emergence of space and the spatial paradigm as a mode of intellectual enquiry is largely due to the rise of structuralism in the French academy in the 1960s. As Edward Soja observed, structuralism is 'one of the twentieth century's most important avenues for the reassertion of space in critical social theory'.[6] Dismissing the nineteenth-century obsession with time and history, Michel Foucault mockingly wrote, 'Space was treated as the dead, the fixed, the undialectical, the immobile. Time, on the contrary, was richness, fecundity, life, dialectic'.[7] In his influential lecture on heterotopias, Foucault claimed that the twentieth century is an epoch of space: 'we are at a moment, I believe, when our experience of the world is less that of a long life developing through time than that of a network that connects points and intersects with its own skein'.[8] Confirming this reversal,

---

5　Michel Foucault, 'Space, Knowledge, and Power', in Paul Rabinow (ed.) *The Foucault Reader* (New York: Pantheon, 1984), 246.

6　Edward W. Soja, *Postmodern Geographies: The Reassertion of Space in Critical Social Theory* (New York: Verso, 1989), 18.

7　Colin Gordon (ed.) *Michel Foucault, Power/Knowledge: Selected Interviews and Other Writings, 1972–1977* (London: Longman, 1980), 70.

8　Michel Foucault, 'Of Other Spaces: Utopias and Hetrotopias', *Diacritics* 16(1) (1986), 22. In this piece, speaking about 'the ideological conflicts' between 'the pious descendants of time and the determined inhabitants of space', Foucault says, 'Writing, over centuries, [t]he great obsession of the nineteenth century was, as we know, history: with its themes of development and of suspension, of crisis, and cycle, themes of the ever – accumulating past, with its great preponderance of dead men and the menacing glaciation

Francois Dosse writes, '[a] planetary, topographic consciousness has repressed a historical consciousness. Temporality has toppled over into spatiality'.[9] In his recent work, *Space in Theory*, Russel West-Pavlov describes this transition as 'one of the fundamental paradigm shifts of modern thought'.[10] By the 1970s, the erstwhile epistemological hegemony of temporality and the totalizing continuity of historical analysis have been largely reversed.

Foucault's work is an excellent point of departure for thinking about geographies of resistance and domination not only because he alerts us to the constitutive entanglement between domination and resistance but also because he provides profound insights into the constitutive and regulative effects of struggle on sovereignty, the subject, and the political. From his enquiry into the spatiality of language to the spatialization of discourse; from his excavation of the historical transformations of modern techniques of power to his investigation of technologies of the self; Foucault offers a particularly instructive spatial paradigm for thinking, writing and performing acts of resistance. This is evident not only in the proliferation of spatial ontologies and metaphors throughout his work but also in his explicit intimations to the spatial dimensions of power and the spatial distribution of knowledge.

Drawing on Bachelard's spatial paradigms, Foucault distinguishes between the exterior space and the interior space, suggesting that the exterior space, the 'space that gnaws and claws at us', is a heterogeneous space that partakes in the configuration and re-configuration of sovereignty, the subject and the political.[11] As he writes, '[W]e do not live inside a void that could be colored with diverse shades of light, we live inside a set of relations that delineates sites which are irreducible to one another and absolutely not superimposable on one another'.[12] Perhaps the most important spatial insight that emerges from Foucault's thought is his formulation of the domain of the episteme (later called 'discursive space') and its three dimensions – the 'epistemological trihedron'.[13] In *The Order of Things*, Foucault identifies the three dimensions as a domain constituted of: (1) the conditions of possibility of discourses; (2) discursive systematicity; and (3) epistemic rupture.[14] These three notions provide useful conceptual instruments

---

of the world ... The present epoch will perhaps be above all the epoch of space. We are in the epoch of simultaneity: we are in the epoch of juxtaposition, the epoch of near and far, of the side-by-side, of the dispersed'.

9   Francois Dosse, *History of Structuralism: The Rising Sign 1945 1966*, translated by Deborah Glassman (Minneapolis: University of Minnesota Press, 1998), 413.

10   Russel West-Pavlov, *Space in Theory: Kristeva, Foucault, Deleuze* (Amsterdam: Rodopi, 2009), 22.

11   Foucault, 'Of Other Spaces', 23.

12   Ibid.

13   Michel Foucault, *The Order of Things: An Archaeology of the Human Sciences* (New York: Random House, 1970), 347.

14   Foucault, *The Order of Things*, xxiii. See also West-Pavlov, *Space in Theory*, 27, 129–34.

of analysis and reflection for political intervention and action. It is precisely for this reason that in his review of *Discipline and Punish*, Deleuze refers to Foucault as the 'new cartographer' and Foucault's notion of power as 'Foucault's diagram'.[15]

Jacques Derrida's deconstruction is another crucial conceptual device for understanding the significance of space and spatial analysis for resistance. Derrida uses the neologism 'espacement' ['spacing'] to deconstruct the traditional literary assumption that the relationship between space and writing, like that between writing and thought, is secondary, neutral and invisible.[16] Derrida argues that space is not merely the underside of writing just as writing is not the underside of thought and speech: 'the economy of writing is not subservient to thought or speech, but actually is productive in its own right'.[17] Derrida deploys the concept of 'spacing' to advance the claim that space is both a product and productive, a force with its own creative agency. He writes:

> Spacing is a concept which also, but not exclusively, carries the meaning of a productive, positive, and generative force. Like *dissemination*, like *différance*, it carries along with it a generic motif: it is not only the interval, the space constituted between two things (which is the usual sense of spacing), but also spacing, the operation, or in any event, the movement of setting aside.[18]

Like Foucault, Derrida too conceptualizes space as something more than just a neutral Euclidean void on which things and events happen: space is a medium with its own productive agency.

There are also several other theorists whose work more explicitly engages with space and offer fascinating insights into the social character of space and its entanglement with power and authority. In a landmark scholarship on the significance of spatiality and spatial imaginations, Henri Lefebvre advances the intriguing proposition that the social space is a social product: '[E]very society – and hence every mode of production ... produces a space, its own space.'[19] Space is a social formation that 'exerts its own variety of agency'. Despite its material and objective appearance, space is not an inert, neutral, and isotropic void that pre-exists human action.[20] As he puts it, 'the social relations of production have a social existence to the extent that they have a spatial existence; they project themselves into a space, becoming inscribed there, and in the process

---

15   Gilles Deleuze, *Foucault*, translated by Seán Hand (Minneapolis: University of Minnesota Press, 1988), 44.

16   Jacques Derrida, *Positions*, translated by Alan Bass (London: Continuum, 2002), 81, 106 (n42).

17   See West-Pavlov, *Space in Theory*, 16.

18   Derrida, *Positions*, 106 (n42).

19   Henri Lefebvre, *The Production of Space*, translated by Donald Nicholson-Smith (Oxford: Blackwell, 1991), 31.

20   West-Pavlov, *Space in Theory*, 19.

of producing that space'.[21] Emphasizing this productive nature of space, Edward Said argued that 'the line separating Occident from the Orient ... is less a fact of nature than it is a fact of human production, which I have called imaginative geography'.[22] Drawing on both Lefebvre and Foucault, Edward Soja calls for an analysis of space that recognizes spatiality simultaneously as 'social product (or outcome) and a shaping force (or medium) in social life'.[23] As a socially produced and culturally mediated space, Soja argues, spatiality is analytically distinguishable from the 'physical space of material nature' or 'the mental space of cognition'.[24] In Soja's analytic schema, then, spatiality is 'simultaneously the medium and outcome, presupposition and embodiment, of social action and relationship'.[25] In a passage that echoes both Foucault and Lefebvre, he claims: 'Spatiality exists ontologically as a product of a transformation process, but always remains open to further transformation in the context of material life. It is never primordially given or permanently fixed.'[26] Building on Lefebvre's paradigm, Fredric Jameson explores the spatial distribution of power and knowledge within a capitalist society. For Jameson, space in a capitalist society is 'the result of a discontinuous expansion of quantum leaps in the enlargement of capital'. Capitalist modes of production generate 'a type of space unique to it'.[27]

What emerges from these brief considerations is the relational, productive and generative character of space. Not the invisible, undialectical, fixed and 'transparent receptacle' for objects and events, space is an active generative medium. It is a set of relations that partakes in the constitution of meaning and the configuration and reconfiguration of sovereignty, the subject and politics. As West-Pavlov put it, '[s]pace is the agency of configuration, and the fabric of configuration is from the outset spatial'.[28] What unites these diverse range of thinkers is what may be called the social-constructivist paradigm that views space both as product and productive. From Foucault's 'discursive space' to Derrida's 'spacing'; from Lefebvre's constructivist paradigm to Soja's 'thirdspace'; from Said's 'imaginative geography' to Jameson's 'cognitive mapping', there is a useful conceptual paradigm filled with implications and insights for thinking about the spatiality of resistance and the courtroom.

It is a paradigm that treats space as a social product and meaning as a function of the spatio-temporal matrix within which it emerges: meaning is

---

21 Lefebvre, *The Production of Space*, 129.

22 Edward Said, 'Orientalism Revisited', in *Reflections on Exile and Other Essays* (Cambridge, MA: Harvard University Press, 2002), 199.

23 Soja, *Postmodern Geographies*, 7.

24 Ibid., 120.

25 Ibid., 129.

26 Ibid., 122.

27 Fredric Jameson, *Postmodernism, or, The Cultural Logic of Late Capitalism* (Durham, NC: Duke University Press, 1991), 418.

28 West-Pavlov, *Space in Theory*, 25.

no longer independent of the space in which it emerges but a function of it.[29] Within this interpretive paradigm, meaning is conceived as socially generated, something specific to time and place, and immanent in the spatio-temporal matrix within which it emerges. According to this perspective, an artefact has no essential or intrinsic meaning of its own. The secret of an artefact lies in the place in which it was produced and the machinery that produced it. Rather than uncovering some hidden truths and juridical meanings, the point of spatial enquiry is to ask how that artefact came to have the kind of reality it now has and what made it possible. It is to strip bare the conditions of possibility of knowledge generation and meaning production as a contingent and heterogeneous process of production.[30]

But resistance is also an irreducibly temporal formation whose consequences could not be fully understood in the immediate aftermath of specific episodes of resistance. As Johan van der Walt's chapter shows, Nelson Mandela's and Bram Fischer's renegade performances at the Rivonia Trial could not be adequately accounted for without a particular attention to time. Only after 'reflection, mirroring, and speculative representation' can we begin to think and make sense of these gestures – only 'when time gives' can we understand the meanings and effects of those moments of madness. Mandela and fellow defendants were renegades who were up to something but did not quite know what they were about, they did not know what those defiant acts and gestures would have meant or achieved within Apartheid's economy of representation, or what Jaco Barnard-Naudé, drawing on Jacques Rancière, calls Apartheid's 'distribution of the sensible'.[31] But it was a performance that touched the world – a kind of gesture that stood for something bigger than the life of the defendants – a performance dedicated to the proposition that South Africa ought to be 'free and democratic'. It is an appeal that is at once a refusal and a demand on the world but whose true meaning and significance we would only know in the future. It was this appeal that we were left with when the event of the trial was closed – an appeal that left behind traces and remainders that remain and repeat. In a memorable formulation, Derrida refers to this appeal as an appeal to humanity, 'to the voice of conscience, to the immediate and unfailing sentiments of justice, to this law of laws that speaks in us before us, because it is

---

29 Ibid., 23.

30 West-Pavlov, *Space in Theory*, 22–23. As West-Pavlov puts it, "An artefact no longer has 'a' meaning, no longer unveils 'a' truth under the stern scrutiny of the scholar, but rather, participates in myriad relations and connections which permit it to be in such a way that it can subsequently be asked to reveal its truth. But before that interrogation, of truth can happen, a more profound interrogation is demanded, one that asks questions about position, location, context, contours, and dimension."

31 Jacques Rancière, *The Politics of Aesthetics: The Distribution of the Sensible*, translated by Gabriel Rockhill (London: Continuum, 2004), 1–3.

inscribed within our heart'.[32] Neither South Africa nor the world fully understood the meaning and significance of Mandela's appeals. Only in time, only in the future, would we come close to understanding or experiencing what that appeal is about. It is in this sense that time, too, becomes a matrix of meaning.

Geographies of the Courtroom: From Domination to Resistance

Law is the preeminent discourse of domination. Its institutional structure and normative content reflects the existing configuration of force relations within society. Law conserves and sustains the founding configuration by codifying it into laws and institutions. In essence, law performatively condenses its violence of inauguration and preservation into legal norms and transforms them into normative relations. As the symbolic personification of the majesty of law and order, the court is law's foremost geography of power whose primary function is to secure the existing distribution of power within the *body-politic*. Despite the enchantment of courts as impartial spaces of truth and justice elevated above and beyond politics, courts have been the primary sites of power-legitimation and order-rationalization. By distinguishing itself from a norm giver and disguising as a neutral norm interpreter, the court conceals the violence of the system and 'dispels the shock of daily occurrences'.

Normative theories of law and the trial conceive the courtroom as a Euclidean space – a physically fixed, dialectically neutral, and transparent space – designed for a rational exchange of ideas necessary for a just and orderly resolution of conflicts. Within this normative frame, the space of the courtroom is a geometrically delineated legal space. Against these strongly normative conceptions, contributors to this volume insist on the multiplicitous and heterogeneous configuration and functionality of the courtroom. Far from being the neutral and apolitical space of adjudication, the space of the courtroom is conceived as material and abstract, singular and multiple, relational and absolute, real and imagined, enabled and enabling, and produced and producing. Despite its appearance of objectivity, materiality and naturalness, the space of the courtroom is an active productive agent mediated by power relations. As Soja aptly put it, 'the appearance of spatial coherence and homogeneity are social products and often an integral part of the instrumentality of political power'.[33] The question remains: how does resistance register in the courtroom and how can we recognize its infinite expressions and manifestations as practices of resistance?

The courtroom is both a geometric and a discursive space. It is both material and abstract, and produced and producing. Not the empty container of Cartesian

---

32 Jacques Derrida, 'The Laws of Reflection: Nelson Mandela, In Admiration', in Jacques Derrida and Mustapha Tlili (eds) *For Nelson Mandela* (New York: Sever Books, 1987), 27.

33 Soja, *Postmodern Geographies*, 126.

or Kantian thought, the courtroom is a generative space of thought and action. It is an epistemological space with innate affinities with truth-bearing discourses of the rule of law, legitimacy, legality and justice. It is a spatial formation capable of creating opportunities for a doubling of language and thought – space capable of sustaining disruptive and transformative interventions. Woven into the spatial configuration of the courtroom are the conditions of possibility of discourses, the systematicity of these discourses, and opportunities for epistemological rupture. These are the spatial configurations that create opportunities for imaginative responses of the subject; activating critique and struggle in the very space where critique is juridically deactivated. When Nelson Mandela asked Apartheid judges – 'Why is it that in this courtroom I face a white magistrate, am confronted by a white prosecutor, and escorted into the dock by a white orderly? Can anyone honestly and seriously suggest that in this type of atmosphere the scales of justice are evenly balanced?'[34] – he is using the spatiality of the discourse of justice to expand the horizons of the imaginable and expose the limit of the symbolic order. The whole enterprise of legal adjudication and the linguistic universe that organizes and structures the terms of the debate, the elements of the trial as process and as event, provides the background against which certain concepts and notions are conceived, spoken and consigned on the archive of the state.

As law's primary site of truth-generation and knowledge production, the courtroom enables both geographies of domination and resistance to take part in the production and generation of their respective modalities of knowledge and meaning. However, in the hegemonic space of the courtroom, resistance and domination are positioned differently and occupy unequal power positions in the process of meaning constitution. Courtroom acts of resistance often express themselves as a diagnosis of the mechanisms, strategies and discursive technologies of the authorized space of law to get around them, to live through them or transform them. To get around the unequal distribution of voice and space, resistance locates itself within or outside law's truth-bearing discourses, works through them or find ways around them, to create alternative spaces of knowledge production. In this way, geographies of resistance use the radical openness of the legal discourse and the site of adjudication to expose normative contradictions and violent foundations of the body-politic. From within these spaces largely defined and regulated by silencing and exclusionary norms, resistance seeks to transform the constitutive system of epistemic organization that renders its claims unintelligible, inaudible and invisible.

A spatial orientation towards the legal space recognizes the complexity, heterogeneity, contingency and multiplicity of the space of the courtroom. Moreover, using space and spatiality as a paradigm of enquiry is critical here because it enables us to situate the trial in its spatial context, to spatialize law's normative closures

---

34   Nelson Mandela, The Incitement Trial, 1962, in *Nelson Mandela's First Court Statement*, available at https://www.nelsonmandela.org/omalley/index.php/site/q/03lv0153 8/04lv01600/05lv01624/06lv01625.htm last accessed 1 April 2015.

and discursive filters, and to re-orient reflections away from its claims about neutrality, objectivity, rationality and autonomy towards more intricate questions of materiality, of relationship, of subjectivity and causality. This account of space enables us to transcend and imagine beyond law's normative closures and open law up for possibilities of progressive change and transformation. Understanding the spatial configuration of topographies of domination and their conditions of possibility allows one to grasp the points at which oppressive discourses become vulnerable and therefore available for intervention and transformation. It enables us to decipher the mode of reasoning and forms of thought by which geographies of domination misrecognize and misrepresent resistant claims. It is the spatial dimension of the courtroom – the conditions of possibility of its discourses, its discursive operations, and the susceptibility of its discourses to epistemological rupture – which makes otherwise unintelligible statements intelligible and marks out the courtroom as an enabling space of resistant thought and action.

In the context of the Rivonia Trial and Mandela's strategic engagement with what he called 'the white man's court', the strategy was to deploy the resources available within law and its meta-level discourses such as justice and morality to expose Apartheid's violent formation. It was a defence strategy crafted to obliterate the mythology of Afrikaner nationalism and law's legitimating functions. Mandela's strategic but trenchant critique of Apartheid was intended to unravel Apartheid's conditions of possibility: how the system constitutes its order of knowledge, formulates its regime of truth, establishes its historical givens and operationalizes its irrational policies.

In celebration of the fiftieth anniversary of the Rivonia Trial, contributors to this volume return to the Rivonia courtroom and other prominent political trials to reflect on the time–space of those constitutive historic spaces. Through an investigation of a range of critical themes and concerns from within different analytic and conceptual frameworks, the book explores the potential of the courtroom as a site of political critique and struggle. The volume is thus both a celebration and a reflection: a celebration of the life and struggle of an extraordinary human being, the late Nelson Mandela; and a critical theoretical engagement with the spatial (and also temporal) dimensions of resistance in the courtroom.

In the opening chapter, Derek Hook problematizes the Nelson Mandela phenomenon and his legacy in 'the libidinal economy' of post-Apartheid South Africa. The name 'Mandela', Hook argues, is a 'master-signifier' that signifies 'a great many different things to a great many different people'. For some, he is the sign and signifier of resistance, freedom, hope and reconciliation. He is 'an emblem of integrity, a touchstone of moral capital, a figure of global renown who transcended the particularity of his political cause to stand for the goals of a universal emancipatory politics'. For others, Mandela is the ANC icon, a radical revolutionary, and a military strategist 'who established Umkhonto we Sizwe'. Hook asks what the commemoration industry and 'the love directed at Mandela' reveal about the South African state and the unique figure of Mandela, the master-signifier. Drawing on insights from psychoanalysis, he argues that the obsessive idealization of Nelson Mandela is a 'crisis of concern that condenses within itself a series of fundamental anxieties underlying the post-apartheid condition'. This uncontainable love both conceals and reveals the guilt, shame and fear that dominate the post-Apartheid imaginary. Hook's reflection on the legacy of Nelson Mandela reconstructs the Mandela brand as a discursive artefact and a spatial configuration that enables and disables competing ideas of society, subjectivity and unity in the post-Apartheid South African imaginary.

People hold strong opinions about the meaning of iconic figures of global renown. As one of the twentieth-century's most iconic figures, people's views of Nelson Mandela manifest either as implicit assumptions or explicit assertions. But as Johan van der Walt shows in his reflection on the meaning of Nelson Mandela and Bram Fischer, two of the most iconic renegades of the Rivonia Trial, true icons are inaccessible, invisible, inexhaustible and unnameable. Through a close re-reading of Derrida's text on Mandela and several recurring themes in Derrida's thought such as the laws of reflection, the performative foundation of the body politic, the notion of the secret, the gift and the sacrifice, Van der Walt problematizes and politicizes Derrida's Mandela. His is a concern with the temporality of resistance and the temporal dimensions of renegade moments (not subject to normative enclosures) and revolutionary moments (appeal to normative ideals). Van der Walt situates these discussions within the broader problematic between the normative and the performative. Working through these Derridean devices, he shows why the figure of Mandela or Bram Fischer cannot be exhausted within the spatial and temporal orderings of a given reflection. 'Mandela's secret' or the 'secret of Mandela' cannot be disclosed by Derrida's deconstructive 'devices of observation'; nor, in fact, is it subject to the very possibility of disclosure. Although this 'irreducible secrecy' remains forever inaccessible, Van der Walt claims, only through deconstruction and its 'devices of observation' can we come closer to understanding or at least experiencing the meaning of Derrida's Mandela or Bram Fischer.

In his famous essay '*fondement mystique de [l']autorité*', Montaigne traces the foundation of authority to mythologies and fictions. In one of his most rehearsed statements, he writes: 'even our law, it is said, has legitimate fictions upon which it founds the truth of its justice'.[35] Working from within the 'law and literature' framework, Peter Leman's chapter examines the constitutive and disruptive functions of institutive myths and fictions in political struggles. Against modernity's disavowal of myth and its celebration of reason and rationality, Leman claims that myths are at the heart of all institutive and regulative instruments or practices. He argues that myths are fragile, partial and precarious, but they do things in the world, filling voids that legal formalism or enlightenment rationality could not: myths provide 'equipment for living'. Setting the myths of the ANC

---

35   Montaigne, in Jacques Derrida, 'Force of Law: "The Mystical Foundation of Authority"', in Drucilla Cornell, Michel Rosenfeld, and David Gray Carlson (eds) *Deconstruction and the Possibility of Justice* (New York: Routledge, 1992), 12.

against those of Apartheid, the myths used to legitimize and validate Apartheid's legal order; Leman's analysis shows how Mandela spatializes and deploys myth to unseat the myths that hold together Apartheid and Afrikaner nationalism. Through the domestication of global myths, and strategic coupling of orature and myth, Mandela both produces and mobilizes myths capable of undermining Apartheid's claims to legitimacy. In his indictment of the Apartheid state, Mandela works with and on myth not only to re-set the terms of speech and action but also to overthrow Apartheid myths and replace them with the myth of a rainbow nation whose conceptual genealogy Leman traces to Mandela's 'ideal of free and democratic society' proclaimed from the dock at Rivonia.

If Mandela is an icon whose name functions as a master-signifier, a figure who has attained a quasi-mythical status; this status cannot be explained, understood or experienced without some account of the events, the spaces and the moments that catapulted him onto the global stage: the Treason Trial, the Incitement Trial and the Rivonia Trial. These are political trials – juridico-political events of historic primacy that embody such paradigmatic stories of law and justice, power and politics, domination and resistance. They are constitutional moments that offered 'the part of no part' the space to ask questions of foundational significance. For Catherine M. Cole, these trials 'represent an extraordinary period of state transformation in South Africa'. In her contribution, Cole traces the genealogy of democratic South Africa to this trilogy of trials. When Apartheid suspended politics proper and turned to the hegemonic geographies of law to secure its authority, law courts became sites of struggle. In Cole's analytic schema, these trials are spatial struggles between domination and resistance 'in which language, costume, gesture, acoustics, space, protocols, dramaturgy, song, and visual culture' emerged as the enabling grid of politics. Cole's chapter works with temporal metaphors such as 'stages', 'transitions', 'befores and afters' and 'transformation', but also draws on spatially oriented vocabularies such as archive, repertoire, displacement and disruption; suggesting that the spatio-temporal coordinates of resistance are more than just the underside of domination. Setting the performative against the enclosure of the normative, Cole both temporalizes and spatializes South African history. Despite law's normative closures and self-reference, she argues, resistance activates itself from within geographies of domination and releases an energy that cannot be properly contained within law's normative framework. Attending to performative repertoires enacted by the accused, she shows how resistance redesigns its map to enable movement between spaces, using their bodies and costumes, to insinuate itself into spaces of the racist state to enact liberationist repertoires of resistance. In this analysis, these trials emerge as moments in history and places on the map where history is made, where the seed of the rainbow nation was laid, a geography circumscribed and constrained by law's silencing conventions but too ambivalent, incomplete, multifaceted and uncontainable to guarantee its complete colonization.

The political trial is an 'essentially contested' space. It has many species and subspecies each with its own shades of politics. But its ultimate aim is the enlargement of space for political action: 'court action is called upon to exert influence on the distribution of political power'.[36] The resort to courts by those who hold the emblem of sovereignty or their foes may be a matter of choice, necessity or convenience. Yet, what provides the political trial proper with its distinctive intensity and its unique spatial formation is the direct participation of the judicial apparatus in the struggle for political power. The court's unique position of trust within society, the generative character of its space, the truth-bearing nature of its discourses, and its vastly superior quality of image creation and saturation makes them such irresistible geographies of power: of domination and resistance. It is precisely this relational nature of geographies of resistance and geographies of domination that orients Catherine Albertyn's chapter.

Taking Foucault's insight that there are no relations of domination without relationships of resistance, Albertyn's chapter engages with the question of space, domination and resistance in the Rivonia Trial. Drawing on Kirchheimer's formulation of the political trial as struggle in power, she locates the Rivonia Trial within the political, economic and ideological conditions of its time. If the political trial is a crisis-formation constituted of struggles, 'ideas, forms, images, and imaginings', we need to pay attention to the local and global networks of power-relations and the particular dialectic between the state and the opposition. In both the Rivonia and Treason Trials, communism, (communist) agitation and violence served as the key political censures around which the Apartheid regime sought to construct knowledge and generate anxieties, fears and prejudices about the means and ends of the struggle. These censures, Albertyn argues, operate to de-legitimize the accused and the ANC as communist and violent while uniting white South Africans and presenting Apartheid as the only bulwark against the onrush of communism in Africa. While the Apartheid regime secured what it wanted in the short run, the trial also enabled the accused to use the courtroom as a site of critique and resistance. Albertyn's chapter shows how spatialities are constitutive not only of geographies of domination but also of resistances, that domination always elicits resistance and spatial configurations play a pivotal role in these configurations. As she concludes, 'As we look back at Rivonia, we no longer see a defeat, but an iconic moment in a momentous struggle for justice'.

Working through Kirchheimer, Judith Shklar, Ron Christenson and others, Mia Swart's chapter develops an analytic category of political trials to account for the specific legal and political conditions that animated the making of the Rivonia Trial and the Treason Trial. The political trial is an elusive and contested concept that cannot be conceptually and analytically delineated and exhausted in one single definition. But it is an inevitable juridico-political enterprise on the fault line of law and politics and understanding its political and social function

---

36 Otto Kirchheimer, *Political Justice: The Use of Legal Procedure for Political Ends* (Princeton: Princeton University Press, 1961), 49.

requires an analytic framework that recognizes the disruptive force of the political trial's spatial configuration. Arguing for a contextual understanding of the political trial, she cautions us against the stigmatization of the political trial and draws our attention to the particular operations, strategies, tactics and mechanisms deployed to appropriate the opportunities immanent in its mode of operation. Within this analytic framework, the Treason Trial and the Rivonia Trial were political trials that took place within a 'modicum of procedural regularity' and for that reason allowed the defence to exploit its conditions of possibility for critique and resistance.

The word 'courtroom' refers to a space both in the material and abstract sense of the term. It is an epistemological space, an institutional space and geometric space. However, the concern here is not so much with what Barbara Piatti referred to as *geospace*,[37] i.e., the real space of the courtroom, but with what Foucault calls the exterior space, the poetic space of imagination produced and enabled by subjects of resistance. The next four chapters take up several critical themes in relation to the political trial's spatial formation – its conditions of possibility and its value for spatially oriented social and political action.

Taking Derrida's astonishing meditation on Mandela, 'The Laws of Reflection: Nelson Mandela, in Admiration' as his starting point, Jaco Barnard-Naudé reflects on the light of Mandela's reflection. Working with and against Derrida, Barnard-Naudés chapter engages with the unsettling and enabling logic of Mandela's opening words: 'I am the first accused.' Far from being a mere confirmation and affirmation of status, this preambular statement is an indictment that 'will always have been an accusation'. It accuses his accusers and situates his adversaries in contradiction with their own professed ideals and values. As a man of law, both by vocation and admiration, Mandela's reflection on law, justice and the coup de force of the Apartheid nation activates a 'supplementary inversion'. Going beyond shining light on the rotten history of South African sovereignty and revealing a fissure in Apartheid's economy of representation, it redefines the accused and transforms him into an accuser, reinventing 'the part of no part' as a subject of resistance capable of disrupting 'the distribution of the sensible'. By re-imagining the South African state on the basis of 'The Freedom Charter' and the will of the 'entire nation', Mandela's accusation, and therefore reflection, seeks to foreground a new body politic and a new epistemic standard. It is this disruptive and transformative force of the light that Mandela's reflection reflects – a reflection that 'reflects the deontology of deontology' – that Jaco Barnard-Naudé's chapter alerts us to.

My own chapter is a genealogical-performative inquiry into the conditions of possibility of the trial for resistance and emancipatory critique. Drawing on Nelson Mandela's critique of Apartheid in the Incitement and Rivonia Trials, I seek to explore the role of spatial configurations and ontologies in mediating, enabling or disabling critique. Departing from forms of critique that are possible and acceptable within law's frameworks and conceptual categories, Mandela both uses and critiques the

---

37   Robert T. Tally Jr., *Spatiality* (Abingdon: Routledge, 2012), 52.

law, resists and claims authority, pleads and indicts, from within a sovereign space elevated above and beyond critique and contestation. Unrelenting and unyielding, Mandela spatializes the legal discourse to conduct a trial within a trial, to enable transformative action 'within the fortress of the enemy'. By submitting himself to the very law he denounces as racist and unjust, positioning himself at aporetic sites and moments, those most fragile frontiers that are so heavily policed from subversive interventions, Mandela exposes the fundamental wrong at the heart of Apartheid's system of epistemic organization. In this sagacious operation, he presents a critique that registers without being co-opted, integrated or domesticated by the discourse and the system it resists. By attending to these strategic moves and the ways in which Mandela orients himself towards contradictions, discursive dynamics and points of tension, my chapter seeks to understand and explain the logic and modes of thought underneath Mandela's skilful appropriation of his trial for progressive political ends.

Joel M. Modiri's chapter is an ambitious attempt at tracing, identifying and retrieving what he calls a 'critical race theoretical critique' in courtroom choreographies of black radical resistance movements. For black radical revolutionaries of Apartheid South Africa and Jim Crow USA, the court is the 'institutional representation' and 'symbolic personification' of white hegemony – its foremost device of legitimation and discipline. Far from being the neutral and transparent repository of truth and justice, Modiri argues, the courtroom is the ultimate expression of power and white domination. Working through Foucault's insight on the uncertain relationship between critique and transformation and Wendy Brown's account of the timeliness of critique, his project explores the strategies by which black resistance is choreographed and performed before the courts of the oppressors. But Modiri's inquiry is not limited to investigating how radical black movements have conceived, perceived, imagined, represented and appropriated the court's spatial matrix for critique and resistance. Going beyond excavating the strategies and cryptic meanings hidden in the archives and repertoires of black liberationist movements, going beyond stripping bare the tautological and self-referential logic of the court, he questions the very premises upon which the turn to the law as a site of resistance is predicated. Modiri upsets this premise by tracing a certain paradox evident in the transition from left critique to left legalism in post-Apartheid South Africa and the increasing juridification of social and political life. By retrieving and comparing the critical race tradition that animated the documented struggles of radical black revolutionaries with contemporary 'left-legalism', his chapter reveals the limits of the legal imagination in recognizing and redressing deep historical injustices.

Alison Phipps's contribution explores the political and cultural meanings of unanswered letters. Phipps's chapter takes its cue from a scene in Mandela's incitement trial where the government's refusal to acknowledge, let alone reply, to the petitions of the ANC, took centre stage. The absent reply, she argues, has a tantalizing hold on the popular imagination. Dissecting this encounter between Mandela and the private secretary to the then Prime Minister Dr H.F. Verwoerd, she argues that Mandela uses this incident to perform 'an archaeology of the indignity symbolized by the letters which have not received a reply'. The absent reply signified contempt and made evident the impossibility of normal relations; exposed the limits of non-violence as a mode of struggle; and marked the transition from petitions into more radical forms of resistance. Phipps's chapter draws on Lacan, Derrida and Zizek, but also brings a liberation theologian's sensitivity, a dramaturge's reading of character and action, and a linguist's sensibility to the economy of words, into a productive conversation with stories of unanswered letters.

While the preceding three chapters were concerned with the discursive and linguistic spatiality of the courtroom and the invisible and often unconscious conditions of possibility it offers, Isolde de Villiers's chapter emphasizes the geometric and architectural dimensions of the Rivonia Trial. It is a spatial analysis of the reciprocal relationship between the city of Pretoria and the Rivonia Trial. The city, she argues, 'is law's greatest testing ground, its loudspeakers and gambling grounds', and retains a unique spatial affinity with law and juridical power more broadly. Drawing on the notion of the lawscape, she investigates the network of spaces and spatial arrangements that constituted Pretoria's geographies of domination and shaped the making of the Rivonia Trial and its haunting ghosts. For de Villiers, the very choice of Pretoria as a venue for several high profile political trials including the Rivonia Trial and the Treason Trial is a deliberate spatial undertaking and is an integral part of Apartheid's geography of power. The relationship between Pretoria and the Rivonia Trial is a mutually constitutive spatial practice. While the Rivonia Trial was shaped by Pretoria's spatial configuration, the trial in turn shaped the architectural, historical, political and economic topographies of Pretoria. Using this spatial lens as its framework of inquiry, de Villiers clarifies and draws out the implication of the law-city quandary for the spatiality of justice, utopia and the legal imagination.

Embedded into all geographies of organized society – the space we inhabit, use and occupy – is a certain degree of inequality and injustice. Every spatial configuration is constituted of complex and contingent struggles and is maintained and preserved not just through armies and police but also through discourses and complex spatial matrices. To use Edward Said's imaginative formulation, these configurations and the struggle to change and transform them is 'complex and interesting because it is not only about soldiers and cannons but also about ideas, about forms, about images and imaginings'.[38] Any possibility of change and transformation is therefore contingent on strategies capable of mapping new spaces of intervention that can insinuate into the fortress of the enemy, on tactics able to create new meanings and identities. Through an investigation of three different trials, the next three chapters show how a spatial orientation towards the courtroom names the unnamable and conceives the inconceivable.

Ted Laros's chapter is a literary exploration of the 1974 Cape Trial of André Brink's novel, *Kennis van die Aand*. Unlike most political trials instigated by the state, this is a trial designed by André Brink, the author, and Buren, the

---

38 Said, *Culture and Imperialism*, 6.

publisher, not only to secure the release of the book but also to use the occasion to scrutinize the legality of censorship, the government's hold on the literary field, and Apartheid's policies and practices more broadly. This trial is a work of imaginative geography. Literature is here reconfigured as a domain of spatial analysis and literary concepts incapable of definitive legal encapsulation – such as 'literary autonomy', 'aesthetic novel', 'engaged novel' or 'littérature engageé', 'likely readership', and the novel as 'hermetically sealed universe' – are used as enabling spatial frameworks to make Brink's and Buren's enunciations utterable and intelligible in the courtroom. Using the spatial ontologies of both literature and the trial as the enabling space of thought and action, Brink and Buren appropriate literature's discursive space, what Foucault calls epistemological space, to contest, subvert and rupture the discursive configurations of Apartheid's oppressive geographies. The literary concepts that were mobilized by Brink and Buren to re-territorialize the courtroom and elaborate new spaces of intervention enabled and made intelligible the subversive meanings the plaintiff sought to generate and circulate. In a sense, what Laros's chapter shows is that literature, because of its affinity with discursive space and the materiality of language, can be a profoundly subversive space and a powerful enabling space of thought and action.

The volume also includes two chapters that explore key themes and ideas on the use of the courtroom as a site of political critique and struggle outside South Africa. The chapters engage with a different kind of problematic and demonstrate that political trials are not unique to authoritarian systems and that trials can be politicized and used to advance a political point within liberal constitutional democracies as well.

Chloé S. Georas's chapter is a postcolonial and performative analysis of the trial of Lorena Bobbitt – a Latina who came to the United States at the age of 18 – for 'malicious wounding'. Georas tells a fascinating story of how an ordinary criminal trial was politicized and turned into a debate over the coloniality of American law and its function in reifying and normalizing 'ethno-racial-sexual hierarchies'. Drawing on law's neo-colonial and culturally hegemonic discourses and rituals, the state prosecution objectified, racialized and gendered the defendant but Bobitt's lawyers re-territorialized and decolonized the courtroom to transform it from being the symbolic personification of white patriarchy and hegemony into a space of citizenship and freedom in which the defendant's experience of history, geography and culture can be heard and registers on the judicial archive. Despite law's conservation, and reproduction of coloniality and cultural hegemony in the post-colonial condition, Georas's account shows that there always remain gaps, tears, points of tension and fissures that offer opportunities for critique and resistance. This spatial reflexivity of the courtroom allowed a gendered and racialized subject of law not only to achieve instant fame but also to wrench the voice and visibility of Latino symbols and cultural productions from the regulative logic of the trans-American imaginary or what Georas, citing Frances Aparicio and Chavez Silverman, refers to as 'hegemonic tropicalization'.

Kanika Sharma's chapter takes up one of India's famous political trials – the Gandhi Murder Trial. Gandhi's murder trial, she argues, is 'a carefully plotted spatial "event"' staged in the iconic Red Fort – a site of great national pride – to achieve political ends that transcend the trial's normative concern with the determination of guilt and innocence. By staging a spectacular political trial at spectacular site of iconic status in the Indian national imaginary, the authorities used Gandhi's murder trial not only to establish and guarantee the continuity of Indian sovereignty but also to ground the new secular state in a deeper and solid foundation. Weaved into the Red Fort is the politics of location which is bounded with history, culture, identity and power. By emphasizing the strategic reconfiguration and re-appropriation of the politics of the place, and the discursive space of the court and its affinity with the image, the spectacular and the ornamental, Sharma shows the entangled relationships between geographies of domination and resistance. The way geographies of domination and resistance converge with one another in this analysis reflects India's colonial history and the coloniality of power. Despite the iconicity and symbolism of the site of this trial, the spectacular trial of the Father of the Nation did more than just re-enacting the glorious history of the past and foregrounding the state in its preferred brand of nationalism: the trial enabled Gandhi's murderers 'to give vent to [their] thoughts'. In the end, the geometric and the poetic configuration of the courtroom enabled both the accused and the accuser to pursue their respective political goals.

What these chapters show is that despite the hegemonic status of geographies of domination, geographies of resistance are not fully determined or encapsulated by the former. As De Certeau put it, there are 'innumerable ways of playing and foiling the other's game'.[39] The resistant subject that has to play within the labyrinth of the legal space appropriates law's own spatialities – its conditions of possibility – to create its own space, to cross into the rigidified spaces of sovereign power with claims that are neither determined nor exhausted by the system against which it stands. Geographies of resistance find ways around law's highly guarded spaces, seek to re-territorialize it, to rework, to re-signify and re-direct the spatial configuration of silencing discourses; to stretch the horizons of the intelligible; to craft new meanings out of hegemonic meanings, and eventually overthrow imposed ontologies. Calling attention to the disjuncture between the normative and the performative, and diagnosing the different ways by which law circumscribes its spaces; using different analytic devices and interpretive paradigms, contributors to the volume urge us to think beyond the normative or to adopt a different orientation towards law's normative closures to appropriate its conditions of possibility for progressive change and transformation.

---

39 Michel de Certeau, *The Practice of Everyday Life* (London: University of California Press, 1984), 18.

Chapter 2

In the Name of Mandela

Derek Hook

Throughout June, July and August of 2013, much of the South African news-media was preoccupied with the question of Nelson Mandela's ailing health. Leaving aside for the time being the question of South Africa's tendency to exhibit a type of media-fixation on a single iconic person – the cases of Oscar Pistorius and Julius Malema being here clear examples – my objective here will be to offer some speculative comments on the social and psychical significance of this period of uncertainty that characterized the run-up to Mandela's death in late 2013. Considering the meaning of Mandela in this period – as opposed to the period immediately after his death – represents a very different line of enquiry to any ostensibly objective assessment of Mandela's political or symbolic legacy. The reason for this is that I broach the topic of Mandela's role in the *libidinal economy* of the South African nation, that is, in terms of the various clusters of affect and unconscious ideation that it represented at the time and beyond.

Social Hagiography

We might begin then by asking: how might one approach the obsessive media speculation concerning Mandela's declining health prior to his eventual death? Popular news-media commentaries on Mandela during the middle of 2013 as a rule wavered between requests that the public honour appropriate cultural customs – to respect the privacy of Mandela and his family – and an unrelenting thirst for ever more details pertaining to the former South African president and his feuding family. The obvious point to note here is that each such impulse effectively undoes the other. A further, related tension was also at play. A variety of political personalities and media pundits made the call – presumably preparing us all for the inevitable – that the public needed to 'let Mandela go', to give him up. Given Mandela's age at the time, and the ordeals he had lived through, this seemed wholly reasonable. The problem however was that once voiced, such sentiments were almost immediately paired with the contrary demand, to the effect that we – as it was then stated – 'can't let him go' (Dawes, 2013).

The commemoration industry that has been built up around Mandela gives one reason to wonder if the country has become vaguely fearful of its many other struggle heroes. None of these men and woman even vaguely approaches the quasi-mythical status attained by the name of Mandela. It is an odd quirk of human psychology and indeed of human sociality more generally that societies so often feel it necessary to predicate an entire social or political order on the image or the legacy of a single person (Adorno, 1991; Freud, 2004). Given the history of fascist, totalitarian and dictatorial regimes of the past century, regimes which unfailingly relied on elevating the figure of a single totemic leader to the place of the sublime *Thing* of the nation, it is understandable that there are many of who feel discomfort at the impulse to thus embody the nation in the figure of a single leader. This gives rise to our first question: despite that Mandela is a hero, a bastion not only of the Left but of global struggles against oppression and colonialism more generally, is it not still somewhat worrying that South African culture seems willing to accord him the transcendent position of the sublime embodiment of the nation? What shortcoming might stem from seeing in Mandela the encapsulation of all that is good in South Africa's history? Are we not in danger of a form of societal hagiography?

Consider the following thought experiment. You are a psychotherapist who has spent hour after hour listening to the adoring praise that one of your patients directs an erstwhile hero. What would your response be? In such a situation, one would be forced to question the function of such praise, and to locate it in reference to an array of affects, to position it, in other words, within a broader libidinal economy. That is to say, when one views idealization of this magnitude one can only suspect that it is proportionately related to – and perhaps even works to conceal – a considerable quantity of shame, guilt, even evil. If one adopts such a psychoanalytic view, then the amount of celebration and love directed at Mandela seems less than innocent, indeed, seems suspect. We can take the argument further: such levels of idealization might even be seen as indications of shame, certainly so inasmuch as possibly functions as the necessary counterbalance to a history that cannot – even now, post South Africa's Truth and Reconciliation Commission – be fully admitted.

I would not be the first person to make the argument that a politics of lionization stands diametrically opposed to Mandela's own emancipatory struggle. Truly progressive political revolutions arguably share this as their aim: not so much to celebrate the icons of the struggle, but to serve the needs of the people. Mandela's struggle as outlined in *Long Walk to Freedom* (1994) was, to risk a simplification, that of attaining a non-racist and democratic state in which the equality and rights of millions of ordinary men and women were protected. It was not, at least in my own view, to set up a class of moneyed political elite or to enshrine the image of a single faultless revolutionary hero. Dawes (2013) has essentially the same point in mind when he notes that Mandela's leadership style was instructive in sending the message that South Africa must be a nation of laws, and of institutions, not of single lauded men and women, and certainly not of one man. In his biography of Mandela, Tom Lodge (2006) makes much the same point:

Neither before nor during his presidency, Mandela neither demanded nor received an entirely unconditional devotion; in power he expected his compatriots to behave as assertive citizens not as genuflecting disciples. (p. 225)

Lodge goes on in fact to credit this as Mandela's single overriding achievement: to prioritize the workings of democratic political processes and institutions – essentially types of participative democracy – over the authority of any one totemic leader. With this in mind, we may go so far as to say that to idolize Mandela is also, in a very significant sense, to undermine him. If a radical and emancipatory politics is about calling attention to those forms of oppression that have been ignored and unchallenged, then the glare of celebratory Mandela fanfare cannot but be seen as diverting attention from forms of human subjugation that are far less edifying to contemplate.

Neurotic Vacillation

Back though to the contrary impulses displayed in public discussions of Mandela's ailing health in mid-2013. How are we to understand this double-step oscillation whereby an instance of action or assertion is immediately paired with its negation (letting Mandela go/refusing to do so, respecting and then undermining his privacy)? Psychoanalytically, one cannot deny the obsessional quality to this self-cancelling set of actions, which clearly represents an impacted ambivalence, a clear 'stuckness', an unwillingness to proceed. This is not, for the most part, an encouraging sign, because it so strongly resembles, as in the case of the classical psychoanalytic model of obsessional neurosis (Freud, 1909), a form of paralysis.[1] Extrapolated to the social sphere, we have a mode of societal stasis in which ambivalence becomes entrenched, where opposing movements counterbalance one another. We have something akin to the dynamic of a perpetual motion machine, continually moving, but never progressing beyond the site to which it is affixed. It is in this way that the obsessional subject avoids the new, forestalls the possibility of making significant choices, and thus, in effect, annuls life. Hence the Lacanian idea of the obsessional as always marking time, as effecting a kind of deadness-in-life (Fink, 1995; Melman, 1980).

Such a deadening of life is typically characterized by ritualization, by structured patterns of living or compulsive behavioural tics (radicalized in the case of obsessive compulsive acts) that ensure that nothing new can ever emerge. It is perhaps unnecessary to add that classically, such a psychic structure or disposition to life often takes the form of the son or daughter chronically over-shadowed by a larger-than-life father figure. Such a symbolic figure – not necessarily of course one's actual father, a man, or even biologically a father at all – is one whose

---

1   The canonical example of obsessional neurosis in the history of psychoanalysis being, of course, Freud's case study of Ernst Lanzer, the so-called 'Rat man'.

influence cannot be metabolized, and who thus remains a model of ambivalent affective responses, typically disguised by processes of idealization. Here another motif of Lacanian psychoanalysis comes to the fore: that of the obsessional, patiently who, despite protestations to the contrary, is essentially waiting for the father to die, so that they can start to live. What this obsessional (and typically unconscious) aspiration overlooks is the fact that the influence of such a father will only grow and attain an ever greater status after their death.

Many questions come to the fore here, not the least of which is whether a society, or, the 'affective economy' of a nation's investment in a given figure, could effectively exemplify a type of obsessional neurosis. Speculation of the sort I have offered can of course be accused of a type of over-extension, of generalizing the observations of the clinic to the political sphere (Fink, 2014; Hook, 2013. One should also point out that there is nothing extraordinary about a temporary period of suspension directly preceding or following the death of a national leader. Indecision and prevarication regarding the future would be unremarkable under such circumstances. Nonetheless, this much can confidently be said: the broader pattern of obsessional neurosis, if we are to except for the moment such an extrapolation from psyche to society, would be ill-suited to a nation for whom ongoing transformation remains such an urgent injunction. For a country still battling to attain the social equilibrium of a genuinely *post*-apartheid era, the prevarications, hidden resentments and repressed ambivalences of the obsessional would prove an immobilizing force. The stultifying mode of life lived-as-death is not one that the post-apartheid nation can afford. Indeed, if Mandela's symbolic and psychical legacy becomes to the nation akin to that of the overbearing father to the obsessional neurotic, then it would be difficult to see how the nation might move 'beyond Mandela' rather than obsessively repeating gestures of his commemoration.

'Mandela' as Signifier of Unity

It would be wrong to dismiss the quasi-hysterical nature of the South African public's concerns over Mandela's failing health in 2013 as an excessive or over-the-top response. To the contrary, this wave of anxiety was deeply significant, although perhaps not in the way it may have appeared. It was a token of a more far-reaching and less easily communicable form of social unease than could have been explained simply by reference to the advancing death of a former president. This behaviour can, in other words, be read *symptomatically*, as a crisis of concern that condenses within itself a series of fundamental anxieties underlying the post-apartheid condition as such. Before elaborating upon this idea any further we need to consider the unique status that Mandela's name and legacy have come to acquire in the psyche of South African and global culture alike.

A name starts to function as a 'master-signifier' when, despite the predominance of a general 'preferred meaning', it comes to signify a great many different things to a great many different people. Moreover, despite the diversity of such personal investments, all related parties – the public as a whole, we might say – remains *identified* with the name in question. They have, in other words, taken it on as a crucial element of who they are or who they would like to be. The emotive signifier in question – it is always an emotive signifier – be it 'Britain', 'the new South Africa', 'God', '*die volk*' or, indeed, 'Mandela', makes a type of subjectivity possible, and anchors an array of beliefs. This constitutive function of the master signifier is often remarked upon in Lacanian discourse theory: in the absence of such a master signifier, there is no committed or believing subject, no subject of the group, indeed, no viable group or constituency at all (Bracher, 1994; Stavrakakis, 1997; Verhaeghe, 2001).

What this means is that the name 'Mandela' represents a point of hegemonic convergence in which a variety of incompatible values and identifications overlap. Frederickson's (1990) comment that Mandela succeeded in fulfilling a symbolic role as the 'embodiment of the nation that transcends ideology, party, or group' (p. 28) has by now become a political commonplace. Lodge (2006) similarly suggests that the moral prestige embodied by Mandela enabled him 'to bring coherence to previously disparate social forces, and in doing so extend [an] exemplary influence across a range of political constituencies' (p. 224). What this means in effect, then, is that for some Mandela is the benign, forgiving father of the nation, the embodiment of hope and reconciliation; for others Mandela is the radical protagonist of the armed struggle, the ANC icon who played his part in establishing the Youth League and *Umkhonto we Sizwe* alike; for yet others is an emblem of integrity, a touchstone of moral capital, a figure of global renown who transcended the particularity of his political cause to stand for the goals of a universal emancipatory politics.

The ability of 'Mandela' to function as an encapsulating signifier that brings together a series of ostensibly incompatible values has its own history. Historically, 'Mandela' stood for: proponent of African Nationalism, representative of African culture and advocate for the sovereignty of African peoples; democrat and student of the values of Western parliamentary democracy; terrorist, communist, anti-capitalist and treasonous enemy of the South African state; ANC leader and representative of the universal ends of justice, non-racialism, equality and freedom. This cross-section of themes is perhaps nowhere better embodied than in Mandela's speech from the dock in the 1964 Rivonia Trial. The event of the trial no doubt proved crucial in transforming Mandela the man into 'Mandela' as master-signifier, and it is worth listening again to sections of his speech in this light:

> I am one of the persons who helped to form *Umkhonto we Sizwe* … I have done whatever I did, both as an individual and as a leader of my people, because of my experience in South Africa, and my own proudly felt African background …
> In my youth … I listened to the elders of my tribe telling stories of the old days.

Amongst the tales they related to me were those of wars fought by our ancestors in defence of the fatherland. (Mandela, 1994, pp. 349–50)

Addressing specifically the questions of violence and armed struggle, Mandela said the following:

I do not ... deny that I planned sabotage. I did not plan it in a spirit of recklessness or because I have any love of violence. I planned it as a result of a calm and sober assessment of the political situation ... We of the ANC have always stood for a non-racial democracy ... *Umkhonto* was formed in November 1961. When we took this decision ... the ANC heritage of non-violence and racial harmony was very much with us ... All whites undergo compulsory military training ... It was in our view essential to build up a nucleus of rained men who would be able to provide the leadership which would be required if guerrilla war started ... The ideological creed of the ANC ... is not the concept of African Nationalism expressed in the cry, "Drive the white man into the sea". The African Nationalism for which the ANC stands is the concept of freedom and fulfilment for the African people in their own land. (Mandela, 1994, pp. 350–51)

Mandela likewise proved adept at placing himself in relation – yet not beholden to – communist allies, whose ideology he carefully distanced himself from. Furthermore, even while espousing fidelity to the African people, he describes himself as a man respectful of Western political institutions:

The ANC['s] ... chief goal was, and is, for the African people to win unity and full political rights. The Communist Party's main aim ... was to remove capitalists and replace them with a working-class government. The Communist Party sought to emphasize class distinctions whilst the ANC seeks to harmonize them. It is true that there has often been close cooperation between the ANC and the Communist Party. But cooperation is merely proof of a common goal – in this case the removal of white supremacy – and is not proof of a complete community of interests ... From my reading of Marxist literature ... I have gained the impression that communists regard the parliamentary system of the West as undemocratic and reactionary. But, on the contrary, I am an admirer of such a system ... I have great respect for British political institutions, and for the country's system of justice. I regard the British Parliament as the most democratic institution in the world, and the independence and impartiality of its judiciary never fail to arouse my admiration. (Mandela, 1994, pp. 352–3)

The 'magic' of the master-signifier – which the above rhetorical performance goes some way to embodying – is that it is able to knit together different constituencies, appealing equally, albeit in very different ways, to a variety of classes who are otherwise opposed in their political agendas. Although in different ways, the signifier 'Mandela' was able to perform something of this task, both in 1964 and –

in a more encompassing fashion – in the post-apartheid years. A master signifier, we can thus say, makes a version of society, a crucial type of social bond, possible. Monqoba Nxumalo's recent (2013) commentary on the different legacies Mandela embodies for whites and blacks seems at first to dispute this idea:

> Mandela of the black community is and will be different to the Mandela of white society. To the black majority, he is a fighter and a radical militant who refused to be broken down even by jail. To them he is a reminder that in order to get justice you must fight because there is honour in struggle. To the white liberal community, he represents reconciliation, forgiveness and peaceful coexistence ... [T]here is a fundamental departure between blacks and whites on what takes precedence in all the things that makes up this icon called Mandela. (Nxumalo, 2013)

What these words suggest is that Mandela is a mediator between racial and class groups whose political ideals are not only very different but are at times diametrically opposed. In this respect, the master-signifier achieves what seems impossible: it engenders a type of hegemonic appeal whereby various social antagonisms might (however temporarily) be overcome. There is a further implication that can be read out of Nxumalo's observations: part of what is anxiety provoking about Mandela's declining health is that South Africa may soon lack a crucial 'class mediator', i.e., a political figure who not only speaks powerfully to black and white groupings but who also enables them to speak with, and engage, one another.

Political theorists such as Laclau (2007) and Laclau and Mouffe (1985) tend to prefer the notion of an *empty* as opposed to a *master* signifier, even though the concept in question is much the same. One benefit of referring to the master-signifier as 'empty' is that it draws attention to the fact that it maintains no intrinsic or essential meaning, first, and second, that it permits for an endless succession of varying applications and uses. A master-signifier, that is to say, can never be totalized; it remains always empty, able to accommodate fresh articulations. This is so obviously the case in respect of Mandela's name – various applications of which are, today in South Africa, seemingly never-ending – that it barely warrants mentioning. Whether in the material form of commemorative architecture or place names; institutions, charities, endowments; commemorative commodities; and even rival political party interests;[2] 'Mandela' is a signifier that can be appended to an endless stream of post-apartheid objects and aspirations.

Although I have cited mainly commemorative and commodity objects above, the true measure of a master-signifier's strength has more to do with the social bonds and subjective investments that it underpins, that is, with its role in consolidating a social mass. Having said that, the symbolic paraphernalia noted above should not be neglected: the symbolic density connoted by such activities

---

2   As in the 2013 attempt of South Africa's Democratic Alliance to appropriate Mandela's image in its own campaigning materials.

and representations is a clear signal that a society is fortifying a mode of belief, concretizing a cherished set of ideals and subjective/societal investments. In short: we don't erect monuments simply to celebrate and affirm what we already know; we build and sustain monuments so that we will continue to know and believe what may otherwise be erased through time, various forms of uncertainty or doubt. So, contrary to assuming that the endless proliferation of Mandela signifiers speaks simply to the historical objectivity, to the *security*, of the Mandela legacy, we might question whether this activity is fuelled rather by *a need to believe*. Moreover, we might question whether it is not propelled by the immanent failure of, or disbelief in, the vision of an integrated South African nation that Mandela championed, and, furthermore, whether this multitude of symbolic gestures attempts – desperately perhaps – to affirm such a unified social reality, despite the mounting evidence of growing social and political divisions.

To extend this point, it is worth briefly remarking upon a change that has occurred in South Africa's relationship to Mandela. Writing in 2006, Lodge commented that:

> Surprisingly ... there is little evidence of a cult of personality. The only public statue of Mandela is located in Sandton ... His image does not appear on banknotes, or postage stamps, and the museum at his birthplace is low key. (p. 223)

All of this, it is safe to say, has changed, and radically so. Mandela's image now adorns South African banknotes; there are now at least museums dedicated to Mandela (at Umtata, Mvezo and Qunu); statues of Mandela in Sandton, Bloemfontein (Naval Hill), Paarl (Groot Drakenstein) – not neglecting of course the Mandela monument in Howick – have now been outstripped by the 9 m statue at the Union Buildings in Pretoria. Why is it then, we might ask, that we need to celebrate and memorialize Mandela now in the immediate aftermath of his death more than ever before? Might it be because now as we advance into a *post*-post-apartheid era we are in a time when the exuberance and enthusiasm of the Mandela-led government of 1994–9 seem already to be dated historical phenomena.[3] To reiterate the point made above, we could say that this surge of commemorative practices and signifiers occurs because we need to believe the Mandela myth now more than ever. Such signifiers indicate less the absolute truth of the political changes Mandela helped bring about, than the fact that without the constant activity of Mandela signification, we might fail to believe in such

---

3   See Walder (2013), for an argument that 2009 represented a turning point in South Africa's recent history. That year saw Jacob Zuma elected as the country's third democratically elected president; the country was plunged into recession; the HIV/Aids pandemic soared to new levels; new crises of unemployment, crime and corruption came to the fore; xenophobia attacks and service delivery strikes swept through the country.

changes – promised or otherwise – and begin to fear that many of the country's divisions of old might resurface in novel post-apartheid forms.

Bailly (2009) adds an important qualification to the notion of the master-signifier which seems here crucial: 'master signifiers usually mask their opposites ... they exist in a polarised form' (p. 63). The openly expressed aspect of the master-signifier props up an ego – that is, the imagined identity of a subject or community – while the unenunciated aspect remains 'buried in the unconscious ... constantly pushing up its opposite number' (p. 63). The function of the master-signifier is thus to redirect potentially painful or anxiety-provoking signifiers, and to do so in such a way 'that a signifying chain with the opposite, bearable, or even comforting meaning emerges' (p. 63). Following the argument developed above, there could barely be a more apt description of how the signifier 'Mandela' is utilized in the post-apartheid context.

The Bonds of Fantasy

Evident in the elevation of Mandela to the realm of 'pure symbol' is the role of a type of mythologization. A master-signifier is never merely objective in its meaning and value, but is animated rather by subjective belief, by the imagination of those who have invested in it. This is to say that the signifier 'Mandela' is today always in part a *projection* of those who have taken pride in, and identified with, the man and his legacy. There is thus some truth, despite the apparent cynicism, in political evaluations that suggest that Mandela's greatness 'is mainly a creation of the collective imagination' (Beresford, 2004). In speaking of Mandela, we have in mind not just the man or Mandela as historical event, but Mandela as focal-point of multiple subjective investments and identifications, Mandela, that is, as shared social fantasy. To make such an observation is by no means to depart from pressing 'real world' political concerns. 'Mandela' has served as a stabilizing signifier, a signifier more able than any other to lend moral purpose and meaning to the social contradictions of the contemporary South African era. Indeed, 'Mandela' enables us to knit together the otherwise discontinuous elements of post-apartheid experience into a narrative of progress.

A crucial qualification should be made here: in psychoanalytic terms, 'fantasy' is not akin to an imaginary flight-of-fancy, an idle illusion, something that should be rejected in favour of the careful consideration of the objective facts of reality. Fantasy is rather what underlies and mediates what we experience as reality; it is what makes reality as such possible. Fantasy is thus indispensable; it provides the lens through which the chaotic and fragmentary nature of subjective and societal reality is afforded a rudimentary narrative coherence. Although not working from a psychoanalytic perspective, Sarah Nuttall's (2013) comments on Mandela's last days point to precisely such a fantasmatic function:

> With the fact of his late old age comes the sense that [Mandela] marks a deep
> void at the heart of a place that has always struggled to mask what it feels might
> be an emptiness at its centre, that has struggled to define itself as a nation and
> to draw together its many fragments into a sustained sense of commonality,
> in the wake of a long racist past. We approach alongside him the anxiety or
> anguish that South Africa is neither a concept nor an idea – just a physical place,
> a geographical accident.

It was in this respect that the demise of Mandela seemed so anxiety-provoking
for the country. It heralded the prospect of a crisis of re-definition, and more than
that, of the divergent strands of post-apartheid society simply failing to cohere.
Or, more dramatically yet – extrapolating a somewhat bleak vision from Nuttall's
conclusion – Mandela's decline may be thought to represent the end of the fantasy,
the point at which the concept of South Africa ceases to work as anything other
than a geographical designation. Perhaps it is the case – easy enough to imagine if
Mandela's legacy were erased from history – that 'South Africa' is no more than
the name for a set of historical events to which no special status, no historical
essence, no grand march of progress can rightly be said to apply.

As sombre as such an eventuality might seem, it is nonetheless one worth
contemplating; it may have 'therapeutic' benefits. How, for instance, might South
Africans see themselves differently; what social, civic and political responsibilities
come to the fore once complacent stories of 'democracy achieved' are interrupted?
What possibilities for self-interrogation emerge once we suspend the narratives
of an extraordinary history and nation that our proximity to the greatness of
Mandela has for so long allowed us to maintain? Despite that fantasy makes a
non-psychotic reality possible, it is also necessary, so psychoanalysis tells us, to
work through those fantasies upon which we have become overly reliant. This
gives us a different relation to those fantasies which have come to function as a
protective shell, those fantasies which routinely obscure disturbing or traumatic
conditions that we would prefer to remain concealed.[4]

The Ways of Love

The question of how – or why – we love Mandela is also crucial. We may distinguish
between several different modalities of love. There is a type of love that is largely
narcissistic in nature and that operates must fundamentally to facilitate self-love.

---

4   The notion of 'traversing the fantasy' sometimes taken as a precondition for a
successful psychoanalytic treatment, entails such a trajectory, namely, a crossing through
the multiple layers of a given fantasy which shields the subject from disconcerting 'reals',
revealing thus the radical contingency of both their given circumstances and of their own
status as subject. Importantly, to 'traverse the fantasy' does not imply that the fantasy be
completely dissipated or destroyed, rather that it be 'passed through', re-situated.

We love those who enable us to maintain an idealized image of ourselves, to bolster and extend the positive qualities of our own self-image. The loved person here is essentially a prop for our own self-regard, a mirror who reflects what (we believe) is best about ourselves and screens out less admirable qualities. Given the function of this type of love, one appreciates both the importance the figure of Mandela plays in the libidinal economy of the nation and, once again, why his prospective demise occasioned so much anxiety. The death of Mandela means – at least in part – the loss of what South Africans feel makes them an exceptional nation, remarkable in the eyes of the world.

There is also the more abstract love of shared social and historical ideals. This type of love concerns those beliefs – what we might call 'to live and die for' values – that not only ground a society, but also link it to its history and set out the ideals that it will continue to strive for. Such a constellation of social and symbolic ideals necessarily exceeds the role of any one person. These comments put us in a position to respond to the question – painful for many – of how, and in what capacity, to let Mandela go. Now that Mandela has died, this may seem a merely academic question; yet his image of course remains, and we should not be too quick to assume that we have in fact relinquished our hold upon him. If it is then the first of the two above types of love that underscores our reticence to give Mandela up, if we love Mandela chiefly as a means of loving ourselves, then, surely, it must by now be time to cut the cord, to bid him a final farewell. We can extend this argument. If we love the image of Mandela in ways that enable us to conceal the injustices and inequalities of the post-apartheid condition and to thus idealize the current social conditions of the country, then it would seem necessary that we leave him behind. More succinctly put: we need to forego the comforting illusions that the *imaginary* figure of Mandela allows us to maintain.

However, inasmuch as Mandela encapsulated a vision of social bonds traversing apartheid's structural divisions, a vision which made the (imperfect) transition from apartheid possible, then it is appropriate that we cherish the unfinished legacy he has left. For, after all, this set of ideals is bigger than any one figure, even if Mandela did more than most to bring these values to life and lend them a recognizable human face. Dawes (2013) makes much the same point, reflecting hopefully on the course that such a permeation of values might take:

> Mandela's long goodbye takes on the form of a return, not as a statue, or as a caricature, but as living potential. That potential is around us in democratic institutions and traditions that, if young, or threatened, are also resilient and powerful ... It is visible in the agonisingly slow, but vital change in the shape of our cities, and the refusal of South Africans to be content with half-a-life, or with the outer forms of freedom, absent its content.

Then again, anxiety may emerge here also, even in respect of Mandela's symbolic legacy. If Mandela made possible 'the post-apartheid', as both political era and mode of subjectivity, then his death cannot but imply the question: What comes after the post-apartheid era, an era which has been synonymous precisely with the figure of Mandela? Furthermore, if we are to credit the notion that Mandela made a version of South African subjectivity possible, then what types of South African subjectivity will be possible in a future where he no longer exists?

Having intimated that love and idealization are rarely innocent, we may now turn to a facet of the public obsession with Mandela that few have remarked upon. The universal outpouring of love and idealization for Mandela in the immediate aftermath of his death has been accompanied by a period of intense vilification directed at his successor as leader of both the ANC and the country, namely Jacob Zuma. These two respective processes – idealization and vilification – are connected; they are part of one and the same dynamic. The more Mandela is idealized, the more Zuma's (not inconsiderable) faults are progressively magnified. Whereas Mandela is lionized, Zuma by contrast, is repeatedly lampooned, reduced to caricature, lambasted as the embodiment of everything wrong with South Africa. This dynamic reflects something of the country's self-ruminations. More to the point yet, it represents the country's inability to bring together what is best and worst, what is most inspiring and most shameful, in our history. One is reminded of the resentful words director Oliver Stone puts into Richard Nixon's mouth in a scene from his (1995) film *Nixon*. Staring with bitterness at a portrait of Kennedy and wondering why the American people loved the younger man so much, he laments: 'When they look at him, they see themselves as they want to be; when they look at me, they see themselves as they are.'

Suffering Idealization

We are all familiar with the figure of the tragic hero, the gallant character who is willing to sacrifice themselves for the good of a cause. Importantly, however, the sacrifice in question may not always be the hero's *life*; it may be of a symbolic sort. That is to say, as in Lacan's notion of being 'between the two deaths', one can die symbolically before one is in fact physically dead. Let us consider a figure – rare at the best of times – that is willing to take on the hate of a community or nation, to assume the role of the villain if this is ultimately what serves the greater public good. One is reminded of the role the psychoanalyst is forced to endure during the travails of the negative transference, in which the patient comes – quite unjustifiably – to see in them everything that they, the patient, most detests and resents. Or, to provide a more dramatic example from within the domain of popular culture, we might follow the argument Slavoj Žižek (2013) makes in respect of the character of Batman in *The Dark Knight Returns*. In order to allow the public to continue to believe in the figure of Harvey Dent, a public prosecutor who is seen as pursuing the ends of justice even in the face of insurmountable odds, Batman assumes the role of the criminal 'public enemy number one' which in fact really belongs to Dent. The heroic here has to do not only with the fact of self-sacrifice, but with the fact that this heroism, this very fact of self-sacrifice, may never be acknowledged as such.

It is not hard to find historical examples of leaders who have had to endure such a treatment, who have been vilified beyond what seems reasonable. Both of Mandela's successors as president –Thabo Mbeki and Jacob Zuma – might be considered cases in point. There is a sense of ethical grandeur that, retrospectively, attaches to such a position, even if it is perhaps not, in the final analysis, fully justified. Hated as one might be in present circumstances, there is always the possibility that what one has done, what one has sacrificed one's self for, will one day by recognized by a future generation.

Lonely as it may be to find one's self in such a position, there is another situation which is potentially even more debilitating. Consider the case of the hero who, rather than being sacrificed for or by the people, is lauded, granted every conceivable honour for qualities and actions that are (at least in part) projections, misrepresentations of who they are. A different type of falsity is involved here, not the falsity of the negative transference (when one is not as bad as has been imagined) but the falsity of the positive transference (when one is not as *good* as has been imagined). Here too, as in the case of the tragic hero, a type of sacrifice is involved, not the sacrifice of one's life, but a sacrifice of what one might privately be, or believe in, for the sake of what people need to see in you. This is part of what Mandela had to undergo: he needed to put himself in the service of the image that others had of him.

Being sublimated in such a way, elevated into the position of 'the most admired person on earth … a secular saint, an embodiment of greatness and an icon of peace and wisdom' (Stengel, 2013) is a necessarily violent process. Such a process would entail the exclusion of many of one's own political values, certain of which one would be obliged to silence so as not to undermine the mythical image one has come to embody. Not all of what one ideally represents, believes, or strives for, can be shown under such circumstances, particularly in respect of one's own more radical views. This, for a man like Mandela, who was so famously prepared to die for what he believed in, was perhaps more difficult than we at first imagine. Moreover, it was not as if Mandela did not hold controversial views. One only needs to consult one of the many muck-racking websites established after his death to see such controversial facts listed: Mandela stood alongside ANC comrades singing 'death to the whites'; Mandela was for many years secretly a member of the South African Communist Party; Mandela was unapologetic of his long-standing friendship with Gaddafi; Mandela condemned the Iraq War and was an ardent opponent of America's aggressive foreign policy; and so and so on (see also, Malan, 2014).

Of course, it can be said that it is better to be *loved* rather than hated for what one is not (that is, for what others have projected upon you). This, surely, is a far more rewarding – even ennobling – form of sacrifice. The rapturous attention of so many might be thought to offset the alienating effects of adopting a persona never quite commensurate with one's own beliefs. Then again, the experience of needing to suffer idealization, to stifle the radical political instincts that had been his lifeblood, cannot have been easy for Mandela.

The Death of the Father

The death of an important father figure – particularly one of the stature of Mandela – can represent a great many things symbolically. It can, of course, result in an ugly series of skirmishes in which various family members and stakeholders struggle for their share of the man legacy's and wealth. This often seems, and has sadly proved, unavoidable. This is not the only outcome that may be predicted of such an event. The death of an esteemed father may represent just as much an auspicious *beginning* as an inauspicious end. This is in fact a well-known literary trope: a grand family story – or historical epic – only in effect really *begins* following the death of a great patriarch. As US soap-operas like *Dallas* and *Brothers and Sisters* demonstrate, little else provides as much by way of interesting new plot developments as does the demise of a powerful and revered father figure.[5]

What most certainly is signalled by such an event is that the father's descendants need to assume responsibility for what had hitherto been his perceived duty. One of Mandela's tasks – perhaps his overriding achievement – was to pull together a radically divided and diverse society, to enable a post-apartheid imaginary that the entire nation could – in very different ways – believe in, and identify with. The signifier 'Mandela' provided the basis – historically unimaginable up until that point – for a type of social consensus that made the post-apartheid public sphere viable. It is this perceived ability to transcend apartheid's lingering culture of hate and separatism, to foster ties of allegiance that crossed the boundaries of race, ethnicity and political allegiance, that characterizes Mandela's lasting greatness. What the 'father of the nation's' demise throws into perspective is the fact that we, as individual citizens, will no longer be able to delegate this task to him. This responsibility, the labour of developing a viable post-apartheid consensus, and indeed, of supporting a shared public sphere, will now fall to those within whom Mandela placed his trust: the people of the country of South Africa.

References

Adorno, T. (1991). *The Culture Industry*. London and New York: Routledge.

Bailly, L. (2009). *Lacan*. Oxford: Oneworld.

Beresford, D. (2004). Mandela's greatness is from being here. *Mail & Guardian*, 7 November.

---

5   In both these TV shows, the 'founding father', that is, the man who has made the wealth and established the name of the large family in question, dies abruptly within the first few episodes.

Bracher, M. (1994). On the psychological and social functions of language: Lacan's theory of the four discourses. In M. Bracher, M.W. Alcorn, R.J. Corthell and F. Massardier-Kenney (eds) *Lacanian Theory of Discourse*, pp. 107–28. New York: New York University Press.

Dawes, N. (2013). Mandela: The long goodbye. *Mail & Guardian*, 28 June.

Fink, B. (1995). *The Lacanian Subject between Language and Jouissance*. Princeton: Princeton University Press.

Fink, B. (2014). *Against Understanding: Cases and Commentary in a Lacanian Key, Volume 1*. London and New York: Routledge.

Frederickson, G. (1990). The making of Mandela. *New York Review of Books*, 27 September.

Freud, S. (1909). Notes upon a case of obsessional neurosis. In J. Strachey (ed.) *The Standard Edition of the Complete Psychological Works of Sigmund Freud, Volume X*, pp. 153–249. London: Hogarth.

Freud, S. (2004). *Mass Psychology and Other Writings*. London: Penguin.

Hook, D. (2013). *A Critical Psychology of the Postcolonial*. London & New York: Routledge.

Laclau, E. (2007). *Emancipations*. London: Verso.

Laclau, E. and Mouffe, C. (1985). *Hegemony and Socialist Strategy*. London: Verso.

Lodge, T. (2006). *Mandela: A Critical Life*. Oxford: Oxford University Press.

Malan, R. (2014). What a lost prison manuscript revels about the real Nelson Mandela. *The Spectator*, 18 January.

Mandela, N. (1994). *Long Walk to Freedom: The Autobiography of Nelson Mandela*. Johannesburg: Macdonald Purnell.

Melman, C. (1980). On obsessional neurosis. In S. Schneiderman (ed.) *Returning to Freud: Clinical Psychoanalysis in the School of Lacan*, pp. 139–59. New Haven: Yale University Press.

Nuttall, S. (2013). The mortality of Nelson Mandela. *Mail & Guardian*, 5 April. http://mg.co.za/article/2013-04-05-00-the-mortality-of-nelson-mandela.

Nxumalo, M. (2013). Mandela for blacks is different to Mandela for whites. *Thought Leader*, July 3. http://www.thoughtleader.co.za/manqobanxumalo/2013/07/03/mandela-for-blacks-is-different-to-mandela-for-whites/.

Stavrakakis, Y. (1997). Green ideology: A discursive reading. *Journal of Political Ideologies*, 2(3), 259–79.

Stengel, R. (2013). Nelson Mandela: Remembering an icon of freedom. *Time Magazine*, 5 December.

Verhaeghe, P. (2001). *Beyond Gender: From Subject to Drive*. New York: Other Press.

Walder, D. (2013). Hysterical nostalgia in the postcolony: From Coming Home to District 9. *Consumption, Markets & Culture*, 17, 2, 143–57.

Žižek, S. (2013). *The Pervert's Guide to Ideology* (dir. S. Fiennes). London: Film 4.

Chapter 3

When Time Gives: Reflections on Two Rivonia Renegades

Johan van der Walt

Introduction

This chapter engages with aspects of the lives of two key figures in the Rivonia trial. The first is Nelson Mandela, one of the accused. The second is Bram Fischer, leader of the defence team. The engagement with Mandela and Fischer will unfold in five sections under the following headings: Mandela and the Laws of Reflection; The Performative, the Constative and the Impossible Foundation; The Gift and the Secret; The Renegade Moment; Bram Fischer's Madness.

The first section consists of a re-reading of the essay Jacques Derrida published on Nelson Mandela when Mandela was still in jail. It engages with the way Derrida situates Mandela within the play of the laws of reflection and how he then moves to contemplate a Mandela who cannot be reduced to or captured and imprisoned by these laws of reflection. The second section moves on to two further themes that Derrida raises in the essay on Mandela, the relation between the performative and the constative in speech acts and the impossibility of foundations or origins. These are key themes in Derrida's thought to which he returns many times in his work. The engagement with these themes in the Mandela essay is significant because of the way it highlights the relation between these themes in Derrida's work, but also because of the way it allows one to trace the boundaries of speculative reflection and to follow a trace to the Mandela who can ultimately not be contained by these boundaries of reflection.

The third section marks these boundaries of reflection with reference to the secret and the gift or the secret of the gift. The concepts of the secret and the gift play a pivotal role in the strand or tradition of philosophical thought that first became known as phenomenology and later as deconstruction. They stand in as reflection-resistant or reflection-resisting articulations of the boundaries of epistemological and normative reflection on and through which existing worlds and their pro- and inhibiting confines are constructed. As such they also point us to a freedom beyond these pro- and inhibiting confines of existing worlds. This freedom cannot be named, but a certain allusion to it is possible through invocation of moments of sheer madness that resist, challenge and rebel against all normative conceptions and ideals of freedom. The fourth section describes these moments as renegade moments, moments that differ from revolutionary moments because they cannot be reduced to the endorsement, postulation and revolving of ancient normative conceptions – the hallmark of revolutions according to Arendt. Ultimately, they simply erupt as instances of an absolute freedom to act. 'Madness beyond insanity', Foucault calls this freedom.

The section on the Secret and of the Gift (third section) already invokes a remarkable renegade moment in the life of Mandela. The last section, 'Bram Fischer's Madness,' turns to a life that was ultimately consumed by a renegade moment. In view of Arendt's assessment of revolutions in terms of the revolving or recycling of ancient normative ideals, renegade moments should be considered as the real or essential inauguration of the newness and new worlds that Arendt's reflections on revolutions and politics also contemplate profoundly. The renegade moment – in the instant of its withdrawal into the madness of absolute freedom – is not concerned with ancient norms and values. It is not concerned. It is simply and exclusively an eruption of unprecedented action. It is the eruption of the unprecedented. If at all related to revolutions, they might be considered as the very seeds from which revolutions ultimately spring. But they ultimately also withdraw from revolutions – and the stale language of revolutions – to return to that which always occurs much earlier. They withdraw to the absolutely unprecedented opening or giving of time from which new times and new worlds derive in the very final or first analysis. They take part in the pure performative, the pure act of withdrawal that 'is' or 'gives' time and through which time gives itself to new times and new worlds by withdrawing from them.

Mandela and the Laws of Reflection

Jacques Derrida published his essay on Mandela in 1987. Mandela was still in jail at the time. The essay reflected then and still reflects today on Mandela's resistance to the apartheid regime, focusing mostly on Mandela's address to the court during the Rivonia trial. The essay turns on three key themes to which Derrida always came back in his work – the laws of reflections and speculation; the relation between the constative and the performative elements in speech acts; and the impossibility of acts of foundation and the need to substitute or at least supplement such 'acts' with retroactive ratifications or consolidations without which they basically remain spectral stirrings with no significant purchase on reality. In this section of this chapter, we shall briefly look at the first of these three themes again and at the way that Derrida articulated it in his essay on Mandela.

Derrida starts off with Mandela's admiration for the law and specifically with Mandela's dismissal of Marxist critiques of the parliamentary system as 'undemocratic and reactionary'. 'On the contrary', stated Mandela clearly during the Rivonia trial, 'I *am an admirer* of [this] system ... [and] *have great respect* for the British political institutions ... and system of justice'. 'The independence of its judiciary never fails to arouse my admiration', he continued. 'Respect', 'admirer' and 'admiration' are the key words here for Derrida and the emphases on these words are his.[1]

Mandela's respect and admiration nevertheless do not make him a 'simple inheritor' of these British institutions. If he is an inheritor, writes Derrida, he is the 'authentic inheritor' who does not simply 'conserve and reproduce' but also 'turn[s the inheritance] upon occasion against those who claim to be its guardians' so as to 'reveal in the inheritance ... what had never seen the light of day'.[2] This 'what had never seen the light of day' would be revealed, if at all, by an 'unheard-of *act* of reflection', says Derrida. It would be revealed, in other words, still by an act of reflection and thus by a certain mirroring, but an unheard-of act of such reflection or mirroring. The act of reflection or mirroring and thus of repetition appears to be inescapable also here in this authentic inheritance, but there is something extraordinary about it, so much so that it is 'unheard-of'. We shall return to this invocation of an 'unheard-of act of reflection' below, for in it is discernible an act that might be called 'purely revolutionary' or even 'pre-revolutionary' because of the way it embodies the very 'seeds' of revolution. Let us first look at what is at stake for Derrida in these mirroring reflections that he also ascribes to Mandela's ad-*mir*-ation of the law.

Derrida's engagement with mirroring and the *speculum* (the Latin for mirror still discernible in the German *Spiegel*, Dutch *Spiegel* and Afrikaans spieël) can be traced back to his engagement with Hegel and Bataille in an early essay on 'restricted and general economies'. Speculative economies are restricted economies, argues Derrida in this essay. They only spend for purposes of investment. The risk they take with others and otherness through the temporary forfeiture of possession has one aim only, and that is to increase possession. The speculation at stake in this investment of the self or the 'own' in the 'other' is aimed at a profitable re-possession of the self. This profitable investment and speculation goes to the heart of Hegel's speculative philosophy, according to Derrida. In Hegel's historical dialectic between spirit and matter or nature, spirit only spends itself (alienates itself/objectifies itself) in nature or matter in order to return to itself as dialectically enriched spirit. It is not an expenditure of spirit in an encounter with matter or nature for the sake of matter or nature. It is not an expenditure of spirit for the sake of losing itself selflessly in that what is strange and foreign to it. The latter expenditure of the self, the complete loss of selfhood, argues Derrida, is what Bataille has in mind with the notion of 'general economy'. At issue in this general economy is an expenditure of the self on the other that envisages or contemplates no profitable return from which selfhood would emerge enriched or enlarged. At issue in the general economy is a pure eroticism, that is, a pure desire

---

1 Jacques Derrida, 'The laws of reflection: Nelson Mandela, in admiration', in Jacques Derrida and Mustapha Tlili (eds) *For Nelson Mandela* (New York: Seaver Books, 1987), 16.

2 Derrida, 'The laws of reflection', 17.

for the other or otherness and a pure desire to merge with this otherness without any consideration of possible consequences. Were Bataille's general economy possible, it would not pay the slightest consideration to economic concerns with survival, let alone concerns of profitability.[3]

Attention to Mandela's mirroring admiration for the law and Western political and legal institutions undoubtedly still confines him (at least for us) to this speculative dialectics of investment. The focus on Mandela's admiration for Western democratic institutions renders him visible as one who risks his life for laudable ideals that we all understand. And this visibility is the beginning of a new confinement. The closing paragraph of Derrida's essay makes this abundantly clear:

> [W]hat remains to be seen ... is also the figure of Mandela. Who is he? We have looked at him through words which are sometimes the devices for observation, which can in any case become that if we are not careful. What we have described, in trying precisely to escape speculation, was a sort of great historical watchtower or observation post. But nothing permits us to imagine this unity as assured, still less the legitimacy of this optic reflection, of its singular laws, of the law, of its place of institution, of presentation or of revelation, for example of what we assemble too quickly under the name of the West. But doesn't this presumption of unity produce something like an effect ... that so many forces, always, try to appropriate for themselves? An effect visible and invisible, like a mirror, also hard, like the walls of a prison. All that still hides Nelson Mandela from our sight.[4]

All the words through the optics of which Derrida endeavoured to observe Mandela in the essay that ends with this passage evidently bother Derrida. They have, he fears, produced an effect. They have constructed an image of Mandela, as if from the vantage point of a watchtower or observation post. And it is from this vantage point that many forces seek to appropriate Mandela. But the unity and legitimacy of this effect is in no way assured, suggests Derrida. In fact, not only is the unity and legitimacy of this effect not assured, the effect effectively hides Mandela from our eyes, insists Derrida. The unitary effect – the picture we get of Mandela through the optic play generated by words of the essay – effectively hides Mandela from our sight, like the walls of a prison. The walls created by the mirroring play of language are as hard as the walls of a prison, he concludes. His choice of words in this regard inescapably reminds one of the self-imprisonment in a hall of mirrors that Calvino describes in *If on a Winter's Night a Traveller*.[5]

The closing paragraph of Derrida's essay on Mandela is truly remarkable, for among the words that went into Derrida's engagement with Mandela in this essay

---

3   Cf. Derrida, *L'Écriture et la Différence* (Paris: Éditions du Seuil, 1967), 369–407; *Writing and Difference* (Chicago: University of Chicago Press, 1978), 251–77.

4   Derrida, 'The laws of reflection', 41–2.

5   Italo Calvino, *If on a Winter's Night a Traveller* (New York: Vintage, 1988), 161–8.

were also words that one might have assessed as an appreciation of the authentic inheritance or unheard-of reflection that at least in some respect transcends the regular reflection or mere mirroring that kept Mandela doubly imprisoned at the time (beyond the brick walls of the prison there were also the hard walls of optic mirroring that kept him incarcerated) and perhaps still keep him imprisoned today. For instance, Derrida also engaged with the Mandela who, in addition to his declaration of respect for Western political institutions, holds up to these institutions a challenging perfection of their ideals of democracy and equality and respect for the individual that he gleaned from 'Marxist reading' and the 'structure and organization of early African societies'. 'The land', Mandela averred in his address to the court, 'then the main means of production, belonged to the tribe'. 'There were no rich or poor, and there was no exploitation of man by man.' In this society Mandela discerned the '*seeds of a revolutionary democracy* in which none will be held in slavery or servitude, and in which poverty, want and insecurity shall be no more'.[6]

Is there not here, in this invocation of the seeds of a revolutionary democracy that Mandela discerned in early African societies, an intimation of the unheard-of reflection that ultimately makes Mandela not just an inheritor but an authentic inheritor of Western democracy that 'reveals ... what has never yet been seen in the inheritance'? One might want to think so, but Derrida does not even exclude *these* observations of Mandela from the 'devices of observation' through which the essay has effectively constructed a unitary image of him. Going by the regular rules and principles of prose and dissertation, Mandela's invocation of the revolutionary democracy that can be gleaned from early African social arrangements is part and parcel of the hard prison and speculative walls that still hide him from our eyes.

In other words, the unitary effect created by the language of the essay on Mandela is not broken by the invocation of Mandela's fascination with early African societies. It is simply completed by it. It only contributes to a more complete unitary effect that also accounts for an element of Mandela's person that is well known and can hardly be ignored without becoming grossly negligent as far as constructing Mandela's portrait is concerned. But the deconstruction of this portrait has surely not yet begun with this completion of it. Paying due attention to Mandela's fascination with the social organization of the societies from which he came is essential for anyone who would like to begin to understand him. But the critical or deconstructive move that would begin to understand Mandela also on this count as an *authentic heir* of the traditions of these societies would have to begin to ask how Mandela does or did not simply 'conserve and reproduce' this inheritance but also 'turn[s or turned it] upon occasion against those who claim to be its guardians' so as to 'reveal in [it] ... what had never seen the light of day'. Derrida's essay does not claim to have begun to do this with regard to either of these two elements of Mandela's double inheritance. The 'unheard-of reflection' that Mandela may have accomplished with regard to the traditions that

---

6   Derrida, 'The laws of reflection', 24, 26.

he admires to 'reveal in [them] what has never seen the light of day' must itself still be revealed. The suggestion at the end of the essay is clear. There is a Mandela that we have not seen yet and may never come to see. For all practical purposes one can call this Mandela the secret Mandela, the one whose secret has not yet been revealed to anyone and will never be revealed.

What are the conditions for talking earnestly about 'the secret Mandela' or 'Mandela's secret'? There are probably more conditions for talking about a secret and for talking in this case about 'Mandela's secret' than can be listed here. But one crucial condition is this one: To remain a secret, the secret may never be revealed and must in fact not at all be subject or susceptible to any possibility of revelation. Only when this condition is fulfilled can one talk seriously about a secret. This is what Umberto Eco tells us in striking fashion in one of his novels, but it is also a crucial element of Derrida's understanding of the secret, contends Jean-Luc Nancy.[7] Can we nevertheless begin to understand better what is at stake in this secret that cannot be revealed? Can one come to understand something of or about a secret without revealing it and thus ruining it? The suggestion in what follows is that this is indeed feasible. The suggestion is in fact that this is what Derrida's work aimed at all along. Deconstruction is an endeavour to alert us to secrets that cannot be revealed and to facilitate an understanding of or at least an experience of these secrets, an experience of their irreducible secrecy that will not allow for any revelation. It is thus only through deconstruction that we might come closer to the secret Mandela that we will never come to see. And that is how we will approach Mandela's un-disclosable secret in what follows – through deconstruction and specifically through two further strategies or themes of deconstruction that Derrida brings into play in the essay on Mandela. The first concerns the relation between the performative and constative in speech act theory. The second concerns the figure of impossible foundational acts.

The Performative, the Constative and the Impossible Foundation

The other two themes of deconstruction announced here, the relation between the performative and constative elements of speech acts and the *impossibility of*

---

7   Jean-Luc Nancy, *La pensée dérobée* (Paris: Galilée, 2001), 63: 'Il veut toucher ainsi au secret … de tout nom et qui est le secret par excellence: celui qui reste secret même quand on le dévoile, surtout quand on le dévoile.' Cf. Umberto Eco, *Foucault's Pendulum* (London: Quality Paperbacks Direct, 1989), 619–20: 'We invented a nonexistent Plan, and They not only believed it was real but convinced themselves that They had been part of it for ages, or rather, They identified the fragments of their muddled mythology as moments of our Plan, moments joined in a logical, irrefutable web of analogy, semblance, suspicion … A plot, if there is to be one, must remain secret. A secret that, if we only knew it, would dispel our frustration, lead us to salvation; or else the knowing of it in itself would be salvation. Does such a luminous secret exist? Yes, provided it is never known.'

founding that haunts all constitutional acts, indeed lead us deeper into the realm of Mandela's secret. Considering that constitutional acts of founding that inaugurate new institutional settings are also speech acts that convey or communicate meaningful content, the two themes are necessarily closely related. Derrida brings the theme of the performative and constative sides of the speech act into play in two regards in the essay on Mandela. The first concerns the failed speech act that marked and marred the constitutionalization and institutionalization of apartheid. The second concerns the revolutionary dream of a purely performative speech act that would never become contained or constrained by the constative acts that result from the performative.

The essay describes apartheid as a failed speech act, an act that was simply too weak to establish the order that it aimed to establish. Speech acts that aim to found new orders perpetrate a minimum or threshold level of violence without which they fail to achieve what they set out to achieve. They have to break down old orders effectively and they have to eradicate all significant resistance to the new order effectively. Only then does the violence that they continue to perpetrate or once perpetrated become inconspicuous or surreptitious enough to be forgotten and only then does the new order begin to appear as an instance of effective order and not as a continuation of disorderly violence. This is what apartheid could never do. It could never perpetrate enough violence, the minimum level of violence required to establish itself. Derrida writes:

> Not all performatives, a theoretician of *speech acts* would say, are "happy". That depends on a great number of conditions and conventions that form the context of such events. In the case of South Aica, certain "conventions" were not respected, the violence was too great, visibly too great, at a moment when this invisibility extended to a new international scene, and so on. The white community was *too* much in the minority, the disproportion of wealth *too* flagrant. From then on this violence remains at once excessive and powerless, insufficient in its result, lost in its own contradiction. It cannot manage to have itself forgotten, as in the case of states founded on genocide or quasi-extermination. Here [in the case of apartheid] the violence of the origin must repeat itself indefinitely and act out its rightfulness in a legislative apparatus whose monstrosity fails to pay back. A pathological proliferation of juridical prostheses (laws, acts, amendments) destined to legalize to the slightest detail the effects of fundamental racism, of a state racism, the unique and the last in the world.[8]

The description or analysis of apartheid that Derrida articulates here evidently turns on a radical *real-political* understanding of political institutionalization. He clearly exempts no institutional foundation from what seems to be an indispensable founding violence. But there are conventions regarding this founding violence that the apartheid regime did not respect. Apartheid's violence was too visible

---

8 Derrida, 'The laws of reflection', 18.

at a time when a certain insistence that violence be kept invisible became an international standard. Derrida's invocation of speech act theory merges here with Walter Benjamin's critique of violence that would become the main focus in his seminal essay 'Force of law'.[9] Benjamin's critique of violence entertains no illusionary ideals about institutionalizations that would not be violent. Derrida would take Benjamin to task in 'Force of law' for entertaining the notion of a final apocalyptic violence – a divine violence – that would finally break out of the cycle of law-creating and law-maintaining violence. But Benjamin's critique remained a functional heuristic for Derrida in 'Force of law' and so it is also here in the essay on Mandela. In terms of Benjamin's critique, apartheid's violence can be analysed as an infinitely insufficient law-founding violence that necessitated an infinitely excessive law-enforcing violence.

It is also against this background of the inevitability of institutional violence of either the founding or securing kind that the bizarre 'liberal' rejection of the ANC's turn to violence in the struggle against apartheid becomes glaringly evident – the rejection of those liberals who worked against apartheid from within the system and insisted that the resistance to apartheid remains 'democratic'. This liberal rejection of the ANC's turn to 'anti-democratic' measures turned on nothing less than a convenient blindness regarding the violence perpetrated by the system of apartheid on a daily basis. The violence perpetrated by the system of apartheid was abominable, these liberals surely acknowledged, but that somehow did not count when it came to taking any kind of concrete action. When the stakes were really up, only the violence that sought to end apartheid's violence counted and warranted enough rejection to cut ties, refuse association and decline support. The violence of apartheid itself did not warrant this principled cutting of ties, refusal of association and denial of support. These liberals continued to work within the system, associated with it and thus supported it despite its quotidian violence. They thus lent apartheid some kind of legitimacy that the resistance to apartheid, on the other hand, did not merit according to them. They insisted that the ANC should join *them* in a democratic struggle against an undemocratic regime. They did not contemplate giving up their institutional and personal security in order to join the ANC. One should also not forget that this was the time that two of the major 'liberal democracies' of the world, the United States and the United Kingdom, the latter being the very democracy whose institutions Mandela singled out in his admiration, labelled the ANC and Mandela as 'terrorists'.[10] It is against this background that Mandela explained the ANC's resort to armed resistance and rejection of this supposedly 'democratic way': 'Only a people already enjoying democratic and constitutional rights has any grounds for speaking of [such] rights. This does not have meaning for those who do not benefit from them.'[11]

---

9   Derrida, *Force de Loi: Le 'Fondament Mystique de L'Autorité'* (Paris: Galilée, 1994).
10 Mandela was only taken off the United States' official list of terrorists in 2008.
11 Derrida, 'The laws of reflection', 19.

However, there is absolutely nothing mysterious or enigmatic about this rejection of democratic rights, principles and measures under circumstances that in any case make a mockery of these rights, principles and measures. It requires little more than common sense to reject the demand to play by rules by which no one is playing. This part of Mandela's person and legacy is therefore neither extraordinary, nor mysterious or enigmatic. It is far from 'secretive'. His stance in this regard was and is still fully visible, transparent and comprehensible. At issue here is surely not an 'unheard-of reflection' that 'reveals what has never seen the light of day'. By taking this stance, the Mandela whom we cannot see has not yet moved one inch closer to the stage that will, in any case, never present or reveal him. What is Derrida getting at then, when he talks about a Mandela that is infinitely shielded from our vision by a wall of mirrors that is as hard as prison walls?

The second invocation of the performative/constative configuration of speech acts and of law founding and securing violence in the essay gives us a clue in this regard. It leads one closer to what might still become 'manifest' as the undisclosed secret of Mandela, the secret that nevertheless will remain undisclosed and unrevealed even while becoming manifest. Derrida returns to the performative/constative thematic in response to the new order that Mandela envisages for South Africa: An order that is founded on 'the will of an entire nation'.[12] According to Derrida, Mandela seems to be invoking Rousseau here without quoting him. He seems to be invoking a general will that is not just the sum of all the individual wills that constitute a people.[13] And we know that Rousseau's general will is a fiction, an idea that has to be presupposed for purposes of entertaining a certain idea of inclusive democracy, but one that has no material reality. Mandela, in other words, appears to envisage for South Africa something that is, going by all realistic expectations, simply impossible. He was not one for real or realistic expectations. He always chose the unexpected route, writes Achille Mbembe poignantly.[14]

Not only is that which Mandela envisages for South Africa realistically speaking impossible. It also runs head-on into the problem of an impossible institutionalization. At issue is a 'performative [institutionalization that] will not appear to refer to any fundamental pre-existing law'. Being an idea of which the material realization is impossible, it would have to 'erase itself from all empirical determination' for it 'seems no more accessible here than anywhere else'. What Mandela envisages for South Africa runs into the same problematic that the foundations of new constitutional orders generally run into, but it also does this so with the stakes raised infinitely higher. To begin with the problem of foundation:

---

12 Ibid.

13 Ibid.

14 Achille Mbembe, 'Nelson Mandela, les chemins inattendus', *Le Monde Diplomatique*, August 2013, 14–15.

This phenomenon marks the establishment of almost all states after a decolonization. Mandela knows that: no matter how democratic it is, and even if it seems to conform to the principle of the equality of all before the law, the absolute inauguration of a state cannot presuppose the previously *legitimized* existence of a national entity. The same is true for a first constitution. The total unity of a nation is not identified for the first time except by contract – formal or not, written or not – which institutes some fundamental law. Now this contract is never actually signed, except by supposed representatives of the nation which is supposed to be "entire". This fundamental law cannot, either in law or in fact, simply precede that which at once institutes it and nevertheless supposes it: projecting and reflecting it! It can in no way precede this extraordinary performative by which a signature authorizes itself to sign, in a word, legalizes itself on its own without the guarantee of a preexisting law. This violence and this autographic fiction are found at work just as surely in what we call individual autobiography as in the "historical" origin of states.[15]

As already mentioned, this theme of the impossible foundation – requiring pre-existing authorization that it will only obtain later, retroactively, etc. – fascinated Derrida endlessly and his work returns to it often.[16] He probably never realized – or if he did never indicated that he did – that he was grappling with a problematic that Hans Kelsen had already addressed squarely and without much ado in his *Reine Rechtslehre* as well as in other writings.[17] Kelsen very lucidly concluded that the *Grundnorm* or foundational norm was nothing more than a presupposition or a fiction that we must maintain for the sake of speaking coherently about law as law. For Kelsen too, the law always lacks a secure foundation. Whatever foundational security it might ever come to claim, has to be extracted from the strength of a presupposition. However, it is from Derrida and Derridean thinkers – especially Jean-Luc Nancy – that we gain a deeper understanding of the dynamics at stake in this presupposition or fiction with which legal systems are sustained. The name of Marcel Mauss – one of the thinkers on whom Derrida himself relied fundamentally for the thoughts that are at issue here, should also be added here. It is from these thinkers that we learn that the presupposition of law on which legal orders depend are ultimately based on either a gift or an act of sacrifice or, most likely, on a combination of gift and sacrifice.[18] And it is here,

---

15   Derrida, 'The laws of reflection', 20.

16   Cf. especially Jacques Derrida, 'Declarations of independence' (1986) *New Political Science* 7–15.

17   Hans Kelsen, *Reine Rechtslehre* (Aalen: Scientia Verlag, 1994), 66–7; Kelsen, *Vom Wesen und Wert der Demokratie* (Aalen: Scientia Verlag, 1981), 31–2.

18   For a more extensive discussion of the distinction between gift and sacrifice, cf. J. van der Walt, 'Timeo Danais et Dona Ferre and the constitution that Europeans may one day have come to give themselves', in J. van der Walt and Ellsworth (eds) *Constitutional Sovereignty and Social Solidarity in Europe* (Baden Baden: Nomos Verlag, 2015), 267–307.

in the region of the distinction between gift and sacrifice, that one draws closer to Mandela's secret, closer to something about Mandela that one will never come to know, notwithstanding the possibility of knowing about it, notwithstanding the awareness that this 'something' is there. However, it will presently become clear that this 'something' is not a thing at all.

The undeniable *logic* of sacrifice makes sacrifice a very likely 'filler' with which the irreducible emptiness or lack that accompanies constitutional foundations can be 'filled'. The logic of sacrifice can very plausibly stand in for the representative contract that should always but never in fact precedes constitutional foundations. It would seem to self-evidently answer the question regarding the identity of the author or authoritative power that gets to decide the foundational rules that inaugurate the new constitutional order. The question opens up, we saw, because we do not have a pre-existing rule in place that stipulates who the author or authoritative power should be. Something must be invoked that fills the space opened up by the absence of a rule so self-evidently that the question regarding the rule does not or cannot even arise properly. The invocation of sacrifice answers the question in advance: We suffered. We sacrificed. So we get to make the new rules, end of story. And this being so, we can also demand that sacrifices now be made by others, by those who made us suffer or caused the suffering. There is such a self-evident logic to all of this that no one in his or her right mind can be imagined to doubt the principle.[19] In fact, the logic of sacrifice seems to negate the need for presupposing Kelsen's *Grundnorm*, the *Grundnorm* on the basis of which the existence of a political people can be assumed. The one who sacrificed through suffering just 'naturally' becomes the *pouvoir constituant* that gets to lay down the new constitutional order; hence also Nancy's acute observation that the history of sovereignty is irreducibly tied to the history of sacrifice.[20] But there is of course nothing 'natural' about the 'idea' that past suffering founds the right to make new rules for the future. Nietzsche, for one, balked at the idea. But Nietzsche

---

19 Ulrich K. Preuss, 'Perspectives on post-conflict constitutionalism' (2006/7) 51 *New York Law School Law Review* 469–70: 'Constitutions come into being after a revolution or war ... After a revolution ... the triumphant forces lay out their principles of how society should be ordered. [They ... impose] their rule upon the defeated groups who are then usually denounced as "counter-revolutionary", "reactionary", or sometimes even as "enemies of the people". Constitution-making after a war is not very different. If the war was lost, then the demoralized masses place the blame for their defeat and sufferings on the ... "old regime". They throw their rulers out of office and ... demand ... a new constitution [that] reflect their needs, hopes and aspirations. But even after a victorious war, a new distribution of power, i.e., a new constitution, is on the agenda of the nation. The people want recognition and remuneration for their *sacrifices* and hence demand a new distribution of the benefits of the social compact' (emphasis added, text slightly paraphrased).

20 Nancy, *Le Sens du Monde* (Paris: Galilée, 1993), 141.

himself was acutely aware how 'self-evident' or 'natural' this idea had become in the course of a history of Christianization.[21]

This logic of sacrifice can indeed take us a long way into the foundation of some constitutional order, no doubt. But there is one essential distance that it cannot cover. It cannot reach what Mandela envisaged for the new South Africa, namely, a constitutional order that would be one laid down by and for 'the entire nation'. Mandela's and Rousseau's counter-factual ideal of a constitution founded by and on a general will that is the will of each and everyone, cannot be realized by the sovereignty claimed solely on the basis of past sacrifices and past suffering. This is so because those who inflicted suffering and demanded sacrifices in the past, however unjustly and obnoxiously so, are still part of this 'entire nation'. If the new constitutional order is to be one for the entire nation, past sacrifices no longer suffice as the obvious foundation for the new constitutional authority and constitutional order. Something else or extra must be assumable and assumed then. Chances are that those who suffered and sacrificed in the past will indeed often or at least sometimes play pivotal roles in post-liberation foundational procedures, but if they are to do so on behalf of 'the entire nation', quite a few assumptions or presuppositions will have to be possible regarding their 'extraordinary wisdom', that is, the 'extraordinary wisdom' – probably obtained through their own suffering – 'not to make the same mistakes', or the like. Quite a few assumptions will have to be possible about their extraordinary generosity, humanity, decency, etc., for none of this will be readily attested by a pre-existing and pre-documented rule or norm that has been signed or ratified by everyone involved.

Imagine those responsible for causing untold suffering in the past ever signing or ratifying the signature of such a document. If there is any of the typical psychological resistance left in them – resistance that might range from regular honour, pride and the understandable wish not to be embarrassed in public, on the one hand, to persistently parochial self-righteousness and pathological inability to own up to any mistakes or misdeeds, on the other – past oppressors will not sign a document that will properly license the hitherto oppressed as the *pouvoir constituant* that can produce a properly grounded foundational norm or *Grundnorm*. And even if they would, what would the dignity and legitimacy of the *pouvoir constituant* and *Grundnorm* gain from the signature of those who signed it, belly up, with no trace left in them of the honour, pride and regular psychological resistance that reside in simple selfhood?[22] Should they – these belly-up signatories – not rather be discarded, Schmittian style, as the 'vanquished enemy' who has nothing further to say about the political future of the people, thereby accepting that they are

---

21   Cf. F. Nietzsche, 'Zur Genealogie der Moral', in *Sämtliche Werke, Kritische Studienausgabe*, vol. 5 (Berlin: Walter de Gruyter, 1999).

22   Recall for a moment Hegel's dialectic of the master and the slave: The master can gain no self-consciousness from the acknowledgement of a slave who has no self-consciousness. Cf. G.W.F. Hegel, *Phänomenologie des Geistes* in *Werke in 20 Bänden, Bnd 3* (Frankfurt a.M: Suhrkamp Verlag, 1970), 145–55.

simply not part of 'the entire nation'? Would this not be less embarrassing to the vanquished and more dignifying to everyone involved?

Circumstances might be imaginable under which this Schmittian resolution may indeed be more 'dignifying' to everyone involved, but they would be limited to cases where the vanquished enemy or oppressor has for all practical purposes no combatant left standing and simply has to sign an unconditional peace treaty and depart from the scene (supposing for the moment signing the treaty would still serve any purpose other than final humiliation). Such cases would, in other words, be restricted to instances of quasi-extermination with regard to which serious questions regarding constitutive and constitutional legitimacy, dignity, etc., would no longer be pertinent and nothing less than distasteful to anyone with any degree of common sense. Whatever one may wish to think of situations like these, this was not the situation in which South Africa found itself towards the end of apartheid. A Schmittian resolution of the conflict, the quintessentially sacrificial resolution,[23] was therefore not an option that Mandela or anyone else could contemplate at the time.

What then, might have made a Kelsenian termination of apartheid feasible? Let us ask more generally: What might make a *pouvoir constituant* and a *Grundnorm* for the *entire nation* assumable or presumable in the absence of the proven and pre-existent title to sovereignty and constitutional authority that we contemplated above? What will make it feasible to presuppose such a *Grundnorm* for the entire nation in the way Kelsen contemplates the presupposition of the *Grundnorm*? The one thing that stands a chance of making this presupposition feasible is a certain retreat from the past that leaves many things undecided and open, open enough to create a space in which an entire nation can commence to simply live together again and find a modus vivendi of the kind that Rawls contemplates as the necessary first step to what may eventually emerge as an overlapping consensus.[24] At issue in this 'leaving things undecided and open' would be a retreat from the logic of sacrifice. This logic, we saw, ties everyone inescapably to the past and to past scores that must still be settled. At issue in the retreat from this logic would be a turn to the rather illogical or at least a-logical dynamic of the gift from which Derrida distinguished the relentless logic of sacrifice.

Why the gift? Why is the gift an alternative to sacrifice, considering the proximity and almost lack of distinction between gift and sacrifice that common sense might stress easily? And why might Mandela be said to have opted for the gift instead of sacrifice? And why might the secret of Mandela and the Mandela that we will never come to see be related to this option for the groundless gift instead of the logically well-grounded sacrifice? Let us consider these questions one by one.

---

23   Cf. Wolfgang Palaver, 'A Girardian reading of Schmitt's political theology' (1992) 93 *Telos* 43–68.

24   Cf. John Rawls, *Political Liberalism* (New York: Columbia University Press, 1996), 142, 154–64.

The Gift and the Secret

Why the gift? How does the gift differ from sacrifice notwithstanding its apparent proximity to sacrifice? Sacrifice ties one to the past, the gift breaks with it. This difference becomes evident in a certain forgiveness that simply breaks with the past and thus allows for the very commencement of a new beginning and a new time. The gift in forgiveness lies in the new time that it makes possible, the time that it gives by allowing a break with the past. The gift in forgiveness is the gift of time, that is, the giving of time and the time that is given. This is a key insight that Hannah Arendt already articulated clearly and which Derrida would revisit extensively and incisively,[25] and it is this insight that casts significant light on Mandela's secret without revealing it. It is the regard for the mystery or secret that attaches to any forgiveness that *simply gives time* that leads one into the vicinity of Mandela's irreducible and unfathomable secret. It is to this link between the secret of the gift and Mandela's secret to which we turn now.

One will never be able to start again if one cannot at some stage just let go of the past, Arendt tells us.[26] At issue in this *general* letting go of the past is a forgiving that has more in common with a Nietzschean forgetting than a Christian forgiveness. Derrida would note the Christianization of forgiveness that would eventually take place in South Africa under the auspices of the Truth and Reconciliation Commission.[27] This Christianized forgiveness still demanded that those who committed crimes confess and come clean. It singled them out for a forgiveness that had to be deserved through confession and remorse, the kind of forgiveness that Derrida unmasked as no forgiveness at all. There is no one left to forgive if the only candidates for forgiveness are those who have already dissociated themselves remorsefully from their misdeeds, he showed us with an exact and exacting conceptual analysis.[28] The argument may well have raised concerns among many that Derrida actually proposed a reckless 'letting off the hook' of criminals, but it surely also created space for – and may well have contemplated – the forceful claim that the regular course of criminal justice provided a sounder alternative to this Christian forgiveness as far as managing or negotiating the transition from apartheid to post-apartheid was concerned.[29] Be

---

25   Cf. Jacques Derrida, *Donner le temps 1. La fausse monnaie* (Paris: Éditions Galilée, 1991).

26   Hannah Arendt, *The Human Condition* (Chicago: University of Chicago Press, 1989), 236–42.

27   Jacques Derrida, *Cosmopolitanism and Forgiveness* (London and New York: Routledge, 2001), 30–32.

28   Derrida, *Cosmopolitanism and Forgiveness*, 32–8.

29   The legitimacy of a criminal justice system that programmatically leaves certain crimes unprosecuted will always remain in question, went the argument. Whether the new sovereign should punish or pardon in the wake of prosecution and conviction is of course a different question. Cf. J. van der Walt, 'Vertical sovereignty, horizontal constitutionalism,

it as it may, this Christianized forgiveness was still much too much bound up with the past and past misdeeds to qualify for the forgetful Nietzschean liberation from the spirit of revenge. It was still too fixated on wrongdoers to facilitate the gift of more time for an entire nation that would consist of both the culpable and the innocent. Moreover, this massively mediatized fixation on a select number of wrongdoers in fact went a long way towards obfuscating the fact that much of that which was fundamentally and structurally wrong in the past was being left untouched in the 'orchestrated' transition that was taking place, as some would argue very forcefully later.[30]

Why can Mandela be said to have opted for a gesture of forgetful forgiving that gave *time* to an *entire nation* and not just to some? Why can he be said to have given an entire nation the first time ever to work out the conditions for a common future that would include everyone involved? The gesture of forgetful forgiving would eventually be authored by a whole generation of ANC leadership. A whole generation of ANC leaders would eventually sit down with leading members of the apartheid government without insisting on confessions or concessions that settled past scores. However, Mandela can be said to have initiated this gift in way that also created the opportunity for other ANC leaders to follow. Why so? A key passage from his biography provides the answer. Mandela and the ANC leadership had already been transferred from Robben Island to the Pollsmoor prison in Cape Town when he was referred to the Volks Hospital for surgery in 1985. The transfer to Pollsmoor was clearly understood as a move of the government to isolate the core leadership of the ANC from the rest of the ANC members incarcerated on Robben Island. After his surgery Mandela was further informed that he would henceforth also be isolated from the other ANC leaders in the Pollsmoor prison. This isolation could have had devastating consequences for the ANC leadership, but Mandela saw in it an opportunity for a renegade moment in which he would break lines with all lines, even with his comrades, in order to break with the past. This is how he explained the situation:

> The change, I decided, was not a liability but an opportunity. I was not happy to be separated from my colleagues … [b]ut my solitude gave me a certain liberty, and I resolved to use it to do something I had been pondering for a long while: begin discussions with the government … This would be extremely sensitive. Both sides regarded discussions as a sign of weakness and betrayal. Neither would come to the table until the other made significant concessions.[31]

---

subterranean capitalism: A case of competing retroactivities' (2010) 26(1) *South African Journal on Human Rights* 118–19.

30   R.A. Wilson, *The Politics of Truth and Reconciliation in South Africa* (Cambridge: Cambridge University Press, 2001).

31   Nelson Mandela, *Long Walk To Freedom* (Randburg: Macdonald Purnell, 1994), 513. Heinz Klug (University of Wisconsin Law School) cast doubt on the veracity of this passage from Mandela's biography in a response to the argument regarding Mandela's

Mandela could easily have alienated himself from the ANC leadership with this risky move. He could easily have sidelined himself, among his peers, as the comrade who had given up the struggle, the one who had become tired and just wanted to get out of prison while he still had some years to live. The language of betrayal, the melancholic language that is always tied to the past, was still in the air. And the apartheid regime could easily have exploited his move by encouraging the interpretation that he had given up the struggle. They could easily have abused his initiative for the sake of some strategic advantage. Mandela nevertheless took this step with the clear conviction that he was doing what he had to do. With this courageous step of selfless leadership and statesmanship he single-handedly precipitated the first essential step in the political transition that produced a constitutional foundation for an *entire* nation. With this unique act of political conviction and courage, Mandela bestowed on South Africa the gift of a new beginning.

Was Mandela's gift well received? This is a key question that leads one to the heart of the gift, the secret of the gift, the gift of the gift, and to the heart of Mandela's secret. The question concerns the very possibility or impossibility of receiving a gift properly or well. Whether something even close to an 'entire nation' ultimately materialized in South Africa is a question that remains contested and will probably remain so until the end of time.[32] That is why this 'entire nation' still has to be assumed or presumed in Kelsenian style whenever the need to talk about a new South African legal order is at stake. Mandela's *gift* has surely not resulted in something that is tangibly given. A lot ended up as patently given in 'post-apartheid' South Africa. A lot finally emerged from the years of transition

---

'mad gift' that follows here during a panel discussion of Mandela's legacy at the 2014 Annual Conference of the Law and Society in Minneapolis (May 2014). Klug suggested that Mandela never broke rank with the ANC cadres and never made any significant move in the negotiation process without due consultation with the rest of the ANC leadership. Would Klug's assessment of this passage (and several similar passages from *Long Walk To Freedom*, as Stephen Ellmann pointed out to me at the time) turn out to be accurate, much of the argument that I base on it would fall apart, and that would leave Bram Fischer the only real renegade invoked in this chapter. The day that Klug's assessment would turn out to be true would be sad and devastating, for it would unmask one of the truly inspiring narratives of the end of apartheid as a cheap myth that was at least co-cultivated or authorized by an ageing and somewhat self-aggrandizing 'patriarch'. Personally speaking I would hope not to live as long as to witness such an unmasking of Mandela's legacy. I, for one, would like to sustain the memory and/or imagination of an isolated old man, who, after having given and/or sacrificed his youth to the resistance against oppression, still had enough renegade madness in him to break rank again, and this right after intrusive surgery that would have left most mortal males of his age content to follow easier routes. The difference between Klug's and my assessment of Mandela's legacy may well be another case of the 'competing retroactivities' that I have described elsewhere. Cf. Van der Walt, 'Vertical sovereignty'.

32   Cf. Van der Walt, 'Vertical sovereignty', 118–19.

as undeniable facts of the new South Africa. Among these facts there would eventually be undeniable signs of significant normative and moral progress. But the gift itself cannot be counted among positive facts, not even among positive facts of positive developments, that is, not even among facts of "progress".

It is the contemplation of the withdrawal of the 'entire nation' from the entire set of positive facts that make up post-apartheid South Africa that leads us into close proximity to a hidden stage, the hidden stage on which Mandela's secret might become manifest, on the one hand, while remaining undisclosed, on the other. It is here that we move into the vicinity, neighbourhood or contemporaneity of the Mandela whom we still cannot see, the Mandela who is still hidden from us – also now after his death – by walls of mirrors and mirroring, so many years after his release from the prison walls that also still hid him when Derrrida wrote the essay on Mandela and the laws of reflection. This is the question that one must ask as one approaches this enigmatic stage: What is the ground for Mandela's graciousness and the ground for Mandela's gift? Why did Mandela become the personification of grace and graciousness in the time we live? We have already mentioned that there is something illogical or at least a-logical about the gift. The gift has no ground in logic. The gift that is always and ever again the *first* gift – it is not a gift if it is not a *first* gift – is groundless, absolutely groundless. Any explanation of Mandela's gift or of his graciousness would ascribe or relate it to some cause or instance of causation. It is very possible to do so. One may ascribe it, for instance, to the 'greater humanity' taught by the African philosophy of Ubuntu about which Mandela must surely have known or learned quite a bit since childhood. One might ascribe it to some sanctification of his person that resulted from years of incarceration, some purification that occurred through long years of personal sacrifice. But what do these ascriptions offer us apart from rather mundane reflections on Mandela in the mirrors of things that we believe we know and understand? What would it tell us about Mandela that would not ultimately reduce him to – and imprison him again in – what *we* make of him? The Mandela whom we need to contemplate and whom we are trying to contemplate here is the Mandela who has always, just like the 'entire nation' that he contemplated all along, been withdrawing from all positive instantiations. The entire nation will always withdraw from its positive instantiations and Mandela, the contemplator of 'entire nations', will always withdraw from all positive instantiations or portrayals of his person.

The tradition of thinking that would engage most consistently and consciously with the gift and the given status of things, the tradition of thinking to which Edmund Husserl gave the name phenomenology, has all along stressed the insight that the gift retreats or withdraws from the given. The gift withdraws from that which ends up, among us, as discernibly or positively given. The title of a recent essay on Heidegger provides one with a succinct articulation. Of concern in this way or method of philosophical thinking is that which gives itself through a withdrawal –

'... ce qui se donne en se retirant'.[33] What ends up among us as discernibly given does so by grace of a purely performative giving that withdraws from the scene of the gift. The gift never becomes part of its own scene. It is not a scene but the end and beginning of the scene that leave the scene behind by withdrawing from it or abandoning it. It is for this reason that it can only be contemplated in positive or constative language through predications that constantly abandon themselves and constantly shed themselves like already dead or dying skin. It is this language – the language through which phenomenology has always sought and still seeks to describe the process of appearance – that eventually also came to be called 'deconstruction'.

The gift exceeds or transcends what is given, but not in the format of a surplus that overflows. The gift exceeds or transcends by grace of a reserve of giving that is never exhaustively given. A negative or inverse excess or transcendence is thus at stake in the gift. And those who are adamantly aware of this reserve of giving that is never given will only approach it with recourse to the least naming of words or words that refuse to name. Among these least naming of words do we find words such as 'secret', the word to which Heidegger, Calvino and Derrida would sometimes resort.[34] Paul Celan would make mention of an 'absurdity' pursued by an impossible poem.[35] Foucault would resort to notions of 'madness', a madness way beyond the medical classification of mental illness. And he would locate in this absolutely foreign madness the possibility of the birth of the first man and

---

33   Cf. Bernard Dov Hercenberg, 'De ce qui se donne en se retirant' (2012) 75(2) *Archives de Philosophie* 311–34. The article is nevertheless not as instructive as its title promises. Nancy's work offers us a much profounder engagement with this thought. There is probably no text of Nancy that does not engage with the giving that withdraws in some way or another, but some of his most forceful articulations in this regard can be found in the essays 'Le cœur des choses' and 'Sens elliptique', both in Nancy, *Une Pensée finie* (Paris: Galilée, 1990). Consider for instance the following passage with reference to both Aristotle and Kant: 'Dans le "il y a" de l'existence, et dans ce qui "y vient" à la présence, il y va donc de l'être, et du sens de l'être. Sous ses deux grandes formes philosophiques, le transcendental a désigné une mise en réserve, un retirement ou un retrait de l'être. L'être d' Aristote est ce qui se réserve en deçà ou au-delà de la multiplicité des categories (prédicaments, ou transcendantaux) par lesquelles l'être est dit "de multiple façons". L'être s'offre et se retire dans cette multiplicité. Et le transcendental de Kant désigne la substitution d'un savoir des seules conditions de possibilité de l'expérience à un savoir de l'être qui soutiendrait cette experience. L'être s'offre et se retire dans cette condition, dans une subjectivité qui ne s'atteint pas comme substance, mais qui se sait (et qui se juge) comme demande.' Consider also the reading of the resurrection and ascension of Christ as a giving that withdraws in *Noli me tangere* (Paris: Bayard Éditions, 2003) to which this chapter is also much indebted.

34   Cf. Calvino, *If on a Winter's Night a Traveller* 192; Martin Heidegger, *Gelassenheit* (Pfullingen: Günther Neske, 1959), 24; Jacques Derrida, *Politiques de l'Amitié* (Paris: Gallilée, 1994), 288–93.

35   Paul Celan, 'Der Meridian', in Celan, *Gesammelte Werke* (Frankfurt a.M: Suhrkamp, 1983), III, 199.

his first step towards freedom – *la naissance du premier homme et son premier mouvement vers la liberté.*[36] Here, in these non-naming or least-naming of words do we find some intimation of the Mandela that we will never see; the secret Mandela; the absurd Mandela; the mad Mandela; Mandela the first free man; the freest man in the world, Derrida calls him; the man beyond sight, beyond the reflections of mirroring languages; Mandela, along with Goya's idiot, the first real man.[37]

From this madness stems his decision to break with friends and enemies and the very distinction between friends and enemies in 1985. And it is with this decision, perhaps more than with anything else, that he began to retreat into the invisibility that Derrida already sensed in 1987. For the friend–enemy distinction is one of the crucial optics of the political. It is the pair of binoculars that render the political possible, insist some.[38] And they do so with more acclaim and endorsement from others than would generally be conceded or admitted, for the friend–enemy distinction reflects a veritable metaphysics of the political that renders the political visible. It is from this visibility that Mandela began to withdraw in 1985.

Beside Mandela in the Rivonia trial, not (yet) as an accused but as counsel, stood another man whose life would be claimed by mad liberty; another man whose fundamental and utter invisibility would soon become manifest. Bram Fischer was his earliest alias. Bram Fischer the Afrikaner revolutionary, the first *vry boer* (freehold farmer), the first Afrikaner beyond language, the first to slip through the language of his ancestors never to return to its confines. It is especially with regard to him, but also still with regard to Mandela, that we will move now to reflect upon the phenomenon of the 'renegade moment'.

The Renegade Moment

When we turn now to take a closer look at what is called here 'the renegade moment' we in fact return again to something that has already been invoked above in another context: 'the seeds of a democratic revolution'. Mandela discerned the seeds of democratic revolution, we saw, in the egalitarian land use arrangements of early African societies. In what follows, we will look for the seeds of revolution, democratic revolution included, elsewhere. We shall look for these seeds in renegade moments, moments on the eruption of which any kind of normative content, the idea of common land use included, has at best secondary or indirect bearing. At issue in these renegade moments is, in fact, a moment of madness, the effect of which on any normative progress or regress hangs, for the moment, completely in the balance. It may come to contribute to considerable or

---

36 Michel Foucault, *Histoire de la folie à l'age classique* (Paris: Gallimard, 1972), 556–7.

37 Foucault, *Histoire de la folie à l'age classique.*

38 Carl Schmitt, *Der Begriff des Politischen* (Berlin: Duncker & Humblott, 1996).

epochal normative progress, as in the case of Mandela's moment of madness that we described above. Or it may contribute to very little or no significant observable moral progress (which of course does not detract one iota from its irreducible dignity), as in the case of Bram Fischer to whom we turn presently.

The crucial point is this: without this moment of madness, no significant shift in the current arrangement of things can be expected. If no one's rational inclination to maintain the security and stability of existing status quos ever gets overwhelmed by a moment of utter despair or sublime inspiration that precipitates a casting off of all shackles of reasonable caution so as to precipitate further a chain of unforeseeable events, nothing significantly new or different will ever happen. Moments of madness are the passages through which new times give themselves to us. It is from moments of madness that we receive the gifts of time. Madness is the pure performative, the purist performative thinkable, the performative that absolutely refuses the constative consolidation of comprehensible language, absolutely refuses any censoring of the somersaulting synapse. Each of the accused in the Rivonia trial will have had this moment of madness that catapulted them into a course of action that exposed them to utter destruction, the moment that abandoned them to persecution and prosecution by a governmental and military force from which they could expect no mercy and no decency. Mandela, we saw above, had another such a moment when he risked becoming branded as a traitor of the people for whom he had been locked up in jail for 27 years. Bram Fischer's moment of madness came 10 years after the Rivonia trial.

Revolutions never bring about significant normative progress. For that, they are much too much driven and informed by normative ideals that are already well articulated and understood in advance, before the revolutionary events commence. This is one of the key points that Arendt makes in *On Revolution*. Revolutions reinstate ancient principles of justice, not new ones.[39] Ancient regimes are taken to task and destroyed by revolutions for reasons of failing to honour principles that basically everyone already knew and grasped well before the first revolts erupted, not for failing to honour principles that only came to be understood and articulated after these revolts. A critical mass of people's support is required for any significant revolt. No mass of people will ever be moved to rebel by some newfangled idea that only few understand. At issue is a point that Gadamer already made well many years ago in his response to Habermas' critique of hermeneutics.[40] A significant critique of traditions are only possible on the basis of values or insights that are as 'traditional' as any other value or insight; hence also the quite traditional reflection/mirroring/admiration of old British democratic institutions and principles in

---

39 Hannah Arendt, *On Revolution* (Penguin Books, 1990), 208–14.

40 Hans-Georg Gadamer, 'Rhetorik, Hermeneutik und Ideologiekritik' and 'Replik', in *Hermeneutik und Idiologiekritik* (Frankfurt a.M: Suhrkamp, 1971), 57–82 and 283–317, especially at 307: 'Veränderung von Bestehendem ist nicht minder eine Form des Anschlusses und die Tradition wie die Verteidigung vom Bestehendem.'

Mandela's justification of his revolt against apartheid. It is evidently not towards revolutions that we must look for the absolutely unprecedented.

Arendt's political thought celebrates the emergence of newness and the birth of new worlds that results from significant political action. It should be clear, however, that this birth of new worlds can hardly consist in the normative innovation that such political action brings about. The most that one can expect from political or revolutionary action is a normative *re*-newal or *re*-generation of some kind. But political or revolutionary action cannot be reduced to these normative renewals or regenerations. Their essence is not exhausted by whatever moral regeneration they bring about. Their essence must ultimately be understood in terms of the sheer freedom to act and the unfathomable desire to act freely, for without this freedom to act and desire to act freely, no normativity will ever induce significant action. People often put up for years with moral discontent – so also the accused in the Rivonia trial – before they finally move to do something about it. When they finally do, something else, something quite apart from moral or normative considerations, spurs them into action. The moral or normative considerations and discontent were there all along. Had this been all that was needed, the action would have followed directly and mechanically from the very first observation that something was amiss. The seeds of revolution – to use again Mandela's rather Aristotelian phrase here – are not contained in the old jars that store normative ideas and ideals. They erupt from renegade moments that withdraw from these jars, withdraws into the mad moment of the pure performative; and it is from here that they give (or fail to give, as they often do) the new worlds that will soon enough describe themselves with old languages again.

What ultimately spurs a person into action belongs to or derives from unfathomable realms of the soul that remain irreducibly unfathomable and secret. It remains so unfathomable and so secret that one may for all practical purposes call it a personal madness that others can never hope to understand. Here erupts the realm of absolute freedom. Here commences the crack. Here shatter the mirrors of personhood and the masks of personae and personality. Here do the mirrors of assigned identities – the social roles and responsibilities that render persons comprehensible – begin to give way to a freedom that knows no bounds. Here is where Antigone entered her cave. Here lurks also, like an unknown animal, the Mandela that we have never seen and will never see, Mandela the freest man in the world. And here too entered Bram Fischer to become, forever, another one of those freest of men; those freest of men (the 'first' or 'only' men, Foucault calls them) who all ultimately withdraw into the other world or worlds from which they come.

Bram Fischer's Madness

Stephen Clingman wrote a brilliant biography of Fischer that concludes with a dismally obtuse remark regarding Fischer's flawed understanding of the 'morally compromised ideology' of communism. Clingman writes:

If the judgment is purely historical – that Bram was wrong because communism failed – it will be contingent and superficial: change the result and we would have to change the verdict. A more telling version is the moral one: Bram's flaw was that he was swayed by a morally compromised ideology, and the specific absolutism it induced produced his particular tragedy. After all, moral blindness is one consequence of the classic tragic flaw, and given the Soviet show trials, the gulag, the invasions of Hungary and Czechoslovakia, perhaps it captures Bram's one failing. Or perhaps, with some greater nuance, Bram's flaw was one of *understanding*, in that he did not fully comprehend the wider resonances and implications – the essential fatalism – involved in his choices.[41]

Perhaps the worst aspect of this flabby bourgeois passage is the consensus regarding the 'morally compromised ideology' of communism that it assumes, for Clingman does not even offer some kind of argument, here or on subsequent pages, why communism is intrinsically a morally compromised ideology and not, as many might think, an ideology with an incidentally bad historical record. He assumes his readers already agree with him. We need not go further into this aspect of the passage for it certainly does not warrant much attention. More relevant for the theme that we are elaborating in this chapter is the question why one might come to think that a flawed understanding of any ideology could have such a decisive influence on someone's life as the influence on Fischer's life choices that Clingman attributes to Fischer's flawed understanding of communism. Why would Fischer's life be *captured* by admiration for and reflections on/of communism, any more than Mandela's life would be captured by admiration for and reflections on/of British political and judicial institutions? This is a question that we have distilled here from Derrida's essay on Mandela, and we cannot fault Clingman for not contemplating it. He is surely no Derridean or deconstructivist biographer and never claimed to be one. However, if we do ask this question here in the context of Clingman's biography of Fischer, it is because this sublime book – sublime notwithstanding its many disappointing moments – provides one with significant thoughts and information with recourse to which Derridean thoughts can surely be thought. One can begin in this regard with an observation that Clingman makes one page after the passage cited above. Here Clingman observes:

Bram's life migrated into fiction ... .[42]

This remarkable phrase introduces a paragraph in which mention is made of a number of literary works that were inspired by Fischer's life – *At the Still Point* by Mary Benson, André Brink's *Rumours of Rain* and *Burger's Daughter* by Nadine Gordimer. But a keener thought lurks here that concerns much more than the impact

---

41   Stephen Clingman, *Bram Fischer Afrikaner Revolutionary* (Cape Town: David Philip, 1998), 450–51.

42   Clingman, *Bram Fischer*, 452.

of Fischer's life on literature. What does it mean when a life really migrates into fiction instead of (or apart from) just becoming a character in some novel? It means much more than one can properly contemplate here, but it surely also means this: A life that migrates into fiction is a life that moves into the vicinity, neighbourhood and contemporaneity of art. It traverses art, but only to slip through its grasp; only to slip away from it. Art is its slipstream. *Such a life enters a different time zone.* Clingman begins his narrative with the following sentence:

> A life begins long before it starts, emerging from other lives before returning to them.[43]

And he returns to this beginning close to the end:

> A life begins long before it starts; it endures long after it ends.[44]

Not all lives begin thus and end thus, but some do. And those that do have time on their side. Commenting on a certain positive side to the subjection of Sholto Cross (member of the South African Communist Party and anti-apartheid activist) to a second period of 90 days' detention without having been charged, Fischer observed:

> In a sense, time is always on our side.

'It is unlikely that there ever was a moment when he surrendered that belief', comments Clingman.[45] True. He knew that he would outlive apartheid, its law, its judiciary, its short-lived convictions and sentences. Consider his words at his own trial:

> Hence, though I shall be convicted by this Court, I cannot plead guilty. I believe that the future may well say that I acted correctly.[46]

Apartheid's judiciary sensed this too. Having just returned to Johannesburg after Fischer's funeral, Issy Maisels (leader of the defence team during the Treason Trial) happened to meet Justice Rumpff (presiding judge during the Treason trial) at the airport. Having told Justice Rumpff where he had been, the judge replied: 'You know, he'll be remembered long after you and I are forgotten.'[47] Indeed,

> [w]e will always remember you ... our children will know that South Africa bore a son like you,

---

43 Ibid., 1.
44 Ibid., 457.
45 Ibid., 344.
46 Ibid., 410.
47 Ibid., 440.

said Lilian Ngoyi, one of the Treason trialists whom Fischer had defended, in her funeral tribute.[48] Perhaps the apartheid prison desperately tried to contain this memory by demanding and retaining Fischer's ashes after his cremation. It is not clear what became of them.[49] But if the idea was to retain or restrain his ghost, the effort was in vain. Time would forever be on Fischer's side.

What does it mean to have time on one's side? This question should be read in conjunction with one that Clingman asks, now at his finest, early in his narrative:

> If there are certain histories in the air, certain examples, gestures, styles, ways of being in the world, what did Abraham Fischer bequeath to his grandson Bram, five years old when he died?[50]

How does a life end that participates thus in histories, examples, styles and ways of being that are in the air, bequeathed from one generation to next and the next? If a life begins long before it starts and endures long after it ends, how can one ever suggest that it has or had an ending, let alone a right ending? This is nevertheless what Clingman suggests at one point, surely also against his own better insights: 'Bram Fischer was a tragic figure indeed; but his story had the right ending.'[51] How can the life of a man whose career and political association had been destroyed by ruthless state oppression, whose friends ended up in jail, whose wife had died in an absurd car accident, who himself spent the last decade of his life ailing and waning away in jail, be said to have ended correctly without making a mockery of either this life or of the meaning of 'correctness'? Clingman again, now closer to the bitter reality:

> Molly was dead, [Bram] was on trial, his career was over, his Party smashed, his friends in jail or exile. It was an end ... and he saw it; going underground was like committing suicide.[52]

Fischer's daughters believed he would never have gone underground had their mother still been alive.[53] *If on a winter's night a traveller ...* . Molly Fischer drowned when the car Bram was driving left the road on an icy winter night in the Free State and ended up in the only pool in miles and miles of arid countryside. Clingman, sublime now:

---

48   Ibid., 442 (the sequence of her words slightly altered in the quotation above).

49   Clingman, *Bram Fischer*, 440–41.

50   Ibid., 27.

51   Ibid., 452.

52   Ibid., 357. The quotation above is a slightly adjusted version of words that Clingman heard form Pat Davidson who became a close friend of Fischer at the time of his trial.

53   Clingman, *Bram Fischer*, 357.

A car goes into a pool and a life is ended. For one person time stops, for another it goes on for ever. The light from that scene travels outwards, and it is travelling still. It will continue forever, and there are stars in the universe where that scene has still not arrived. It will never end. In Bram's mind it would not go away.[54]

This endless scene will never attain shape; it will forever remain nameless. '*For one person time stops, for another it goes on for ever.*' Thus also can time always remain on one's side: as infinite and interminable loss that cannot be suffered in one lifetime only. As bearers of infinite and interminable loss do some lives endure long after they end. Thus do they migrate, not into, as we shall see shortly, but *through* fiction, through the most cathartic of narratives imaginable. Talking about the correctness of an end under these circumstances is as sacrilegious as talking about the 'unreality' or the 'error of understanding' that ultimately accompanied and solicited this end; as sacrilegious as relating any of this to the 'morally compromised ideology' of communism:

A life begins long before it starts; it endures long after it ends.

Bram's life migrated into fiction … .

We will always remember you … our children will know that South Africa bore a son like you.

A car goes into a pool and a life is ended. For one person time stops, for another it goes on for ever. The light from that scene travels outwards, and it is travelling still. It will continue forever, and there are stars in the universe where that scene has still not arrived. It will never end.

[T]here are certain histories in the air, certain examples, gestures, styles, ways of being in the world.

These are the silent traces of a sublime thought embodied in Clingman's narrative of Bram Fischer's life. But this thought must still be thought and only becomes thinkable in the wake of a Derridean resistance to the laws of reflection, mirroring and speculative representation. For this purpose we need to break into Clingman's language and even invert it. For Bram Fischer still remains invisible to us, notwithstanding Clingman's sublime portrait. Artaud's madness does not enter the work of art, writes Foucault.[55] Fischer's madness will not enter any biography. His life also never *migrated into* fiction for no fiction will ever have accommodated or reached him. He only traversed fiction – slipped into it only to slip out of it again.

---

54   Ibid., 326.

55   Foucault, *Histoire de la folie* 556: 'La folie … ne se glisse pas dans les interstices de l'œuvre; elle est précisément l'*absence d'œuvre*' (Foucault's emphasis)

Like Antigone (who of course only slipped from and never into fiction), Fischer went underground. He slipped through and away from all histories in the air, all examples, gestures, styles and ways of being in the world. He will, in fact, never be remembered because he never entered any memory. Having never entered memory he cannot be forgotten either. His life is unforgettable life.[56] There will only be memories that will remind us of those who can neither be remembered nor forgotten and among those there is one of whom the first of several aliases was 'Bram Fischer'. 'The light from [this] scene travels outwards, and it is travelling still. It will continue forever, and there are stars in the universe where [it] has still not arrived. It will never end.' Time is therefore always and irreducibly and interminably on his side. Time cannot abandon him, for he bears an infinite burden and the burden of the infinite.

Thus did Fischer's mad liberty become the passage of the infinite's withdrawal from the finite, the withdrawal of the temporal into eternity. And thus did he/does he cross the threshold of the visible and the invisible.

This, then, is how time gives. This is the way times are given. Through Bram Fischer, and through those with him. Through their madness. '[Par] cette folie qui noue et partage le temps.'[57]

---

56   Cf. Giorgio Agamben, *The Time that Remains* (Stanford: Stanford University Press, 2005), 39; cf. also Maurice Blanchot, *Lécriture du Désastre* (Paris: Gallimard, 1980), 44–5: 'Lorsque nous somme patients, c'est toujours par rapport à un malheur infini qui ne nous atteint pas au présent, mais en nous rapportant à un passé sans memoir.'

57   Foucault, *Histoire de la folie*, 551.

Chapter 4

Nelson Mandela and Civic Myths: A Law and Literature Approach to Rivonia

Peter Leman

Introduction: Myth and Orality in Law and Literature

A key text in the law and literature movement, Herman Melville's novella *Billy Budd, Sailor* (which he began writing in 1888 and was published posthumously in 1924) describes the trial and execution of its eponymous character on the HMS *Bellipotent* in 1797. Billy's captain, Edward Fairfax Vere, loves the young man described as the "Handsome Sailor," but feels compelled to observe the law when Billy kills the master-at-arms in a fit of anger. In the chapter following Billy's execution, the narrator quotes Vere, in one of the most famous passages from the book, stating his legal philosophy. Commenting on the "disruption of forms going on across the Channel and the consequences thereof" (i.e., the French Revolution and its aftermath), Vere observes, "With mankind, forms, measured forms are everything; and that is the import couched in the story of Orpheus with his lyre spellbinding the wild denizens of the wood" (1986: 380).

Literary critics and legal scholars have debated the meaning of this statement, and one of the more persuasive accounts is offered by Brook Thomas who insists that Vere's "measured forms" are an expression in favour of legal formalism, of which the "central doctrine ... is that freedom can be guaranteed only by maintaining the institutions supporting the formal order of the law" (1991: 230). What interests me most about Vere's statement, however, and what is most important to this chapter is not his insistence upon legal formalism as such, but the fact that he connects law's forms to the classical myth of Orpheus. What does it mean to assert that the "import" of legal formalism—an eminently rational, even scientific, form of jurisprudence—is to be found in the myth of a magic lyre? Thomas relates the Orpheus allusion to one made earlier by Thomas Carlyle about the French Revolution and the need for the "Lyre of some Orpheus, to constrain, with the touch of melodious strings, these mad masses in to Order" (qtd. in Thomas 1991: 230). One might respond, then, that for Captain Vere the comparison is strictly metaphorical—he is not saying formalism functions by magic, but that just as Orpheus' powerful song is able to bring order, so too can the power of the law's forms bring order to disorder. Or, perhaps he is instead emphasizing the performative nature of the law: law is characterized by speech acts that can bring order through their performative power, as does Orpheus' song. I find these compelling but still insufficient interpretations due to the overdetermined quality of the metaphor that juxtaposes formalism, which is rationally based and tends to be embodied in the written word (even performative utterances in modern law have their lasting force in being written afterwards), and a myth that describes divine power expressed through song. Melville, I argue, recognized a fundamental tension in modern law arising out of its simultaneous denial and incorporation of myth, which in the legal context is intimately related to orality, or pre-literate forms of cultural expression.

In addition to embodying this tension, Vere's statement also embodies a myth fundamental to the history of Western law, particularly in contexts of imperialism such as those of Great Britain in the eighteenth century and, for example, South Africa in the twentieth: namely, the myth of a defining divide between "civilized" and "uncivilized" parts of the world. (Indeed, according to Mahmood Mamdani, in colonial Africa "civilization ... meant the rule of law" [1996: 109].) This "white mythology," as Peter Fitzpatrick calls it (1992: x), quoting Derrida, maintains that those with the law must bring it to or impose it upon those without and that those who rebel against the established authority (as in the French Revolution or the anti-apartheid movement) are "wild denizens" and "mad masses" in need of constraint and order.

Now, why am I beginning a chapter about Nelson Mandela and the Rivonia Trial with a nineteenth-century American novella? It is an unlikely choice, I admit, but not an arbitrary one. Primarily, I believe Melville's text usefully introduces a number of concepts that have been important in the law and literature movement as well as some that have yet to be examined fully, and each of these concepts is useful in helping us develop a law and literature perspective on what Nelson Mandela accomplishes in his statement before the dock, a statement that, I argue, is deeply attentive to and engaged with the forces of myth in apartheid South Africa. Just as a tension emerges in the way Captain Vere connects the forms of the law to mythology, so too are there tensions and contradictions in the colonial system of apartheid, the laws of which only appear legitimate within the context of the political mythology of Afrikaner nationalism and the anti-communist mythology of the Cold War. One of Mandela's strategies, as I will show, was to sabotage (conceptually, as Umkhonto we Sizwe [MK] had done physically) these mythic foundations. Furthermore, whereas Captain Vere associates Orpheus with the forces of power and civilization and the wild denizens with those who resist such power, there is a marked irony in the fact that it is among the so-called "uncivilized" parts of the world where orality and song actually have the force of law. In other words, it does not necessarily make sense to locate the "import" of Western law, with its absolute dependence upon the written word, in the story of Orpheus, poet, singer, and orator. Compare, instead, what Ugandan poet Okot p'Bitek says about poets, singers, and orators in Africa: "The [traditional African] artist proclaims the laws but expresses them in the most indirect language: through metaphor and symbol, in image and fable. He sings and dances his laws" (1986: 39). Okot meant this literally: poets and singers are law-makers in indigenous

African cultures, not only in Uganda but throughout the continent. In other words, orature—the myths, songs, stories, poems, proverbs, etc. that comprise an oral tradition—can actually be law. Orature archives normative wisdom and shapes traditional procedures. Elsewhere, I have studied this phenomenon, which I call "orature-as-law," at length,[1] and for our purposes here, a recognition of orature's relationship to law suggests that there is a sense in which Vere's observation turns against itself when read in the context of an oppressive situation like that of apartheid. During Rivonia, the state no doubt believed itself to be imposing "forms, measured forms" on the "wild denizens" who resisted and repeatedly disobeyed its laws. However, in his statement at the dock, Mandela invokes African oral traditions in subtle but important ways, leading Jacques Derrida to describe him as a "man of the law by vocation"—by calling and profession, of course, but also by the power of his voice, his vocality, his orality, and the forms of African orality that he invokes (1987: 29). Thus, Mandela's Orphean speech challenges the law directly by confirming and rationally justifying his participation in forming Umkhonto we Sizwe, but also indirectly—and in a sense more powerfully—by destroying the myth upon which Captain Vere's and the apartheid state's laws were based. He demonstrates, ultimately, that the wild denizens who lack and are in need of the law are not the African people, but, ironically, the Afrikaner oppressor who in "scorning his own law ... gives the law over to be scorned" (Derrida 1987: 32).

In the remainder of this chapter, I will examine how Mandela frames his speech with oral conventions in such a way that allows him to judge the apartheid system and dismantle its myths from the standpoint of an alternative basis of law. Additionally, more than solely employing a "negative hermeneutic" of unmasking the myths and ideologies of apartheid (Thomas 2007: 10), Mandela also seeks to generate new myths, or new ways of understanding the origin, destiny, and potential unity of South Africa as a nation.

Mythology and Modernity

Before examining Mandela's speech as a civic myth, it is necessary first to say a bit more about the concept of myth itself and its relationship to law and the state. In thinking about myths, I have been influenced primarily by Brook Thomas' *Civic Myths: A Law and Literature Approach to Citizenship* (2007), whose title is clearly echoed in my own, as well as Peter Fitzpatrick's *The Mythology of Modern Law* (1992) and Leonard Thompson's *The Political Mythology of Apartheid* (1985). All three scholars begin with a similar point, which, I believe, was also Melville's: although modernity is assumed to be opposed to myth, or to have replaced *myth*

---

1   See Leman (2009), "Singing the law: Okot p'Bitek's legal imagination and the poetics of traditional justice and Leman (2011) "African oral law and the critique of colonial modernity in *The Trial of Jomo Kenyatta.*"

with *truth* (historical, scientific) during the Enlightenment, myth is "vibrantly operative in modernity" (Fitzpatrick 1992: ix). In fact, the great myth of modernity is its very denial of myth. Or, as Thomas puts it, summarizing Blumenberg, "the Enlightenment's great myth was the belief that, by replacing myth with truth, it could leave myth behind" (2007: 13). Our civic and political mythologies today may not have the same interest in the supernatural or the transcendent as so-called "pre-modern" mythologies, but their patterns and functions are nevertheless similar. We tell stories and construct and assume narratives, sometimes but not always factually true, that make sense of, render coherent, and/or justify as natural particular states of affairs that may otherwise be contradictory. In fact, Thomas asserts that civic myths are "a particular version of ... cultural narratives. Stories without specific authors, cultural narratives help give meaning to social practices that cannot necessarily find a basis in rational logic" (2007: 6). Because myths can be used to render contradictions meaningful and coherent, we may be tempted to see them in terms of ideology—in other words, as potentially dangerous falsehoods that must be unmasked and critiqued. Inasmuch as myths are pervasive features of any oppressive regime, this is, in fact, true, and as I will show, one of the strategies that Mandela uses in his speech is such a critique of myth.

However, myths are not all bad. Not all myths serve nefarious functions, and in many respects, myths are necessary in our world today. As Thomas writes, the "relentless reliance" of ideological criticism "on a negative hermeneutic of 'unmasking' has limited its range, as evidenced by recent turns to both aesthetics and religion. Even critically skeptical citizens need something to believe in, some stories that serve as 'equipment for living'" (2007: 10). Thomas's response, therefore, is to employ a method that he finds in the work of Hans Blumenberg of working "on/with myth" (2007: 12–13). To work *on* a myth is to continue the necessary labor of unmasking, of debunking dangerous myths that can be used to justify and perpetuate oppression and inequality. But once a myth is removed, it is not replaced automatically with truth or fact—often a void remains, a place where people need stories to help them make sense of their place in society, of their relationship to the whole and its various component parts. Therefore, we need to work *with* myths and not just against them. "Following Blumenberg's lead," Thomas asserts, "scholars and teachers should continue their quest for complex truths, but they should also explore the process by which those truths can generate civic myths to rival the ones they debunk" (2007: 13).

One way of exploring this process, according to Thomas, is by turning to works of literature, which naturally interact with myths in ways that are both challenging and generative, and this is one additional reason I chose to begin this chapter with a work of literature. However, imaginative literature is not an obvious source for understanding the mythological complexities of Mandela's statement and the trial in which it was delivered, although Nadine Gordimer and Alan Paton were both briefly involved (Gordimer in editing biographical notes of the accused for the press, and Paton in standing as a mitigation witness [see Broun 2012: 123–6]). My method for reading Mandela in terms of civic myths departs here somewhat from Thomas'—whereas he works on/with myths by turning to works of literature that can be read in the context of specific legal problems related to citizenship, I am interested in identifying how Mandela himself works on/with myths in the immediate context of a legal event that, in a sense, is also about citizenship, or what it means to be a citizen (or a subject) in South Africa. Mandela *is*, therefore, the literary text, although there are some interesting comparisons to be made between his strategies as a "man of the law by vocation" (Derrida 1987: 35) and those of authors such as Herman Melville, as we have seen already, and also Nurrudin Farah and Ngũgĩ wa Thiong'o, who similarly work on/with myths in contexts of oppression. Like them, Mandela was able to begin generating new forms of myth to replace old ones without sacrificing a core commitment to truth. In his text (in him *as text*), myth and truth work together, and this may be one reason why the Rivonia statement and Mandela himself have, today, achieved such mythic status.

Orality, Myth, and Law in the Rivonia Trial

The content of Mandela's speech during the Rivonia Trial is highly significant, of course, but so too are its formal elements and the form of its presentation, or performance. As noted earlier, Mandela frames his speech with elements of orality, which, along with his choice to deliver a statement rather than submit to cross-examination, provides greater legitimacy to his effort to put apartheid on trial. The assumption behind Mandela's choice to deliver a statement was, in part, that apartheid law itself was illegal—that its legitimacy was a myth, in other words—and that he and his people were not bound by its forms. In *The Political Mythology of Apartheid*, Leonard Thompson describes in detail the powerful mythic dimensions of Afrikaner nationalism which were foundational to the apartheid state. Among the most influential civic myths for the state were the myth of the Afrikaner people's divine origin and destiny and the classic imperial myth that separates "us" from "them" along lines of race and civilization. These myths informed the core myth of the state that any disagreement with and resistance to its policies could not have a legitimate basis and must, therefore, be criminal and even terrorist in nature. The tendency of the government to react in this way—expressed, for example, through the extreme powers of the Sabotage Act—reflects the myth of the *laager*, as Mandela notes, or the protective wagon circle with its closed loop and defensive posture that was an actual mechanism of defence for nineteenth-century settlers in South Africa and that, in the twentieth century, became such an important symbol in Afrikaner political discourse.

Mandela works *on* these myths, first of all, by turning the tables on apartheid and assuming its assumption of absolute legitimacy to be wholly incorrect. He expresses this more directly in statements prior to his speech at Rivonia: in his earlier trial statement in 1962, for example, Mandela began by challenging "the right of this court to hear [his] case" because, as he said, "I consider myself neither legally nor morally bound to obey laws made by a parliament in which I have no representation" (2013). Additionally, when asked whether he pled guilty or not guilty to the charges during the Rivonia Trial, Mandela and his co-defendants responded, "My Lord, it is not I but the government that should be in the dock. I plead not guilty" (1994: 310). A similar claim opens the Freedom Charter, and what is significant about the idea of declaring a government illegal is not simply the declaration itself and the way it counters core myths, but that it is done from an alternative position of authority, or from the jurisdiction of an alternative system of law. This both undermines the myth that Africans are "wild denizens" without law and authorizes them to *take action* against the infringing body.

Several literary texts explore these concepts in fascinating ways and are worth bringing in here for the sake of comparison. Furthermore, as works of narrative and performance, these texts can help us better recognize and understand the significance of the narrative and mythic elements of Mandela's speech. For example, in Nurrudin Farah's novel *Close Sesame* (1983), the final text in his trilogy collectively titled *Variations on the Theme of an African Dictatorship*, two of the main characters, a father and a son, begin the novel with a discussion of the concept of *lex talionis*, or the law of retribution. The current dictator—a fictionalized version of Siyaad Barre—has led a brutal regime, and the son, Mursal, is interested not simply in overthrowing the dictator in a fit of naked power against naked power, but in discovering an actual legal justification for ending the regime. Mursal, a professor of constitutional law, looks to traditional and Islamic law in order to declare the regime illegal. He asks: "does the state in Somalia as we know it have a traditional base in Somali thought? Does the régime of Somalia today have any Islamic legitimacy?" (1983: 11). The answer is no, of course, and Mursal and his co-conspirators make several efforts to carry out—legally, according to their reasoning—a death sentence against the dictator. Similarly, in Ngũgĩ wa Thiong'o and Mĩcere Mugo's play *The Trial of Dedan Kimathi* (1976), the main character—the last Mau Mau general captured by the British during Kenya's State of Emergency—refuses to acknowledge the legitimacy of the court in which he is being tried. The Judge reads the charges against Kimathi and asks how he pleads. Kimathi then declares, echoing Mandela, "I will not plead to a law in which we had no part in the making" (1976: 25). The Judge replies, "Law is law. The rule of law is the basis of every civilized community. Justice is justice." "Whose law? Whose justice?" Kimathi demands, insisting that the Judge's tautological explanation conceals the particularity, rather than the universality, of colonial law and its role as a means of protecting the rights of the white minority and denying the rights of the black majority. The parallels with South Africa are, no doubt, clear. Like Farah and Ngũgĩ, Mandela situates himself in such a way as to argue that his resistance to apartheid law through the ANC and MK was not illegal, but, in fact, was the only lawful thing for a "man of the law by vocation" to do (Derrida 1987: 29).

With this invocation of "vocation," I want to turn now to Mandela's voice and the question of orality. Farah and Ngũgĩ's texts aid in this transition, in fact, because in both cases, not only do the authors articulate challenges to oppressive laws, but they draw heavily upon oral traditions as a way of exploring the potential of orature-as-law to facilitate imagining new, or renewed, forms of myth, law, and modernity. Though it may seem to be a mundane detail or part of the expected logic of telling his personal story, Mandela's early reference in his speech to oral traditions is, in my view, highly significant. After freely admitting that he helped form Umkhonto we Sizwe and after denying that he did so under the influence of "foreigners or communists," Mandela insists that he acted "as an individual and a leader of my people, because of my experience in South Africa and my own proudly felt African background" (1963). He then states:

> In my youth in the Transkei I listened to the elders of my tribe telling stories of the old days. Amongst the tales they related to me were those of wars fought by our ancestors in defence of the fatherland. The names of Dingane and Bambatha, Hintsa and Makana, Squngathi and Dalasile, Moshoeshoe and Sekhukhune, were praised as the pride and the glory of the entire African nation.

Mandela then credits these stories—these myths and histories within the Xhosa oral tradition—with giving him the desire, as he says, to "make my own humble contribution to [my people's] freedom struggle." He then adds a crucial observation: "*This is what has motivated me in all that I have done in relation to the charges made against me in this case*" (emphasis added). Mandela's motivation to fight apartheid, in other words, can be traced back to the tales and stories he heard as a youth. And, if orature is a form of law and if these tales are part of the oral tradition, then we can say that Mandela violated the law in the name of another law: that law expressed and embodied in African oral traditions. As Jacques Derrida observes, "He [Mandela] presents himself in his people, before the law. Before a law he rejects, beyond any doubt, but which he rejects in the name of a superior law, the very one he declares to admire and before which he agrees to *appear*" (1987: 27, emphasis in original). Elsewhere Derrida discusses the fact that Mandela "declares his 'admiration' ... for the 'structure and organization of early African societies in this country'" (25), and I therefore wish to speculate that the "superior law" in whose name Mandela rejects apartheid law is not—or at least, not *only*—the sort of abstract, higher law of morality and conscience, but the actual moral and legal authority of his inherited cultural myths and oral traditions.

Derrida's 1987 essay "The laws of reflection: Nelson Mandela, in admiration" is worth examining in greater detail at this point—I have been quoting his description of Mandela as a "man of the law by vocation," and I am fascinated by the concept of "vocation" in this context: vocation, vox, vocare, vocal, voice, calling, to call or be called. Derrida repeats the phrase several times, clearly fascinated by the concept himself. He means, on the one hand, that Mandela is a man of the law by calling, and not just by profession—in other words, that he possesses and is driven by an innate sense of justice; Mandela's voice is "a voice which never ceases to appeal to the *voice of conscience*, to the immediate and unfailing sentiment of justice, to this law of laws that speaks in us before us, because it is inscribed within our heart" (1987: 27).[2] On the other hand, however, Derrida is clearly aware of and interested in the voice within "vocation" and in the performative possibilities of that voice as a voice of conscience and a voice of law. Elsewhere, Derrida has written about the "mystical foundation of authority," describing the conditions for the emergence of forms of law that rival those of the state. Writing of strikes and revolutions, Derrida observes, "What the state fears (the state being law in its greatest force) is not so much crime or *brigandage* ... The state is afraid of fundamental, founding violence, that is, violence able to justify, to legitimate, or to transform the relations of law, and so to present itself as having a right to law" (1992: 34–5, emphasis in original). Earlier he writes about the "performative and therefore interpretive violence" of the founding moment of the law (1992: 13), and I'd like to suggest (remembering, of course, that Mandela had already been convicted of inciting strikes before being charged with sabotage) that there may be an element of this performative violence in Mandela's voice, which Derrida finds so fascinating and admirable. The Sabotage Act, with its absolute forms of detention and prosecution, seems to be a clear expression of the fear Derrida describes: fear not of crime, but of violence able to justify itself as having a right to law, violence that must be put down through greater violence. Mandela describes MK's violence in the context of his own motivations, which are tied to Xhosa oral traditions that, I argue, are also a kind of legal tradition. Thus, the real threat that Mandela and MK presented was violence able to transform the relations of the law and present itself as having a right to law. Their violence did this, in part, because it directly attacked aspects of apartheid mythology. As Thomas and others note, political mythologies are not only given expression through stories, but also through material objects such as flags, statues, monuments, and buildings—symbols of national unity or government power. MK's objective, as Mandela explains, was to disrupt the country economically through acts of sabotage, but also to destroy "Government buildings and other *symbols* of apartheid"; "These attacks," he says, "would serve as a source of inspiration to our people" (1963, emphasis added).

What the state mistakenly believed in responding to these attacks, however, was that violence able to transform the law could only be physical and, therefore, that such violence could be stopped through excessive legal measures and a sufficient

---

2   There is another literary comparison begging to be made here: that with Sophocles' *Antigone*, in which the eponymous heroine deliberately violates the positive law of Creon, justifying her actions with an appeal to a higher divine or natural law (i.e., comparable to what Derrida calls "the law of laws that speaks in us before us"). It is significant that *Antigone* has been an important cultural intertext for many freedom struggles throughout Africa, including the struggle against apartheid: Athol Fugard cleverly re-wrote *Antigone* in his short play *The Island* (1973), in which two political prisoners on Robben Island perform *Antigone* for a prison talent show as an act of protest. *The Island* is typically grouped with Fugard's two other plays *Sizwe Bansi is Dead* (1974) and *Statements After an Arrest under the Immorality Act* (1974), both of which also dramatize powerful critiques of apartheid law.

show of force. To the contrary, Mandela's voice, with its invocation of orality and powerful critique of the *mythical* foundations of the government's authority, also constituted or carried out a form of founding violence able to transform the relations of the law. As I noted earlier, Mandela's speech is framed by orality: he begins by referencing the stories of revolutionary heroes in his youth and he concludes by abandoning the written text of his speech. As Mandela himself describes it: "I had been reading my speech, and at this point I placed my papers on the defense table, and turned to face the judge. The courtroom became extremely quiet. I did not take my eyes off Justice de Wet as I spoke from memory the final words" (1994: 322). He then utters the famous final paragraph of his speech in which he declares his readiness to die fighting for the "ideal of a democratic and free society." Mandela's gesture at this moment—setting his papers down and speaking from memory—is small but powerful. The effect of the words themselves is remarkable, particularly because Mandela and his co-defendants were under real threat of being sentenced to death. However, I wish to suggest that part of the power of Mandela's final statement is that, in a sense, he relies briefly but entirely on orality, which formally ties his conclusion back to the stories he enjoyed as a youth, to what he claimed has motivated him in everything he has done up to this point.

Furthermore, because orature is law, there is a sense in which Mandela here speaks as "a man of the law by vocation," as one whose voice has the Orphean force of law. Judgments of innocence or guilt and subsequent acts of sentencing are paradigmatic speech acts in the law. In committing an act of performative violence in his speech and in declaring himself prepared to accept death, if necessary, there is a sense in which Mandela undermines the potential force of the death sentence, should the state decide to declare it. Antecedent to that potential sentence, Mandela willingly and courageously accepts it, rendering it powerless as a punishment and, instead, investing it with potential energy as a means of creating martyrs and making Mandela and his companions even greater symbols of the freedom struggle. It is performative, inaugural violence, indeed, if it can so thoroughly change the force and meaning of a death sentence—in effect, transforming the relations of the law—even before it is uttered. Thus, Mandela's voice demonstrates the violent, ordering power of Orpheus spellbinding the "wild denizens" of the apartheid state and contributes, in part, to his sentence and that of his co-defendants being changed to life in prison despite all indications that they would receive the death penalty.

Thus far, we have primarily focused on the ways in which Mandela, from this position as a man of law by vocation, works *on* apartheid civic myths, dismantling and conceptually sabotaging the mythical foundations of the legal system from the position of an alternative legal and mythical tradition expressed in and through African orality. Now, I would like to examine the ways in which Mandela works *with* civic myths as well as on them. He not only exposes the contradictions of apartheid mythology and undermines their force, but he offers new myths to replace them. I will, therefore, turn to one crucial example of such a civic myth in order to demonstrate how the complex intersections and contestations of myth in the trial have left a legacy both positive and, by some accounts, negative in South Africa today.

From Red to Rainbow: Working On/With Cold War Myths

At the beginning of his speech, Mandela makes three main points in quick succession: the first and third we have already examined, namely that he organized MK and was motivated by the oral traditions of his youth. The second point I have mentioned, but now will consider more fully: Mandela denies the state's claim that "the struggle in South Africa is under the influence of foreigners and communists" (1963). As Kenneth S. Broun makes clear in his recent book on the Rivonia Trial, the South African government was at pains to portray Mandela, the ANC, and MK as nothing more than communist puppets, and the state prosecutor, Percy Yutar, made frequent attempts during the trial to prove that the ANC was controlled by the Communist Party. Broun observes that "the portrait of Rivonia painted in the world's media was complex, contradictory, and very much influenced by Cold War politics" (2012: 25). Indeed, Broun's third point—at least—could be said of the trial itself, not solely its portrayal in the media, only I would add "myths" to "politics." The Cold War was a war not just of politics and ideologies but of ideologies structured, reinforced, and propagated by myths of various kinds. The government's effort to pin Mandela as a communist was, largely, an active exploitation of Cold War myths in order to win support from the Western states upon which it depended economically and otherwise.

The contesting mythologies of the Cold War were primarily voiced by the world's two major superpowers—and their allies—following World War II: the US and the USSR. Expressing and reinforcing mutual distrust and national anxieties about the threat that each nation posed to the other, Cold War myths also portrayed the national self as ideal and universal. As James G. Richter puts it, both the US and the Soviet Union in the years following World War II "relied heavily on universalistic ideas to create a national identity and both justified their foreign policies not only as a means to protect the national interest but also to protect and even propagate the way of life (whether Soviet-style socialism or liberal democracy) these ideas would prescribe" (1992: 276). These "legitimating myths," as Richter calls them, constituted the foundation for "prevailing myths about the unconditional hostility of the other" (1992: 298). In other words, to the US, the Soviet Union was perceived and portrayed as essentially hostile and a threat to the ideals of freedom and democracy; similarly, the Soviet Union depended upon "an entrenched image of an aggressive enemy existing in the other superpower" (1992: 299). This contest, of course, was led by but not limited geographically to these two superpowers, and the African continent was one of the many areas of the world affected by Cold War politics and myths. However, only recently have scholars begun to examine fully the effect that the Cold War had on South Africa and, in turn, the role that South Africa played in that global conflict.

For example, in her introduction to a 2009 collection titled *Cold War in Southern Africa: White Power, Black Liberation*, Sue Onslow clearly demonstrates how crucial it is to understand the apartheid years in relationship to the larger contexts of global politics. She argues that the "ideological contest between the global economic systems, which intersected with the process of European decolonization, intensified and prolonged the struggle between the remaining white minorities in power and black nationalist movements" (2009a: 1). The nationalist movements found ready allies among the communist nations—as did decolonization movements throughout Africa—and members of the Communist Party in South Africa played key roles in the struggle, including the formation of MK and as members of Mandela's defense team.[3] At the same time, the South African government perceived (or chose to perceive) communism's presence as control rather than support and solidarity. It consequently formed policy toward and told stories about the ANC and other liberation entities as though they were manifestations of the global threat to Western civilization: in other words, they incorporated Cold War myths into their anti-ANC/black liberation strategy. Doing so courted "Western solidarity with the apartheid state" (Onslow 2009a: 4), and allowed the government to "divert domestic and international attention from the real causes of opposition to racist rule" (Onslow 2009b: 9). A submission to the Truth and Reconciliation Commission from a former member of the South African security forces powerfully articulates the consequences of this diversion. Major Craig Williamson stated:

> The South African security forces gave very little cognizance to the political motivation of the South African liberation movements, beyond regarding them as part and parcel of the Soviet onslaught against the 'civilised/free/democratic' Western world. This fact, I believe, made it easier for the most violent actions to be taken against the liberation movements and their supporters because such violence was not aimed at our people but at a 'foreign' enemy ... my security force colleagues and I did not see the liberation movements and their members as fellow citizens of our society. We regarded them as an alien enemy. (qtd. in Daniel 2009: 35)

This same strategy of alienation (in the literal sense of *"making alien"*)—a kind of domestic xenophobia—is at work in the Rivonia Trial: the prosecution attempts to demonstrate that Mandela and his co-defendants are communist-controlled and, therefore, non-citizens. Successful alienation of the defendants would allow the

---

3 Denis Goldberg and Rusty Bernstein, for example, were two of Mandela's co-accused and active members of the Communist Party, and Bram Fischer, lead counsel for the defense team, was also "an ardent Communist" (Broun 2012: 16).

state to achieve more easily its aims in putting down the liberation movements and would justify the use of extreme measures in the process.

A great irony of this myth of the "citizen-as-alien-enemy" was that the people propagating it were themselves historically alien to the African continent. As noted earlier, civic myths can be used to resolve contradictions in society; or, put differently, contradictions in society often lead to the creation of narratives that help make sense of "social practices that cannot necessarily find a basis in rational logic" (Thomas 2007: 6). Brook Thomas writes that "the concept of citizenship itself is inhabited by contradictions that generate civic myths, which, in turn, help give meaning to the practices of citizenship within particular cultures. Those contradictions can arise out of tensions between different models of citizenship." During apartheid, and during the Rivonia Trial, there were different models of citizenship in tension, and the government's strategy for making sense of the contradiction between the National Party's model of citizenship, which privileged the white minority, and the ANC model of citizenship, which petitioned for the rights of the indigenous black majority, was to generate a civic myth that localized the global myths of the Cold War and cast anti-apartheid activists as a foreign threat to Western civilization and "legitimate" (i.e., white) citizens within South Africa. This was a powerful means of overriding or simply ignoring the implications of the blatant fact that black Africans were the original inhabitants of the region.

This myth of alienation was deeply influential in apartheid politics, but it was not invulnerable. In contrast and in response to the government's strategy of alienation through localizing Cold War myths, Nelson Mandela employs a strategy—and generates a myth—of *domestication*.[4] In other words, what the government makes foreign and threatening (i.e., communism), Mandela makes domestic and homely. However, he does this in a complex way that allows him both to work *on* the government's myths in order to undermine their power and expose their contradictions and to work *with* new myths in order to provide "equipment for living" to the South African people. Mandela's first step in working on the myths is simply to deny that the ANC and MK were governed by "foreigners and communists," and the second is to assert the fact of his status as a rightful citizen of South Africa. As discussed earlier, Mandela refers to his "proudly felt African background" and the oral tales of his youth that inspired and motivated him to

---

4 I have deliberately avoided using the more obvious binary of "foreignization" and "domestication" here in order to avoid confusion with the sense of these terms in the translation theories of Lawrence Venuti and others. For Venuti, foreignization refers to the technique of emphasizing and remaining loyal to the source language rather than the target language in the practice of translation. This is, according to Venuti, a more ethical practice. Domestication, which emphasizes the target language, thus has a negative sense in his usage, whereas domestication is a much more positive and ethically driven term in the sense I am using to describe Mandela's response to the apartheid government's ahistorical and illogical strategy of mythologizing the domestic and indigenous as foreign or alien. See Venuti (1995), *The Translator's Invisibility: A History of Translation*.

struggle against apartheid. Not only do these stories allow Mandela to speak from a position of alternative law in critiquing the mythical foundations of apartheid, but they also fix from the outset his position as someone who is most certainly *not* alien to Africa and is *not* motivated by allegiance to anything other than his own people.

Later in the speech, Mandela continues to work on the government's alienation myth, stating that the allegation about communism's influence "is false" and that it was "an old allegation which was disproved at the Treason Trial, and which has again reared its head." He then proceeds to describe in detail the "ideological creed" of the ANC, as expressed in the Freedom Charter, and to explain how markedly it differs from the ideologies of communism. Noting differences in approaches to nationalization and private enterprise, Mandela asserts that the Freedom Charter "is by no means a blueprint for a socialist state" and the "ANC has never at any period of its history advocated a revolutionary change in the economic structure of the country, nor has it, to the best of my recollection, ever condemned capitalist society." Furthermore, he argues, "The Communist Party sought to emphasize class distinctions whilst the ANC seeks to harmonise them." In other words, the ANC is *not* controlled by the Communist Party, nor would Mandela want it to be because the philosophies of the two organizations are so dramatically different, at least with regard to economics and class relations.

Given how much the apartheid government feared (or proclaimed to fear) the threat of communism, it almost appears as though Mandela confirms or agrees with part of the Cold War myth. By denying so thoroughly that the ANC is communist-controlled, is Mandela buying into, or reinforcing, the anti-communist mythologies of the state? No—in fact, quite the opposite. This is because his denial is immediately followed by the myth of domestication. As soon as he demonstrates that the ANC and the Communist Party are at odds on some issues, Mandela states that on other important issues they are in complete agreement, sharing "a common goal – in this case, the removal of white supremacy." Mandela then proceeds at length to describe cooperation with communists as though it were the most natural thing in the world, and not just for the ANC. First taking a historical perspective, Mandela notes that throughout the world, there are examples of communist and non-communist nations working together toward common goals: he points out that Great Britain, the US, and the Soviet Union worked together in fighting Nazi Germany; he describes how communists "have played an important role in the freedom struggles fought" in formerly colonized countries throughout the world; and he concludes that the same has happened in South Africa as communists and the ANC shared short-term goals in fighting apartheid. Mandela acknowledges how difficult it must be for white South Africans, with their "ingrained prejudice against communism," to understand how and why the ANC would work hand-in-hand with communists, but for Africans, he insists, it makes perfect sense. This is because, he says, "for many decades communists were the only political group in South Africa who were prepared to treat us as human beings and as their equals; who were prepared to eat with us; talk with us, live with us, and work with us."

This is the most powerful aspect of Mandela's response to the Cold War myth: he denies that the ANC is communist-controlled, but then he works with a new myth, the myth of domestication, telling a story that illustrates how natural it was that the liberation movement would work hand-in-hand with communists. Mandela's imagery reinforces the myth: communists and Africans are eating together, talking with one another, working side-by-side, and living as equals. There is no foreign enemy here, just a quotidian partnership founded on equality, mutual support, and common sense. Thus, in response to the government's myth of alienation, which relies on bias, sensationalism, and fear, Mandela critiques that myth and then offers in its place a myth of domestication. In this way, he resolves at a local level an issue that had global implications: the global Cold War myths pitting Western civilization against socialism and communism are reconciled in relative microcosm as Mandela is able to articulate and justify through his new myth the seemingly impossible act of non-communists simultaneously disagreeing and cooperating with communists.

A myth whose aim is to demonstrate that people with vastly different beliefs and long-term goals can live and work peaceably together is precisely the kind of myth that was needed not just for apartheid South Africa, but even more importantly for *post*-apartheid South Africa. Thus, the myth of domestication, I argue, prefigures, anticipates, and perhaps even provided a foundation for myths about the utopian potential of reconciliation between whites and blacks in the years following apartheid. These myths found their most potent articulation in the myth of the rainbow nation. When Mandela was released from prison, it was significant that he concluded his first speech with the famous final paragraph of his Rivonia statement. Not only did this restate his beliefs and ultimate commitment to the cause of ending apartheid, but it also recalled and reinforced the myths that his speech had created, reintroducing them in the new context of his release. However, it was his later appropriation of a phrase attributed to Archbishop Desmond Tutu that ultimately became the hopeful (and, later, cynical) keyword in conversations about the post-apartheid state.[5] In his 1994 Presidential Inauguration speech, Mandela describes the "depth of the pain" his people experienced during the apartheid era, but he does not dwell on it (2011). Instead, he says, "The time for the healing of the wounds has come. The moment to bridge the chasms that divide us has come. The time to build is upon us." One of the strategies he uses to inaugurate not just his presidency but this moment of building and bridging

---

5   Archbishop Tutu is generally credited with coining the phrase "rainbow nation" in several speeches in 1989. In one speech, he called on "the South African government and its police [to] come here now and look at the people of South Africa ... This is how our country will be: Technicolor, a rainbow, a country where black and white hold together" (1994: 175). In a later speech, he made a similar statement, calling on F.W. de Klerk and other government leaders to "Come and see what this country is going to become" (1994: 187). Tutu then declares, "This country is a rainbow country! This country is Technicolor. You can come and see the new South Africa!"

chasms is, of course, myth, and he soon articulates the myth that will carry his and the nation's hopes for peace and prosperity in the wake of apartheid:

> We have triumphed in the effort to implant hope in the breasts of the millions of our people. We enter into a covenant that we shall build the society in which all South Africans, both black and white, will be able to walk tall, without any fear in their hearts, assured of their inalienable right to human dignity – a rainbow nation at peace with itself and the world.

In contrast to the basically dichromatic character of the nation under apartheid, Mandela offers the rainbow nation as a corrective civic myth that allows and embraces people and beliefs of many kinds. It is a civic myth of multiculturalism, of a society where black and white, communist and non-communist, Christian and Muslim and Hindu, etc., can live together and work toward common goals for the benefit of all. Wole Soyinka describes the rainbow nation as a "formulation" that "lays claim to a fusion of humanity or, at the very least, a communal blending, and offers the prospect of an integrated consciousness that speaks to a collective identity or, at least, one that is in formation" (2006: 24). Crucially, Mandela uses the present perfect tense in describing their success in giving people hope—i.e., "We *have triumphed*"—and then uses the present tense in making a "covenant" for something that has yet to be done, or, as Soyinka says, is "in formation." Mandela thus concludes in the future tense, saying we "*shall* build" and all "*will* be able to walk tall." The myth of the rainbow nation is future-oriented, in other words, as myths often are. It does not describe current conditions; rather, it gives form to a narrative that envisions and provides a roadmap for ongoing resolution of the contradictions and complications of current conditions.

Given this forward-looking orientation, it is interesting to note that the rainbow nation has frequently been described in recent years as a myth in the pejorative sense: i.e., as a fiction, falsehood, or thin veneer that conceals a more complicated reality in the present. As early as 1997, commentators have described the rainbow nation as a myth. Adam Habib wrote, for example, "The politics of the rainbow nation is unlikely to realise the consolidation of democracy. That it would do so is perhaps one of the biggest myths of the South African Transition" (1997: 31). More recently, however, it has become increasingly commonplace for critics in the media to describe the rainbow nation as a myth in the negative sense. In 2008, Wesley Buthelezi reported on a poll for IOL News that asked its readers "Is the Rainbow Nation a myth?" Eighty percent of respondents voted "yes." Catrina Yu wrote for *The Perspectivist* in 2010 that the "myth of the 'Rainbow Nation'" has blinded the international community to the realities of violence and racism still rampant in South Africa. The same year, a debate was held in Cape Town to commemorate Archbishop Desmond Tutu's retirement from public life; the topic: "South Africa as the Rainbow Nation: Myth or Reality?" (Tay 2010). Mamphela Ramphele told the audience that the myth of the rainbow nation "obscures reality" and has had the dangerous tendency of diverting people's attention from the original "vision and purpose" of those who first voiced the myth. Ramphele quipped, "I don't see any rainbow" (qtd. in Tay 2010). Finally, though there are likely many more examples, Ngwenya Witness asked in March of 2013, "Is the rainbow nation a myth?" and she answered by noting the prevalence of both racial *and* gender discrimination in South Africa today. For so many South Africans, the rainbow nation is a myth only in the sense of its unreality and unfulfilled promises of peace, equality, and prosperity.

One obvious fault that these criticisms share is a focus on the present rather than the future: each assumes that the rainbow nation is supposed to be now, is supposed to have happened already, whereas Mandela's first articulation of the myth cast it as an aspirational ideal, something for which the nation must continually strive. At the same time, however, perhaps these critics have a point: have the post-apartheid moment and even Mandela himself been so thoroughly idealized and mythologized that the government failed to make those basic necessary changes that would pave the way for actually realizing the rainbow nation? Is the rainbow nation even worthwhile as an ideal if it is ultimately unattainable? It is possible that the myth is undergoing the inevitable changes that all myths undergo over time. Few civic myths are perpetually resilient and relevant, and when one has outworn the context that gave it meaning, it becomes necessary to look for, or generate, another. However, perhaps it would be best to see current anxieties about the rainbow nation as an opportunity to reflect critically on the myth as a *civic myth* before hastily discarding it as a weak articulation of an unattainable ideal. And the focus of such critical reflection should not just be the future, but also the past—in other words, at this moment, particularly as we commemorate the fiftieth anniversary of the Rivonia Trial, we should recognize that the rainbow nation as a civic myth has a conceptual genealogy that reaches back to that trial and to Mandela's civic myth of domestication, which told the story of people with widely divergent beliefs working together toward common goals. However, unlike the rainbow nation, the myth of domestication was not purely aspirational; it was descriptive. It told the story of actual, successful cooperation between people who shared common goals but not common origins, politics, or systems of belief.

Taking such a historical perspective on the myth of the rainbow nation may reinvigorate its viability as a civic myth and may also allow us to raise important questions about why it worked as a strategy during apartheid but has been more difficult to implement since. Is the rainbow nation less viable as a civic myth today because its goals are long-term whereas those of the myth of domestication were short-term? Did the common enemy of white supremacy during apartheid simply allow *some* groups to unite, whereas today the myth of the rainbow nation faces the greater task of uniting *all*? What "equipment for living" was made available by the myth of domestication, and where has that equipment gone in the rainbow era? Can that equipment be recovered or made anew? Whatever the answers to such questions, there is much to be gained by rethinking current civic myths in South Africa in light of those of the past: those of apartheid and, more importantly, those that Mandela and the ANC worked with during the Rivonia Trial and throughout their campaign to end legalized racial discrimination. That campaign was successful, in part, because of their attention to the power of civic myths and the relationship of those myths to the legal order. By focusing our attention on such myths today, we will better understand not only the various roles that they have played in South Africa's history, but also the necessary roles that they still play and will continue to play, particularly in the development and administration of our systems and cultures of law.

References

Broun, Kenneth S. *Saving Nelson Mandela: The Rivonia Trial and the Fate of South Africa*. Oxford: Oxford University Press, 2012.

Buthelezi, Wesley. "Rainbow nation is a myth." *IOL News*. September 3, 2008.

Daniel, John. "Racism, the Cold War and South Africa's regional security strategies 1948–1990." In *Cold War in Southern Africa: White Power, Black Liberation*. Edited by Sue Onslow. London and New York: Routledge, 2009, pp. 35–54.

Derrida, Jacques. "The laws of reflection: Nelson Mandela, in admiration." In *For Nelson Mandela*. Edited by Jacques Derrida and Mustapha Tlili. New York: Seaver Books, 1987, pp. 13–41.

Derrida, Jacques. "Force of law: The 'mystical foundation of authority'." In *Deconstruction and the Possibility of Justice*. Edited by Drucilla Cornell, Michel Rosenfeld, and David Gray Carlson. New York and London: Routledge, 1992, pp. 3–67.

Farah, Nuruddin. *Close Sesame*. Saint Paul, MN: Graywolf Press, 1983.

Fitzpatrick, Peter. *The Mythology of Modern Law*. New York and London: Routledge, 1992.

Habib, Adam. "South Africa – the rainbow nation and prospects for consolidating democracy." *African Journal of Political Science*, 2:2 (1997): 15–37.

Leman, Peter. "Singing the Law: Okot p'Bitek's Legal Imagination and the Poetics of Traditional Justice." *Research in African Literatures*, 4:3 (Fall 2009): 109–28.

Leman, Peter. "African Oral Law and the Critique of Colonial Modernity in *The Trial of Jomo Kenyatta*." *Law & Literature*, 23:1 (Spring 2011): 26–47.

Mamdani, Mahmood. *Citizen and Subject: Contemporary Africa and the Legacy of Late Colonialism*. Princeton: Princeton University Press, 1996.

Mandela, Nelson. "'I am prepared to die': Nelson Mandela's statement from the dock at the opening of the defence case in the Rivonia Trial." 1963. *Nelson Mandela Centre of Memory*.

Mandela, Nelson. *Long Walk to Freedom*. Boston: Little Brown and Co., 1994.

Mandela, Nelson. "Statement of Nelson Mandela at his inauguration as president." 2011. *African National Congress*.

Mandela, Nelson. "'Black man in a white court': Nelson Mandela's first court statement – 1962." *Nelson Mandela International Day* (UN website). March 15, 2013.

Melville, Herman. *Billy Budd and Other Stories*. Edited by Frederick Busch. New York: Penguin, 1986.

Ngũgĩ wa Thiong'o and Mĩcere Githae Mugo. *The Trial of Dedan Kimathi*. Oxford: Heinemann, 1976.

Okot p'Bitek. *Artist, the Ruler*. Nairobi: Heinemann, 1986.

Onslow, Sue. "Introduction." In *Cold War in Southern Africa: White Power, Black Liberation*. Edited by Sue Onslow. London and New York: Routledge, 2009a, pp. 1–8.

Onslow, Sue. "The Cold War in Southern Africa: White power, black nationalism and external intervention." In *Cold War in Southern Africa: White Power, Black Liberation*. Edited by Sue Onslow. London and New York: Routledge, 2009b, pp. 9–34.

Richter, James G. "Perpetuating the Cold War: Domestic sources of international patterns of behavior." *Political Science Quarterly*, 107:2 (Summer 1992): 271–301.

Soyinka, Wole. "Views from a palette of the cultural rainbow." In *The Meaning of Mandela: A Literary and Intellectual Celebration*. Cape Town: HSRC Press, 2006, pp. 24–40.

Tay, Nastasya. "South Africa no rainbow nation – Ramphele." *Business Day*. October 14, 2010.

Thomas, Brook. *Cross-Examinations of Law and Literature: Cooper, Hawthorne, Stowe, and Melville*. Cambridge: Cambridge University Press, 1991.

Thomas, Brook. *Civic Myths: A Law and Literature Approach to Citizenship*. Chapel Hill: University of North Carolina Press, 2007.

Thompson, Leonard. *The Political Mythology of Apartheid*. New Haven: Yale University Press, 1985.

Tutu, Desmond. *The Rainbow People of God: The Making of a Peaceful Revolution*. Edited by John Allen. New York: Doubleday, 1994.

Witness, Ngwenya. "Is the rainbow nation a myth?" *news24*. March 29, 2013.

Venuti, Lawrence. *The Translator's Invisibility: A History of Translation*. London; New York: Routledge, 1995.

Yu, Catrina. "The myth of the rainbow nation." *The Perspectivist*. August 11, 2010.

Chapter 5

Justice in Transition:
South Africa Political Trials, 1956–1964

Catherine M. Cole

Apartheid: a harsh, mean word that resounds in one's ears like a trapdoor opening beneath a gallows.[1]

And before June 12, 1964, there was November 7, 1962. And before November 7, 1962, there was March 21, 1960, and before the day in Sharpeville and before and before there was December 1952, and before the trial for treason there was 1948, and before the infamous apartheid laws there were so many befores. And Nelson was born July 18, 1919. And afterward there was Wednesday, June 16, 1976. And after the day of Soweto, there was September 1977. And after the death of Steve Biko, there had been ... .[2]

There have been so many milestones in the history of resistance to apartheid in South Africa that when one tries to speak on the subject, one often feels the impulse to provide a litany of dates and laws or to hurry, breathlessly, back and forth in time as Hélène Cixous does in the text that opens this chapter.[3] Taken from Cixous' fictional imagining of the life together (and mostly apart) of Nelson and Winnie Mandela, the passage lurches in time, disrupts chronological order, and moves from the realm of the individual to that of the national, from the birth of Mandela to the death of Black Consciousness Movement activist Steven Biko. "And before ... and before ... and before ...," the sentence runs on. The narrator then shifts to an "afterward," a time for which there is no conclusion, just a trail of ellipses. Cixous wrote this story in the mid-1980s, before Nelson Mandela was released from prison in 1990, before the passage of the interim constitution in 1993, before the first democratic elections in 1994, and before the commencement of the Truth and Reconciliation Commission (TRC) in 1995–6. She wrote prior to

---

1   Michel Leiris, "Apartheid," in *For Nelson Mandela*, edited by Jacques Derrida and Mustapha Tlili (New York: Seaver Books, Henry Holt, 1987), 71.

2   Hélène Cixous, "The Parting of the Cake," in *For Nelson Mandela*, edited by Jacques Derrida and Mustapha Tlili (New York: Seaver Books, Henry Holt, 1987), 213.

3   See, for instance, Leslie and Neville Rubin, *This is Apartheid* (London: Christian Action, 1966). This pamphlet defines apartheid solely through a litany of extracts from apartheid legislation.

the momentous day of December 5, 2013 when the great tree of Madiba finally fell even as his towering legacy still stands as a humbling measure of us all.

This chapter focuses on three occasions Cixous referred to: the long-running Treason Trial held from 1956 to 1961, a 1962 case against Nelson Mandela that I will call the Incitement Trial,[4] and the Rivonia Trial of 1964. This trilogy of trials represents an extraordinary period of state transformation in South Africa. As apartheid became ever more suffocating and restrictive, law courts became battle grounds where the accused performed as gladiators.[5] In these political and highly politicized trials, the state's shifting norms, its new constitution, as well as the cascade of apartheid legislation that continued to flow forth were both performatively enacted and performatively resisted. Law courts became stages of transition in which language, costume, gesture, acoustics, space, protocols, dramaturgy, song, and visual culture served as critical elements in an improvised script. During a period of state transition into an increasingly authoritarian regime, these three trials were occasions of both promise and blasphemy. Theorist of political justice Otto Krichheimer has said, "By utilizing the devices of justice, politics contracts some ill-defined and spurious obligations. Circumstantial and contradictory, the linkage of politics and justice is characterized by both promise and blasphemy."[6] As I argue in my book *Performing South Africa's Truth Commission*, the performative qualities of these trials also set the stage for the repertoires that would dominate South Africa's transition out of an authoritarian regime and into a new democratic dispensation in the 1990s through the Truth and Reconciliation Commission process.[7] While it may seem blasphemous to consider political trials staged by the apartheid state as sharing a genealogical heritage with the Truth and Reconciliation Commission, it is also accurate to say both share a heavy investment in the conjunction of politics and theater. Returning to these trials at the time of Madiba's passage forces us to look anew at the ways in which Mandela, as a lawyer as well as a consummate performer, enacted and embodied a new dispensation long before this imagined future went into constitutional effect.

The charges levied in the Treason, Incitement, and Rivonia trials ranged from treason, incitement, and sedition to attempting violent overthrow of the state. In each case, however, the accused and their counsel and anti-apartheid spectators transformed the proceedings by means of performance through songs, gestures,

---

4   The 1962 trial of Nelson Mandela is often confused with the earlier Treason Trial and also with the later Rivonia Trial, I suspect in part because the 1962 trial has no comparably recognizable name. Hence I have given it one: the "Incitement Trial," indicating the chief charge against Mandela on this occasion.

5   Joel Joffee, quoted in Mac Maharaj and Ahmed Kathrada (eds) *Mandela: The Authorized Portrait* (Kansas City: Andrews McMeel Publishing, 2006), 121.

6   Otto Kirchheimer, *Political Justice: The Use of Legal Procedure for Political Ends* (Princeton: Princeton University Press, 1961), vii.

7   Catherine M. Cole, *Performing South Africa's Truth Commission: Stages of Transition* (Bloomington: Indiana University Press, 2010).

costumes, and speeches.[8] These performed dimensions of human behavior constitute what Diana Taylor calls the "repertoire"—the embodied expressions that stand in relation to historical traces left behind in transcripts, documents, and recordings in the archive.[9] Taylor's book *The Archive and the Repertoire: Performing Cultural Memory in the Americas* provides new terminology for old conundrums. Whereas in the past theater and performance studies scholars tended to polarize text and performance in ways that were both artificial and rigid, Taylor's approach provides terminology that is more elastic and flexible. The archive consists of objects such as documents, letters, archeological remains, and maps—objects that seem "real," concrete, and able to transmit memory over space and time. The "repertoire," by way of contrast, is embodied memory: "performances, gestures, orality, movement, dance, singing – in short, all those acts usually thought of as ephemeral, nonreproducible knowledge."[10] Taylor posits the relationship between the archive and repertoire neither as a dichotomy nor as being sequentially related (first repertoire, then archive). Rather, the archive and the repertoire are parallel and overlapping realms. The repertoire *seems* less stable or concrete than the archive, though if we look further this contrast breaks down. As the history of the TRC archive makes abundantly evident, documents can mysteriously disappear, and the collection and classification process is intensely mediated, as is the process of requesting, granting, and denying access.

What *is* dichotomous between the realms of archive and repertoire are the biases and expectations people tend to bring to their reception: in scholarship, the archive is given pride of place. The archive is perceived as a rich repository of meaning that is worthy of precise and in-depth analysis, whereas the repertoire is not. The archive is seen as immutable, reliable, and unmediated. While intellectual bias tries to locate the repertoire only in the present, it too transmits knowledge from the past and into the future. The scholarly tendency, Taylor claims, is to banish the repertoire to the past, to see it as false, unreliable, and primordial—or worse, entirely devoid of meaning. "The dominance of language and writing has come to stand for *meaning* itself," according to Taylor, while embodied practices not based in literary codes are seen as having no claims to meaning.[11]

This chapter takes as a foundational assumption the idea that embodied practices *do* have significance and meaning and hence demand our analytical

---

8   Philippe-Joseph Salazar has argued that dissident rhetoric in apartheid South Africa was confined to three sites for codified and public expression: universities; judicial commissions and high courts at the trials of so-called terrorists; and churches, especially via homilies delivered at funerals. Philippe-Joseph Salazar, *An African Athens: Rhetoric and the Shaping of Democracy in South Africa* (Mahwah: Lawrence Erlbaum Associates, 2002), 8.

9   Diana Taylor, *The Archive and the Repertoire: Performing Cultural Memory in the Americas* (Durham, NC: Duke University Press, 2003), 19.

10   Ibid., 20.

11   Ibid., 25.

attention. While various studies have mentioned the repertoires enacted by the accused and their supporters at the South African political trials of 1956–1964 in passing, as sorts of colorful accents to the "real" story of the trials, I instead approach these performative repertoires as meaningful and coherent discourses in their own right. An examination of this repertoire gives a fresh perspective on the ways that performance and the law were deployed during a period of intense political transition. Justice and performance were used (and abused) in this era as South Africa devolved from following the rule of law into a police state. More than three decades later, justice and performance were deployed once again when the Truth and Reconciliation Commission enacted "transitional justice" as a means to restore the rule of law.

I argue that an intensity of meaning worthy of analytical attention occurs at precisely those moments when the archive and the repertoire explicitly converge, as they did during the political trials of the late 1950s and early 1960s. For example, the Treason Trial ended in acquittal in part because the police proved so spectacularly inept at documenting the live improvised speeches of African National Congress leaders at their political rallies, the content of which was alleged to be treasonous.[12] The problem of incoherent reportage came to light through the disparities between longhand and shorthand transcriptions. One of the accused, Helen Joseph, said that her fellow accused were most distressed by the longhand writers, who were, without exception, "White and non-reporters [whose] garbled, inadequate, reports drew scathing comment from the Judge President even during the trial." He testily chided the prosecution for its shoddy research methodology: "Sometimes the State employs shorthand writers, sometimes recording machines, sometimes Africans are sent who may or may not be qualified. Sometimes they are not qualified. *I* am not going to make people employed by the State qualified if they are not qualified."[13] Who would have predicted that the outcome of the largest and most high-profile trial in South African history would depend upon an arcane conundrum of performance studies: how to document live performance?[14]

The political trials of 1956–1964 must be seen as central to the performance genealogy of the TRC. The concept "performance genealogy" has its own intellectual heritage, with a lineage one can trace most directly to Joseph Roach, who in turn inherits from Nietzsche and Foucault.[15] Seeing political trials as part of the performance genealogy of the TRC is important not so we can discover an essence of form or clarify, once and for all, whether the TRC did, in fact,

---

12   Thomas G. Karis, "The South African Treason Trial," *Political Science Quarterly* 76, no. 2 (1961): 21.

13   Helen Joseph, *If This Be Treason* (London: Andre Deutsch, 1963), 37.

14   See, for instance, Peggy Phelan, *Unmarked: The Politics of Performance* (New York: Routledge, 1993), 146–8; Taylor, *The Archive and the Repertoire*; and Philip Auslander, *Liveness* (New York: Routledge, 1999).

15   Joseph R. Roach, *Cities of the Dead: Circum-Atlantic Performance* (New York: Columbia University Press, 1996), 25.

produce "real" truth or viable reconciliation, whether its justice was restorative or a travesty. Genealogy, in the Foucauldian sense, is not about getting to the bottom of things. Rather, performance genealogy provides a means for seeing the TRC's complex inheritance as multiple, contradictory, and more complex than has previously been understood. As Roach writes, genealogies of performance attend to "counter-memories" as well as to "the disparities between history as it is discursively transmitted and memory as it is publicly enacted by the bodies that bear its consequences."[16]

In South Africa prior to the TRC, the discursive practices of officially sanctioned history had been overwhelmingly logocentric while the practices of resistance had been largely located in performance—that is, in the realm of the body. This dichotomy was both racialized and racist, and the state was the chief agent in that racialization. The state passed a torrent of laws aimed at limiting, circumscribing, or eliminating altogether the discursive practices of those who most acutely bore the consequences of apartheid: nonwhites. Black cultures in South Africa had long-standing oral and performed traditions that far pre-dated apartheid. But under apartheid, embodiment came to be linked to either resistance/transgression *or* to compliance. Hence, the trials staged, in essence, a confrontation between the archive and the repertoire. By the time of the TRC, 35 years later, the gap between the written record of history preserved in the archives and the countermemories recorded in repertoires had become a chasm. The Truth and Reconciliation Commission was intended to bridge this chasm, and it did so by drawing on many resources. Among these were the international traditions of transitional justice, the high-profile quasi-juridical events of the past such as political trials, and the repertoires of resistance cultivated by the anti-apartheid movement.

Befores and Afters

If we consider South Africa's Truth and Reconciliation Commission as a stage of transition *out* of a period of gross violations of human rights, when did that period begin? "Apartheid" is surely central to the answer. In addition to being "a harsh, mean word that resounds in one's ears like a trapdoor opening beneath a gallows," in Michael Leiris's phrase, apartheid is an Afrikaans word that means "racial apartness." Dr. Hendrik Frensch Verwoerd, the South African leader who is usually considered the architect of apartheid, once described it as a policy of "good neighborliness," a statement that was much parodied afterward.[17] The inception of apartheid is usually dated to the 1948 ascendancy to power of the Afrikaner

16   Ibid., 26.
17   "Exit Sighing," *Time*, March 24, 1961, available at www.time.com (accessed July 21, 2008).

National Party, which inaugurated an "avalanche" of security legislation.[18] The Prohibition of Mixed Marriages Act of 1949, the Population Registration Act of 1950, the Group Areas Act of 1950, the Suppression of Communism Act of 1950, the Bantu Authorities Act of 1951—these and many related laws made apartheid ideology operational by tightly proscribing where nonwhites could live and work, whom they could marry and have sex with, what they could say, and what type of education they could receive.[19] Apartheid as an official policy was articulated and systematically enforced after 1948, though it was simply an extreme version of racial practices already in place. The fact that the African National Congress was formed in 1912 is a testament to the earlier need of blacks for representation, for even then land seizures and labor practices were racially driven. Under the post-1948 rule of the National Party, apartheid was made manifest performatively through passbooks, separate amenities, separate school curricula, and separate living areas, known as townships in cities and as homeland reserves in the country. The amount of legislation needed to bring apartheid into being was breathtakingly extensive, as evidenced by a huge wall—a monumental monolith—at the present-day Apartheid Museum in South Africa that is covered with plaques inscribed with acts of apartheid legislation. A "pathological proliferation of juridical prostheses," Jacques Derrida calls them.[20] Such prosthetics were necessary to prop up a state that had amputated morality from the law.

While state repression escalated and intensified in the 1950s, the early 1960s were a crucial turning point. Most important was the massacre at Sharpeville in March 1960, during which 69 Africans were killed and another 180 wounded while peacefully protesting, brutally gunned down by the police during an anti-pass law demonstration. "Previously, nearly every ANC leader had been deeply committed to non-violence," says historian Leonard Thompson. "But nonviolence methods had achieved nothing except a series of defeats at the hands of a violent state."[21] The two leading anti-apartheid organizations, the African National Congress and the Pan Africanist Congress, were banned. The government declared a state of emergency and conducted mass arrests, facilitated by new legislation that permitted arrests without warrants and detention without trial. The prison

---

18   Christopher Merrett, *A Culture of Censorship: Secrecy and Intellectual Repression in South Africa* (Macon: Mercer University Press, 1995), 21.

19   In his influential history of South Africa, Leonard Thompson includes two chapters on the apartheid era that together span the period 1948 to 1989. See Leonard Thompson, *A History of South Africa*, 3rd edn (New Haven: Yale University Press, 2000), 187–264.

20   Jacques Derrida, "The Laws of Reflection: Nelson Mandela, in Admiration," in *For Nelson Mandela*, edited by Jacques Derrida and Mustapha Tlili (New York: Seaver Books, Henry Holt and Co., 1987), 18.

21   Thompson, *A History of South Africa*, 211.

populations exploded. Anti-apartheid activists began to call the years before 1960 "the legal days"; afterward, everything was illegal.[22]

For over 50 years the ANC had tirelessly and patiently fought oppression through nonviolent means. But after Sharpeville its policy changed. The ANC formed a military wing known as Umkhonto we Sizwe (MK, or "Spear of the Nation"), which endorsed certain acts of violence as part of the freedom struggle. In 1961, the South African government chose to leave the British Commonwealth and become the Republic of South Africa. The republic's first act was to pass a new constitution under which one-fifth of South Africa's people—its whites—determined the fate of the country's entire population, 81 percent of whom were not white.[23] Protesting against this new constitution—an unconstitutional constitution if ever there was one—landed Nelson Mandela in court for his Incitement Trial of 1962.

Not only does 1960 serve as a meaningful historical frame for understanding the period out of which the TRC was intended to be a transition, this year is also the historical frame for the TRC's mandate: the commission was charged with examining gross violations of human rights that took place after March 1960, the date of the Sharpeville massacre. Even at the time, many recognized Sharpeville as a historic watershed. "The old book of South African history was closed at Sharpeville," said Paul Sauer just two weeks after the shootings.[24] Thus, the Sharpeville massacre marks the beginning of the 34-year period the Truth and Reconciliation Commission was charged to investigate. Of course, gross violations of human rights did not *begin* in South Africa in 1960.[25] However, 1960 was seen by the authors of the interim constitution as a logical starting point for the Truth and Reconciliation Commission's investigations.[26]

---

22   Albie Sachs, foreword to Ruth First, *117 Days* (New York: Monthly Review Press, 1989), 11. For an overview of the early apartheid period, see Thompson, *A History of South Africa*, 187–220; Leslie Rubin, *This Is Apartheid* (London: Victor Gollancz, 1960); and Philip Bonner, Peter Delius, and Deborah Posel (eds) *Apartheid's Genesis, 1935–1962* (Johannesburg: Ravan Press and Witwatersrand University Press, 1993). Deborah Posel argues that between 1959 and 1961 apartheid "shifted gear into a discrete second phase" that should not be simply seen as a continuation and extension of what came before it. See Deborah Posel, *The Making of Apartheid, 1948–1961* (New York: Oxford University Press, 1991), 227–55, quote on 227.

23   Akil Kokayi Khalfani and Tukufu Zuberi, "Racial Classification and the Modern Census in South Africa, 1911–1966," *Race & Society* 14, no. 2 (2001): 166.

24   Paul Sauer quoted in Karis, "The South African Treason Trial," 236.

25   Anthony Sampson, *The Treason Cage: The Opposition on Trial in South Africa* (London: Heinemann, 1958), 41–52.

26   TRC, *Truth and Reconciliation Commission of South Africa Report*, vol. 1 (London: Macmillan, 1999), 55.

South Africa in the Dock

The 1950s and early 1960s were a time of intense political change. As the government exerted increasing control over the domain of writing, anti-apartheid opponents responded by means of performance through songs, slogans, and codified gestures, traditions that would become defining features of the anti-apartheid movement during subsequent decades. The state passed repressive laws and Africans broke them. When Africans broke the law, they were put on trial. Yet, in Nelson Mandela's view, "Our appearances in court became the occasion for exuberant political rallies."[27] In the face of state repression and censorship, the anti-apartheid struggle cultivated a rich and multifaceted repertoire of resistance. Embodied expressions, songs, gestures, dances, and speech acts were its weapons, especially in the early days of nonviolent protest before the ANC began throwing stones and wielding AK-47s. Performed repertoires of resistance attained national and international visibility during the political trials of 1956–1964 and were to remain a common feature of political trials during subsequent decades, much to the irritation of the state. How and what did anti-apartheid activists perform at political trials from 1956–1964, not just with words, but also with their bodies, voices, gestures, clothing, and use of physical space?

"Awful, wonderful, inspiring and boring beyond words," said defendant Hilda Bernstein of the Treason Trial, which began in 1956, when 156 people were arrested for treason and for planning to violently overthrow the government.[28] The accused, identified by the state as 105 blacks, 21 Indians, 23 whites, and seven coloreds, included the leaders of all the major resistance organizations, among them the African National Congress, the Coloured People's Congress, the Congress of Democrats, the South African Indian Congress, and the South African Congress of Trade Unions. (These organizations were collectively known as the Congress Alliance.) They faced charges of high treason and of setting up a countrywide conspiracy to topple the government and install a communist state. The trial droned on for nearly five years before ending in mass acquittals. Then, in 1962, Mandela alone was tried for inciting Africans to participate in a strike and for leaving the country without a passport. Found guilty on both counts, he was sentenced to five years in prison. Halfway through his sentence, he was again brought before a court, this time with several others, in the so-called Rivonia case. Their alleged crime was sabotage, which carried the threat of the gallows. The Rivonia Trial was Mandela's final appearance in court before he disappeared from public view for 25 years.

Although South African political trials transpired in what were ostensibly courts of law, the accused freedom fighters often argued that the courts in which they

---

27   Nelson Mandela, *Nelson Mandela: An Illustrated Autobiography* (Boston: Little, Brown and Co., 1996), 46.

28   Hilda Bernstein, *The World That Was Ours: The Story of the Rivonia Trial* (London: SAWriters, 1989), 20.

were tried were not, in fact, legal. In addition, the audience these courts addressed went beyond the judges, advocates, prosecutors, and spectators present in the room. The courts spoke also to an audience beyond the walls of the courtroom, to a national and, indeed, a global audience. L.J. Blom-Cooper, a British observer of the Treason Trial, remarked, "Not since the burning of the Reichstag in Berlin in 1933 – with the notable exception of the special trials at Nuremberg – has a trial attracted such international attention."[29] South Africa's political trials were platforms, show trials, juridical events both inside and outside the law. They dealt with the law not just on an operational level but also on a philosophical one. The trials used semantic opacity, ephemerality, and locus in the body of performance to mediate between conscience and the law.

The Treason Trial

The state inaugurated the Treason Trial as a spectacle with a mass arrest at dawn of over 140 people. Lionel Forman, one of the accused, recalls the highly publicized event:

> One hundred and forty families were wakened that morning – Africans, Indians, Europeans, Coloureds; doctors and labourers, teachers and students, a university principal, a tribal chief. And if the names and occupations were analysed, here was a complete cross-section of South Africa. Afrikaaners, Englishmen, Jews, Zulu, Xosa, Basutho, Hindu, Moslem, young and old; sick and healthy; university graduate and illiterate.[30]

Specially arranged trains and military planes whisked the accused off to Johannesburg, where they were met by a squadron of soldiers "armed as for war."[31] The accused were shipped off to the Old Fort Prison In Johannesburg in a *kwela-kwela* van, and as they rode, they launched into performative repertoires that became characteristic of political trials.[32] Forman recalls, "Now we are swinging in the huge kwela-kwela towards the Fort. They are singing, and I am singing too: 'Izokunyathela iAfrika' ... 'Afrika will trample you underfoot'. Unrepentant. People seen through the mesh: surprise and dawning understanding. The thumb raised in reply. 'Mayibu'ye iAfrika!'" The arrest was a spectacle orchestrated

---

29 L.J. Blom-Cooper, "The South African Treason Trial: R. v. Adams and Others," *International and Comparative Law Quarterly* 8, no. 1 (1959): 59.

30 Lionel Forman and E.S. Sachs, *The South African Treason Trial* (New York: Monthly Review Press, 1958), 11.

31 Ibid., 19.

32 The term *kwela* is derived from the Zulu for "get up," though in township slang it also referred to the police vans, the *kwela-kwela*. See "South African Music: Kwela," available at http://www.southafrica.info/about/arts/922564.htm (accessed April 4, 2009).

by the state, but those arrested and their supporters used song and gestures to transform military spectacle into a festival of resistance.

When the prisoners arrived at the Fort and assembled in a big hall, the atmosphere was one of elation and pandemonium. "It was like a great May Day picnic, or the most representative of national conferences," recalls Forman.[33] Anti-apartheid activists came together from Johannesburg, Durban, Cape Town, and Port Elizabeth, sometimes meeting for the first time. Forman writes:

> Warders wandered about with batons, not quite knowing what to do. White men and black men hugging each other. Black professors and doctors and lawyers. Ministers of religion, a member of parliament. Men being introduced to one another and formally shaking hands as if they were at a braaivleis [barbeque]. Warders had never seen anything like this in the Fort before. They stopped wandering about and huddled together in a whispering group.[34]

This scene is emblematic of the dueling spectacles that characterized the Treason Trial. The National Party government tried to whip the public into a state of hysteria about "treason" and a "communist threat." The arrests at dawn, the secret military air flights, and the spectacular headlines in the press were all intended to dramatize the magnitude of this threat as well as the state's overwhelming capacity to suppress opposition. The trial was also implicitly a rationale for the state's increasing infringement on civil liberties—its intimidation and surveillance via the new Special Branch secret police. But the Treason Trial spectacle backfired. "It was the oddest paradox," writes Anthony Sampson, an editor of *Drum* magazine, an important voice in the anti-apartheid struggle, "that in the very court where they were being tried for treason, the Congress leaders were able to hold their biggest unbanned meetings for four years."[35] For the first time the opposition leaders had a central office—the Drill Hall, where the trial was held. This cavernous military building in Johannesburg was hastily fitted as a satellite court since no existing courtroom could accommodate 156 defendants in its dock. The accused were so numerous that the arrests and legal proceedings had the unintended consequence of fostering relationships among opposition leaders. Nelson Mandela notes:

> Our communal cell became a kind of convention for far-flung freedom fighters. Many of us had been living under severe restrictions, making it illegal for us to meet and talk. Now, our enemy had gathered us all together under one roof for what became the largest and longest unbanned meeting of the Congress Alliance in years.[36]

33　Forman and Sachs, *The South African Treason Trial*, 22.
34　Ibid.
35　Sampson, *The Treason Cage*, 203.
36　Nelson Mandela, *Long Walk to Freedom: The Autobiography of Nelson Mandela* (Boston: Little, Brown and Co., 1994), 201.

The great miscalculation of the political trials of 1956–1964 was that in seeking to break political opposition, the government instead succeeded in strengthening it.[37]

In the face of the state's escalating censorship of expression, the anti-apartheid movement developed an extraordinarily adaptable, enduring, and politically efficacious repertory of resistance. The freedom songs, the thumbs-up "Afrika! Mayibuye!" salute, and other, more subtle performed interventions in the drama of the trial were all means of protest that the state seemed incapable of regulating, a fact that was increasingly vexing to state officials. The protest repertory was deployed in myriad ways, and song was of primary and enduring importance throughout all three trials. As the musician Abdullah Ibrahim notes, South Africa's may well have been the first revolution ever conducted in "four-part harmony."[38] There was the "singing music box" that Forman and others describe—the vans that invariably rocked with freedom songs as they transported prisoners to and from the Treason Trial and later the Rivonia Trial as well. Helen Joseph remembers the latter days of the Treason Trial:

> The men came pouring out of the goal gate and into the back of the van. I couldn't see them but I could feel the lorry rocking as they clambered in, and the singing started. The beautiful melodies and the incomparable harmonies as we rode through the streets of Pretoria. Our van was known as the 'singing lorry' and the driver was so proud that he sometimes drove us round Church Square, 'Sing up, sing up, chaps!' he shouted, 'I'm taking you for a ride!'[39]

Joseph's story suggests the extent to which prisoners' singing of freedom songs affected onlookers, even the wardens directly charged with their imprisonment.

What was this strange efficacy of song? Hilda Watts, wife of one of the accused, recalls the arrival of vans in Pretoria:

> Soon there is a sound of singing, we look up – the buses have arrived! The songs, the raised thumbs, the spirit of courage and unity, all this arrives with the accused in their buses, just as it came with the *kwela* that morning more than a year and a half ago when they were first brought from the prisons to the Court.[40]

Memoirs of political prisoners speak eloquently and often of the importance of song as a means of communication while in solitary confinement, as a way of creating a sense of community among individuals of disparate backgrounds, and as

---

37 Sampson, *The Treason Cage*, 5.

38 Quote from the jazz pianist Abdullah Ibrahim in the documentary film *Amandla! A Revolution in Four-Part Harmony* (2002, ATO Pictures/Kwela Productions; dir. Lee Hirsch).

39 Joseph, *If This Be Treason*, 91.

40 Hilda Watts quoted in ibid., 26.

a way of knitting together moments in time during the long struggle for freedom.[41] During the 1962 Incitement Trial, the crowd that assembled each day often left the courtroom by breaking into song, reportedly "rocking" the courtroom as they spontaneously sang "Nkosi Sikelel i'Africa" ("God Bless Africa").[42] Even at the end of the Rivonia Trial, as the accused who had been sentenced to life in prison were being ferried away, Albertina Sisulu stood outside the court in traditional dress leading a crowd singing "Nkosi Sikelel i'Africa."[43]

Another technique of the repertoire of resistance was the manner in which the accused and their supporters performed courtroom protocol. When the Treason Trial defendants first arrived in the magistrates' court for their remands, they saw that a huge audience had gathered in the gallery. The spectators whispered slogans of support and raised their thumbs in the air, despite the magistrate's warning that such gestures could lead to charges of contempt.[44] As a way of expressing solidarity with the accused, the audience refused to sit even after the magistrate did so. In the spirit of improvised collective action, the accused spontaneously devised another and more subtle means of performed resistance, as Lionel Forman narrates:

> The prosecution called out the names one by one. The first few answered with a simple 'yes' but then one responded in deep and formal Zulu and the idea caught on at once.

> In a variety of languages and in every form of subtle irony came the reply.

> 'I am here if it may please your worship', said Archie Sibeko, Secretary of the Congress of Trade Unions in dignified si-Xosa.

> 'My lord, I have the pleasure to be in court', said Cleopas Sibande in Sesutho. 'Ich bin do', said Hymie Barsel in Yiddish.

> 'Ndi Lapa' – 'I am here' – said Chief Luthuli.

---

41   See Mandela, *Long Walk to Freedom*, 202; and Jeremy Cronin, "Death Row," in Jeremy Cronin, *Inside* (Johannesburg: Ravan Press, 1983), 26–31. Ruth First, who was detained for 117 days, said, "Those held in prison pending political trials or during the 1960 State of Emergency and the days of the 1961 Mandela strike, had emerged from a spell of community jail life with morale marvelously unimpaired. Every new stretch of prison for a group of political prisoners gave birth to a new batch of freedom songs." See First, *117 Days*, 140.

42   "Mandela Wins Week's Adjournment," *Cape Times*, October 15, 1962, 3. I am grateful to research assistant Bianca Murillo for her painstaking work in locating this and many other articles on the political trials of 1956–1964 in South African newspapers.

43   Joel Joffe, *The Rivonia Story* (Cape Town: Mayibuye Books, University of Western Cape, 1995), 205.

44   Forman and Sachs, *The South African Treason Trial*, 34.

For a long time there was no Afrikaans, the language of [Prime Minister] Strijdom, but the morning was not to pass without a symbol that there are Afrikaners in the freedom movement too.

'Ja, ek is teenwoordig', came the reply when Jan Hoogendyk's name was called, and the magistrate's head snapped up.

Once again the roster had demonstrated that the 'traitors' speak in all the voices of South Africa.[45]

This moment inaugurated the juridical space as a forum in which the agon between the apartheid state and anti-apartheid resistance would play out. Here we see a call-and-response that set the paradigm for much of what followed: the prosecutor calls the names of the accused and they respond in unexpected ways, their language and tone asserting individuality, difference, and irony. The audience is called to stand and they do so, but then they refuse to sit according to normal courtroom protocol. Spectators introduced hand gestures (the thumbs-up sign) and slogans ("Mayibuye") from another public sphere—the political rally.

The Treason Trial was a spectacle that attempted to respond most directly to a counterspectacle, the political rallies being staged throughout the country by the anti-apartheid movement. The political rally was what the political trials were intended to curtail. The charges of the Treason Trial largely resulted from an extraordinary gathering in Kliptown held in 1955, when a great tide of anti-apartheid delegates from across the country met to write the Freedom Charter, a document that would serve as a prototype for the future constitution. "There had been bigger political meetings in South Africa, but the Kliptown gathering was and still is unique in our history," according to Raymond Suttner and Jeremy Cronin.[46] "Seven thousand spectators watched the proceedings. This was certainly the most representative gathering there has ever been in South Africa. It was a real people's parliament, with one difference. It was not, of course, sovereign."[47] The political trials of 1956–64 were an attempt by the state to stage a spectacle that would compete with and ultimately suppress the spectacles of political rallies, people's parliaments that were assembling with incredible force and magnitude throughout the country.

---

45   Ibid.

46   Raymond Suttner was a political prisoner from 1975 to 1983, imprisoned for his activities with the ANC. He is now a professor at the University of South Africa. Jeremy Cronin was also imprisoned during the apartheid era for his political activities with the South African Community Party. He is a well-known poet and presently serves as a Deputy Minister of Parliament in South Africa.

47   Raymond Suttner and Jeremy Cronin (eds) *30 Years of the Freedom Charter* (Braamfontein: Ravan Press, 1986), 86.

When the preparatory examination for the Treason Trial commenced, these two arenas of spectacle converged. A great throng of protestors pushed right up to the doorstep of the hearing. Thousands had assembled in the streets outside the Drill Hall. Yet they were not allowed in. Apartheid reigned inside the courtroom: only a third of the seats had initially been allocated to non-Europeans, and these were revoked when the European audience exceeded the hall's capacity. "The whites were allowed to take up all the seats meant for the blacks. And the thousands of Non-Europeans who stood patiently in long lines extended round several city blocks—who had stood there for many hours—were left to stand," recalls Forman.[48] When the accused were led into the courtroom, there was not one non-European in the audience. And yet somehow the masses of non-Europeans outside the hall knew with incredible precision what was happening inside the courtroom. The dueling spectacles had finally converged—the courtroom and the rally—and a disarming call-and-response ensued that momentarily connected the juridical space and the political rally. "How word got out to the streets is a mystery," Forman writes:

> But the people out there knew of every move in the court as soon as it was made. They knew the moment the court orderly called out: 'Rise in court', and the magistrate strode in. There was a hush outside, and with miraculous timing, just as he sat down there was a swelling sound of ten thousand voices singing "Mayibuye, Afrika", and then silence once more.[49]

Once again we see a kind of oddly antiphonal structure, with the state initiating a "call" and Africans answering in unexpected ways. On this particular day, the rally outside the courtroom won the duel. Their booming voices combined with the horrendous acoustics of the Drill Hall, creating such a din that nobody inside the courtroom could be heard, and the court was adjourned until loudspeakers could be found.[50] The next day, the state erected a five-foot-high mesh cage for the accused and police dispelled the crowed with batons and gunshots.[51] "Everyone in the court stood up and the accused pushed forward in their cage," writes Forman, adding, "The police were shooting the people outside. The police were shooting the people," an alarming declaration that we can read in retrospect as a premonition of the state's new techniques of repression, for shooting into crowds

---

48   Forman and Sachs, *The South African Treason Trial*, 49.

49   Ibid. See Sampson, *The Treason Cage*, 11. For news service film coverage of this disruption, see *Hearst Telenews*, issue 9, tape 256, which shows images of demonstrators disrupting the Treason Trial in Johannesburg on December 24, 1956. Footage located at the UCLA Film & Television Archive, Los Angeles, California.

50   Anthony Sampson, *Mandela: The Authorized Biography* (New York: Alfred A. Knopf, 1999), 12.

51   Sampson, *The Treason Cage*, 13–14; Forman and Sachs, *The South African Treason Trial*, 51–3; Blom-Cooper, "The South African Treason Trial," 60.

gathered at rallies would eventually replace transcription of speeches at rallies as the state's primary technique of suppression. In the battle of spectacles, day two of the hearings went to the state. In *The Treason Cage*, his book on the proceedings, Anthony Sampson describes an encounter that is in many ways emblematic not only of the Treason Trial but also of the many political trials in South Africa that followed. One day during the lunch break, Sampson was sharing a meal with Professor Z.K. Matthews, one of the most distinguished Africans among the accused. Sampson recalls:

> Two young Afrikaner sportsmen wandered in during the lunch-hour and, seeing the hall full of natives, walked up to one of them who was sitting having lunch with me. 'What are these trials about, eh? Who is it they are trying?' one of them asked. 'The whole of South Africa is on trial', replied Professor Matthews, looking up darkly from his soup. 'You're on trial, we're all on trial. It's ideas that are being tried here, not people'.[52]

Matthews responded to the casual Afrikaner observers by telling them they were not innocent bystanders: they too were on trial, sportsmen or no. And he made it clear that the primary defendant in this trial was not people but ideas, a sentiment echoed by defense counsel Vernon Berrangé in his opening address to the court:

> A battle of ideas has indeed been started in our country. A battle in which on one side – the accused will allege – are poised those ideas which seek equal opportunity for, and freedom of thought and expression by, all persons of all races and creeds; and, on the other side, those which deny to all but a few the riches of life, both material and spiritual, which the accused aver should be common to all.[53]

Accusations of communism and treason were central to the government's case. By simply hurling the accusation "communist" at an individual or organization, the state could utilize the powers of the Suppression of Communism Act, passed in 1950, which included, as Christopher Merrett describes:

> The liquidation of unlawful communist organizations; the listing of their office- bearers, members and active supporters, and the forced resignation and/ or exclusion of such persons from other organizations, including legislative bodies; a prohibition on printing, publication and circulation of documents emanating from or reflecting the aims of communist organizations; seizure of documents; proscriptions of meetings; banning of persons from gatherings and from specified areas; and ... deportation.[54]

---

52 Sampson, *The Treason Cage*, 28.
53 Vernon Berrangé quoted in Joseph, *If This Be Treason*, 16.
54 Merrett, *A Culture of Censorship*, 22.

The act allowed the state to unleash a torrent of security legislation that curbed civil liberties in every arena. The accused contended that their ideas were not communist but rather were concerned with fundamental issues of human rights, liberty, and representative government. Their approach to the trial was to shift the focus from purported communism to the ideology of apartheid, which institutionalized gross socioeconomic inequities and violations of human rights.

If the Treason Trial was a battle of ideas, a conflict between firing guns and freedom songs, and a duel of spectacles between the courtroom and the political rally, it was also a battle between the domain of the archive and the domain of repertoire. Until 1956, the anti-apartheid struggle was conducted openly with public meetings and a firm commitment to nonviolence. And yet it was largely conducted in the realm of performance, for possessing written documents that the state could confiscate and scrutinize was a liability. In addition, unequal access to education ensured that many of those most acutely impacted by apartheid could not read. So the anti-apartheid struggle was a movement that deployed body and voice as primary instruments of communication. The state, on the other hand, was imposing itself upon its citizenry through escalating degrees of documentation. This burden was nowhere more potently expressed than in the passbook system, which required all non-Europeans to carry identity documents that defined where they could live and work.

But the state's attempts to document (to archive) the supposedly treasonous speeches (the repertoire) of anti-apartheid activists were often woefully inadequate. Early on in the Treason Trial, it became clear that the state's primary evidence of treason hinged upon speeches so poorly transcribed that they were "incomprehensible, incoherent and illiterate."[55] These speeches had been recorded by police who had infiltrated and spied on political rallies. But their methods of transcription were erratic and inept, especially among those who could only write in longhand. Political speeches were improvised performances. As theater and performance studies scholars well know, performance presents acute methodological challenges, for it is notoriously difficult to record. In the 1950s in South Africa, the police had access primarily to handwritten transcriptions. "During those years it was rare for our speakers to use prepared notes," explains Helen Joseph. "And some of the speeches that were being so mangled and maimed in the Court had been made all of seven years ago – and none less than four. But *we* knew what our leaders used to say; and it wasn't this garbled gibberish, this double-Dutch, this blood-and-thunder nonsense."[56] So painful did the accused find the Crown's gross mangling of their speeches that they sometimes even sent notes of clarification to the front of the courtroom as some detective "fumbled through penciled notes," according to Anthony Sampson.[57]

---

55 Forman and Sachs, *The South African Treason Trial*, 88.
56 Joseph, *If This Be Treason*, 38.
57 Sampson, *The Treason Cage*, 30.

But the problem of documentation was not the only difficulty these performed speeches presented to the state. Language in South Africa's radically multilingual environment was also a profound issue. At one point in the Treason Trial, the prosecutor produced a witness who read to the court a text he claimed was an accurate transcription of a speech given by a Mr Press. Lionel Forman writes:

> The detective who was reporting it could not understand English well enough to write down the actual words. But fortunately the speech had been translated into Sesutho for the audience [at the rally]. The detective didn't understand Sesutho either, but the Sesutho had been translated into Zulu. And the detective understood that. But there was no point in him writing the speech down in Zulu because his officers didn't understand Zulu. So he had translated the translation of the translation of the speech into his own English while the speech was still on.[58]

So the spy's transcription of the speech was three generations removed from its original source—as the text went from English to Sesutho to Zulu and back to the detective's "own" version of English, with all the potential for error and inaccuracy compounded with each reiteration. If not for the fact that this witness was called by the state to testify in a case about the most serious of offenses, that of High Treason, for which the accused could potentially be executed, this episode would stand as one of the most comical in South Africa's legal history.

Such absurdities were not uncommon in the early years of the Treason Trial, which, despite its spectacular beginnings, was largely boring. Tedium was relieved by fleeting moments of drama or humor. On more than one occasion, the magistrate had to admonish, "This is not as funny as it seems."[59] But perhaps the Treason Trial's most bizarre convergence (or failed convergence) of archive and repertoire was not a debate about the methodological challenges of transcribing live performance but rather a demonstration and performative reenactment of this very problem. Advocate Berrangé, during his cross-examination of African Secret Police boss John Tabata, contended that the witness was too illiterate to record a speech in English, even if he had an interpreter. Berrangé promised to put Tabata to a test: Tabata said he took his notes while sitting on a motorcycle and so, very well, Berrangé would have a motorcycle brought into court and everyone would be able to see how he fared transcribing under such conditions. "Little wonder then that there was an air of expectancy in the court the next morning," said Lionel Forman. "The proceedings are deadly monotonous and the idea of having a motorcycle in the witness-box complete with detective perched on it, was one which appealed to everyone."[60] The motorcycle when it came had a sidecar and was too

---

58 Forman and Sachs, *The South African Treason Trial*, 88.
59 Sampson, *Mandela*, 27.
60 Forman and Sachs, *The South African Treason Trial*, 123.

wide to fit through the doorway.[61] Yet the "show" had to go on. Tabata sat on a chair instead and transcribed a speech delivered by advocate Berrangé which was then translated into not just one but two different African languages:

Berrangé: Afrika! Sons and daughters …

Magistrate: Tabata seems to be agitated.

Berrangé: I think he is very worried.

Magistrate: I know you think it is simulated.

Berrangé: No, no. Not at all. I'm sure it's genuine.

Tabata: I would like another interpreter.[62]

In this metatheatrical moment of the performed "play" within the trial, the magistrate and advocate Berrangé observe the witness's comportment and discuss whether he is "simulating" (i.e., acting) his emotions of panic or whether these are indeed genuine. Berrangé continued with his recited speech, and this time the accused in their cage also began to play along. The courtroom became a theater, a performed replication of a political rally. Berrangé said: "Afrika! Sons and daughters of Africa, just as the sun rises in the East, it is sure that through all our vicissitudes we will achieve the aims of the Freedom Charter."[63] Then, as Lionel Forman recalls, "There was a pause for realistic applause, and a cry of '*Afrika! Mayibuye!*' came from the back, until the accused remembered that they were still in court."[64] They were performing the repertoire of resistance. As A.S. Chetty, a former executive member of the Natal Indian Congress explains, such exclamations were essentially one's membership card in the freedom struggle. "The moment you give them [African people] the sign, you're a comrade. You say: '*Afrika!*' and they return it: '*Mayibuye!*' Straight away you're a comrade. Open, come into the house and talk."[65]

At the Treason Trial, this demonstration of a rally was staged in order to reveal the inability of the police to document the crimes they alleged. Yet this moment also created a convergence of the two domains vying for preeminence throughout: the trial and the rally. For a few brief moments, the courtroom became a political rally. It also became a theater, with the proceedings not just *telling* what had happened but also *showing* through reenactment. The theater of the Treason Trial involved

---

61 Sampson, *The Treason Cage*, 24.
62 Forman and Sachs, *The South African Treason Trial*, 126.
63 Ibid.
64 Sampson, *The Treason Cage*, 24.
65 A.S. Chetty quoted in Suttner and Cronin, *30 Years of the Freedom Charter*, 48.

role-playing: the defense advocate played the role of the accused by delivering one of their political speeches; the accused played the role of spectators, which in South African anti-apartheid rallies was not passive but rather required active vocal interaction; and the policeman played himself. Ironically, the only person who was not "acting," the policeman, was exposed through this dramatization as a fraud. At the end of Berrangé's 12-minute, 533-word speech, Detective Tabata had managed to record 144 words, or 27 percent of the speech.

"One thing stood out as clear as the pimple on the end of Strijdom's nose," Lionel Forman writes. "The Nationalists had bitten off more than they could chew."[66] The high spirits and confidence of the early days of the Treason Trial, however, gave way to boredom and stress as the proceedings dragged on for years and took a toll on the finances and families of the accused. When, after years of preliminary hearings, the actual trial began in August 1958, the venue was moved from Johannesburg to Pretoria, creating further hardship for the accused, who were forced to endure long commutes in addition to hours of tedium sitting in the courtroom. Crowd reduction was certainly the government's chief motivation for changing locales; the new location also made it far more difficult for the rallying masses of supporters to attend the hearings.

That the Treason Trial was no ordinary trial was evident in many ways: the number of the accused, the spectacular nature of their arrest, the wire cage constructed for their confinement in court, the deluge of supporters who thronged the streets outside the courtroom and disrupted the juridical proceedings with songs, and the squadrons of armed police officers who were stationed outside to suppress the rally. But the quasi-juridical nature of the proceedings, the way that the trial existed both inside and outside the law and charted new territory in the nationalist government's devolution into a police state, was perhaps most vividly expressed in the physical venues chosen for these proceedings. The Treason Trial took place in two locations, neither of which was originally built to be a courtroom: first in a converted military hall in Johannesburg and later in the Old Synagogue in Pretoria. The Drill Hall was a "bare barn of a place with a corrugated iron roof," according to Anthony Sampson. It had "an old-fashioned military appearance[,] and a few desultory soldierly activities, such as cleaning of ancient guns, went on in the outhouses."[67] The acoustics were terrible, a problem compounded by the thundering noise from the roof when it rained. Nor was the Old Synagogue in Pretoria particularly well suited to juridical purposes. The first synagogue to be constructed in Pretoria, it was "expropriated" by the government in 1952 after the Jewish population migrated to the suburbs and the building fell into disuse. The government converted it into a special Supreme Court intended to be used "for cases relating to the security situation, the activities of the black opposition

---

66   Forman and Sachs, *The South African Treason Trial*, 20. J.G. Strijdom was South Africa's prime minister from 1954 to 1958.

67   Sampson, *The Treason Cage*, 10.

movements and socialist/communist alliances."[68] Its "appalling" acoustics aside, the Old Synagogue was designed in a style that did little to mitigate "the hot and airless Pretoria climate."[69] The building's high narrow galleries, ornate columns, and elaborate moldings contrasted markedly with the Drill Hall's modest functionality and informality, and the transfer of venue coincided with a similar change in tone within the trial.[70] However, the chief purpose for the venue change was to deter the boisterous crowds that assembled outside the court. Pretoria is a remote city that is inconvenient to Johannesburg and certainly to the black townships where many of the accused and their supporters lived.

Although the Drill Hall and the Old Synagogue had been converted from military and religious spaces into judicial spaces, they were still ghosted by their former functions. This ghosting, though probably unanticipated or unintended by the state, provides a revealing perspective on the trial. One of the witnesses in the Treason Trial, M. Mkalipe, brought his Bible into the witness box and to the surprise of the judges read eight verses from the book of Daniel. "The names of Shadrack, Meshack and Abednego rang once more in the Old Synagogue," reflects Helen Joseph. "I looked at the three judges, scarlet-robed, sitting there, where once a rabbi stood alone, perhaps reading these very words to his assembled congregation."[71] Mkalipe was perhaps deliberately invoking the history of the Old Synagogue, a religious space distinct from the Calvinist Dutch Reformed roots of the National Party apartheid regime but nevertheless sharing with it the Judeo-Christian tradition. How can we read the symbolic significance of these venues? The use of nonjudicial spaces for the administration of justice may have been merely a pragmatic choice by the government. Given the poor acoustics of both venues, we can at least surmise that the state intended its political trials to be seen but not heard. However, these venues were nevertheless symbolic of the trial's quasi-judicial status; they inhabited a space that was simultaneously inside and outside the law. The state's expropriations of the Drill Hall and the Old Synagogue expressed a profound transition that was occurring in South Africa: the law of the land was expropriating other areas of civil society, including the military and religion, to fulfill white supremacist ambitions.

The turning point of the Treason Trial came not with its venue change but rather with the Sharpeville massacre in March 1960 and the declaration of a state of emergency. After that, the trial switched course: the accused were incarcerated

---

68   Quoted from "Pretoria, South Africa," available at http://www.edwardvictor.com/pretoria_main.htm (accessed October 24, 2006). George Bizos confirmed this history of the Old Synagogue in an interview with the author, Johannesburg, July 25, 2006.

69   Hilda Bernstein, "No. 46 – Steve Biko," available at http://www.sahistory.org.za/pages/library-resources/online%20books/biko-no46/vi-inquest.htm (accessed April 4, 2009).

70   Joseph, *If This Be Treason*, 25.

71   Ibid., 103. After the Treason Trial, the Old Synagogue was also the site of the Mandela Incitement Trial of 1962 and the inquest into the death of Steven Biko in 1977.

and were often held in isolation. Escalating repression from the security police prevented defense witnesses from testifying without fear of reprisal, and defense attorneys were afraid to communicate with their clients. In his private correspondence, lead advocate Bram Fischer despaired of the restrictions the state of emergency placed on the ability of the defense to bring witnesses to testify:

> Almost every justification of Congress policy and every attack on government policy would constitute a subversive statement. Hence we could never know that any witness could testify without fear. Nor could any witness testify without subjecting himself and his friends to arrest because of an admission of Congress membership or of participation in Congress activity ... Who could ever prove that he had been detained because of something said in court and not some other reason?[72]

In the face of legal obstacles, including obstruction of access to their attorneys, the accused took over their own defense.[73] This development infused the proceedings with moments of excitement and exhilaration, for it enabled the accused to turn the courtroom into a platform for their own ideas. "In many ways, these were the glory days for the accused," recalls Nelson Mandela, "for our own people were on the stand fearlessly enunciating ANC policy."[74] Acting as their own counsel, the accused could be assertive and proactive, not merely passive witnesses who had to wait to be asked a question before they could speak. Mandela says, "Our strategy was simple and defensive in nature: to drag out the case until the State of Emergency was lifted and our lawyers could return ... In practice, this strategy became rather comical."[75] Since each of the accused was entitled to conduct his or her own defense, each witness called to the stand would be cross-examined by 27 other defendants, the ones remaining from the original 150 who had been charged. "At that rate," Mandela recalls, "we would be at trial until the millennium."[76]

---

72 Bram Fisher to Rev. Canon L. John Collins, May 2, 1960, Treason Trial Documents, I3/S/726, Mayibuye Archives, Historical Papers Archives, University of Western Cape–Robben Island.

73 Mandela described in *Long Walk to Freedom* how "consultations between the accused and our lawyers [became] virtually impossible. Our lawyers, who were based in Johannesburg, had trouble seeing us in prison and were unable to prepare our case. They would often drive up and be informed that we were not available. Even when we were able to see them, consultations were harassed and cut short." Mandela, *Long Walk to Freedom*, 246. Because of the state's obstruction of contact between the accused and their attorneys and the risks that anyone faced who testified on behalf of the accused under the State of Emergency, the accused decided to have their attorneys withdraw from the case and conducted their own defense.

74 Mandela, *Long Walk to Freedom*, 253.

75 Ibid., 247.

76 Ibid.

The toll of the trial's length wore on all the defendants, however, with months, then years, spent worrying about families, struggling with finances, and being plagued by uncertainty about what was going on outside prison or what course the trial would take or how much longer it might go on. "It's four years ago today since we were arrested at dawn on this charge of high treason," wrote Helen Joseph in her prison diary. "*Four years – and* we are still sitting here."[77] Then abruptly the trial ended in mass acquittals. What began as grand spectacle and high drama ended suddenly with a fizzle. Many first-hand observers resort to theatrical metaphors when describing the atmosphere and tone of the Treason Trial. "The prologue to the drama which began to unfold with mass arrests at dawn, December 5th 1956, has been spectacular," reported Forman and Sachs. "The vast audience watching the stage responded with boos and catcalls for the producers and directors who expected applause."[78] Anthony Sampson, too, sees the Treason Trial as a stage, one that the whole world was watching:

> The opening of the treason trial hearings in Johannesburg raised the curtain, not only on this most extraordinary trial, but on the whole drama of the African opposition and the emergence of a new Africa beneath the old. The group of African politicians in prison, wobbling between the East and the West, between the black world and the white were likely to play a decisive role, not only in the country, but in the continent.[79]

Yet the great clarity of the drama and the attention it garnered somehow "came adrift."[80] By the time the trial ended, the case had "lost all significance on the political scene," according to Hilda Bernstein. "It was a played out drama bearing little relations to the surroundings in which it was enacted."[81]

Was the show trial over or was it just a first act? As we shall see, the Treason Trial was mainly a prologue to a much longer saga, one that would unfold over two more political trials during an epoch of atrocity. One could argue that this story came to an end only with the elections in 1994 and the beginning of the TRC in 1996. But the Treason Trial set the tone for what followed: the state's use of a judicial space to stage a direct encounter with the anti-apartheid movement, its use of the political trial to vanquish the political rally. These dueling spectacles as well as the battle between the state-controlled domains of the archive and the opposition's repertoires of resistance can be seen in many subsequent political trials and indeed in the proceedings of the TRC.

---

77   The quote is from Helen Joseph's diary entry for December 5, 1960. Joseph, *If This Be Treason*, 133.

78   Forman and Sachs, *The South African Treason Trial*, 201.

79   Sampson, *The Treason Cage*, 6.

80   Joseph, *If This Be Treason*, 17.

81   Bernstein, *The World That Was Ours*, 20.

Incitement Trial

Having failed to make its case in the Treason Trial, the South African government tried a new legal strategy in 1962. The Treason Trial had faltered, among other reasons, because of its large scale and vague charges that alleged no single acts of conspiracy or violence.[82] Two years later, when the government charged Nelson Mandela, it did not make the same mistakes. One person alone was accused, and he was charged on two clear counts: incitement and leaving the country without a passport. Yet in focusing on one person, the government inadvertently created an icon, for this legal battle also focused the energies, frustrations, dreams, and hopes of a multitude of the oppressed onto the person of Mandela, someone whose extraordinary capacities as a leader were only then being discovered.

Just as the state's legal strategy in the Incitement Trial was far more precise and focused than it had been in the Treason Trial, the opposition's approach to this second trial was far more subtle and particular. For nonwhites in South Africa, close attention to physical behavior could be a matter of life and death, and they habitually watched white bosses to "detect the slightest hint of unease: the brushing of the back of the head with the hand in a moment of bewilderment, the fumbling of papers," as Anthony Sampson explains.[83] Nelson Mandela was a particularly astute observer of behavior. When he first entered the courtroom, he "stared at the magistrate, who was transfixed like a mongoose looking at a snake," said ANC counterintelligence operative Wolfie Kodesh. "It took the magistrate two minutes to get his strength back."[84] Mandela paid close attention to the physical expressions of the prosecutor and judge. He noticed that during the proceedings, the magistrate was "diffident and uneasy" and would not look at him directly. Mandela notes in his memoir:

> The other attorneys also seemed embarrassed, and at that moment, I had something of a revelation. These men were not only uncomfortable because I was a colleague brought low, but because I was an ordinary man being punished for my beliefs. In a way I had never quite comprehended before, I realized the role I could play in the court and the possibilities before me as a defendant. I was the symbol of justice in the court of the oppressor, the representative of the great ideals of freedom, fairness and democracy in a society that dishonored those virtues.[85]

Mandela decided to serve as his own counsel, a decision no doubt informed by his experience serving in this same capacity during the Treason Trial. As a lawyer, he knew how to utilize the mechanisms of the courtroom to his advantage. And he

---

82 Karis, "The South African Treason Trial," 234.
83 Sampson, *The Treason Cage*, 30.
84 Sampson, *Mandela*, 171.
85 Mandela, *Long Walk to Freedom*, 317.

understood, through the subtleties of his oppressors' physical behavior, the role in which he could cast himself, not just in the courtroom but also in the drama playing out in the nation and, indeed, on the global stage. "By representing myself I would enhance the symbolism of my role," Mandela realized. "I would use my trial as a showcase for the ANC's moral opposition to racism."[86] Mandela quite deliberately turned the trial into a showcase, a stage, and a political platform.

Mandela also introduced a new technique to his courtroom behavior: unexpected clothing. He already had a reputation as natty dresser, always "immaculately" turned out in Western suits he commissioned from the famed tailor Alfred Kahn.[87] At his Incitement Trial, however, he donned instead a Xhosa leopard-skin kaross, signaling a dramatic departure in his self-presentation. He also wore a thick band of yellow and green beads, the colors of the ANC.[88] He entered the defendant's dock, as is the tradition in South Africa, by climbing stairs from the holding cell below. "As he came up, there was a complete hush," said Wolfie Kodesh. "Even the policemen, I honestly think they went pale, to see this huge black man standing there in his national costume."[89] "The kaross electrified the spectators," Mandela later wrote, well aware that his appearance mesmerized the courtroom.[90] His entrance into the Old Synagogue was ghosted by his previous appearance in this same building just two years before, as an article in *New Age*, the leftist newspaper, reminded readers:

> In Pretoria the last time there was such concentrated excitement outside the Old Synagogue converted to a court was when the treason accused were acquitted after four years – Nelson Mandela among them ... At 10.20 as Mandela came into the court the crowd of spectators rose to its feet including even the press gallery. Mandela in leopard skin kaross was an impressive, upright figure and his ringing voice dominated the proceedings as he stated the grounds for a remand of the case.[91]

Anthony Sampson, Mandela's biographer, sees his subject's use of costume in this trial in explicitly theatrical terms: "He was now playing a more flamboyant role,

---

86   Ibid.

87   On Mandela's reputation as an impeccable dresser, see Sampson, *Mandela*; and Martin Meredith, *Nelson Mandela: A Biography* (New York: St. Martin's Press, 1997), 106.

88   "Mandela Wins Adjournment," *The Cape Times*, October 15, 1962, 3. Mandela describes the skin he was wearing this day as a Xhosa leopard-skin kaross. However, Winnie Mandela's biographer says Nelson was dressed in a lion skin, "the traditional garb of a chief, which had been a gift from the paramount chief." See Anne Marie du Preez Bezdrob, *Winnie Mandela: A Life* (Cape Town: Zebra Press, 2003), 108.

89   Wolfie Kodesh, interview with John Carlin, available at www.pbs.org/wgbh/pages/frontline/shows/mandela/interviews/kodesh.html (accessed October 26, 2006).

90   Mandela, *Long Walk to Freedom*, 324.

91   "Bombs, Protests as Mandela Trial Opens," *New Age* (Cape Town), October 18, 1962, 3.

using the magistrates' court as his theater."[92] Mandela further explains his sartorial strategy: "I had chosen traditional dress to emphasize the symbolism that I was a black African walking into a white man's court. The kaross was also a sign of contempt for the niceties of white justice. I well knew the authorities would feel threatened by my kaross as so many whites feel threatened by the true culture of Africa."[93] As Mandela returned to his cell, a Colonel Jacobs ordered him to hand over his "blanket."[94] Mandela responded in the language of lawyers, informing Colonel Jacobs that he had no jurisdiction over Mandela's attire and that, if necessary, Mandela was prepared to take the matter all the way to the Supreme Court. After this encounter, Mandela was allowed to wear his kaross—but only in court and not while traveling to and from court, for according to newspaper accounts, it would "incite" other prisoners if they saw the traditional garment.[95]

Every day when Mandela appeared in the Old Synagogue, always wearing his kaross, a crowd of 150–200 African supporters gathered in the well of the court, the segregated area for nonwhites. As Mandela entered the courtroom, his supporters stood as one and raised their fists in the air. Mandela intoned the now-famous call of the struggle, "*Amandla!*" (Power!), which elicited from his supporters in the galley the lower-pitched response, "*Ngawethu!*" ("To the people!").[96] In the years between the Treason and Incitement trials, when the ANC switched its policy on the use of violence, the performed repertoire of the anti-apartheid crowds apparently changed. Whereas the crowds at trials formerly gave a thumbs-up salute, by the time of the Incitement and Rivonia trials they raised their fists in the air. Whereas formerly they had shouted "*Afrika! Mayibuye!*" ("Africa! Come Back!"), they now chanted "*Amandla! Ngawethu!*" ("Power! To the People!").

Mandela was not alone in wearing African costume. On the first day of the proceedings his wife Winnie wore clothing typical of Thembu royalty: a beaded headdress and an ankle-length skirt, which the opposition press described as "regal."[97] In an attempt to legislate the realm of performance, an arena of behavior that as we shall later see the apartheid government seemed impotent to control, the minister of justice served Winnie notice that she would be barred from court if she appeared again wearing "native" dress.[98] Afterward, like a chameleon, Winnie changed her attire each day, often wearing clothing that Nelson had brought back from his travels, including the national dress of Ethiopia, a yellow Indian sari, the

---

92   Sampson, *Mandela*, 173.

93   Mandela, *Long Walk to Freedom*, 325.

94   Colonel Jacobs used the word "blanket." Mandela wrote: "The colonel never again tried to take my 'blanket', but the authorities would permit me to wear it only in court, not on my way to or from court for fear it would 'incite' other prisoners." Ibid.

95   Ibid.

96   "I Am Guilty of No Offence," *New Age* (Cape Town), November 1, 1962, 6.

97   Mandela, *Long Walk to Freedom*, 324. See also "Bombs, Protests as Mandela Trial Opens," *New Age* (Cape Town), October 18, 1962, 3.

98   Bezdrob, *Winnie Mandela*, 108.

black skirt and blouse of the anti-apartheid Women's Federation, or a Dior-style skirt with white cap.[99] The thousands of African supporters who turned out at the Old Synagogue also wore a range of traditional African clothing, as photographs published in local newspapers amply document.[100]

Wearing traditional African clothing was an unusual step for Mandela and for the African National Congress, which was firmly committed to a policy of nonracialism. This strategy originated from the ANC's founding days, when "tribal jealousies" and bitter grievances over the past among various South African ethnic groups were put aside for the larger cause of fighting white domination.[101] Anthony Sampson writes of the Bloemfontein Conference of 1912, at which the ANC was founded:

> It was the first time, not only in South Africa but in the whole continent, that African tribes had dropped their traditional loyalties to form a common nation of black people. It was, in fact, the birth of African nationalism: not in the sense of militancy or chauvinism, for the new Congress was obsessed by the need for moderation, white friendships and constitutional methods; but in the sense of a common nationhood of Africans distinguished not by tribes but by race.[102]

By donning traditional clothing, Nelson Mandela and his supporters may have seemed to be putting emphasis on ethnic specificity and departing from the long-standing ANC policy of nonracialism. Winnie Madikizela-Mandela's use of Xhosa clothing, in which she began appearing publicly before the Incitement Trial (as a photograph taken on Afrika Day and printed in the opposition newspaper *New Age* in April 1962 attests), provoked consternation in at least one observer.[103] Paul Mathabe wrote in a letter to *New Age*:

> I think that this tribal dressing is turning the struggle into a Xhosa struggle. To the onlooker and the one who mixes with the crowds, [the] Congress struggle is being relegated to the Xhosa tribe. Now that is defeating the very aim and efforts of the leaders. We have heard remarks made by enemies of the struggle that Mandela was a Xhosa, Sisulu was a Xhosa, Nokwe was a Xhosa, Xuma was a Xhosa, and the predominant tribal dress was Xhosa ... Traditional dress and items should be left to the Theatre and stage, the preservers of culture.[104]

---

99   "I Am Guilty of No Offence," *New Age*, November 1, 1962, 6.

100   See in particular "I Have Nothing to Regret," *New Age*, November 15, 1962, 4–5. This is an extensive article with photographs.

101   See Sampson, *The Treason Cage*, 45.

102   Ibid., 47–8.

103   "Mrs. Mandela on Afrika Day," *New Age* (Cape Town), April 26, 1962, 3.

104   Paul Mathabe, "Tribal Dress," *New Age* (Cape Town), November 1, 1962, 2.

In his autobiography Mandela explains that he wore the kaross to impress upon the court the "true culture of Africa," thus stressing a continent-wide sense of authenticity rather than an ethnic particularity such as his Xhosa identity or, more specifically, that of his clan. It is likely that most white observers in the courtroom saw his clothing as representing a nonspecific African "otherness," one that stood in contrast to European identity. Yet Mandela also knew that his kaross would be seen and interpreted by many people who *would* notice its ethnic particularity and that such an emphasis on ethnicity was likely to raise precisely the objections Paul Mathabe voiced. So while Mandela has written that he wore the kaross to show that he was a "black man in a white man's court," it would seem that the clothing was also signifying that he was an *African* man in a European court, an *indigenous* person in an imported forum, and a *Xhosa* man—and royalty at that—forced to operate within a British-derived legal structure.

So what were Mandela and his supporters trying to tell ANC members through this particular use of clothing at the Incitement Trial? Mandela may have been influenced by his recent trip to other African countries where an emphasis on African nativism was central to the anticolonial struggle. Yet I think this is unlikely, as Mandela returned from his travels convinced that "South Africa is different to all the countries of Africa ... because our population is different, and the whole structure of the country is different. Economically and politically in every way."[105] Mandela's commitment to nonracialism remained as strong as ever. Mandela may have been influenced by the recent popularity of the rival South African opposition party, the Pan Africanist Congress (PAC), which did not share the ANC's policy of nonracialism. Perhaps this was a gambit to try to lure some PAC followers to the ANC. But this also seems unlikely. The most plausible explanation can I think be found on three fronts. First, Mandela's choice of clothing in the courtroom was intended very deliberately to stand in relationship to the rhetorical thrust of his words, especially his speeches during this trial, as I shall explain below. Second, this clothing was consistent with the rhetorical strategies often used by the opposition during the political trials of this era to invert apartheid's reasoning. In this case, the apartheid state made great hay over ethnic differences, using such divisions as a way to divide and conquer the nonwhite population through such policies as separate homelands. Using a "native" costume called the apartheid state's bluff, in a sense. How could it prohibit what it in fact seemed to embrace: so-called natives behaving in native ways?

Finally, this use of traditional clothing was a tactic that allowed both Mandela and his supporters to circumvent stringent press regulations that severely restricted what local newspapers could print about the trial and banned altogether public rallies in Mandela's name. In order to suppress public demonstrations at trials, the government decided just before the start of Mandela's 1962 Incitement Trial to ban all meetings relating to Nelson Mandela and to add his name to a list of 102

---

105 These words are Wolfie Kodesh's paraphrase of Mandela in Wolfie Kodesh, interview with John Carlin.

persons whose statements could not be published. Minister of Justice B.J. Vorster, using the classically performative phrase "I prohibit," authorized legislation just two days before the commencement of the Incitement Trial that ensured that there would be no publication of Mandela's words in the South African newspapers.[106] As a result, journalists were sometimes awkwardly forced to write "what Mandela said here cannot be reported."[107] A "Free Mandela" campaign mobilized supporters by means of pamphleteering, graffiti paintings on the streets, and silent poster demonstrations outside the Durban City Hall and the Pretoria Union building.[108] Yet this resistance via text was forbidden: members of the Special Branch wrote down the names of those taking part. Likewise there could be no gatherings in Mandela's name, a "gathering" being defined as "two or more people coming together for a common purpose."[109] However, the performative dimensions of the hearing—the songs, fashions, gestures, and actions of Mandela and his supporters—*could* be freely reported, and they were, lavishly, with many pictures. And a crowd gathered wearing traditional dress could not necessarily be labeled a political gathering. They were just "tribes" being their native selves. Supporters of Mandela thus circumvented the restrictions by means of performance. Clothing seems to have been a chief strategy of resistance by Mandela's supporters, but song continued to play an important role. At the close of trial, the throng of supporters left the court singing "Nkosi Sikelel i'Africa," a song that was to become the national anthem of the new democratic South Africa three decades later. And they marched up the street singing "Tshotsholoza Mandela" ("Carry on Mandela") in flagrant disregard of the government's ban on public demonstrations for Mandela.[110]

Mandela's approach to his courtroom appearances during the Incitement Trial succeeded in two ways: visual appearance through costume and verbal impact through the spoken word. By serving as his own counsel, Mandela secured a venue in which to deliver a political speech unimpeded and uninterrupted at an extremely high-profile public gathering—the trial. Mandela gave a lengthy plea of mitigation during the Incitement Trial, an hour-long speech that explained who he was and why he had done what he had done. During the subsequent Rivonia Trial, Mandela chose not to take the witness stand at all but rather to deliver a speech from the dock. Under South African law, a defendant can make such a statement without cross-examination. The testimony carries less legal weight, but Mandela had

---

106   "Vorster Bans All Mandela Meetings for Two Days; Trial Switched to Pretoria," *The Star* (Johannesburg), October 13, 1962. See also "Mandela on the List," *The Star* (Johannesburg), October 12, 1962, 1.

107   "Verwoerd's Secretary Speaks at Mandela Trial," *The Star* (Johannesburg), October 22, 1962, 3.

108   "Release Nelson Mandela!" *New Age* (Cape Town), August 16, 1962, 1; and "Mandela Slogans in Jo'burg," *New Age* (Cape Town), August 16, 1962, 1.

109   Bernstein, *The World That Was Ours*, 2.

110   Nelson Mandela, *We Accuse: The Trial of Nelson Mandela* (London: African National Congress, 1962), 36.

no intention of fighting the case legally. Instead he manipulated the courtroom, transforming it into platform for communicating with his followers to whom he could not otherwise speak. Mandela followed the strategy of using his trials as "a continuation of the struggle by other means,"[111] and his speeches at the Incitement Trial and the Rivonia Trial implicitly and ingeniously raised a question: were not these political trials themselves a public gathering in his name?

The text of Mandela's speeches from the Incitement Trial deserves careful analysis, and it is fortunate that such an analysis has been provided by Jacques Derrida.[112] Derrida contends that Mandela used admiration as a force of persuasion. "He becomes admirable for having, with all his force, admired, and for having made a force of his admiration, a combative, untreatable, and irreducible power."[113] In a famous oration that became known as the "Black Man in a White Man's Court" speech, Mandela stated that he admired the principles inaugurated by the Magna Carta, the Universal Declaration of Human Rights, parliamentary democracy, the doctrine of the separation of powers, and the independence of the judiciary. In short, he admired the intellectual, legal, and political principles central to Western society, principles and traditions that the South African state in fact claimed to inherit. Using painstakingly careful logic, incisive legal reasoning, and his characteristically measured voice, Mandela cogently demonstrated that the most recent South African constitution, that of 1961, was in fact an inversion, or perversion, of its imported model. "A terrifying dissymmetry," Derrida called it. Mandela told the courtroom he admired the law, was devoted to the law, and was a man of the law—even if he had had to oppose certain specific laws in order to defend the law. "Taking as his witness humanity as a whole," Derrida writes, Mandela addressed himself to the "universal justice above his judges of one day only."[114] Thus Mandela also used inversion: his apparent contempt for the law, he argued, signified his supreme respect for it. In his brilliant analysis of Mandela's speech, Derrida takes no particular notice of Mandela's clothing. However, if we consider the kaross a meaningful rhetorical strategy, one intended to function in tandem with the spoken word, we can see yet an-other inversion performed by Mandela. His "native" African costume signified a radical otherness before the Western law he professed to admire, yet his words—their content, logic, and refined manner of delivery—demonstrated that he was, in fact, a more legitimate heir to the Western traditions of the law than were the white judges in their flowing robes who sat before him.

---

111 Mandela, *Long Walk to Freedom*, 360.

112 For the text of the speech, see Nelson Mandela, "Black Man in a White Man's Court," in *No Easy Walk to Freedom*, edited by Ato Quayson (New York: Penguin Books, 2002), 105–42. For an important reading of this speech, see Derrida, "The Laws of Reflection," 13–42.

113 Derrida, "The Laws of Reflection," 15.

114 Ibid., 27.

The Rivonia Trial

At the end of the Incitement Trial, Mandela was found guilty and sentenced to five years in jail. However, before he had served his full sentence, he was once again pulled into court, once again in Pretoria. This third trial of Nelson Mandela was held in the Palace of Justice rather than in a converted judicial outpost like the Drill Hall or the Old Synagogue. Mandela was charged along with 11 others with sabotage in a case known by the name Rivonia, referring to a farm outside of Johannesburg where the arrests had taken place and the alleged sabotage had been planned. The atmosphere at the Rivonia Trial was sober and restrained. The repertoires of resistance available to the accused were far more circumscribed than they had been in any previous trial. The accused were charged with over 200 acts of sabotage "aimed at promoting guerrilla warfare and armed invasion," and this time, unlike in the Treason Trial, they were in fact guilty as charged.[115] The punishment for such crimes was the death penalty, and the very real threat of the gallows cast a pall over the proceedings.

In terms of theatrical genres, the Treason Trial could be characterized as a farce with an enormous cast that lasted too long. The Incitement Trial was a more realistic drama with a single protagonist and a style subtle enough to depict intricacies of expression, gestures, eye contact, clothing, and precise dialogue. The audience came more clearly into view in the Incitement Trial as two halves of the segregated courtroom became the chorus that Mandela addressed. In both trials, there was an acute sense of the audience outside the courtroom: in the Treason Trial, it was the masses standing at the door of the Drill Hall; in the Incitement Trial, it was the growing international attention the trial was garnering in the world at large. The Rivonia Trial represented a progression as global spectatorship became even more intense and the range of performative repertoires available to both spectators and the accused narrowed significantly. If the Treason Trial was a farce and the Incitement Trial a realistic drama, then the Rivonia Trial could perhaps be most closely compared to an ancient tragedy, as even the *Rand Daily Mail* seemed to recognize: "The case has captured the imagination because it seems to tell a classic, ancient story of the struggle of men for freedom and dignity, with overtones of Grecian tragedy in their failure."[116]

At the Rivonia Trial, the crowd was once again a factor. It descended upon the Palace of Justice daily, despite police use of force and intimidation: they demanded passbooks and took surveillance photographs. By 1963 the state seemed to have become more astute in its attempts to control the dramaturgy of the trial. A special dock was constructed to change the physical layout of the courtroom so the accused had to sit with their backs to the audience. The dock had been made with sufficient room that each defendant could be guarded by two private warders, "sitting like

---

115   Tom Lodge, *Mandela: A Critical Life* (New York: Oxford University Press, 2006), 108.

116   Quoted in Bernstein, *The World That Was Ours*, 240.

footmen in attendance."[117] Mandela's first appearance in court contrasted markedly with the proud robust figure in a royal African kaross last seen at the Incitement Trial. As Mandela entered the courtroom, fellow accused Dennis Goldberg recalls:

> He was in leg irons and handcuffs, wearing sandals, no socks, short trousers, a jacket that looked like a house boy's jacket. Now, you know, to put a man into the dock like that is to create an immediate prejudice. He was usually so elegant, such a snappy dresser, and they set out to humiliate him in his clothes, but he held himself so ramrod straight, so dignified. He had lost an enormous amount of weight in prison.[118]

Yet the black audience sitting in their segregated area of the courtroom was not deterred. "There was a ripple of excitement amongst the public" at the first sight of Mandela.[119] He faced the spectators, raised his clenched fist, and shouted "*Amandla!*" which immediately elicited a chorus of "*Ngawethu.*"[120] The courtroom was packed with officers and security guards and Security Branch policemen, sitting in the benches and guarding every door. They were completely surprised and incapacitated by this verbal outburst from the accused and their supporters. "None of this vast army," advocate Joel Joffe recalls, "was fast enough on their feet to cope with this unexpected demonstration."[121] But shortly thereafter, a new procedure was instituted for the start of each court date. The judge was brought in before the accused, hence putting an end to struggle salutations.[122]

The arena in which the accused might practice their repertoires of resistance was becoming more and more tightly circumscribed. Mandela's primary strategy at the Rivonia Trial was to speak very little until one appointed moment. Unlike at the Treason and Incitement trials, he did not serve as his own counsel. In addition, he refused to give testimony or submit to cross-examination. Instead, he exercised his right to give a speech from the dock, a ploy that enabled him to circumvent the state's draconian and ever-escalating repression of speech. Mandela inaugurated a tradition at South African political trials, as speeches from the dock thereafter became a tactic replicated by many other political prisoners.[123] "The courtroom is often the last forum in which freedom fighters speak out against tyranny and justify their actions not only to the judge but also their fellow citizens and the

---

117　Joffe, *The Rivonia Story*, 37.

118　Dennis Goldberg quoted in Mac Maharaj and Ahmed Kathrada (eds) *Mandela: The Authorized Portrait* (Kansas City: Andrews McMeel Publishing, 2006), 116.

119　Joffe, *The Rivonia Story*, 37.

120　Ibid.

121　Ibid.

122　Ibid., 58.

123　For a moving compilation of these statements, see Mary Benson (ed.) *The Sun Will Rise: Statements from the Dock by Southern African Political Prisoners*, rev. and exp. edn (1974; London: International Defence and Aid Fund for Southern Africa, 1981).

world at large," says advocate George Bizos, who made a career of defending political prisoners, including the Rivonia accused.[124]

Although a speech from the dock may have been one of Mandela's only means of exercising the repertoire of resistance at this trial, he exploited the possibilities of this speech to their maximum potential. And the impact of his speech was enhanced by the superior acoustics of the Palace of Justice compared with previous trial venues. Also audible was the profound silence of everyone else. "It was amazing to sit through Mandela's speech," recalls advocate Joffe. "There was tremendous silence in the courtroom when he stood and he spoke for a long time, around five hours. He went to the dock ready to die."[125] Mandela had handwritten his speech and conferred with compatriots about its content. His delivery was slow, in a "flat even voice," according to Joffe, which contrasted markedly with the tone prosecutor Percy Yutar usually adopted in the Rivonia proceedings. Yutar is reported to have squeaked, whined, and crackled his way through the Rivonia Trial, often resorting to the falsetto registers. Mandela was, in contrast, calm, unwavering, and steady, the antithesis of a hotheaded radical revolutionary. "At no stage did he raise his voice very much, or change from the slow, measured speech with which he had started," says Joffe. "His voice carried clearly across the court. Gradually as he spoke the silence became more and more profound, till it seemed that no one in the court dared move or breathe."[126]

Mandela's statement from the dock is legendary. He spoke for three hours (though many remember it being four or five hours long). The text of the speech is widely available, and legal scholar James Boyd White, among others, has provided incisive analysis of its content.[127] My focus here is rather on the reception of the speech, the audience's silence, especially during the final lines. Mandela concluded by saying the now famous words: "During my lifetime I have dedicated myself to the struggle of the African people. I have fought against white domination, and I have fought against black domination. I have cherished the ideal of a democratic and free society in which all persons live together in harmony and with equal opportunity."[128] At this moment, Joffe remembers, Mandela paused, a long pause, in which one could "hear a pin drop in the court," and then he looked squarely at the judge as he finished:

---

124   George Bizos, "Reflection on the Past," *Sunday Times* (Johannesburg), May 11, 2003.

125   Joel Joffe quoted in Maharaj and Kathrada, *Mandela: The Authorized Portrait*, 121.

126   Joffe, *The Rivonia Story*, 131.

127   See Mandela, *No Easy Walk to Freedom*, 105–42; James Boyd White, *Acts of Hope: Creating Authority in Literature, Law, and Politics* (Chicago: University of Chicago Press, 1994), 275–94.

128   For a complete transcript of this speech, see chapter 15, "The Rivonia Trial," in Mandela, *No Easy Walk to Freedom*, 143–70.

'It is an ideal which I hope to live for and to achieve'. Then dropping his voice, very low, he added:

'But if needs be it is an ideal for which I am prepared to die'.

He sat down in a moment of profound silence, the kind of silence that I remember only in climactic moments in the theatre before the applause thunders out. Here in the court there was no applause. He had spoken for five hours and for perhaps thirty seconds there was silence. From the public benches one could hear people release their breath with a deep sigh as the moment of tension passed. Some women in the gallery burst into tears.[129]

Dennis Goldberg describes the moment: "It was terribly moving. Nobody said anything. Even the judge didn't know what to say. I knew it was a moment of history. He emerged then as a great leader."[130] Throughout the political trials of the late 1950s and early 1960s, the opposition leaders and supporters had deployed a tremendous range of repertoires of resistance. Yet this particular speech and the silences in and around this speech proved the most classically theatrical and performative moment of all. Not only was the speech dramatic, it did things, it changed the political landscape profoundly. With this speech, Mandela became a singular personification of the anti-apartheid struggle, even as he physically disappeared from public view for the next 25 years.

Mandela's noncompliance with expected protocol and his masterful manipulation of South Africa's legal procedures transformed the courtroom into a media event and, more important, into a trial not of himself or of the ANC but of the racist apartheid government. If, as Mandela argued in the Rivonia case, the trial was a show trial, then the state (and not its so-called saboteurs) was the show. Mandela and his followers contested apartheid and its agents through performance; through performed behaviors, songs, chants, and clothing; and through rhetorically effective speech acts that profoundly affected those who were present in the courtroom and even more profoundly transformed audiences outside the courtroom, who heard reports of the speeches or read clandestinely published pamphlets that reproduced his words. In the townships, people even re-performed his speech by reciting it out loud.[131] Mandela's trial speeches—especially their touchstone phrases such as "black man in a white man's court" from the Incitement Trial and "I am prepared to die" from the Rivonia Trial—reverberated throughout

---

129   Joffe, *The Rivonia Story*, 133.

130   Recording of interview reproduced in "The Underground Movement," part 2 of the five-part series *Mandela: An Audio History*, an audio documentary by Joe Richman and Sue Johnson, available at http://www.npr.org/templates/story/ story.php?storyId=1851882 (accessed March 17, 2009). This series originally broadcast on National Public Radio in the United States in 2004.

131   Bernstein, *The World That Was Ours*, 198.

the world and throughout history. His declaration of his willingness to accept the death penalty for the sake of the ideal of a free and democratic society is one of the most famous phrases of the twentieth century. Mandela not only articulated an ideal of a democratic and free society but he actually played a central role in bringing such a society into being. His speeches in these courtrooms were performatives in the Austinian sense.[132] Mandela "did things"—big things—with words. His speeches were extraordinary inasmuch as the words articulated a new constitutional order, one that had yet to come into being.

Conclusion

While the apartheid government demonstrated breathtaking persistence in circumscribing speech, it seemed incapacitated by the challenge of trying to legislate control of song and gesture at political trials. Minister of Justice J. Kruger complained about political trials to parliament in 1978:

> The accused ... enter the hall singing and with clenched fists, take up their places in the dock and, standing, turn to the audience, whereupon all of them—accused and audience—then sing inflammatory songs. Brief speeches are also made ... When the hearing is adjourned, the accused and the audience all leave the court-room singing, and the entire procedure is repeated with every adjournment and resumption of the trial. The supporters frequently continue their activities outside the court building and in the adjoining streets. To accompany the singing and the clenched-fist salutes, there is dancing, slogans are shouted and posters are displayed for the express purpose of attracting the attention of the Press, film and television photographers.[133]

Kruger's complaint came in the wake of the Stephen Biko inquest and a full 14 years after Mandela was put in prison for life. As minister of justice, Kruger was one of the most powerful figures in South Africa. His comments reveal not only the impotence of the government to control performed repertoires of resistance but also the extent to which the political trials of the late 1950s and early 1960s set a precedent. Those trials essentially defined the "genre" of the political trial in apartheid South Africa and, in turn, profoundly shaped the type of transitional justice that South Africa embraced as, moving out of apartheid into democracy, it created the Truth and Reconciliation Commission.

---

132   J.L. Austin, *How to Do Things with Words*, 2nd edn (Cambridge, MA: Harvard University Press, 1975).

133   Entry for May 12, 1978, in Parliament of South Africa, *Debates [of the House of Assembly of the First Parliament of the Republic of South Africa]* (Cape Town: Parliament of South Africa, 1978), 6846.

While the apartheid regime found songs, gestures, and dance (both in and out of the courtroom) to be uncontrollable, even more striking is how political trials sanctioned revolutionary speeches, the content of which would otherwise have been banned, suppressed, and confiscated. As Oliver Tambo notes, "By 1960 virtually every African leader was muzzled and restricted by Government decree."[134] Yet political trials proved the last outpost of unfettered speech, the final and most potent platform on which Mandela and many freedom fighters who stood trial after him found an opportunity to articulate publicly their objectives and rationale.[135]

If we accept that the TRC inherited the performance genealogy of South African political trials, it is not at all puzzling that on the occasion when TRC chairperson Desmond Tutu publicly presented the truth commission's final report to President Nelson Mandela in 1998, "the two elderly statesmen started to dance—in exultation and celebration."[136] Rhetorician Philippe-Joseph Salazar, noting that this dancing "seemed out of place, out of beat with the dignity of the occasion," speculated that the dance by Mandela and Tutu was a symbolic rebuttal of the "deadly toyi-toyi dance, often performed at mass killings ... as a tool for gross human rights abuses on the part of the liberation movements themselves."[137] Yet the dance has far greater significance than a rebuttal or inversion of the *toyi-toyi*. Dancing at the formal presentation of the TRC's final report was entirely in keeping with the repertoires of resistance that had been enacted within the courtrooms of South Africa for decades.

At the trials of Nelson Mandela, the inquest of Steve Biko, and countless other political trials in the history of the resistance movement, dance was central to the judicial encounter between the political opposition and the apartheid state. This is why Minister of Justice Jimmy Kruger complained in 1978 that dancing, clenched-fist salutes, and the singing of inflammatory songs had become standard fare at political trials. Song, gesture, and dance were core elements of the repertoire of resistance, both inside and outside courtrooms. While it is true that one dance, the *toyi-toyi*, became quite prominent in the 1980s and its history is connected to black-on-black violence within the townships, Tutu and Mandela's dancing at the presentation of the TRC summary report was about much more than dancing as a prelude to violence in the townships. This celebratory dance at the conclusion of a quasi-judicial proceeding was a continuation of a decades-long tradition of dance in and in front of judicial spaces at political trials. Dance was an enduring accompaniment to trials within the liberation struggle.

The trials of 1956–1964 that I have examined here mark the beginning of a violent militarized epoch of South African history, a period that lasted for over three decades, concluding with the first democratic elections in 1994 and the

---

134   Mandela, *No Easy Walk to Freedom*, xxv.
135   Benson, *The Sun Will Rise*.
136   Salazar, *An African Athens*, 76.
137   Ibid., 85–6.

formation of the Truth and Reconciliation Commission shortly thereafter. These early political trials and the TRC were highly visible public rituals. They each served a legitimizing function for a new nation-state—for the Union of South Africa that was declared in 1961 and for the democracy of South Africa that was voted into power in 1994. During his trials of the 1960s, Mandela acted on the assumption that a compelling performance could overcome and overthrow unjust laws. Though it took many decades, these changes did in fact happen.

That both the Treason Trial and the Truth and Reconciliation Commission coincided with the writing of a new constitution (in 1960 and 1994) is expressive of how deeply transitional both periods were. Constitutions bring a state into being through what Jacques Derrida calls "properly performative" acts, iterations that must "produce (proclaim) what in the form of a constative act it merely claims, declares, assures it is describing."[138] Examining the TRC within the frame of the early political trials illustrates that during times of political transition, constitutions in and of themselves may not be performative enough. During both transitions, a convergence of performance and the law was necessary—performance not just in the sense defined by the speech-act theory of J.L. Austin but rather performance in all of its physical expressiveness, including reenactments, singing, tone of voice, and subtle expressions of physicality. The Truth and Reconciliation Commission and the political trials of 1956–1964 repeatedly—and in all their operations, public hearings, and textual reports—made manifest the values and assumptions of a new political dispensation. The public and juridical events that transpired in the Drill Hall, the Old Synagogue, and the high court and (in the case of the TRC) the quasi-judicial series of events that took place in town halls, churches, and schools throughout the country provided physicalized and visible signs of the inward character and identity of a newly constituted state.

"Why was this abortive trial ever staged?" Helen Joseph, one of the accused, asked of the Treason Trial. "Why was it pursued so relentlessly until almost the very end, when the Court itself brought the proceedings to a close? Why were the arrests carried out in such a dramatic, spectacular fashion?"[139] One might ask similar questions of the Truth and Reconciliation Commission: why was the political transition from apartheid to democracy enacted so publicly on stages, in town halls and churches, in front of live audiences and television cameras? Why were live hearings broadcast so extensively to the citizenry? Why did spectators at the hearings participate so vocally and viscerally?

South Africa's Truth and Reconciliation Commission was unprecedented in many regards: it was the first truth commission in the genre's history of more than 30 years to offer conditional amnesty and the first to embrace public hearings as a defining feature. Within South Africa, the Truth and Reconciliation Commission is often perceived as an import from abroad. Yet the TRC can be productively considered as sharing a genealogy of performance that is as beholden to South

---

138   Derrida, "The Laws of Reflection," 18.
139   Joseph, *If This Be Treason*, 14.

African political trials as it is to international transitional justice models.[140] The TRC's performance genealogy can be traced to the Treason, Incitement, and Rivonia trials, during which the South African state tried to enforce the ever-expanding powers of the white minority and justify its increasing erosion of the powers and rights of the African majority. In high-profile political trials, the state met its opposition head on before an audience of witnesses that was both national and international. Anti-apartheid defendants used the courtroom performatively to resist and to offer a counterdiscourse that included the principles of the Freedom Charter, a constitutional speech act that in the mid-1950s could only implement the future perfect tense, a speech act that remained infelicitous for decades to come.[141]

One should be clear: the political trials of 1956–64 were conducted in courts of law and the TRC was not. Further, it would be misguided to suggest equivalence between a truth commission sponsored by a nonracial and democratically elected government and political show trials promulgated by a racist and authoritarian regime. But if one accepts Mandela's contention that the law of South Africa by which he was tried in the early 1960s was at odds with the Universal Declaration of Human Rights (a document that, interestingly, was admitted by the Crown as part of its evidence against the ANC in the Treason Trial), we can see that these political trials—like the TRC—put the issue of human rights at center stage.[142] The second issue at center stage was the fate of the South African state, which in 1961 had recently departed from the British Commonwealth and had been newly constituted as an independent nation. By putting anti-apartheid leaders in the dock in highly publicized trials, the government inadvertently put South Africa itself on trial in the court of public opinion. British and African newspapers, including

---

140   This genealogy also includes a history of commissions of inquiry within South Africa, of which there have been over a thousand. For an analysis of key South African commissions from 1903 to 1981, see Adam Ashforth, *The Politics of Official Discourse in Twentieth-Century South Africa* (New York: Oxford University Press, 1990), especially 15n5. The TRC acknowledged this legacy by printing in its report a list of South African commissions of inquiry from 1960 to 1995; see TRC, *Truth and Reconciliation Commission of South Africa Report*, 1: 498–510. On the history of truth commissions internationally, see Pricilla Hayner, *Unspeakable Truths: Confronting State Terror and Atrocity* (New York: Routledge, 2001).

141   Suttner and Cronin, *30 Years of the Freedom Charter*. "Infelicitous" here refers to the work of speech act theorist J.L. Austin, who proposed that performative speech acts are those in which one *does* something by *saying* something, such as when one says "I do" during a wedding ceremony. Such speech acts are, in Austin's terminology, either felicitous (successful) or infelicitous (unsuccessful). If one said "I do" during the wedding ceremony and was actually already married to someone else, this would be an infelicitous speech act. See Austin, *How to Do Things with Words*.

142   Nelson Mandela, "'Black Man in a White Court': Nelson Mandela's First Court Statement, 1962," available at www.anc.org.za/ancdocs/history/mandela/1960s/nm6210. html (accessed March 17, 2009). On the evidence presented by prosecution at the Treason Trial, see Sampson, *The Treason Cage*, 21.

Ghana's *Daily Graphic*, discerned clearly that South Africa was on trial at these proceedings.[143] The British *Daily Telegraph* reported that the Rivonia Trial was not the end but "rather the beginning of debate on the larger moral issue. It is the law itself that the South African Government has to justify at the bar of the civilized world."[144] South Africa stood at that bar of public opinion for decades, and it was only through the perceived success of the Truth and Reconciliation Commission that the case finally concluded. Final judgment was neither acquittal nor conviction but rather a complex, uneven, often impenetrable report. The unwieldiness of the TRC's final report and its neglected status as a document of the commission suggest that perhaps the report's conclusions and recommendations were not really the "point" of the proceedings. But if the commission's analysis and conclusions were not the point, what was? The answer to that question, I believe, lies in the power of performance itself—in its ability to captivate and persuade an audience; its ephemeral nature enacted very much in the present tense; its agon between opposing sides; its ability to produce empathy and identification as well as terror, pity, and fear among spectators; its human scale; and finally in its ambiguity, simultaneity, and layering of meanings.

Just as the TRC bears the imprint of the many truth commissions that preceded it (and of the Nuremburg and Tokyo trials before them), it also inherits a genealogy of performance from important South African political trials. In examining the Treason, Incitement, and Rivonia trials, I have focused on three aspects that I believe have great relevance to our understanding and interpretation of the Truth and Reconciliation Commission: (1) the opposition movement's cultivation of repertories of resistance and how these became codified and internationally recognizable; (2) moments when the archive and the repertoire explicitly converged and the implications of this convergence for our interpretation of the TRC; and (3) how political trials facilitated a complex process of surrogation, mediating the relationship between particular iconic figures and the masses.[145] While in the Treason Trial 156 people represented the opposition movement, by the time that the Rivonia Trial concluded, one person, Nelson Mandela, had come to stand in for the disenfranchised millions. Over 30 years later, the Truth and Reconciliation Commission attempted to profoundly reconfigure this surrogation through its public hearings. In the TRC, formerly disenfranchised masses (whom Chairperson Tutu called without irony the "little people") would represent themselves as well as the millions of others whose human rights were violated in both "gross" and minor ways.

Activist Joe Slovo has characterized the judicial confrontations of the 1950s and early 1960s as happening on a "gentlemanly" terrain: "There was still a rule of law. You had a fair trial in their courts. Nobody could be kept in isolation. Up to 1963 I know of no incident of any political prisoner being tortured. The whole

---

143   "South Africa on Trial," *Daily Graphic* (Accra), October 24, 1962, 5.

144   Quoted in Bernstein, *The World That Was Ours*, 239.

145   On the idea of surrogation, see Roach, *Cities of the Dead*, 2–3.

legal structure which existed lulled us into feeling that we could do much more than we eventually discovered we could."[146] After Sharpeville and Rivonia, everything changed. In the words of George Bizos, "The acquittal of the political leaders at the end of the Treason Trial in 1961 probably marked the end of the administration of justice in accordance with generally accepted procedural safeguards, such as habeas corpus."[147] In 1963, the government imposed a law authorizing 90-day detention without trial, which was later amended to 180 days. Finally, in 1967, with the authorization of Section 6 of the Terrorism Act, the police acquired the right to detain suspects for an indefinite period without any trial at all, thus effectively shutting down the courtroom as a primary stage for the state's enactment of power.

The first reported death in detention was that of Looksmart Solwandle Ngudle, a man in good health at the time of his arrest who was found dead in his cell some 40 days later on September 5, 1963. Thereafter, torture became the new staging ground for confrontation between the archive and the repertoire, between the document and the body. Unlike trials, these confrontations took place behind closed doors, with no rules and with virtually no witnesses beyond the police and prison warders and the victims themselves. Along with torture behind closed doors, inquests into the growing number of deaths during detention also replaced trials as a key nodal point, a public site of contestation. Under South African law, an inquest must be held for any unnatural death.[148] The record of Looksmart Ngudle's inquest is chilling, hauntingly evocative of hundreds of stories heard over 30 years later during the proceedings of the Truth and Reconciliation Commission. Mrs Maria Ngudle testified at the inquest about how she went searching for her son:

> I was shown the prison in Pretoria by some people. I said to the African policeman, 'I have come for Looksmart's funeral'. The policeman took down my name. He asked me if Looksmart was sentenced to death. I said I did not know. I only knew he was arrested. The policeman said he would go and look. He came back. 'We have buried him already because we can't keep a dead person. How can we help you?' I said, 'I want his clothes'. He said there were none.[149]

The policeman then sent her to another prison where she asked the same questions, and those authorities, in turn, sent her back to the first prison, where she saw the same black policeman, who then sent her upstairs to see a white policeman. Mrs

---

146   Joe Slovo quoted in Thomas G. Karis and Gail M. Gerhardt (eds) *Nadir and Resurgence, 1964–1969*, vol. 5 of *From Protest to Challenge: A Documentary History of African Politics in South Africa, 1882–1990* (Stanford: Hoover Institution Press, 1997), 24.

147   George Bizos, *No One to Blame? In Pursuit of Justice in South Africa* (Cape Town: David Philip Publishers; Bellville: Mayibuye Books, 1998), 3.

148   Ibid., 4. Bizos wrote that "between 1963 and 1990s, 73 detainees are known to have died in detention," the youngest of whom was 16 and the oldest 63 years of age (6). His book details his own experience serving as advocate for many of these cases.

149   Mrs Maria Ngudle quoted in First, *117 Days*, 84.

Ngudle recalled, "I felt they were playing me for the fool. I went home. I could not find out what the cause of death was."[150]

Mrs Ngudle's story is emblematic of many stories heard later by the TRC: her frantic and frustrating search from place to place, lack of immediate access to legal counsel, forthright demands for the clothes of her dead son, and determined quest to find the cause of death. Also typical was the state's delay in providing information, the hasty burial of the body, the evasion of the police, the delayed and then abruptly scheduled inquest, the coercion of Mrs Ngudle to sign a statement State Security had crafted, and the sudden banning of the deceased so that even his name could not be published in the newspapers.[151] "Dead Man Banned" was all the Johannesburg evening newspapers could say.[152] Fellow prisoners of the banned person were likewise banned, which meant they could make no public statements or be quoted, so witnesses to the treatment of Ngudle by the police during his detention could not testify in court. Attorneys for the Ngudle family withdrew at the beginning of the inquest because, they said, the banning orders meant that many potential witnesses, including fellow prisoners, could not testify without fear of prosecution.

But at the Ngudle inquest the state had not yet refined either its techniques of torture in isolation (to ensure that there were no witnesses) or the rules of engagement for inquests. At the start of the inquest, Minister of Justice Vorster made a series of rulings he may have come to regret. He determined that a court was a privileged forum, that courts could hear statements by banned persons, and that an inquest proceeding was a court. Therefore, banned persons could testify at an inquest without fear of reprisal. "Suddenly the stillness enveloping the fate of the detained in their cells was broken," recalls Ruth First, an anti-apartheid activist and scholar who was eventually assassinated by a parcel bomb. "The bush telegraph in the jails began to work."[153] Fellow prisoners came forward at Ngudle's inquest, and their tales provided evidence of a widespread pattern of police interrogation by means of torture. Fellow detainee Isaac Tlale testified of his ordeal:

'I was handcuffed. There were two chairs joined together. I was to sit on those two chairs. I was sitting this way …'. Tlale indicated how he had sat, with his

---

150 Ibid., 85.

151 In South Africa, banning was "an administrative action by which publications, organizations, or assemblies could be outlawed and suppressed and individual persons could be placed under severe restrictions of their freedom of travel, association, and speech. Banning was an important tool in the South African government's suppression of those opposed to its policy of apartheid." "Banning: South African Law," *Encyclopædia Britannica Online*, available at www.britannica.com/EBchecked/topic/52092/banning (accessed April 4, 2009).

152 First, *117 Days*, 86.

153 Ibid., 86–7.

knees up, his arms wrapped around them. 'My hands were handcuffed', he continued, 'and in between my knees they inserted a broom handle'.[154]

The police inserted the broom handle above his arms and below his knees, so that he was immobilized. They covered his head with a bag and subjected him to electric shocks while they hounded him to make a confession. When more evidence of police torture was heard from other detainees, the state prosecutor finally objected, saying that evidence of the conditions and treatment of other detainees was "irrelevant." The court agreed and declared such evidence inadmissible.[155] The final verdict was that Looksmart Ngudle had committed suicide and that his death was not caused by "any act or omission involving or amounting to an offence on the part of any person."[156] In other words, "no one was to blame," a refrain that families of deceased prisoners and their advocates such as George Bizos were to hear repeatedly for decades to come.[157]

What one sees in the Treason, Incitement, and Rivonia trials is the way law courts became highly theatrical spaces for public acknowledgment of the changes sweeping the country. As the few liberties blacks had were gradually being eroded, including any rights to free speech, the courtrooms became, ironically, spaces that put into the public record the voices, speeches, and perspectives of the opposition. Trials also made visible the direct confrontation between the powerful and the powerless. These were theaters of power. But as the state of emergency went into effect after the Sharpeville massacre, blacks' limited freedoms of speech were ever more tightly circumscribed, even in the courtroom. Protesters who flocked to the courtroom to support Mandela and others could not speak his name, so they resorted to nonverbal means of communication: posters, buttons, costumes, gestures, and song. The opposition's expressive culture was forced into the nonverbal domains of performance.

As the 1960s wore on, the state's methods became more clandestine, calculated to avoid the theatrical and highly public encounters staged by political trials. The number of days the state could detain prisoners without trial kept increasing and the state's methods of oppressing those detained were concealed in prison cells and torture chambers, leaving little documentation except damaged bodies. The primary stage of encounter between the opposition and the state was not in the public space of the trial but in inquests, where the prisoner could no longer speak but where his body could provide testimony through forensic evidence.

Theatricality and performance must be central to our analysis of justice during periods of regime change and political transition. Who would have predicted, for instance, that the Treason Trial, which seemed to be a calculated "attempt to silence and outlaw the ideas held by the accused and the thousands whom they represent,"

---

154 Isaac Tlale quoted in Bizos, *No One to Blame*, 12.
155 First, *117 Days*, 95.
156 Ibid., 96.
157 Bizos, *No One to Blame*, 13.

to quote defense advocate Berrangé, would in fact document for the first time the history of the anti-apartheid struggle? "The unwritten history of the struggle for freedom has gone into the record of this trial," Helen Joseph wrote, adding, "It's a macabre university in which we study, facing a capital charge."[158] But then, who would have predicted that in 1996 a marathon state-sponsored public airing of a nation's past atrocities—its systematic killings, tortures, lynchings, and daily violations of human rights committed over three decades—would be expected to lead, of all things, to reconciliation? The paradoxes of justice during times of political transition are indeed many, and these paradoxes are often most vividly perceived when the archive and the repertoire converge.

---

158   Joseph, *If This Be Treason*, 131.

Chapter 6

The Rivonia Trial:
Domination, Resistance and Transformation

Catherine Albertyn

> *Where there is power, there is resistance, and yet, or rather consequently, this*
> *resistance is never in a position of exteriority in relation to power. Should it be*
> *said that one is always "inside" power, there is no "escaping" it, there is no*
> *absolute outside where it is concerned, because one is subject to the law in any*
> *case? ... This would be to misunderstand the strictly relational character of*
> *power relationships.*[1]

Introduction

The Rivonia trial is the story of domination and resistance, of despair and hope, of endings and beginnings. It was, without question, a devastating blow for the African National Congress (ANC) and its allies. Four years after the organisation was banned in 1960, and after thousands of arrests, detentions and trials of opponents to apartheid and white rule, the leadership of the ANC was arrested, tried and imprisoned for life, others fled into exile and internal resistance to apartheid all but ended. A white community that had been ambivalent towards the authoritarian policies of apartheid found some consensus around the censure of African political aspirations as fermenting violence and revolution, and some comfort in an economy that had shrugged off the uncertainty generated by the protests and state of emergency of the early 1960s to enjoy unprecedented levels of growth. In this climate, apartheid became less contested and more entrenched.

If the trial signified an unprecedented white consensus, it was also a site and focus of struggle and resistance. It closed a chapter of internal struggle in which the ANC and its allies had shifted from petitions, to boycotts and civil disobedience and, finally, to sabotage. But the legal space of the trial enabled a full justification of the turn to sabotage, and of the liberation struggle itself. The trial – especially Mandela's opening statement for the defence – provided the opportunity to oppose the criminalisation and censure of resistance by the state, to (re)write the history of the struggle and to provide an enduring rallying point for future struggles that culminated in the unbanning of the ANC in 1990 and the first democratic elections in 1994. In many ways, Rivonia marks the beginning of our contemporary memory of domination, resistance and democracy.

---

1   Michel Foucault, *The History of Sexuality* (1979).

This chapter develops a theoretical framework, that understands political trials within a broader dialectic of domination and resistance, and that recognises the spaces for resistance that are possible in the state's repressive and, especially, ideological mechanisms that seek to delegitimate and eradicate political opposition. It employs the idea of 'censure' to hone it on the particular discourses of communism and violence that were used to target and criminalise aspirations of equality, non-racialism and democracy, and to illustrate the manner in which these labels were opposed and resisted. These censures form part of wider political and economic struggles in which political trials must be located and understood. The third section of the chapter discusses the political struggles of the 1950s that provide a context to the Rivonia trial, highlighting briefly the development of the censure of communism and its contestation in the 1956–61 Treason trial. The following section turns to the early 1960s to discuss the crisis of legitimacy that momentarily faced the apartheid state in 1960, and the subsequent authoritarian response to this crisis. It focuses on how the Rivonia trial can be understood in the context of relations of power and resistance in the early 1960s, and how it came to signify a new, although incomplete, white consensus over the censure of black aspirations, and a new basis for resistance. The chapter concludes by reflecting on the trial as a space for domination, resistance and transformation.

Political Trials as Sites of Domination and Resistance[2]

In his classic 1961 text on political trials, *Political Justice*, Otto Kirchheimer locates political trials squarely within the 'fight for political domination':

> Court action is called upon to exert influence over the distribution of political power. The objective may be to upset – fray, undermine or destroy – existing power positions or to strengthen efforts directed at their preservation.[3]

Of course the court is only one site of political control, but it is one that has particular rewards. Not only can it eliminate political opponents, it may also have significant ideological effects that enable political regimes to legitimate political action and 'integrate the population into their political goals'.[4] Power-holders will seek to mobilise public opinion by surrounding the legal defeat of their political opponent with 'a wider framework of historical and moral justification'.[5] But even

---

2   This section is based on the theoretical framework developed in C. Albertyn, *A Critical Analysis of Political Trials in South Africa: 1948–1988* (1994) PhD thesis, University of Cambridge.

3   *Political Justice* (1961) 49.

4   Ibid., 17.

5   Ibid., 422.

as they do so, those in opposition will endeavour to use the courtroom to win support for their explanations and justifications.[6]

Where political trials are not the 'telephone justice' of show trials whose outcomes are known in advance, but constitute a 'more civilised political game' in which procedural and substantive norms limit a state's capacity to punish its opponents, they provide a more uncertain judicial contest.[7] Indeed, legal procedures and the dictates of the rule of law enable procedural standards that offer some protection, the possibility of alternate versions of evidence, and even acquittal.[8] While these trials pose higher risks, the allure of legality, fairness and the rule of law promises more glittering rewards, especially in their educative effects.

Kirchheimer's insistence on the political nature of law and on the educative effects of a trial is fundamental to understanding the role and effects of political trials. However, Kirchheimer tends to limit his enquiry to the immediate effects of a trial – rather than its place in longer political and economic struggles. As I hope to demonstrate in this chapter, political trials are best understood in the longer term, especially in understanding the resort to law, its form and substance, and the deeper political and ideological battles that the trial serves. In other words, if Kirchheimer inclines to a more instrumental and functional idea of the state, law and power,[9] I argue that political trials, as well as the use, form and content of law in these trials, can best be understood within the changing nature of political and economic struggles, the dialectic between the state and its opposition, and a more relational understanding of power. Political trials should be analysed and understood within the political, ideological and economic conditions of their time. In particular, we should understand how the delegitimation of political opposition, that occurs through a specific trial, is located in wider discourses of disapproval and censure that are rooted in broader political and hegemonic struggles.

The location of the trial in political struggles highlights the dual nature of political trials as a form of political domination and as a site of struggle and resistance. The trial is a repressive and an ideological attempt at domination. However, if we understand power as relational, rather than merely instrumental, then in those forms of repressive and ideological control lie the possibilities, modes and strategies of resistance.[10] In each instance, the particular forms and methods of domination and of resistance will be historically contingent, with historically specific effects.

---

6   Ibid., 49.

7   Ibid., 424; 50.

8   Ibid., 120.

9   See Albertyn (note 2 above) chapter 1, 12–17.

10   This, of course, is Foucault's approach to power, first identified in *Discipline and Punish* (1977) and developed in *The History of Sexuality* (1979).

Technologies of Apartheid Era Political Trials:
Ideology, Relational Power and Political Censures

At the heart of political trials is the criminalisation of political opposition and dissent, and resistance to that label. The criminal label is a complex one, located in wider ideas, attitudes and discourses. Criminological literature has long understood the links between the public understanding of a crime, social attitudes, the shifting use of the crime against different groups and activities, and how the 'criminal' label is used to 'prepar[e] the ground for ... the exercise of legal restraint and political control'.[11] To illustrate the links between crime, ideology and control, Sumner has suggested that categories of crime and deviance be analysed as 'negative ideological categories with specific material application' called social censures.[12] By this he refers to ideas that are part of everyday language and appeal to general moral principles, such as 'slut', 'mugger' or 'pervert', with general, predictable moral and political targets that they seek to marginalise, denounce and control. Sumner further argues that these tend to express the moral and political disapproval of the dominant class, gender, race, etc., and to affirm dominant norms and ideologies. Thus censures can be understood within the 'ideological discourse and social interests which support and constitute them ... the phenomena they interpret and classify, and the historical conjuncture within which they are applied'.[13]

Sumner argues that political censures target political movements, ideas, individuals and activities that challenge the dominant social relations of class, race, nation, gender, etc. As Mahabir wrote, colonial and neo-colonial elites:

> often use their power as lawmakers to undermine (oppositional) movements ...
> They label as serious crime social phenomena such as resistance movements,
> labour strikes, mass demonstrations (and) rallies, acts of civil disobedience ...
> They refer to participants as subversives, conspirators, terrorists, communist
> instigators, as dangerous criminals committing treason and sedition, as
> instigators of riot.[14]

Generated in political struggles and social practices, political censures have particular sets of meaning and historical resonances. In South Africa, the dominant political censures of the period under review included communism, (communist)

---

11   Stuart Hall, C. Critcher, T. Jefferson, J. Clarke and B. Roberts, *Policing the Crisis: Mugging, the State and Law and Order* (1978) 189.

12   C. Sumner, 'Re-thinking Deviance: Towards a Sociology of Censures', in S. Spitzer (ed.) *Research in Law, Deviance and Social Control* (1983) 187; C. Sumner and S. Sandberg, 'The Press Censure of "Dissident Minorities"; the Ideology of Parliamentary Democracy; Thatcherism and "Policing the Crisis"' (1990) 163.

13   Sumner (note 12 above) 196.

14   C. Mahabir, *Crime and Nation-Building in the Caribbean: The Legacy of Legal Barriers* (1985) 190.

agitation and violence. Each was articulated in a variety of institutions, discourses and practices before becoming institutionalised in different ways in the criminal law. On their own and in legal provisions, they are composite ideological categories with multiple ideological inputs. Their power derives from the fact that they arise out of and link into everyday norms, feelings, fears and moral principles as well as the political and legal discourses of the state. Hence their deployment in courts can trigger a range of fears, prejudices and ideas about the necessary political and social order, thus rendering them particularly powerful forms of condemnation and ideological control.[15]

The composite nature of censures and their ability to trigger particular ideas, fears and prejudices means that they can be used to unite people around particular issues, against a particular group and/or set of ideas, and in favour of a specific course of action. Not only can censures be powerful images of disapproval, operating to condemn and exclude; but equally significant is their potential to affirm and defend a desired political order and way of life.[16] Giddens argued that the power to distinguish between what is political and what is criminal, together with the ability to define which political programmes, policies and practices are in the 'general', 'public' or 'national' interest and the articulation of historicity (the ability to 'invent' the history of the nation-state, the myth of origins, the common destiny), encapsulate critical ideological dimensions of the modern nation-state.[17] Political censures can play an important role in struggles around the definition of nation, citizenship and the appropriate social and economic order.

Most importantly, censures are contested categories. As Sumner notes, censures can only be properly socialised to the extent that their generalised and authoritative dissemination is unopposed by oppositional ideologies and organisations. Censures are part of wider hegemonic struggle, and are always contested and changing, requiring constant renewal, defence and modification. 'Certain meanings and practice are chosen for emphasis', others 'neglected and excluded'.[18] Writing about the use of the criminal label in colonial and post-colonial society, Mahabir notes that '[t]hese terms (of the state) are counteracted ... by members of the subject populations with terms such as organizers, nation-builders, freedom fighters and political prisoners'.[19] In South Africa, ideas of criminality, communism and violence were part of the repertoire of the apartheid state in delegitimating the political opposition and its ideas of racial equality and universal suffrage. In

---

15 Sumner and Sandberg (note 12 above).

16 Ibid.; A. Young, '"Wild Women": The Censure of the Suffragette Movement' (1988) 15 *IJSL* 279.

17 A. Giddens, *A Contemporary Critique of Historical Materialism Volume Two: The Nation-State and Violence* (1985) 211–12.

18 R. Williams, 'Base and Superstructure in Marxist Cultural Theory' (1973) *New Left Review* 31, 39.

19 Mahabir (note 14 above) 190. See Kirchheimer (note 3 above) 24.

response, the political opposition resisted the label and sought to justify its own ideas of non-racialism, equality and political rights.

Censures are particularly powerful when located in a wider system of criminal justice and judicial pronouncements which claim to represent a universal social order.[20] When political censures are targeted at selected groups and individuals through the medium of law and a trial, they play an important role in the struggle for hegemony. And just as the state uses courts to denounce its opposition, so the opposition exploits law and courts as sites of struggle and resistance, challenging the censures of the state, creating a platform for political programmes, and justifying its aspirations, acts and ideas. It thus participates within a hegemonic struggle for legitimacy, and the ability to define and claim the nation.

The Techniques of Domination and Resistance: Developing and Contesting the Censure of 'Communism' in the 1950s

The pre-democratic South African state was consumed by the need to address the 'native question'. When the National Party (NP) assumed power in 1948 on a platform of racial 'apartheid' (literally separateness), the white community was divided over the appropriate shape of capitalism and society, and how to address growing claims for political and economic inclusion by black South Africans. On the one side, the NP advocated for legally enforced social segregation, greater controls on the movement of black workers and a racially segregated workforce, and opposed political inclusion and racial equality. On the other, the United Party (UP) opposed legally (rather than socially) enforced segregation and supported fewer controls over movement and a settled, less racially stratified workforce. Following the Cape liberal tradition, it opposed full racial equality, adopting a paternalistic lobby for 'white leadership with justice' and the gradual incorporation of black South Africans into political and economic life through a qualified franchise, negotiation and evolving economic rights in line with the interests of capital.

The NP used its slim parliamentary majority[21] to implement apartheid through laws that imposed an increasingly repressive and segregated labour framework; enforced social separation;[22] and limited black political aspirations.[23] Its repeated attempts to remove coloured voters for the voters' roll generated significant

---

20   Sumner (note 12 above) 196.

21   Although the NP triumphed with a majority of parliamentary seats in 1948, it was with a minority of electoral support (37 per cent versus the UP's 49 per cent). The NP remained a minority in percentage terms until 1966 due to the uneven demarcation of rural and urban wards.

22   The Population Registration Act 30 of 1950 was the centre of this, but see also the Reservation of Separate Amenities Act 49 of 1953 and Groups Areas Act 51 of 1950.

23   Important here was the removal of all direct political representation (the remaining votes of coloureds in the Cape Province) and the development of homelands and traditional authorities as the political home of black South Africans.

resistance from white South Africans.[24] But its core ideas of white supremacy and apartheid conflicted directly with the demands of black South Africans for non-racialism and equality. Indeed, the post-war period saw the intensification of political struggle as the ANC eschewed constitutional means of protest to adopt more militant extra-parliamentary means and campaigned for full equality, based on 'universal suffrage, equal rights, the rule of law, a mixed economy and the provision of social welfare'.[25] As the NP ratcheted up the implementation of apartheid, so resistance to these policies grew and organisations joined the ANC in a broad-based 'Congress Alliance' that called for a National Convention to decide on an inclusive future. The Congress Alliance challenged the state with passive resistance, boycotts, strikes and civil disobedience, culminating in the Defiance Campaign of 1951–2, the largest non-violent resistance seen in South Africa, and in the adoption of the Freedom Charter at the Congress of the People in 1955. The Freedom Charter was a comprehensive statement of a non-racial South Africa and asserted a common nationality, a non-racial democracy, equal rights, and redress and redistribution to secure full equality.[26]

Of course such resistance spurred deeper repression and ideological censure, within the constraints on an increasingly thin notion of the rule of law. Two features stand out. First, the passage of the Suppression of Communism Act 44 of 1950 (SoCA) outlawed the Communist Party of SA (CPSA) and enabled the state to criminalise a broad range of political activities as 'communist' and to act against persons and organisations associated with 'communism'. Second, in the Treason trial the state sought to criminalise the entire struggle as communist and, therefore, treasonous.

The Censure and Criminalisation of Black Political Aspirations as 'Communist' in the 1950s

Formed in 1921, the CPSA was committed to full racial equality.[27] It was a racially integrated political organisation that attracted a range of activists, black and white, and elected (white) members to parliament and city councils. While

---

24   T. Karis and G. Carter, *From Protest to Challenge: A Documentary History of African Politics in South Africa. Vol. 2 Hope and Challenge 1943–1952* (1973) 405.

25   D. Everatt, *The Origins of Non-Racialism: White Opposition to Apartheid in the 1950s* (2009) 125.

26   See generally N. Steytler (ed.) *The Freedom Charter and Beyond: Founding Principles for a Democratic South African Legal Order* (1991).

27   The Communist Party Manifesto, 1921 included a commitment to racial equality in organising workers 'of all ranks and races' to 'propagate the Communist gospel'. In 1928 the CPSA resolved to struggle for complete equality of rights and the abolition of racially discriminatory laws. South African Communist Party 'Fifty Fighting Years: The Turn to the Masses', available at http://www.sacp.org.za/main.php?ID=3943.

its manifesto linked it to global communist ideals, its acceptance of a 'two-stage revolution' meant that its immediate goals in South Africa were full political equality and democracy, thus placing it 'squarely on the side of the ANC and national liberation'.[28]

As with many political censures, the criminalisation of communism in the SoCA followed decades of political, capitalist, bureaucratic and social concern over the influence of communists amongst black miners, ex-servicemen and in extra-parliamentary politics. In the growing East/West divide of the post-war world, it is not difficult to see why the South African government acted against the CPSA in 1950, at least in the traditional interpretation of communism. However, the passage of the SoCA was accompanied by a growing censure around communism extending well beyond its conventional meaning. Despite prominent references to the international context, the 'intense and deadly struggle, creating turmoil throughout the world',[29] communism had its own distinctive set of meanings and targets in South Africa. The SoCA was not a means to control a few communists but a weapon to suppress all extra-parliamentary dissent and censure all forms of multi-racial political activity. This was made explicit by a Nationalist MP in the parliamentary debate:

> (Communism) causes troubles among the Natives ... it incites the Natives and ... it preaches equality. Now when one preaches equality it means that all the Natives will eventually have to get the franchise ... on the same basis as the European, then this will not be a white republic or a white dominion but it will be a black republic ... That is why we come here and state in the definition ... that a person is not allowed to cause trouble between Europeans and Non-Europeans.[30]

The wide definition of communism criminalised a broad spectrum of political activities and included any doctrine or scheme which aimed at:

> bringing about any political, industrial, social or economic change within the Union by the promotion of disturbance or disorder ... unlawful actions or omissions the encouragement of feeling of hostility between European and non-European races of the Union the consequences of which are calculated to further the aims of [communism].

Any person deemed to further the aims and objectives of communism, as defined, could be listed, banned, prevented from attending meetings or from meeting

---

28   South African Communist Party 'Fifty Fighting years. The Turn to the masses' available at http://www.sacp.org.za/main.php?ID=3943.

29   Minister of Justice, Second Reading Debate *Hansard* 1950 col 8910.

30   MP Boltman from the rural Cape constituency of De Aar/Colesberg. *Hansard* 1950 col 9378.

another banned persons, restricted to particular areas or banished to others, while organisations could be proscribed and their assets seized.

Communism was a complex censure whose meanings differed for different sections of the white group. The Nationalists had fought the 1948 election on the basis of 'oostroming' (engulfment) and 'swart gevaar' (black peril). Both found expression in the communism censure and since racial equality was seen as the inevitable concomitant of British Imperial liberal capitalism, anti-communism combined both anti-black and anti-British sentiment.[31]

By linking communism to integration and non-racialism, the communist threat referred to real fears and interests protected by segregation and apartheid, particularly in respect of black urban migration and integration in the workplace. The struggle to preserve the privileges of the white working class and the identity of the Afrikaner nation was defended as the fight against integration and communism. Thus to oppose apartheid was to support non-racialism and communism, and tantamount to treason. As NP member of parliament, F.S. Steyn, said:

> If South Africa were to fall into the hands of a Black Bantu government, our economic pattern our material pattern ... our whole cultural heritage ... our language will be destroyed. Everything which gives form and concept to the South African state will disappear. But this propaganda is being made by Luthuli and other people in South Africa with complete freedom, in order to bring about this more revolutionary destruction of the South African state than is contemplated by the act of high treason ... I say that in our time and in our country, it is the most probable and the most dangerous form of high treason to try and shift the power of the government from the present White hands to the Bantu hands.[32]

The English-speaking UP was also committed to an anti-communist discourse, but with a narrower, and more conventional, content. The dangers of international communism gave meaning to and justified the UP policy of 'white leadership with justice'.

> Caught up in a duel for the minds of men between the free countries in the world and communist countries ... therefore it will be fatal to divide the country into white nationalism and black nationalism ... In short the UP policy is one of willingness to share western civilisation with all our peoples in this country, but not at the expense of civilisation already achieved by many of our people. And we are convinced that in order to maintain this standard, European leadership is essential.[33]

---

31 T.D. Moodie, *The Rise of Afrikanerdom: Power, Apartheid and the Afrikaner Civil Religion* (1975) 25.

32 *Hansard* 1959 col 5719.

33 Sir De Villiers Graaf (United Party) 'Policy Statement' (1960) United Party Archives, University of South Africa Archives, Pretoria.

Despite the differing content of the censure, the common rejection of communism and support for white rule meant that the censure was a potentially powerful weapon in delegitimating extra-parliamentary opposition, diverting dissent from government policies and cementing a white consensus. Its strength lay in its grounding in real fears, interests and values and real historical struggles and practices. It was made plausible by the fact that communists were had consistently struggled alongside blacks. The CPSA was the only party 'that had no colour-bar and united diverse racial and social groups',[34] and communists shared a common commitment to non-racial democracy. As Mandela noted later in the Rivonia trial: 'For many decades communists were the only political group in South Africa to treat Africans as human beings and as their equals.'[35]

Initially used against ex-CPSA members and unionists, the scope of the SoCA widened to include members of Congress Alliance and liberals, thus dubbing all opposition as communist, irrespective of its nature or content. Eventually communism became the central censure of the Treason trial, as the escalation of political resistance led to the arrest of 156 people on a charge of treason in December 1956.

Domination and Resistance in the Treason Trial: 1956–1961

In the Treason Trial that commenced with a year-long preparatory examination in 1957, the apartheid government sought the 'glittering rewards' of a show trial, hoping to portray the activities and aspirations of the Congress Alliance as communist and treasonous. The difficulties in doing this are illustrated by the fact that only 30 accused were actually charged with treason.[36] This charge alleged a countrywide conspiracy in which:

> The accused ... prepared to subvert the existing state by illegal means including the use of force and violence; and to replace [it] with a state founded on principles differing fundamentally from those on which the present state is constituted.[37]

This new state was alleged to be 'a Communist state, in the form of a People's Democracy or a People's Republic, or some other state'.[38]

---

34   H. Bernstein, *The World that was Ours* (1967) 5.

35   Rivonia Trial Record. *S v Mandela and Others*, University of the Witwatersrand, Johannesburg, Vol. 19, 39–40. Mandela's statement is also available at http://www.anc.org.za/show.php?id=3430.

36   At the end of the preparatory examination, 91 people were indicted for treason, but only 30 eventually went to trial. Charges against the rest were withdrawn after the state failed to supply further particulars.

37   *Treason Trial Bulletin* no. 12, 3.

38   *Crown v F Adams and 29 Others* Indictment 4. Treason Trial Record, University of the Witwatersrand, Johannesburg.

The charge of treason was directed at the extra-parliamentary opposition in general, and the ANC in particular. Despite the fact that the legal definition of communism condemned advocacy for equal rights, it was technically not unlawful to seek to achieve this, except by unlawful means. Hence the charge of treason sought to demonstrate that advocacy for equal rights and a multi-racial society was inevitably connected to unlawful means (violence) and an unlawful end (the achievement of a communist state). As such, it was alleged, the struggle for equality was neither legitimate nor constitutional, but must have been a struggle that had intended violent revolution.

In the political and legal environment of the 1950s, these charges were impossible to sustain. The defence was able to limit the issue to one question – Did the Congress Alliance pursue a policy of violence? – which it was able to refute.[39] In contrast to the picture of violent and communist oriented struggles, the defence successfully characterised the struggle as non-violent, non-communist and committed to liberal democracy. In the end, the judge found that, although the accused might have contemplated illegal methods, there was no policy of violence[40] nor was it proved that the Freedom Charter (alleged to be a communist blueprint) envisaged a communist state. While there was a strong left-wing tendency in ANC, it was not a communist organisation.[41] And so a major show-trial failed in its core intention: to criminalise ideas of, and advocacy for, racial equality and democracy as communist, violent and treasonous.

Despite this legal failure, the effects on politics were complex. The government's attempt to criminalise ideas of equality and a multi-racial society as communist and (inevitably) violent, and thus foreclose possibilities of change through constitutional means, cast a wide shadow. Caught up in these censures were not only communist and socialist ideas of the left, and the social-democratic and liberal ideas of the ANC and Liberal Party, but also the more conservative, incrementalist approach of the UP. All were implicated in the anti-communist discourse (directly or as 'fellow-travellers') as the government sought to affirm its apartheid policies and construct a new hegemony around racially separate development. Thus even as the acquittal was welcomed by many whites as a triumph of the rule of law,[42] its indirect effects deepened the divide between white politics and the ANC. Indeed, the court's findings of left-wing tendencies, the desire for a state based on the Freedom Charter, the role of communists and the use of unconstitutional methods confirmed that the ANC was unacceptable to a white electorate whose idea of a multi-racial society was based on economic rather than political equality and 'white leadership with justice'.[43]

---

39   Maisels opening statement *Treason Trial Bulletin* no. 8.
40   Rumpff J. Reasons for Judgment 11–12. Treason Trial Record (note 38 above).
41   Ibid., 60.
42   Albertyn (note 2 above) chapter 3, 138.
43   Ibid., chapter 3.

For those on trial, there was both opportunity and constraint. Political action was limited and ideas constrained by the straitjacket of legal defence. Preoccupied with legal procedures, the leadership was restricted in its ability to assess political forces and formulate appropriate strategies, especially in the difficult conditions of 1960.[44] However, the trial also catapulted the ANC into international headlines and provided space to defend its aspirations and demands. It forged common purpose amongst the opposition and brought people together in a way that was difficult in the repressive atmosphere of increased restrictions and bannings.[45] Importantly, it demonstrated at home and abroad the nature and extent of extra-parliamentary opposition to apartheid.

> For the first time since Union, the African opposition to White Government had taken an unmistakeable shape … (T)he greatest single upshot of the Treason hearings was emergence, both in black and white minds, of the name "Congress" as a real force of black power, concentrated in one place, capable of strikes, boycotts and perhaps even of treason, where before it had been an intangible, amorphous body, scattered over half a million miles.[46]

The trial thus provided a rallying point for resistance. Although there was no public voice in the mainstream media, the alternative (and to some extent the international) press, and networks of informal and word-of-mouth communication publicised the ideas of the trial at the time. And the documentation of a hard-fought legal case and courtroom records preserved an archive of resistance that has formed the basis of ongoing writing, research and story-telling about the national liberation struggle.

The Rivonia Trial

As the Treason trial continued into 1961, the world changed around it. On 21 March 1960, 50 people were shot dead and 169 injured by police at Sharpeville. It remains an iconic moment in South African history, signifying a deepening resistance to the apartheid state and the possibilities of an authoritarian and violent state response. Yet in 1960, the state was relatively weak with an economy that had barely begun to emerge from a period of stagnation before it experienced the massive outflow of capital in the wake of Sharpeville, high levels of popular resistance and a white community whose ideological divisions were brought to the fore by Sharpeville. By 1964, a confident state was embarking on a vigorous

---

44   R. Lambert, 'Black Resistance in South Africa: 1950–1961: An Assessment of the Political Strike Campaigns' (1978) 6. Southern African Societies Seminar Group, Institute of Commonwealth Studies, London.

45   A. Luthuli, *Let My People Go* (1962) 148; 154.

46   A. Sampson, *The Treason Cage* (1958) 4–5.

programme of restructuring society, with political opposition crushed and unprecedented economic growth accompanied by growing white unity. During this period at least 2,000 people were jailed and possibly twice as many prosecuted for political offences.[47] It is within this movement from political and economic crisis in 1960 to political confidence and economic growth in 1964 that the second iconic moment of the 1960s – the Rivonia trial – can begin to be understood.

From Sharpeville to Rivonia: Repression and Resistance

The non-violent, extra-parliamentary methods of the 1950s, described above, were partly driven by a belief in the irrationality of apartheid and inevitability of its demise in the context of a decolonising world. But the optimism of this public voice concealed a more complex reality as the intransigence of government and increasing numbers of whites became apparent. As we learn later in the Rivonia trial, this intransigence gave rise to discussions of strategy, and support for militant and even violent methods of struggle began to emerge. Tensions over strategy, multi-racialism and the influence of whites resulted in the splitting of the Pan African Congress (PAC) from the ANC in 1959. Opposed to white supremacy and communism, the PAC found support amongst the black working class and migrant labour force. In 1960, it pre-empted the ANC in a call for a mass defiance campaign against the pass laws. An initially peaceful demonstration escalated, after the killings at Sharpeville, in mass protest action and countrywide strikes.

The response to these protests was mixed. The state declared a state of emergency, deployed the army and police to break the strikes and detained up to 11,000 people.[48] In a move supported by the official opposition, the ANC and PAC were censured as violent and subversive and declared unlawful organisations:[49]

> (The ANC and PAC) represent less than 1% of the Bantu population of South Africa ... They are just a small coterie of terrorists ... the barbaric and merciless reign of terror which these two organisations ... have succeeded in conducting in recent times, is being pursued against the wishes of the vast masses of peace-loving Bantu in South Africa. Their aim is to bring to its knees any white government in South African which stands for white supremacy ... (They) do not want peace and order ... What they want is our country.[50]

But events around Sharpeville also shook ruling circles to an unprecedented extent. Despite some unity on the need to deal repressively with the situation in the short-term, it precipitated public debate over the direction of the country with a powerful body of opinion calling for change. The incorporationist constituency

---

47 See Albertyn (note 2 above) 168.
48 As confirmed by the Minister of Justice in Parliament, *Hansard* 1960 col 6818.
49 The Unlawful Organisations Act 34 of 1960.
50 Minister of Justice *Hansard* 1960 cols 4302–3.

of parliamentary opposition, capital and the English press were joined for the first time by enlightened elements in the NP and Afrikanerdom[51] in calling for reform of the pass laws and the treatment of urban blacks. This resurgence of tensions over responses to the 'Native Question' occurred amidst the most severe economic crisis since 1932.[52]

But the 1960s is, if nothing else, the story of Nationalist triumph over political and economic crisis brought to the surface by Sharpeville. Over a few years, the government thrust aside opposition to establish the stability necessary for economic growth and the implementation of apartheid. The eradication of extra-parliamentary opposition and the construction of greater consensus in the white community were central to this.

Although the outlawing of the ANC and PAC drastically curtailed political action, it brought no immediate change in the policy of either organisation. Each continued to operate within a framework of non-violence with the object of gaining white support for its policies. There was also continuing protest against apartheid from parts of the white community against sectional Afrikaner politics and in favour of consultation with blacks.[53] This opposition was strengthened by the NP's decision in 1961 to declare South Africa a republic and remove it from the British Commonwealth. Seeking to capitalise on a divided white community, the ANC called for a national convention for a multi-racial South Africa, failing which a national stay-away would be implemented. This was premised on the belief that 'these are the means of peaceful pressure either to force the government to conform to civilised standards or to give to one which will'.[54] As Mandela wrote to leader of the opposition: 'It is not too late to turn the tide against the Nationalist created crisis. A call for a national convention from you would well be the turning point in our country's history.'[55]

The state responded with the full force of its ideological and repressive repertoire. Characterising opposition as violent and subversive, the NP rushed a law through parliament,[56] *inter alia* to authorise detention without trial for 12 days, and criminalise the organisation of prohibited gatherings. Between 8,000 and 10,000 people were arrested and detained.[57]

Of course, many in the Congress Alliance were not optimistic about the possibilities of the National Convention. Forms of violent opposition had been discussed before 1961 and in December 1960, the SACP decided to pursue

---

51   Albertyn (note 2 above) 173.

52   Foreign investment plummeted, strikes, massive outflow of foreign capital and continuous growth since 1920 came to almost complete halt. Ibid., 174.

53   Ibid., 198.

54   N. Mandela, *New Age* (1961) 4–5.

55   T. Karis and G. Carter, *Challenge and Violence 1953–1964* (1977) vol. 3, 636.

56   The General Law Amendment Act 39 of 1961.

57   *Rand Daily Mail*, 25 May 1961.

economic sabotage to be followed, later, by guerrilla warfare.[58] After the repression of early 1961, Umkonto we Sizwe (MK) was formed by Nelson Mandela and others to participate in controlled forms of violence under the political guidance of the ANC. According to evidence presented at the Rivonia Trial, sabotage was aimed at persuading whites to bring about a common society. Two other organisations also adopted violent methods in the early 1960s. POQO, a PAC-inspired organisation said to be the largest clandestine organisation in the 1960s,[59] adopted terrorist methods and a policy of killing people to free South Africa of white rule.[60] The African Resistance Movement (ARM) was an organisation of white liberals and radicals who believed that symbolic acts of sabotage would elicit a change in attitudes of government and the white electorate.

As evidence of sabotage and violence emerged, the constraints of existing laws were abandoned with the creation of new political offences of sabotage and military training, 90-day detention and an extraordinary criminal procedure for political trials.[61] These new legal weapons, especially the use of 90-day detention to isolate, torture and obtain information, resulted in wide-scale arrests and trials. This repressive campaign was accompanied by state discourses that sought to delegitimate the extra-parliamentary opposition, justify state action, and defend white interests and security. Central to this were the political censures of communism, violence and revolution and the trials through which these were publicised and confirmed. The fruits of this campaign were measured in declining opposition to the censures of violence and revolution and draconian legal measures, as well as a new white consensus by the mid-1960s.

However, this was not an inevitable progression to authoritarianism. It was in response to the struggles of the black majority that the state and legal system was transformed and an authoritarian consensus constructed. Changes in law had to be worked out and justified, opposition marginalised and delegitimated, a white public educated and a new consensus constructed around law and order. Poulantzas has argued that the construction of an authoritarian state requires restructuring of dominant ideologies and involves ideological work.[62] As Greenberg notes:

> [If there was an] ideological coherence and broadening support, apparent by the mid-sixties … (it) did not come easily. The ideology had to be elaborated and integrated, supporters had to be educated and brought along, and opponents had to be silenced. The government had to forge a broad base of support, both within the state apparatus and outside of it.[63]

---

58 Lambert (note 44 above) 6.

59 T. Lodge, *Black Politics in South Africa* (1983) 241.

60 See generally ibid., 241–55.

61 General Law Amendments Acts of 1962 and 1963.

62 B. Jessop, *Nicos Poulantzas: Marxist Theory and Political Strategy* (1985) 89.

63 S. Greenberg, *Legitimating the Illegitimate: State, Markets and Resistance in South Africa* (1987) 129.

Political censures and political trials, especially the Rivonia trial, were to play a significant role in the construction of this authoritarian consensus.

Deepening Political Censures

Expressed in parliament, the media, the courtroom and on various public platforms, the political censures of the early 1960s were composite, overlapping categories conjoining various themes and expressing moral values, political ideas and multiple white fears. These were not new, but historically rooted and given more meaning, plausibility and legitimacy by shifts in political and economic relations. Most important were the related censures of communism, violence, agitators and intimidators.

Communism continued to play a dominant role. The portrayal of the ANC as a communist organisation and African nationalism as communist inspired and directed, both apparent in the Treason trial, remained prominent. For example, in the debate on 1963 security measures, the Minister of Justice outlined the history of communism in the ANC and alleged that the ANC and Congress Alliance were '[o]ut and out communistic, in some case communist inspired ... (with the Freedom Charter) ... nothing else but the communist blueprint for South Africa'.[64] As the 1960s progressed, the growing intolerance of all forms of dissent and its censure as communist began to encompass liberal opposition and any person who 'befriends blacks'.[65]

The censure of communism was rooted in white social consciousness and given new meaning in the context of changing forms of resistance, the presence of white communists in the extra-parliamentary opposition (demonstrated in the Treason trials and others), evidence of communist influence in African liberation struggles and the continuing Cold War. The ruling party attempted to convince white South Africa and its international allies that the government faced a real threat from international communism and was thus worth supporting: 'South Africa has taken its stand unequivocally against the onslaught of communism. It is the one country in ... Africa on which the West can rely absolutely.'[66] Thus opposition to the NP government was characterised not as a product of inequitable social and economic system, but as the domestic extension of a world communist conspiracy.

Communism was highly plausible to whites, although there were differences in parameter and content. For the NP, communism was still linked to the threat of black rule and by extension to multi-racialism and integration. Communism, external manipulation, racial conflict and the fears of engulfment, conquest and chaos were ever-present. For the UP it was narrower, feeding into the international communist threat and fears of isolation on the African continent. The UP tended

---

64 *Hansard* 1963 col 4640.

65 Sir De Villiers Graaff *Hansard* 1963 col 30.

66 Department of Information Pamphlet, 'The Safety of the State is Priority No. 1' (1962) 1.

to distinguish between communism and other forms of opposition such as African nationalism. However both were seen to constitute a threat to white leadership and western values.

Perhaps the most powerful political censure was *violence*, and its more historically specific form of sabotage. It was against violence that the white group found most unity, as became apparent in the Rivonia trial. Here actual and planned violence by the extra-parliamentary opposition lend credence to the censure and assisted the state in justifying the draconian measures of the early 1960s. It portrayed acts of sabotage as senseless, immoral and revolutionary, demonstrating no commitment to 'civilised' standards. In this way it disconnected sabotage and violence from its political and moral context – a context that the defendants in the Rivonia trial sought to provide. The state also portrayed the violence of all extra-parliamentary opposition as a seamless form of aggression towards whites. In this respect, state censures were given plausibility by the attacks on whites by POQO in 1962 and the conflicts surrounding decolonisation in Africa.[67]

Closely linked to the above was the specific targeting of *agitators and intimidators*, in contrast to the mass of 'peace-loving' and 'uneducated' blacks. The extra-parliamentary opposition was portrayed as a small group of agitators:

> The membership of these bodies is not large. On … occasions they attract masses of Natives who are not under their control and who are not members of their bodies; they do so by incitement and by misleading the masses and by emotional incitement to which obviously the Bantu in his relative ignorance is more susceptible than other people who have already learnt self-control.[68]

This, together with the frequent portrayal of agitators as white communists, effectively denied the reasons for black dissent and the legitimacy of black aspirations and grievances. The state thus insisted that subversion was very limited and that blacks were not, in fact, oppressed.

The Rivonia Trial: Repression and Censure of the National Liberation Struggle

The years 1963 and 1964 were decisive in crushing resistance, beginning with mass trials of POQO and the PAC, then trials of MK and ANC leadership and, from 1964, trials of the ARM and white members and office-bearers of the SACP. At least 4,505 arrests took place under various laws, of these 2,438 people were tried, 1,604 convicted and 1,167 released without trial.[69] These reflected different steps in the struggle – the pass campaign, the stay-away strike of 1961 and incitement, and the trials of sabotage and military training.[70] Rivonia was the most important

---

67 Albertyn (note 2 above) 208; 213–20; 248.
68 *Hansard* 1960 col 3881–2.
69 Albertyn (note 2 above) 210.
70 Ibid., 191–226.

of these and demonstrated the multiple political effects that major show-trials can have in the right conditions. In this trial, nine accused were charged with 222 counts of sabotage. In essence, all were alleged to be members of the National High Command of MK who had conspired with the ANC, SACP and MK to overthrow the government of South Africa by violent and revolutionary means.

Rivonia was crucial in delegitimating the ANC and its call for multi-racialism, equality and democracy in the eyes of the white electorate. In doing so, the state sought to prove that the ANC and its allies were the communist, violent agitators that it had long claimed them to be. The trial opened amidst banner headlines about rebellion, civil war and sabotage,[71] and the prosecution launched an extraordinary attack – that went well beyond the legal charges – in its opening address, alleging sabotage was only the first step in an armed revolution intended to bring 'chaos … disorder and turmoil', in which 'Moscow had promised every sort and manner of assistance'.[72] As discussed below, the accused admitted to acts of sabotage, but firmly resisted any idea of moral guilt and exploited the legal space of the trial to contextualise, explain and justify their actions and political aspirations.

In legal terms, the die was cast. As anticipated, the judge found the accused guilty of sabotage. While accepting explanations on the limited extent of violence,[73] he confirmed the dominant censures of communism and violence. He found that the ANC was a 'communist dominated organisation' and that 'many, if not the majority of the members of the ANC and Umkonto … also belonged to the Communist Party'.[74] He found further that there was no moral justification for their actions, no validity to the claim that their struggle was to overcome the oppression of black South Africans:

> I have heard a great deal … about the grievances of the non-European population. The accused told me … who are all leaders of the non-European population (that they) have been motivated entirely by a desire to ameliorate these grievances. I am by no means convinced that the motives of the accused were as altruistic as they wished the court to believe. People who organise a revolution usually plan to take over the Government, and personal ambition cannot be excluded as a motive.[75]

In simple terms, the arrests at Rivonia and subsequent convictions provided the occasion that the state had been waiting for. In one fell swoop, it imprisoned the

---

71   '11 Accused Of Organising Rebellion: State Alleges Rivonia Men Planned Invasion – 222 Sabotage Charges', *The Star*, 9 October 1963; 'State says Rivonia was Headquarters for Civil War: They Wanted 210 000 Grenades and 48 000 Personnel Mines', *The Star*, 3 December 1963.
72   Rivonia Trial Record (note 35 above).
73   Ibid., Judgment 36.
74   Ibid., 2.
75   Ibid., 1.

political leadership, it delegitimated (in the eyes of the white electorate) the ANC's claims for equality and democracy, and labelled those who made such claims as violent, communist and subversive.

But as Foucault argues, where there is power, there is also resistance. What space, then, existed for resistance in such a trial?

Resistance and Contestation in Rivonia

As discussed above, the state's attempt to label the ANC and its allies as communist and violent had been resisted throughout the 1950s and early 1960s, not only by the Congress Alliance but also the English-speaking press and parliamentary opposition. But as the struggle moved underground and the platforms for open political opposition were eroded by repressive measures, the courtroom became one of the few legal sites of political resistance available to the extra-parliamentary forces. As such the political trials of the 1960s were often fiercely contested sites of struggle. If the courtroom was a place where the state could demonstrate the 'truth' about violence and revolution and the benefits of apartheid, for the opposition it was a platform of resistance where the censures of the state were opposed and ideas of nationhood, rights, justice and democracy explained and justified.

Thus a fundamental battle of ideas ensued in the Rivonia courtroom, apparent from the opening plea of each accused: 'The government should be in the dock and not me. I plead not guilty.'[76] The defence was primarily a political one as the inevitable legal convictions were undercut by the rejection of moral guilt and the possibility of a deeper political victory.

Against the state's version that the accused were members of the ANC, under the control of communists, who sought to incite a black community that was satisfied with its lot, the defence asserted the reality of oppression and the legitimacy of black grievances, and thus of their struggle for equality and justice. The defence was geared towards explanations and justifications for their actions. They would not deny what they had done, truthful evidence would be admitted and no apology would be made. However, sections of the state's case that were incorrect or which were thought to strengthen the case for the death sentence would be attacked. These included the crucial links between the censure of communism and violence: that MK was part of the ANC, that the ANC was a tool of the SACP, and that MK had actually adopted a military plan (Operation Mayibuye) and intended to embark on guerilla warfare.[77] Rivonia attorney, Joel Joffe, argues that, in this way, a narrow line was pursued between not compromising the political integrity of the accused and avoiding the death sentence.[78]

---

76 James Kantor, a lawyer caught up in the trial, pleaded not guilty and was subsequently discharged.

77 Opening address of defence, Bram Fischer QC, Rivonia Trial Record (note 35 above).

78 Interview Joel Joffe, August 1987.

The relatively open nature of the trial and legal procedures provided significant space to the defendants to advance their views. Thus, the leadership of the underground was afforded a unique opportunity to communicate its policies and aspirations to a wider audience. Indeed, the government relaxed its restrictions on Mandela to allow publication of his evidence, the opening salvo of the defence. In a four-hour carefully constructed statement, Mandela admitted to his actions, explained the history and aspirations of the African people and liberation struggle, and provided the reasons for the formation of MK and adoption of violent struggle. It was a direct challenge to the definitions and censures of the state, and a powerful communication of an alternative version of the situation of black South Africans and their struggles, and the ideas of morality, politics and vision of state that this implied.

Central to this defence was to counter the state's censure of arbitrary, reckless and immoral violence, and to explain how the escalating repression of the state and closing down of the space for legal action had led to a rational and considered decision to adopt limited forms of violence, based on considerations of morality and justice. In Mandela's words:

> A government which uses force to maintain its rule teaches the oppressed to use force to oppose it … (We adopted violence) not because we desired such a course but because the government left us with no other choice.[79]

> I did not plan it in a spirit of recklessness, nor because I have any love of violence. I planned it as a result of a calm and sober assessment of the political situation that had arisen after many years of tyranny, exploitation and oppression of my people by whites … It was precisely because the soil of South Africa is already drenched in the blood of innocent victims that we felt it our duty to make preparations for a long-tern undertaking to use force in order to defend ourselves against force.[80]

Other defendants followed this lead to place the responsibility of the state in limiting options for resistance and to claim the morality of their actions. Thus Sisulu, cross-examined extensively on MK, stated that 'the African people like all oppressed people have got a moral right to revolt against oppression',[81] whilst Kathrada placed the responsibility for violence on the state:

> I believe that violence is becoming inevitable, and when the people resort to violent methods they will be justified … Because of the actions of the Government in making other methods impossible.[82]

---

79   Rivonia Trial Record (note 35 above) vol. 19, 14–15.
80   Ibid., vol. 19, 6; 25.
81   Ibid., vol. 20, 12.
82   Ibid., vol. 26, 2–21.

In resisting the powerful censure of communism and communist agitators, Mandela was careful to distinguish between communism and the aims of the national liberation struggle.[83] In doing so, he provided an alternative understanding of communism and the nature of resistance. He suggested that 'communists have always played an active role in the fight by colonial countries for their freedom, because the short-term objects of communism would always correspond with the long-term objects of freedom movements'.[84] Importantly, he asserted the links between communism, freedom and equality as sources of empowerment and solidarity for black South Africans:

> For many decades communists were the only political group in South Africa to treat Africans as human beings and as their equals ... who were prepared to work with Africans for the attainment of their political rights ... Because of this many Africans tended to equate communism with freedom.[85]

Thus he inverts the censure: if the state sees the equation of communism with racial equality as the core of the problem, the accused see this as a reason to hold communism in high esteem, whilst clearly separating the aims of communism form those of national liberation.

Finally, in contrast to the state's image of agitators whipping up a satisfied black majority, Mandela argued that:

> Our fight is against real and not imaginary hardships or to use the language of the state "so-called hardships". Basically, my lord, we fight against two features which are hallmarks of African Life in South Africa, and which are entrenched by legislation which we seek to have repealed. These features are poverty and lack of human dignity and we do not need Communists of so-called "agitators" to teach us these things.[86]

The aim of the ANC and its allies was thus not to ferment violent, criminal and communist revolution, but to achieve equality and democracy:

> We want a just stake in ... South Africa; we want security and a stake in society. Above all, my lord, we want equal political rights, because without them our disabilities will be permanent. I know this sounds revolutionary to whites ... because the majority of voters will be Africans. This makes the white man fear democracy. But this fear cannot be allowed to stand in the way of the only solution which will guarantee racial harmony and freedom for all ... Political division, based on colour, is entirely artificial, and when it disappears so will

---

83   Ibid., vol. 19.
84   Ibid.
85   Ibid., vol. 19, 39–40.
86   Ibid., vol. 19, 48.

the domination of one colour group by another ... This ... is what the ANC if fighting (for). It is a struggle of the African people ... It is a struggle for the right to live.[87]

All defendants followed Mandela's lead in asserting their interpretations and beliefs, rejecting as Mandela had done the laws, censure and categories of the state. Unlike the Treason trial where the defendants accepted the categories of the state (but denied their relevance), the Rivonia defendants rejected the validity of the censures and attacked the system of politics and morality underlying them. Whereas the state portrayed their actions within a decontextualised framework of gratuitous violence and communist conspiracies, the defendants asserted an alternative system of morality and politics in justifying their actions. In doing so, they (re)wrote the history of resistance.

Effects of Rivonia: Domination and Resistance

Rivonia was a powerfully human trial with two languages, two sets of norms and two audiences. Perhaps more than any other political trial in South Africa, it reveals the Janus-faced nature of such trials, signifying both domination and resistance.

For the state, the 'glittering rewards' of the trial saw the immediate elimination of its political foe and significant ideological effects in the confirmation of its censures. The consensus amongst whites was that the accused were guilty of criminal not political acts and had been properly convicted in a fair trial. It was accepted that there had been 'concerted attempt to stage a revolution in South Africa'[88] and that the ANC was a violent and communist-dominated organisation. Few grasped the political and moral context of sabotage, as the censures of communism and violence successfully mystified the real issues of the trial, and shifted the debate from the terrain of political rights to that of senseless, revolutionary violence, criminal communist conspiracies, and law and order.

In reproducing these dominant ideologies in an 'independent' court, the trial contributed to a hardening of white attitudes. In this sense, it was a culmination of a wider ideological campaign against the extra-parliamentary opposition and gave it lasting meaning. It worked for the state because the censures were rooted in real, lived experiences and fears brought about by fundamental shifts in political relations: the events around Sharpeville, the terrorism of POQO, the violence in the decolonisation of Africa and now the admission and proof of actual acts of violence and plans for guerrilla war in the trial. All of this gave material meaning to the censures of the state as whites unified around them.

In the long term, the Rivonia trial initiated a process of social amnesia, signifying the beginning of white memory of the ANC where the censures of violence and communism were merged into the public image of the ANC. It

---

87   Ibid., vol. 19, 19; 54.

88   *Rand Daily Mail*, editorial, 12 June 1964.

also marked the beginning of a white failure to distinguish between violent and non-violent political action and the censure of all oppositional ideas – liberal, social-democratic and socialist – as linked to violence. If the ANC had enjoyed some recognition as representing black aspirations in 1960, it was now regarded as beyond the pale. Even the more liberal Progressive Party concluded by 1966 that calls for consultation with the ANC were an 'electoral liability ... [and] proceeded to condemn African nationalism as a danger on a par with "communism" and "totalitarianism"'.[89] Thus the Rivonia trial was of long-lasting value to the state and could be invoked throughout the ensuing decades to instil the images of violence, communism and revolution as synonymous with the ANC and the national liberation struggle.

In the contested space of the trial, the accused were able to explain their actions and challenge the censures and interpretations of the state. As noted, it was a rare opportunity for the leaders of the ANC and MK, as underground movements, to explain their actions publicly. Importantly, the lifting of restrictions on Mandela allowed full media coverage of his statement.[90] There is little documented on the reaction of black South Africans in those repressive times. However, Hilda Bernstein, communist activist and wife of one of the accused, described it thus:

There is jubilation in the African townships when the speech is read. [It] is a triumph, a vindication breathing confidence over the shattered battlefields, restoring hope in the face of defeat.[91]

Black support at the trial was visibly high, with public galleries packed. Despite a huge police presence and show of force, intimidation and arrest of spectators, the interest did not flag. More than 2,000 people packed Church Square outside the courtroom on the day of sentence with banners proclaiming 'Sentence or no sentence. We stand by our leaders',[92] and Chief Luthuli made the following public statement:

They represent the highest in morality and ethics in the South African political struggles ... Their policies are in accordance with the deepest international principles of brotherhood and humanity; without their leadership, brotherhood and humanity might be blasted out of existence in South Africa for long decades

---

89   B. Hackman, 'Incorporationist Ideology as a Response to Political Party Struggle: The Progressive Party on South Africa 1960–1980', in S. Marks and S. Trapido, *The Politics of Race, Class and Nationalism in Twentieth Century South Africa* (1987) 377.

90   For example, *The Star* devoted two full pages to the statement ('Rivonia: Mandela's Story. "We had to Turn to Violence"', 20 April 1961).

91   Bernstein (note 34 above) 165. Rusty Bernstein was granted bail, allowing him to escape to the United Kingdom.

92   Albertyn (note 2 above) 249–52.

to come. They believe profoundly in justice and reason; when they are locked away, justice and reason will have departed from the South African scene.[93]

An underground pamphlet entitled 'The Message of Rivonia' circulated, describing the trial as follows:

> The trial of the Rivonia men and all those others accused of sabotage will only make the struggle more relentless. We will never surrender – we cannot. We are backed by all of Africa – and the whole world. Nationalist oppression is hated and despised by the majority of people inside the country and everyone outside, White supremacy is doomed.[94]

During the trial, therefore, the battle of ideas was central: political action was justified and alternative interpretations asserted. A local (mostly black) and international audience regarded the accused as heroes, their aspirations as just, their actions vindicated.

Of course, we should not forget that the national democratic movement was ideologically and organisationally weakened by this and other trials in 1964. Without doubt, Rivonia represented a 'momentous defeat for the national liberation struggle. With one blow, the state completed its grip on the political arena, by capturing key leaders of the ANC and MK'.[95] With the elimination of political leadership by imprisonment and exile, and little real depth of organisation in black communities, there was virtually no political resistance to apartheid in South Africa for a decade.

But where there is domination, there is also resistance. In Rivonia, this was present in and outside the courtroom. And in this resistance were the seeds of future struggles. As the accused made history in the courtroom by offering their version of events, so a new history was written and the stories and heroes of Rivonia became the inspiration and lasting rallying point for future struggles, from the first campaign to release our leaders in the early 1970s,[96] to Nelson Mandela walking out of gaol on 11 February 1990. Unlike the Treason trial, whose legal strategies were defensive and sought to rebut the allegations of the state, the Rivonia trial saw a powerful assertion of equality, universal suffrage and non-racial democracy. In this sense, it is Rivonia that drew a deep line in the sand: between domination and resistance, inequality and equality, authoritarianism and democracy. On the one side were white South Africans, whose fears and interests drove them to support a state based on inequality, oppression and injustice. On the other, was a non-negotiable demand for justice, equality and self-determination that was

---

93   Described thus and cited in *Wits Student*, 30 May 1970.

94   'The Message of Rivonia', South African Institute of Race Relations Papers. University of the Witwatersrand.

95   H. Wolpe, *Sechaba*, July 1983.

96   G. Moss, *The New Radicals* (2014) chapter 6.

vindicated 30 years later in 1994. So resistance in the Rivonia trial became the basis for a new set of aspirations in a democratic South Africa.

Conclusion: Domination, Resistance, Transformation

Read as part of a longer story, the Rivonia trial emerges out of post-war global and local struggles around communism, apartheid and self-determination in South Africa. The events that precipitated the trial – the turn to sabotage, the state's authoritarian and repressive response – only make sense in the context of longer struggles around the nature and form of the South African state. Within this relationship of struggle, and of domination and resistance, law takes on changing forms and provides an important space for the expression of power, authority and legitimacy, as well as opposition, resistance and injustice. Despite the repression that surrounds the Rivonia trial, the leadership of the national democratic movement is able to counter the interpretations of the state with its own version of truth and justice. The political trial is simultaneously a place of domination and resistance.

The different forms that this resistance takes, its short- and long-term possibilities, are both historically contingent and variable. It is interesting to contrast the Treason trial with Rivonia. The latter trial is characterised by legal loss, imprisonment and immediate political defeat, whilst the former is signified by legal and (albeit) uneven political victory. Yet it is the legacy of the Rivonia trial that survives to sustain another three decades of struggle. Here it seems that the possibility of legal victory in the Treason trial played a constraining role, as the accused and their lawyers played a necessarily defensive game. Legal defeat was certain in Rivonia, thus enabling the defendants the opportunity of political victory: the ability to tell their own story, on their own terms, in a public court of law. As public record, the story survives, grows and takes on new meanings. As we look back at Rivonia, we no longer see defeat, but an iconic moment in a momentous struggle for justice. The lens of history reverses the trial's content and meaning as equality and non-racial democracy come to the fore, and the inequality of apartheid is criminalised and rendered illegitimate. In the resistance of the Rivonia trial are the seeds of transformation, but it is in the nature of the struggles that succeed the trial that the potential for such transformation is nurtured.

Chapter 7

'The Road to Freedom Passes Through Gaol': The Treason Trial and Rivonia Trial as Political Trials

Mia Swart*

This Court ... is a pointless institution from any point of view. A Single executioner could do all that is needed.[1]

Introduction

The year 2013 was an auspicious one in South African history. It marked the fiftieth anniversary of the Rivonia trial. It was also the year of the death of Nelson Mandela, struggle icon and symbol of South Africa's liberation. In the weeks after Mandela's death, Mandela's statement from the dock during the Rivonia trial[2] was frequently referred to in obituaries.[3] This is but one indication that the Rivonia trial has become integral in popular perceptions of South Africa's freedom struggle, liberation and transition. In many ways Rivonia represented a watershed moment: the moment when the South African justice system was publicly and defiantly called racist and unjust. It is the *public* nature of the political trial that allows it to function not just as an *object* of resistance but also as a space of political critique and a space of struggle. The mere fact that such a trial can attract

---

* I wish to thank the reviewers of this chapter for their helpful and insightful comments.

1 Franz Kafka, *The Trial* (1992) 154.

2 Mandela's speech ended with the famous words: 'During my lifetime, I have dedicated myself to this struggle of the African people. I have fought against white domination, and I have fought against black domination. I have cherished the ideal of a democratic and free society in which all persons live together in harmony and with equal opportunities. It is an ideal which I hope to live for and to achieve. But if needs be, it is an ideal for which I am prepared to die.' In his book Mandela, *The Authorised Biography* (1999) Anthony Sampson described the speech as the most effective speech of Mandela's career.

3 See for example the obituary by George Bizos, 'Mandela's Trial and Tribulations', *Mail & Guardian*, 6 December 2013, available at http://mg.co.za/article/2013-12-06-00-geo rge-bizos-mandelas-trial-and-tribulations/. See also Paul Vallely 'Nelson Mandela Obituary: Madiba – the Father of South African Democracy', *Independent*, 6 December 2013, available at http://www.independent.co.uk/news/obituaries/nelson-mandela-obituary-madiba--the-fa ther-of-south-african-democracy-8654396.html.

significant publicity to the cause of the accused means that a trial of this kind can be politically instrumentalised in a positive way for the accused.

During the Defiance Campaign protestors against the judicialisation of the protests held up posters proclaiming 'The Road to Freedom Passes through Gaol'.[4] The demonstrations accompanying political trials as well as the media coverage of the trials reflected and heightened the political value of the trial. It was clear to the protestors that the state was engaged in the criminalisation of the political opposition through trials.

Those who stigmatise political trials fail to acknowledge the positive ripple effects of such trials when such trials allow the accused to strategically use the trial process in their favour. I will conclude that the positive publicity benefits of a political trial will always be limited because it will be circumscribed by what the state allows. In spite of the different kinds of political trials and in spite of the fact that the particular political circumstances surrounding such trials will always differ, the state will almost always dictate the outcome of the trial. Although some consequences of political trial might be unforeseen, the state always wins. What was remarkable about the Treason and Rivonia trials, however, was that clever and creative defence lawyering could achieve a more powerful public impact than the state could have foreseen. The Treason trial is a particularly atypical form of political trial since the accused were all acquitted.

Significantly, the term political trial has been applied in a wide variety of contexts. Albertyn writes that political trials can occur in authoritarian regimes as well as liberal democracies. She points out that 'they have been conducted under the most rigorous and substantive requirements of the rule of law and in conditions where the trial form has provided a flimsy veneer of legality over an underlying reality of violence and torture'.[5] Shklar uses Nuremberg as an example of a classic political trial that served liberal ends because of its implicit promotion of legalistic values to lay the foundation for future constitutional politics.[6]

This chapter is primarily concerned with the notion of the 'political trial' and the extent to which this label applied to the Rivonia and Treason trials respectively. But trials are not only a means of deciding political disputes. The meaning or definition of the concept of the political trial in itself is also strongly contested. The contested nature of the concept of the political trial will first be discussed.

After an examination of the history and meaning of the term 'political trial' I will distinguish between different kinds of political trials after which I will turn to an analysis of the extent to which the Rivonia trial and the Treason trial merit the

---

4   The slogan refers to public protests during the Defiance Campaign of the early 1950s. During the preliminary examination in the magistrate's court the long corridors of the buildings were packed with supporters with slogans such as these. See also George Bizos, *21 Icons*, available at http://www.21icons.com/twentyone-icons/profile/george-bizos.

5   Cathi Albertyn, 'A Critical Analysis of Political Trials in South Africa', unpublished PhD thesis (1988), 1.

6   Judith Shklar, *Legalism: Law, Morals and Political Trials*, 2nd edn (1986).

description of a political trial. The question of whether and to what extent the trials also benefitted the ANC will receive attention.

What is a Political Trial?

What might political trials teach us about our normative commitment to legality and the rule of law? Barbara Falk provides one answer to this question: when legal norms are followed, rather than deliberately, covertly or systemically undermined, the legitimacy of legal decisions is enhanced.[7] Whereas the political direction and manipulation of courts is a hallmark of authoritarian regimes, law and politics are *not* as separate in liberal democracies as one might expect.

The term political trial is often used quite freely and loosely.[8] Eric Posner writes that the term political trial may refer to any trial in which a person is tried for engaging in political opposition. In Posner's view, a trial is also characterised as political when it presents a question that transcends the narrow issue of guilt or innocence by implicating larger societal and cultural considerations.[9] This type of trial can of course also take place within a democratic state. This can also be called the 'democratic' version of the political trial that Albertyn referred to when she stated that political trials can also take place in liberal states. This understanding of the term 'political trial' extends the applicability of the term to cases one would not traditionally consider to merit the description of a political trial.

While there might be some truth in the proposition that all trials contain elements of the political in that they reflect the values of the political system within which

---

7   Barbara Falk, *Making Sense of Political Trials, Causes and Categories* (2008) 2 Occasional Paper No. VIII available at http://munkschool.utoronto.ca/wp-content/uploads/2013/05/Making_Sense.pdf.

8   The term 'political trial' has been used to describe trials such as the corruption trial of Jacob Zuma. See *Jacob Gedleyihlekisa Zuma v National Directorate of Public Prosecutions* Case 8652/08. See in this regard, Mia Swart, 'Why is Zuma's Trial "'Political"?', *Mail & Guardian*, 1 August 2008. Davis described the Zuma case as proof that judicial institutions in South Africa were engulfed by party political contest. It emerged from the evidence used for the conviction of Schabir Shaik that in the time between October 1995 and September 2002, Shaik made substantial payments of money to Zuma. It was announced in 2005 that the NPA would prosecute Zuma. This decision led to numerous litigation attempts to ensure that Zuma would not be prosecuted. According to Davis and Le Roux 'the case was set up in the public discourse as a case of vicious factional party politics being fought out in the courts'. See Dennis Davis and Michelle le Roux, *Precedent and Possibility: The (Ab)use of Law in South Africa* (2009) 190–94.

9   Eric Posner 'Political Trials in Domestic and International Law', *Duke Law Journal* 55 (2005) available at http://scholarship.law.duke.edu/cgi/viewcontent.cgi?article=1266&context=dlj.

courts operate, such a generic approach does not allow us to retrieve features unique to the concept of the political trial and multifaceted manifestations.[10]

Political trials fall on the faultline of law and politics.[11] The term political trial is notoriously difficult to define.[12] Whereas some authors distinguish between various forms of political trials, Falk sets out a list of criteria she considers potential markers of political trials. These criteria include: an obvious political motive for the trial, the fact that the accused are political enemies of the state, the trial is ideologised and sensationalised by the media, the use of secret evidence, etc.[13] But she emphasises that the historical and political context and the facts of a case are ultimately more determinative of whether a trial is a political trial.

In political theory the term 'political trial' has a specific meaning. The jurist Otto Kirchheimer wrote in his seminal study *Political Justice: The Use of Legal Procedures*:[14] 'Throughout the modern era, whatever the dominant legal system, both governments and private groups have tried to enlist the support of the courts for upholding or shifting the balance of political power.'[15] Kirchheimer suggests that political trials are trials in which 'the courts eliminate a political foe of the regime according to some prearranged rules'.[16]

To Kirchheimer the prototype of a political trial has been the criminal trial of a political adversary for political reasons.[17] Kirchheimer argued that political trials serve to legitimise state action most successfully when the legal procedures coincide with the dictates of the rule of law. It can be argued that this analysis applies especially to the South African political trials under Apartheid. Ironically, in the case of the Treason trial and Rivonia trial the Apartheid state could have benefitted more if these trials departed more from the rule of law. Albertyn refers to the 'still dominant ideology of the rule of law' at the time of the Treason trial.[18] The fact that some minimal fair trial guarantees were upheld could have helped the trials to appear more legitimate. The trials would not have been decided the way they were under a substantial 'thick' understanding of the rule of law.[19]

---

10   Falk (note 7) 3.

11   See Shklar (note 6).

12   Since the term political is often used too loosely, it is important to clarify terminology. In discussions on political trials, the following terms are often used interchangeably with the term political trial: show trials, security trials and partisan trials.

13   Falk (note 7) 4.

14   Otto Kirchheimer, *Political Justice: The Use of Legal Procedure for Political Ends* (1961).

15   Ibid., 47.

16   Ibid.

17   Kirchheimer (note 14) 46.

18   Albertyn (note 5) 129.

19   See Tom Bingham, *The Rule of Law* (2011).

Of relevance here is what the scholar Ronen Shamir identified as the legitimising role of 'landmark decisions'.[20] Shamir explores how courts can support the dominant political interests and at the same time appear impartial.[21] In the context of the Israeli occupation Shamir shows how in the majority of the cases the Israeli High Court of Justice upholds the decisions of executive, however, in order to maintain the legitimacy of the court, it intervenes in a few landmark cases.[22] He argues that the majority of landmark decisions of this kind in Israel were symbolic rather than substantive.

Following Christensen I will argue that a distinction should be made between those political trials which are totally unsupported by law and those which, while proceeding with a political as well as a legal agenda, are within the rule of law.[23] It can be argued that both the Treason trial and the Rivonia trial took place within a context of procedural rule of law but not substantive rule of law.[24] To an extent the Rivonia trial even lacked aspects of the procedural rule of law.[25]

Although the Rivonia and Treason trials may be the best documented of South Africa's political trials during Apartheid, it is important to keep in mind that there were many other 'political' trials that did not receive the same attention. Ahmed Kathrada has pointed out that the Rivonia trial overshadowed many other important trials.[26] It will be clear from this chapter that one can learn as much from the Treason trial as from the Rivonia trial.

---

20 Ronen Shamir, '"Landmark Cases" and the Reproduction of Legitimacy: The Case of Israel's High Court of Justice', *Law and Society Review* 24 3 (1990).

21 Ibid., 783.

22 Since the beginning of the occupation residents of the West Bank have been allowed to petition the High Court of Justice to ask the court to review a range of state actions and policies. See *Dawikat et al v Government of Israel* (1979) as an example of such a 'landmark case'. Ibid., 784.

23 R. Christensen, 'A Political Theory of Political Trials', *Journal of Criminal Law and Criminology* (Summer 1983) 551.

24 For more on this distinction see Bingham (note 19).

25 The substantive version of the rule of law has also been referred to as the 'thick' version of the rule of law whereas the procedural version of the rule of law has been described as the 'thin' version of the rule of law. 'A "thicker" version of the rule of law denies that mere procedural formality can protect individuals or groups from oppression and insists that effective rule of law requires a deeper set of constitutional and legal norms.' See Meryl Chertoff and Michael Green, 'Revitalising the Rule of Law', *Harvard International Review*, 30 September 2012.

26 Khadija Patel, 'Rivonia Treason Trial: Commemorating a Vital Turn in SA History', *Daily Maverick*, 25 November 2013.

Typologies of 'Political Trials'

To Kirchheimer, political trials are clearly about using judicial devices to attain political objectives. Political trials are instances in which 'court action is called upon to exert influence on the distribution of political power'.[27] It is striking that Kirchheimer therefore does not necessarily define political trials as trials which are used for the sole purpose of consolidating the power of the state. It is clear that Kirchheimer defined political trials in quite a broad way.

Rather than accepting one definition of 'political trials', scholars have distinguished between different types of political trials. Christensen, for example, differentiates between political 'trials' (involving violations of due process guarantees), the 'political' trial (camouflaged as a criminal trial) and the politically motivated political trial.[28] The distinction between the second and third of these kinds of trials can of course be very subtle.

I will primarily distinguish between four kinds of political trials: the first species of political trial I will be concerned with is the political trial in the strict sense of the term. Such trials are characterised by the fact that they are completely arbitrary[29] and that all standards of fairness, justice and due process are disregarded during such trials. Notorious political trials of this kind (also called partisan trials) would be the trials by the *Volksgericht* in Nazi Germany and the purge trials of Stalinist Russia, where many of the judges, prosecutors and defence attorneys served as instruments of terror and propaganda for totalitarian systems in which the legal process and the space of the courtroom are mobilised to rationalise and justify the rule of the absolutely corrupt.[30] Kirchheimer argues that the image-creating effect of certain instruments of a political system serve the purpose of manipulating and rallying public opinion in accordance with the political needs of the moment.[31] Leora Bilsky refers to these kinds of political trials when she describes political trials as sham legal proceedings designed by authorities to dramatise specific political campaigns and/or to eliminate prominent individuals.[32]

A second type of political trial is the trial initiated as a result of particular kinds of political legislation. It usually takes the form of a criminal prosecution of a political opponent of the ruling party for breach of a law designed to ensure

---

27　Ibid.

28　Christensen further categorises political trials into four categories: trials of dissenters; trials of corruption; trials of nationalists; and trials of regimes. Christensen (note 23) 554.

29　I will heed the warning of Noam Chomsky who wrote that comparisons with Nazi Germany evoke such ghastly memories that rational discussion becomes impossible. Chomsky, Paul Lauter and Florence Howe, 'Reflections on a Political Trial', *New York Review of Books*, 22 August 1968.

30　Christensen (note 23) 547.

31　Kirchheimer (note 14) 424.

32　Leora Bilsky, 'Political Trials', in *International Encyclopedia of the Social and Behavioral Sciences*, 2nd edn (2014).

the maintenance of the status quo, generally termed a 'security law'. Trials that fall into this second category of political trials do not violate the rule of law to the same extent as the first or 'pure' kind of political trial. It can be said that whereas the first type of trial does not even possess the veneer of the procedural rule of law, the second type of trial can at least claim to observe the procedural rule of law. Typical examples of such forms of political legislation in the South African context would include 'security' legislation and anti-communism legislation such as the Suppression of Communism Act,[33] trials initiated under anti-terrorism legislation such as the 1967 terrorism trials under the Terrorism Act[34] and legislation implementing states of emergency. Political legislation of this kind is often drafted very widely and vaguely to encapsulate almost any type of behaviour the state finds undesirable. The trial of Julius and Ethel Rosenberg was an example of this kind of trial.[35] In the view of Christensen post-war trials such as the trial of Dreyfus and that of the Rosenbergs can be described as 'products of hysteria'.[36] Within this category the state can allow for varying degrees of due process ranging from trials in which fair trial guarantees are only nominally observed to trials in which good lawyering still have some limited ability to affect the fate of the accused.

The third kind of political trial is the trial that may take the form of a defamation action designed to destroy the credibility of a political figure, what Kirchheimer called the 'derivative political trial'. In certain circumstances the prosecution of an ordinary criminal offence could also be a 'political trial'. This would be the case if a trial attracts a significant amount of public attention or when a crime was motivated by race or gender discrimination, for example. Examples of such trials would include the O.J. Simpson trial, the Kastner trial in Israel,[37] and the trial of Lorena Bobbit.[38]

---

33   No. 44 of 1950.

34   No. 83 of 1967.

35   The US Supreme Court, in a six-to three decision, refused to stay the execution of the Rosenbergs. President Eisenhower refused clemency, explaining that 'the Rosenbergs have received the benefit of every safeguard which American justice can provide ... I can only say that, by immeasurably increasing the chances of atomic war, the Rosenbergs may have condemned to death tens of millions of innocent people all over the world'. Christensen (note 23) 551.

36   Ibid., 550.

37   Leora Bilsky, 'Justice or Reconciliation: The Politicisation of the Holocaust in the Kastner Trial', in Emilios Christodoulids and Scott Veitch (eds) *Lethe's Law* (2001).

38   As Chloe Georas writes in this volume, both the prosecution and the defence succeeded in portraying Lorena Bobbit in terms of stereotypes. The defence ultimately racialises Lorena by 'inscribing her in a cultural space of stupidity, backwardness and psychotic irrationality'. Lorena's infantilisation as a 'woman who was young, almost child-like in terms of her lack of life experiences' invites a paternalistic gaze to protect her pathologised vulnerability and completely obscures the complex agency of her actions. The

I argue that the Apartheid era political trials described in this chapter constitute a fourth form of political trial. Trials such as the Rivonia trial and Treason trial fall into a category of their own because they contained elements of the other three forms of political trials but can be distinguished in one critical way: the fact that the accused in the Treason Trial were acquitted means that, unlike in the case of other political trials, the outcomes were not a fait accompli.

Throughout the Apartheid era there was a widely held belief that the South African Apartheid judiciary was independent. As a retired judge wrote, 'It is high time that the world realised the South African judiciary is independent and that its judges are not amenable to pressure from government, public or another source'.[39] According to Cathi Albertyn, the debate on the political trial in South Africa is complicated by the fact that judicial decisions in South Africa were not the result of a conspirational collusion between government and the judiciary. It has been suggested that judicial decisions should rather be understood as the result of a more complex process. Although the South African judiciary had to uphold (at least cosmetically) basic fair trial standards, the outcome of trials were deeply influenced by the fact that the judges shared the ideologies of those in power.[40] The more political the legislation was the judges had to interpret, the more the backgrounds and beliefs of the judges determined the outcome of a case.[41]

The term political trial is not necessarily pejorative and political trials do not always serve the interests of the state or the prosecution. Occasionally a defendant and a defendant's lawyers can reconfigure and appropriate the discursive and spatial openness of the courtroom in their programme to contest the normative legitimacy of the political order, to subvert or undermine the legal system, and generate political capital for their political goals. With the exception of the first category (the *Volksgericht* variety), all political trials can, to varying extents, be re-signified and used by the defence.

Bilsky shares the view of various scholars[42] that trials, whether domestic, international or transnational, inevitably have political consequences. If this is

---

prosecution reifies Lorena as belonging to a culture of lawlessness, barbarity and chaos where the 'biggest knife wins'.

39   Judge President of the Natal Provincial Division, Frances Boome.

40   Albertyn (note 5).

41   See the study by Hugh Corder on the executive mindedness of South Africa's judiciary in the early part of the twentieth century. Hugh Corder, *Judges at Work: The Role and Attitudes of the South African Appellate Judiciary 1910–1950* (1984). See also Christopher Forsyth, *In Danger for Their Talents: A Study of the Appellate Division of the Supreme Court of South Africa from 1950–80* (1985).

42   Bilsky (note 32) refers to Shklar, Douglas, and Nouwen and Werner in this regard. See J. Shklar, *Legalism: Law, Morals, and Political Trials* (1964); Lawrence Douglas, 'Shattering Nuremberg, Toward a Jurisprudence of Atrocity', *Harvard International Review*, 21 November 2007; Sarah Nouwen, and Wouter Werner 'Doing Justice to the Political: The International Criminal Court in Uganda and Sudan', *European Journal of International Law* 21:4 (2012) 941–65.

the case, the question of whether a trial is political or not obscures more than it reveals. In essence she argues that the characterisation of a trial as a political trial is not inherently pejorative. Instead, she argues, we should ask what sort of politics each type of trial promotes, and what kind of procedures and legal doctrines are available to the court to balance the politics while fighting niches of immunity.[43]

Christensen agrees that political trials can have positive value. In his opinion:

> Political trials serve a free society by bringing together for public consideration the basic contradictions which arise from the clash of conflicting values and loyalties. The tensions over the relationship of the private to the public realms, the rightness of policy and of dissent, the nature of representation, and the legitimacy of government are all present in any political system. Especially in crises, these tensions must be faced.[44]

In the Treason and the Rivonia trials 'the accused became the accusers'.[45] The trials would therefore meet Christensen's criteria of trials that serve a free society.

The *Volksgericht* (1934–1945) and Stalinist Show Trials (1936–1938)

The German *Volksgericht* or People's Court[46] was essentially Hitler's court. The court was created by Hitler in 1934 as a *Sondergericht* or special court. The court was created as a direct result of the controversy surrounding the Reichstag fire and Hitler's dissatisfaction with the fact that all but one of the accused in the so-called Reichstag fire trial were acquitted.[47] An important function of the court was to intimidate the German public. The court was clearly an instrument of terror and propaganda. This section will merely serve to highlight some of the most egregiously political features of this court.

Although the Nazis intended to make the *Volksgericht* a reliable instrument for conducting propaganda trials, the use of professional jurists on the court indicated that (at least initially) they were hesitant to violate the tradition of (or at least the perception of) an independent judiciary.[48] This changed rapidly as

---

43 Bilsky (note 32).

44 Christensen (note 23) 577.

45 See Bizos (note 3).

46 The German word Volk is often translated as 'nation' and has strong nationalistic connotations.

47 Hitler hoped to prove the existence of a communist conspiracy. William Sweet, 'The Volksgericht', *Journal of Modern History* (June 1974)

48 Ibid.

Hitler consolidated his grip on power. Christensen points out that five of the seven People's Court judges were chosen from the Nazi Party, the SS or the military.[49]

As pointed out by William Sweet, the *Volksgericht* was 'an entirely constitutional creation'.[50] Article 105 of the Weimar Constitution forbade the creation of courts for the trial of individually determined cases, but not special courts for trying general categories of cases.[51] The Court had jurisdiction over 'political offences' and primarily passed judgement on cases including treason against the Third Reich.[52] The court often handed down a large number of death sentences, especially under Judge-President Roland Freisler. With very rare exceptions, the court almost always sided with the prosecution. Significantly, defence attorneys had to get permission to appear before the court and could be disqualified from the start of a trial. Even if defence counsel was admitted, counsel for the defence usually remained silent during trials. There was no possibility of appealing a judgment. Furthermore, Hitler and Goering retained the right to quash the criminal proceedings in the event the result would be unfavourable.[53]

The *Volksgericht* was initially created only as a 'temporary expedient'[54] and later made permanent. It was only after 1940 that the court adopted prejudicial and inquisitorial procedures. The famous *Volksgericht* trial of Sophie Scholl and her fellow White Rose activists[55] illustrates the working of the *Volksgericht* at its most aggressively prejudicial stage. This trial has been described as even less than a show trial because the entire trial was concluded in less than an hour without evidence being presented or any arguments being made on either side.

The show trials that took place during Stalin's rule of the USSR also constitute examples of trials that were so far removed from any notion of substantive and procedural legality that they can be described as completely arbitrary. The purpose of these trials was to target Stalin's enemies – both real and perceived. For example, anyone associated with Trotsky was considered an enemy of Stalin, and this brought with it imprisonment and death. The NKVD[56] (the law enforcement agency of the Soviet Union) was handed a list of those who were labelled 'enemies of the state' – effectively the Bolshevik Party's Old Guard. Stalin viewed these men as potential rivals and they were charged with plotting to kill him. Anyone associated with these men was also under suspicion.

---

49   Christensen (note 23) 552.

50   Sweet (note 47) 314.

51   Ibid.

52   Ibid., 315–16.

53   Christensen (note 23) 552, citing G. Dimitrov, *The Reichstag Fire Trial* (1969).

54   It was pointed out that the Volksgericht borrowed its prosecution staff from the Reichsgericht and that its judges retained positions on other courts. Sweet (note 47) citing Hans Richter, 'Das Gesetz zur Anderung von Vorschriften des Strafrechts vom 24. 4. 34', *Deutsche Justiz* 96 (1934) 604.

55   See Jacob Hornberger, 'The White Rose – A Lesson in Dissent', available at http:// www.jewishvirtuallibrary.org/jsource/Holocaust/rose.html.

56   Narodny Komissariat Vnutrennikh Del or People's Commissariat for Internal Affairs.

The first trial that formed part of the 'Moscow trials' took place in 1936.[57] The trial involved 16 members of the 'Trotskyite-Kamenevite-Zinovievite-Leftist-Counter-Revolutionary Bloc'.[58] The two main defendants were Grigory Zinoviev and Lev Kamenev. The primary accusations against the defendants were that they had, in alliance with Trotsky, been involved in the assassination of Sergey Kirov in 1934, and of plotting to kill Stalin. After confessing to the charges, all were sentenced to death and executed.[59]

The show trials had to prove the guilt of the defendants, preferably with a very public admission of betraying the revolution and therefore the people.[60] The trials were carefully staged. If defendants refused to 'cooperate', i.e., to admit guilt for their alleged and mostly fabricated crimes, they did not go on public trial, but suffered execution nonetheless. Interestingly, foreign journalists were invited to these highly public trials and were there to prove to those in the USSR that 'enemies of the state' still existed and that leaders such as Stalin were at risk. After the conclusion of these show trials, Stalin had managed to bring both the party and the public to complete submission to his rule.

The Treason Trial

The Treason trial was the longest and probably the most complex political trial in South African history. It was also the first South African treason trial to be heard in conditions of peace. For the ANC the case had important political implications.

If one compares the Rivonia and Treason trials one cannot fail to be struck by the difference in outcome of the two trials: whereas all the defendants in the Treason trial were acquitted, most of the accused in the Rivonia trial, including such struggle stalwarts as Nelson Mandela, Walter Sisulu and Ahmed Kathrada, were convicted, narrowly escaped the death penalty and were sentenced to life imprisonment. The juxtaposition of the 1963 Rivonia trial and the five-year-long Treason trial, which concluded in 1962, raises the obvious question: given the close proximity in time, how could the outcome of the Treason trial have been so different from the Rivonia trial? Although this question will receive attention, it will not form the focus of this chapter.

In his brilliant analysis of the Treason trial, Stephan Clingman discusses two motivations the state might have had for initiating the trial: first, the state, alarmed at the swell of resistance politics through the 1950s, including the Defiance

---

57   See K R Bolton 'The Moscow Trials in Historical Perspective', Counter Currents publishing available at http://www.counter-currents.com/2013/02/the-moscow-trials-in-his torical-context/

58   Ibid.

59   Ibid.

60   'The Show Trials in the USSR' available at http://www.historylearningsite.co.uk/ ussr_show_trials.htm.

Campaign and the Congress of the People, 'felt a compelling need to counteract and literally delegitimise' resistance politics.[61] Second, there was the backdrop of the Cold War which increased the state's interest in proving that communism motivated the actions of the accused. In the view of Clingman these motivations helped to legitimise the South African state and its policy of Apartheid.[62]

As Albertyn highlights, the censure and discourses on communism in South Africa in the 1950s 'had a distinctive set of meanings, interpretations and targets'.[63] It was clear from this that the Suppression of Communism Act was not merely a means to control a few communists but a weapon to suppress all extra-parliamentary dissent.[64] Communists were identified as those who supported multi-racial and integrated society. As is typical of security legislation, the Suppression of Communism Act created an extremely wide definition of terrorism. The definition included any doctrine or scheme:

> Which aims at bringing about any political, industrial, social or economic change within the Union by the promotion of disturbance and disorder ... unlawful actions or omissions ... or which aims at the encouragement of feelings of hostility between European and non-European races of the Union the consequences of which are calculated to further the achievement of one of the aims of any object referred to (in the definition).[65]

In December 1956, the state arrested 156 leaders of the Congress Alliance and charged them with treason.[66] In the view of Albertyn, this meant that the state was finally 'taking the struggle into the courtroom'.[67] From the beginning the charge of treason was problematic for the state and it struggled to formulate an indictment. The initial indictment was withdrawn after two months as a result of the defence's attack on the indictment. Of the initial group of 91 only 30 went to trial.[68] The defence had already secured a small victory against the government at the start of a widely followed juridico-political event. The strategy of Maisels QC was to challenge the charges on both legal and procedural grounds. This led to successive

---

61   Stephan Clingman, 'Writing the South African Treason Trial', *Current Writing* 22:2 (2010), available at http://www.thefreelibrary.com/Writing+the+South+African+trea son+trial.-a0244951480.

62   Ibid.

63   Albertyn (note 5) 108.

64   Ibid.

65   Section 1 (1) 2 9b) and (d) of the Suppression of Communism Act no. 44 of 1950.

66   The 156 people included almost the entire executive of the African National Congress (ANC), Congress of Democrats, South African Indian Congress, Coloured People's Congress, and the South African Congress of Trade Unions (collectively known as the Congress Alliance).

67   Albertyn (note 5) 133.

68   The indictment against the others were quashed after the state did not give further particulars.

changes to the indictment as well as the nature and admissibility of evidence. This strategy undermined the state's case from early on. Clingman writes, 'From the start the defence was resolute and relentless'.[69]

The defence relied on the fact that despite the fact that communism was censured and the advocacy of equal rights and equality was similarly censured, it was technically not unlawful to promote or seek to achieve this, except by unlawful methods.[70] But by charging the accused with treason the prosecution sought to demonstrate that the advocacy and demand for equal rights and a multi-racial society was inevitably connected to unlawful means (violence) and an unlawful end (the achievement of a communist state). The essence of the charge was that there was a countrywide conspiracy that:

> the accused (acting in concert and through the instrumentality of their organisations) … prepared to subvert the existing state by illegal means including the use of force and violence; and to replace the existing state with a state founded on the principles differing fundamentally from those on which the present state is constituted.[71]

The main issues at the trial crystallised into whether there had been such a conspiracy and whether the policy of the ANC and the Congress Alliance was one of violence. Essentially the question was limited to whether the policy of the ANC was one of violence. It was the exceptional skills of the defence counsel, which led the court to limit and constrain the legal question in this way. The prosecution argued that the course taken by the accused and the belief in 'freedom in our lifetime' would inevitably result in a violent collision with the state. On its part, the defence described the trial as political right from the start. Vernon Berrange, for the accused, argued that the trial constituted an attempt to silence and outlaw the ideas held by the accused. The defence to the charge of violence was straightforward:

> The Defence case will be that it was not the policy of the ANC, or of the other organisations … to use violence against the state. On the contrary the defence will show that all these organisations had deliberately decided to pursue their ends by peaceful means only.[72]

Stephan Clingman describes Maisels' approach. Essentially Maisels believed that the defence case had to be run on legal and not political grounds.[73] Adopting such

69   Albertyn (note 5) 125.
70   Ibid.
71   Treason Trial Bulletin no. 1 at 3.
72   Maisels Opening Statement, Treason Trial Bulletin, 1959
73   Clingman (note 60).

a perspective might have seemed counterintuitive in what was so far the major political trial of the century in South Africa. In Clingman's view:

> it was also a perspective based on a certain reading and an intention to author the trial. The allegations were already a text – but the question was, did the prosecution understand the legal implications of its own narrative?[74]

On 29 March 1961 the state's argument was interrupted by Judge Rumpff when he said that the state failed to prove its case since it did not prove the necessary facts.[75] On the question of communism it was found that the ANC and Congress Alliance were:

> working to replace the existing state with a fundamentally different form of state based on the demands of the Freedom Charter ... (It) had not been proven that the form of state pictured in the Freedom Charter (was) a communist state.[76]

The court was not convinced that the ANC had acquired a policy causing it to cross the dividing line between non-communism and communism in the spectrum of socialist belief.[77]

The defence succeeded in their argument that their methods were not violent. It can however be asked whether the defence argument and strategy was a true representation of their goals and motives.[78] It was already clear at the time of the Treason trial that the ANC planned to resort to violence since peaceful methods of resistance were not succeeding. It is interesting that the armed wing of the ANC, Umkhonto we Sizwe (MK), was established on 16 December 1961. Nelson Mandela was one of its co-founders.[79]

Clingman writes the following on the mood at the conclusion of the trial:

> And that too meant this was catharsis: a moment of release and purgation, of transcendence and renewed promise filled with the significance of an experience

---

74   Ibid.

75   Albertyn (note 5) 125.

76   Rumpff J Judgment at 4–5.

77   Rumpff J, Reasons for Judgment at 60.

78   See Albertyn (note 5) 125.

79   In his Rivonia defence in 1964, Mandela justified the establishment of MK as follows: 'Firstly, we believed that as a result of Government policy, violence by the African people had become inevitable, and that unless responsible leadership was given to canalise and control the feelings of our people, there would be outbreaks of terrorism which would produce an intensity of bitterness and hostility between the various races of this country which is not produced even by war.' See Mandela's Statement from the dock, available at http://www.anc.org.za/show.php?id=3430.

whose result could well have been otherwise. This was why, at the end of the trial, Isie Maisels and Bram Fischer were lifted on the shoulders of the accused.[80]

After the trial and the subsequent State of Emergency and banning of the opposition movements, the ANC went underground and adopted a version of the armed struggle it had been accused of.[81] The scene for this strategy was set by the creation of MK towards the end of the Treason trial. The significance of the Treason trial lay partly in the definite emergence of a black opposition after the trial.[82] Anthony Sampson, who observed the trial, traced the gradual disillusion and hardening of African leaders against white rule back to the Treason trial. The defence would pay a high price for its ingenuity and success in the Treason trial. The state's determination to clamp down on its opponents was strengthened after this trial and played itself out in the Rivonia trial.

The extent to which the trial could be seen as a failure for government depended on the publication of the case which of course affected the level of awareness of the general public. The coverage the case received in the South African media 'strengthened' the government's case and political message. The initial arrests were front page news and the progress of the trial was widely reported in the Afrikaans and English press. According to Young the local media coverage took place in a complex political context where the public was both ally and adversary.[83] Whereas the local media coverage reflected the limitations of political news coverage in South Africa, the international media played a crucial and critical role in promoting the ANC's cause. The international media showed an unusual degree of interest in the case. The international media coverage of the trials played a significant role in increasing international pressure on the Apartheid government. Newspapers such as the *New York Times* and the *Guardian* covered the trials from the start.[84] Commenting on the Rivonia trial, the *New York Times* wrote: 'Most of the world regards the convicted men as … the George Washingtons and Benjamin Franklins of South Africa, not criminals deserving punishment'.[85]

In spite of the ability of the defence to successfully exploit the political nature of the case and in spite of the acquittal, the case was not an unmitigated victory for the defence. Even though the state lost the case the state was successful in polarising political relations in many ways. Ironically the detention and trial also allowed the ANC leaders to consult and decide on the direction of their struggle.[86]

---

80   Clingman (note 60).

81   Ibid.

82   Anthony Sampson, *The Treason Cage* (1958).

83   Sandra Young, 'Rehearsing Trauma: The Reader as Interrogator in Prison Narratives', *Journal of Literary Studies* (July 2013).

84   See Kenneth S. Broun, *Saving Nelson Mandela: The Rivonia Trial and The Fate of South Africa* (2012).

85   http://www.anc.org.za/show.php?id=3764.

86   Elinor Sisulu *Walter & Albertina Sisulu* (2011)

It can be argued that in the same way Hitler set up special courts in reaction to the Reichstag trial, the Apartheid government set up the Rivonia trial in reaction to the Treason trial. According to Albertyn the costs and benefits were equally weighed against each other.[87] Significantly, the banning of the ANC midway through the proceedings in 1960 meant that by the end of the trial the trial was about an organisation that no longer had legal existence. Because of the repressive laws enacted during the time of the trial South Africa became a police state by the time the trial was concluded. Nelson Mandela wrote that the outcome of the Treason trial pushed the South African government into a new and heightened level of conflict with anti-Apartheid movements: 'During the Treason Trial, there were no examples of individuals being isolated, beaten and tortured in order to elicit information. All of those things became commonplace shortly thereafter.'[88] After the Sharpeville massacre a State of Emergency was proclaimed by the government and over 20,000 people were detained. By the end of the Treason trial the South African state had changed the political narrative and the political framework and so had the South African resistance. The fact that the accused in the Rivonia trial offered a political rather than legal defence was an indication of this new narrative. The shift corresponded with the changed logic and the changed narrative of the time.

Although the Treason trial was intended and constructed to be a major show trial it did not turn out to be such a trial. Falk writes that political trials determine verdicts on the basis of 'evidence organised into a prosecutorial metanarrative'.[89] To a great extent, the Treason trial however departed from the narrative the prosecution intended to construct.

Clingman described the trial as a last attempt, at least in the South African judicial context, to redeem qualities of progress and reason.[90] The inability of the state to frame charges, the length of the trial, the fact that the defence was able to exploit the legal procedure to their benefit and the eventual acquittal of the accused amounted to a failure for the state.[91] The tactics of the defence helped to contest the criminalising 'vocabulary' of the state security system.[92] But the political clampdown on the opposition that followed the trial meant that the authoritarian state always wins.

---

87   Ibid.
88   Nelson Mandela, *Long Walk to Freedom* (1994).
89   Falk (note 7) 10.
90   Clingman (note 60).
91   Ibid.
92   Young (note 82).

The Rivonia Trial

The Rivonia trial has been described as 'the trial that changed South Africa'.[93] The timing of the trial was important. The fact that the trial followed about five years after the Treason trial had important historical consequences. As David Dyzenhaus writes, the 1950s was the decade in which the Apartheid divide was legislated; in the 1960s, the security apparatus to repress opposition to Apartheid was legislated and eventually consolidated.[94] The trial followed the Sharpeville massacre and the declaration of the subsequent State of Emergency in March 1960. The trial was also preceded by an auspicious historical event: the declaration of South Africa as a republic on 21 March 1961. Nationalistic sentiments ran high. State repression of anyone resisting the policies of the Apartheid state was at its most intense. Since being outlawed in April 1960, the ANC had been operating underground, one month after the Sharpeville massacre of 67 protestors by police.

In contrast with the Treason trial, the accused were not charged with treason but with two counts of sabotage. The state believed that a charge of sabotage would prevent claims that the trial was a 'Reichstag trial'.[95] It has been argued that the reason for the state's sensitivity to this issue was its consciousness of the foreign media's criticism of the Treason trial.[96] Many years after the trial the prosecutor Percy Yutar explained why treason was not included in the charges. In his view the fact that the Treason trial ended disastrously with the acquittal of all the accused was a major reason for switching the charge from treason to sabotage.[97]

The 11 defendants were Nelson Mandela, Walter Sisulu, Govan Mbeki, James Kantor, Raymond Mhlaba, Andrew Mlangeni, Lionel Bernstein, Elias Motsoaledi, Ahmed Kathrada, Bob Hepple and Denis Goldberg. The defence team comprised of Joel Joffe (the instructing attorney); Bram Fischer QC (leading the defence) as well as Vernon Berrange, Arthur Chaskalson and George Bizos (Junior Counsel). The trial judge was Justice Quartus de Wet. The prosecution was led by Dr Percy Yutar.

Mandela and his fellow defendants were charged with 221 acts of sabotage designed to 'ferment violent revolution'.[98] The initial charge sheet alleged 192 separate acts under the Sabotage Act and a third charge in terms of the Suppression of Communism Act.[99] The fourth charge concerned the financing of MK activities. It was alleged that the accused had conspired to acts of guerilla warfare, giving

---

93   Joel Joffe, *The State v Nelson Mandela: The Trial that Changed South Africa* (2013).
94   David Dyzenhaus, '"With the Benefit of Hindsight": Dilemmas of Legality', in Scott Veitch (ed.) *Lethe's Law* (2001) 70.
95   Albertyn (note 5) 227.
96   Ibid.
97   Albertyn interview with Yutar, 1987.
98   Davis and Le Roux (note 8) 41.
99   Ibid.

assistance to military units of foreign countries who would invade South Africa and a general participation in violent revolution in South Africa.[100]

As is typical in trials of this kind, charges were framed very vaguely and contained very few specific or detailed allegations. Bram Fischer QC, lead counsel for the defence, objected to the charge sheet on the basis that the charges set out were too vague.[101] Fischer immediately applied for a postponement. This step was probably motivated by the success the defence had with this strategy in the Treason trial. Since the charge sheet did not contain sufficient particular and detailed allegations to substantiate the charges, Judge de Wet had little choice but to grant a three-week postponement. Three weeks later Fischer again attacked the indictment.[102] Again, the judge found for the accused, admitting that the indictment was vague and full of generalisations.[103]

The Rivonia trial opened in the Pretoria Supreme Court amidst intense publicity. The prosecution emphasised the role of communism and the SACP, claiming that the ANC was completely dominated by the SACP. The state argued that according to the documents found during the raid on Rivonia, 'Moscow had promised the accused every sort and manner of assistance in the campaign'.[104] The prosecution's case was summarised as follows by Percy Yutar:

> The accused deliberately and maliciously plotted and engineered the commission of acts of violence and destruction ... The planned purpose thereof was to bring about in South Africa chaos and disorder and turmoil, which would be aggravated according to their plan by the operation of thousands of guerilla warfare units deployed throughout the country at various vantage points. These would be joined in the various areas by local inhabitants, as well as specially selected men posted to such areas. Their combined operations were planned to lead to confusion, violent insurrection and rebellion followed at the appropriate juncture by an armed invasion of the country by military units of foreign powers.[105]

Yutar tailored his opening address not only to the judge but to the white electorate and a broader communist-fearing Western audience.[106] He asked for his

---

100   The specific charges were: (1) recruiting persons for training in the preparation and use of explosives and in guerrilla warfare for the purpose of violent revolution and committing acts of sabotage; (2) conspiring to commit the aforementioned acts and to aid foreign military units when they invaded the Republic; (3) acting in these ways to further the objects of communism; and (4) soliciting and receiving money for these purposes from sympathisers in Algeria, Ethiopia, Liberia, Nigeria, Tunisia, and elsewhere.

101   See Glenn Frankel, *Rivonia's Children* (1999) 196.

102   Ibid.

103   Ibid., 43.

104   Trial record state opening address.

105   Rivonia trial record, volume 4, p. 1.

106   Davis and Le Roux (note 8) 45.

opening address to be broadcast live on SABC radio.[107] Judge de Wet refused this request – another small victory for the accused.[108] The reason for de Wet's refusal was probably the fact that he realised that Yutar saw such publicity as an instrument for self-promotion.[109] This put an end to Yutar's plan to use the state-controlled radio to inflict damage on public perceptions of the accused.[110]

The defence admitted to portions of the state's case but challenged some important points. The defence did have the space and opportunity to put forward their own version of the case. Some of the connections between communism and violence were challenged. The defence denied that they decided that they were engaged in guerilla warfare but they admitted that they decided that if all else failed they might resort to guerilla warfare.[111] The defence challenged the argument that the ANC was a tool of the Communist Party. Fischer stated that the leaders of MK and the ANC decided to keep the two organisations separate and that MK had never adopted the military plan Operation Mayibuye.

The defence was primarily of a political nature. To a large extent the accused accepted the inevitability of their legal defeat but kept believing in the possibility of a deeper political victory. The defence decided that they would not apologise for their actions, instead they would justify and explain their actions.[112] Joel Joffe argued that a narrow line was followed between not compromising the political integrity of the accused and avoiding the death sentence.[113] It was clear that the defence wanted to maximise the trial's potential as a political forum. Mandela had a growing international reputation and the ANC sought to use the trial to win worldwide support and attention.

After Fischer gave the opening statement he immediately stated that the defence case would begin with Mandela (as accused number one) speaking from the dock. Yutar, who thought that Mandela would present himself for cross-examination, was visibly disappointed by this strategic move to address the court from the dock.[114] In his five-hour statement Mandela directly challenged the political authority of the government. Mandela aimed to expose the truth about the oppression of the people of South Africa by an illegitimate regime, but also to appeal to the world at large that they had no choice.[115] He admitted to what the ANC and MK had done. He explained the history, aims and aspirations of the African people. Mandela made

---

107   Yutar was fond of publicity and enthusiastically courted the press. Kenneth Broun, *Saving Nelson Mandela* (2012) 19.

108   Ibid.

109   Author's interview with Nic Wolpe, 3 March 2014.

110   Ibid.

111   Joffe (note 92) 146.

112   See Frankel (note 100) 254.

113   Joel Joffe (in interview with Cathi Albertyn) 1987 as documented in Albertyn (note 5).

114   Davis and Le Roux (note 8) 48.

115   Bizos (note 3).

it clear that he would take responsibility for whatever the ANC and MK had done and delivered an apology in the true sense of the word – a justification for what had been done, rather than an expression of regret or a plea for mercy. He said 'Above all, we want equal political rights, because without them our disabilities will be permanent'. Unusually, the government allowed Mandela's statement to be published. Whereas ordinarily the press was not allowed to broadcast Mandela's statements because he had been banned, local and foreign publication gave extensive coverage of the speech.[116] By making his statement from the dock, Mandela appealed to the world jury to acquit them of any moral wrongdoing and to convict the regime of committing crimes against humanity.

The National Party government was hoping that the accused would get the death penalty. Under the new General Law Amendment (Sabotage) Act of 1962 and the Suppression of Communism Act, the defendants faced the threat of the death penalty. The defence lawyers therefore informed their clients from the outset that they should expect the worst.

On 12 June 1964 eight of the accused (Nelson Mandela, Walter Sisulu, Govan Mbeki, Andrew Mlangeni, Raymond Mhlaba, Elias Motsoaledi, Ahmed Kathrada and Denis Goldberg) were convicted and sentenced to life imprisonment.[117] In convicting the accused Judge de Wet gave the censures of the state the stamp of legitimacy.

Mandela was found guilty on four charges of sabotage. All eight were imprisoned to life imprisonment. In the aftermath of the convictions, the United Nations Security Council condemned the trial and began moves towards international sanctions against the Apartheid regime which eventually led to South Africa's isolation by the 1970s. After the imprisonment of the leaders of MK, the liberation movements strengthened their underground networks. The movements also continued to create organisational capacity abroad.

As in the case of the Treason trial, the courtroom became a new site of struggle for the accused. The defendants' daily appearances in court drew large crowds in the street outside the court.[118] The media coverage of the Rivonia trial was significant. From the very first day of the trial the media was documenting the trial almost every step of the way. The United Nations issued statements to the South African government appealing against the death sentence, which many expected.

---

116   David McQuoid Mason, 'The Chicago Seven Trial Reloaded: Using the Chicago Seven, Nelson Mandela and Saddam Hussein Trials to Teach about the Role of Lawyers, Judges and Accused Persons in the Criminal Justice System', in S. Hoctor and P.-J. Schwikkard (eds) *The Exemplary Scholar: Essays in Honour of John Milton* (2007) 291.

117   John Dugard, *Human Rights and the South African Legal Order* (1976) 218.

118   Many supporters were in violation of numerous influx control regulations, and the courts for them too, became new sites of struggle. See http://www.sahistory.org.za/topic/rivonia-trial-1963-1964.

The trial drew large crowds that filled up the courtroom and streets outside the court. Many of the supporters who travelled to the court to protest or to show solidarity with the accused were themselves in violation of numerous influx control regulations. The courts for them, too, became new sites of struggle.[119]

Cathi Albertyn described the Rivonia trial as an example of a 'major show trial'.[120] As the most prominent of South African political trials, it demonstrated the impact political trials can have.[121] The accused lost their personal liberty and were constrained for many decades in their political activity. From this specific point of view the political impact of the Rivonia trial could be described as negative. The impact could further be described as negative or retrogressive in terms of the way in which it was used to entrench the state's authority. The Rivonia trial not only helped to justify repressive state action but also helped to cement white unity. But resistance movements often measure success from a different perspective. From a longer-term political and historical perspective it would be wrong to glibly describe the impact of the trial as merely 'negative'. Mandela's speech from the dock as well as the bold and unapologetic strategy of the accused and defence counsel sent a vital symbolic message to South Africa and the world. As Awol Allo puts it, 'Mandela found words to register the grievances and injustices that the hegemonic language of law is incapable of hearing or representing'.[122] The trial, and specifically Mandela's speech, played a major role in exposing and publicising the injustices of the Apartheid system. It was this publicity that led the international community to mobilise and to pressurise the South African government to dismantle Apartheid. As many expected, the United Nations issued statements to the South African government appealing against the death sentence.[123]

Conclusion

The Treason and Rivonia trials are clearly examples of political trials. In the spirit of Kirchheimer, the Apartheid government enlisted 'the support of the courts for upholding or shifting the balance of political power'. However, the same space and discourse deployed by the state to eliminate its adversaries were redirected and used to indict and call to account the state to answer for its oppressive policies. The press coverage of the trials (particularly by the American and British media)

---

119   South African History, available at http://www.sahistory.org.za/topic/rivonia-trial-1963-1964.

120   Albertyn (note 5) 191.

121   Ibid.

122   Awol Allo, 'Nelson Mandela's "I am prepared to Die Speech" Fifty Years On', *Open Democracy*, 22 April 2014, available at http://www.opendemocracy.net/awol-allo/nelson-mandela%E2%80%99s-%E2%80%98i-am-prepared-to-die%E2%80%99-speech-fifty-years-on.

123   See http://www.sahistory.org.za/topic/rivonia-trial-1963-1964.

played a major role in exposing the oppressive policies of the state and the state's appetite for clamping down on its political adversaries by means of the courts.

The active role of the media, especially foreign media, in publishing and broadcasting the views of the accused to the world were factors that contributed to the 'success' (albeit limited) of the accused in the Treason trial. Other such factors were excellent and creative defence lawyers, the scope, although limited, that the South African legal system provided for the exercise of fair trial rights, and the public and eloquent expression of the position of the accused. Leading international newspapers described Mandela, Sisulu and Mbeki as the George Washingtons and Benjamin Franklins of South Africa, and as great patriots who should not be punished.[124] The eloquence of the accused and defence lawyers helped amplify the ANC's message. The defence lawyers helped shape the trial by insisting on clear definitions of crimes. Words spoken in the shadow of the gallows always have great dramatic impact. These factors contributed significantly to the symbolic victory of the accused in the Treason trial. The impact of the Rivonia trial was limited because of the fact that it did not take place within the framework of the rule of law – not even the limited procedural version of the rule of law that existed during the Treason trial. But in terms of the publication of the views of the accused the Rivonia trial is one of the best examples of a political trial in which the accused successfully used the trial to carry a political message across. If the trial was a narrative then the defence helped to shape the plot and the tone. The trial was therefore not a completely 'pointless institution' in the sense described by Kafka in the epigraph at the outset of this chapter.

To Christensen a political trial is a 'central moment' for understanding a nation.[125] Studying the Treason and Rivonia trials helps one understand the political mood of the late 1950s and early 1960s in South Africa, the agenda of the Apartheid state as well as the character of the strategy of the liberation movement. The trials also illustrate political and legal idiosyncrasies unique to South Africa and the existence of islands of bravery and morality in a sea of mass scale executive mindedness and cowardice. In the words of Bob Hepple the sacrifices of Mandela and others remind us of Mandela's words that 'there are few misfortunes in this world that you cannot turn into a personal triumph if you have the iron will and necessary skill'.[126]

---

124   *New York Times* (1964). Bizos 'Mandela's Trials and Tribulations', *Mail & Guardian*, 6 December 2013.

125   Christensen (note 23).

126   Bob Hepple, *Young Man with a Red Tie* (2013) 167.

Chapter 8

'I am the first accused': Seven Reflections (and a Postscript) on Derrida's Mandela

Jaco Barnard-Naudé

The domain of the rules was no longer enough for you; you were unable to live any longer in the domain of the rules; so you had to enter into the domain of the struggle.[1]

I

In 1985 Jacques Derrida published a text in a collection of protest 'tributes' that he co-edited with Mustapha Tlili, entitled *For Nelson Mandela*. Derrida's own tribute was published in English under the title 'The laws of reflection: Nelson Mandela, in admiration'.[2] On the day of Nelson Mandela's death, I chose to subvert/remirror Derrida's title by way of re-ordering its words. I wrote a tribute entitled 'Nelson Mandela, in reflection: the laws of admiration'.[3]

My motivation for the violence that I knowingly committed against Derrida's title and, thus, against his text, was inspired by the overwhelming impression that the day of Mandela's death was in South Africa, at least, perhaps more a day of and for reflection rather than for admiration or, if you will, for reflection precisely *by way of admiration* – and reflection, then, on the laws of Mandela, which in the end *are*, by his own account and in reflection, the laws of admiration. By changing the title to refer to the laws of admiration, I wanted to foreground precisely what Derrida first taught us about Mandela – that he was a man *of* admiration and, in reflection on his death, that it is there, with this fact, that we ought to begin (again), asking ourselves once more what could be learned not so much *in* admiration of Nelson Mandela, but rather *about* the admiration he reflected so vividly. What, finally, could reflecting on Mandela on the day of his death, teach us about how he could be admired (more) faithfully, about admiration generally, and about the relationship between the law and admiration, specifically? Reflection, admiration,

---

1   Michel Houellebecq (2011) *Whatever.* Serpent's Tail: London, p. 11.

2   Jacques Derrida 'The laws of reflection: Nelson Mandela, in admiration', in Jacques Derrida and Mustapha Tlili (eds) (1987) *For Nelson Mandela.* Seaver Books: New York, p. 13.

3   Jaco Barnard-Naudé (2013) 'Mandela in reflection: the laws of admiration'. *Mail & Guardian Thoughtleader*, available at http://www.thoughtleader.co.za/jacobarnardnaude/2013/12/06/nelson-mandela-in-reflection-the-laws-of-admiration/.

its laws and the Law. These are, then, the terms – even, the series – that come to light when we put Nelson Mandela in the light of Jacques Derrida. Or is it the other way around? Jacques Derrida in the light of Nelson Mandela? Or, in a gesture of fidelity to the 'both, and' logic for which deconstruction is (in)famous,[4] is it not more accurate to say that these are the terms that come to light when these names are viewed in each other's light? When we reflect on the laws that the Nelson Mandela reflected by Jacques Derrida will have given us in admiration? I hear the accuser asking as the police[5] flashlight shines blindingly in my eyes: 'What difference does it make?' I proceed in this light, this light in which I also stand accused, to reflect, then, on the opening words (which are initially read as a confirmation and an affirmation) of Nelson Mandela's statement from the dock in the Rivonia trial: 'I am the first accused.' The words, I hope to show, that made all the difference.

II

At the beginning of his text on Mandela, Derrida asks: 'Why does he seem exemplary and admirable in what he thinks and says, in what he does or in what he suffers? ... Why does he also *force* admiration in this manner? This word presupposes some resistance, for his enemies admire him without admitting it. ... So, this is the question: where does that force come from? Where does it lead?'[6]

Derrida answers by arguing that we see in the force of this admiration a 'line of reflection' which is first of all a force of reflection. In other words, the force of admiration *is*, derives itself from, another force: the force of reflection. Mandela seems always to blend his experience and passion with theoretical reflection: 'about

---

4   In Jacques Derrida (1990) 'Force of law: The "mystical foundation of authority"', 11 *Cardozo Law Review* 921, the 'both, and' logic of deconstruction is famously brought to bear upon the relationship between law and justice. Through the discussion of a series of aporia in this relation, Derrida ultimately arrives at the conclusion that law is both justice and injustice, that justice is both law and not law.

5   I am alluding here to Jacques Rancière's argument that the police (as opposed to the low-level police force) constitutes that system of forces that aims at the abolition of politics proper ie disagreement by putting into position a general law 'that divides the community into groups, social positions, and functions' that separate those who are considered to have a legitimate position as partakers in the operation of politics from those who are excluded from this operation. Politics, for Rancière, consist in the disruption of the police order by 'supplementing it with those who have no part in the perceptual coordinates of the community' as it is set by the police, thereby modifying the 'aesthetico-political field of possibility', that is, the parameters of what can be seen, heard and said within such a field. Jacques Rancière (2004) *The Politics of Aesthetics: The Distribution of the Sensible*. Continuum: London, pp. 3, 89.

6   Derrida, 'The laws of reflection', pp. 13–14.

history, culture, and above all jurisprudence'.[7] Mandela was a man of reflection and, for that very reason, forced admiration. The force of his reflection generated the force of admiration (*for* him, in both senses of the phrase). Derrida accordingly puts two senses of Mandela's admiration into play: 'the one he inspires and the one he feels'.[8] In short, Mandela is admired (even, albeit secretly, by his enemies) for having himself admired so forcefully. And what is it that he has admired so forcefully? Derrida answers that it is the Law and that jurisprudence is what inscribes this Law in discourse and in history.[9] Jurisprudence, then, as a kind of optics, is what *reflects* the Law in discourse and in history. The 'line of reflection' here connects the two points: jurisprudence with law. And, by the force of his reflection on and admiration (an admiration, as we shall see, that is by no means uncritical, is *reflexive*) of the Law, Mandela has been a man of Jurisprudence. In fact, Derrida, who will explicitly bring to light the intricate connection between this admiration of the Law and the call of conscience, shows us that Mandela has always known the meaning of Jurisprudence as itself a line[10] that connects two points: 'the prudence, the *phronesis* of *jus* (law), law's consciousness *and* conscience', 'the exploration of law's justice and of an ideal law or equity at the bar of which state law is always judged'.[11] 'In all the senses of this term Mandela remains, then, a *man of the law*. He has always appealed to the law even if, in appearance, he has to oppose himself to such-and-such specific legality and even if certain judges have made of him at certain moments an outlaw.'[12] As the first accused before the positive law in the Rivonia trial, Mandela, the man of Jurisprudence, found himself to be an outlaw, appealing to a consciousness of law's conscience.

And it is because Mandela is a man of Jurisprudence as the line of reflection between law's consciousness and conscience, that the reader of Mandela's words/ reflections can be led to an understanding that, in his appearance before the Apartheid court and in his writing about it, Mandela reflects 'specular paradoxes in the experience of the law'.[13] This is an understanding of these paradoxes, moreover, that is *enabled* by admiration. What is a 'specular paradox'? What does it mean to understand it? Stephen Curkpatrick argues that in his work on law and justice, Derrida avoids an equation of justice with particular manifestations of legal justice. This is the case because we are always 'behind' on justice. Justice always already overtakes the particular instantiations of its demand articulated

---

7   Ibid., p. 14.

8   Ibid., p. 15.

9   Ibid.

10   My reflections on the line are inspired by Carrol Clarkson's *Drawing the Line: Toward an Aesthetics of Transitional Justice* (2014) Fordham University Press: New York.

11   Costas Douzinas and Adam Gearing *Critical Jurisprudence: The Political Philosophy of Justice* (2005) Hart Publishing: Oxford, p. 3 (emphasis added).

12   Derrida, 'The laws of reflection', p. 26.

13   Ibid., p. 14.

in terms of a particular case and even positive law in general.[14] In short, there is always more justice to be done. One 'specular paradox' in Mandela's experience of the law, then, is the injustice of law: the reflection that justice must be done and yet it cannot be done. One way in which this paradox is reflected by Mandela's appearance in the dock at the Rivonia trial is that whilst he is summoned as first accused before the law of Apartheid in a supposed rendering of justice, he summons the very law which he is accused of transgressing, 'in a spectral trial within a trial' 'to justify itself before his conscience and testimony',[15] to reflect that justice cannot be done and yet that it must be done, to account for its historical determinacy (here, as Apartheid), even in the face of his admiration for the Law. In Mandela's call upon the Law, then, he places the law in question: it is no longer Mandela before the law, but the law before Mandela.

Derrida proceeds to quote from Mandela's speech from the dock (in which he 'prosecutes those who accuse him') in order to explain what notion of law (now as positive, historically determined law) is at stake in Mandela's admiration. Of the parliamentary system, the Magna Carta, the Petition of Rights and the Bill of Rights Mandela says that he is an 'admirer'. And speaking of 'the independence and impartiality' of the judiciary under a system of justiciable rights he says that it never fails 'to arouse my admiration'.[16] But here, before him, in *this* court, the law that he admires stands accused and accused of having betrayed itself, of having betrayed justice.

III

At this point in his text, Derrida asks that we consider whether this law that Mandela admires is essentially 'a thing of the West' and whether the white, European struggle against Apartheid amounted to a 'domestic war that the West carried on with itself, in its own name'.[17] Derrida will answer by way of a detour that begins by pointing out that Mandela is an authentic inheritor of this legal tradition in that he 'respects the logic of the legacy enough to turn it upon occasion against those who claim to be its guardians'.[18] It is here where we begin to see that Mandela's admiration of the democratic, constitutional law of the West never was an uncritical one, that in his eyes, the constitutional law of the West in its colonial and Apartheid instantiation, always stood accused of betraying the very principles upon which it relied for its justification. Curkpatrick believes that for Derrida, Mandela 'is a spectre of justice that haunts European law, made and preserved for

---

14   Stephen Curkpatrick, 'Mandela's "force of law"' (2001) 41(2) *Sophia*, p. 85.
15   Ibid., p. 97.
16   Derrida, 'The laws of reflection', p. 16.
17   Ibid.
18   Ibid., p. 17.

human dignity, yet inadvertently underpinning the presuppositions of apartheid in Eurocentric humanism'.[19]

For instance, Mandela turns the legacy against the guardians by causing the ANC's – as a resistance movement's – structure and paradigm closely to resemble the parliamentary democracy that he admires. And the Freedom Charter – as a resistance manifesto – matches the democratic commitments of the Universal Declaration and other bills of rights, similarly revered. Yet, Mandela refused to 'maintain the struggle within the constitutional framework' of Apartheid South Africa which was itself modelled on the Westminster system, because he recognized the *coup de force* – the failure of the law – of the white minority at the heart of the establishment of this constitutional law; a *coup de force* that could not, like others, be forgotten or covered over by retroactive acts of legitimacy.

To this *coup de force* of white occupation Mandela opposes the 'entire nation' and, in so doing, intends to refound, by way of the Freedom Charter, the founding act of law which is 'necessarily alegal in itself'.[20] Whilst it is true that the moment of any founding of the law is neither authorized nor unauthorized[21] – a certain *coup de force* – the point about the South African founding was that it '*remained* a coup de force'. The disparity between the fiction of the 'unity of a nation' and the reality of the particular will – that of a white minority – that it always had, exclusively, in mind, was simply too excessive, too transgressive: 'The white community was *too* much in the minority, the disproportion of wealth *too* flagrant.'[22]

However, in South Africa the Freedom Charter would have done more than simply refounding the law. It would have *reflected* against the white minority the very principles 'from which it was claiming to be inspired, whereas *actually* it never ceased to betray them'.[23] This reflection is an accusation and this accusation is redoubled. It is not simply that Mandela and his people stand accused before any law – Mandela and his people stand accused before a law that has betrayed itself, before a law that is no longer a law, a law that has contaminated itself from within. And it is for this reason that Mandela and his people accuse and accuse by way of a witnessing of and a testimony about this betrayal. Mandela accuses by way of reflection. This becomes most clear in Derrida's reading of the part of the speech from the dock where Mandela describes how the white government refused even to acknowledge receipt of his and other ANC members' letters addressed to them. This refusal constituted a betrayal on the part of the whites of the very laws of 'civility' that they made and invoked in justification of Apartheid. In his speech, Mandela effectively acknowledges the receipt of this refusal to acknowledge receipt and in so doing reflects the government's own barbarism: 'He reflects

---

19 Curkpatrick, 'Mandela's "force of law"', p. 84.
20 Derrida, 'The laws of reflection', p. 21.
21 Derrida, 'Force of law', p. 927.
22 Derrida, 'The laws of reflection', p. 18.
23 Ibid., p. 21.

somehow, by accusing, by answering, by acknowledging receipt, the scorn of the whites for their own law.'[24]

In actual fact, Mandela's reflection reveals that the adversaries accuse themselves in the very act (or, as the law would have it, omission) of not acknowledging the receipt of the petition. The accusation that sets the scene ('I am the first accused') is reflected back onto the white minority, the Apartheid system. *It* stands accused by the force of its own accusation. It accuses itself. Thus the prosecution of which Derrida speaks – the true prosecution in the Rivonia trial – institutes itself.

IV

This reflection that accuses 'would oblige us to see what was no longer seen or was not yet to be seen. It tries to open the eyes of the whites; it does not reproduce the visible, it produces it'.[25] The accusation is political because it is aesthetic – it tries to produce the visible, it tries to open eyes. It disrupts the distribution of the sensible and thereby changes it, it produces the part of no-part as an actor on the stage: Mandela, the man but also the symbol of the 'entire nation' to whom is opposed the white minority and its government. If the 'political autobiography, his and that of his people' is 'indissociable', then so is the accusation. 'The "I" of this autobiography establishes himself and justifies himself, reasons and signs in the name of "we".'[26] 'I am the first accused' is thus also 'We are the first accused'. Derrida notes how Mandela 'always says "my people"', 'especially when he asks the question of the subject responsible before the law'[27] and, in this way 'presents himself in his people, before the law'.[28] It is as if, when Mandela speaks the words 'I am the first accused', the 'entire nation' rises up and speaks in one voice: 'I am the first accused' and then, by the reflection of the sharpest light, the constative transforms with the force of reflection into a performative: 'I accuse.'

We cannot but recall here Emile Zola's *J'accuse* in the wake of the Dreyfus affair. In that case there was also a first and falsely accused. In that letter there is also admiration of and high respect for the law, expressed in the language of light: 'your star which, until now, has shone so brightly'.[29] And there is reflection of and upon this light and reflection of a type similar to the reflection that Mandela achieves with his 'entire nation':

---

24 Ibid., p. 32.
25 Ibid., p. 23.
26 Ibid., p. 26.
27 Ibid.
28 Ibid., p. 27.
29 Emile Zola, 'Letter to the President of the Republic: I accuse!' (1898) available at http://www.marxists.org/archive/zola/1898/jaccuse.htm.

Today is only the beginning, for it is only today that the positions have become clear: on one side, those who are guilty, *who do not want the light to shine forth*, on the other, those who seek justice and who will give their lives to attain it. I said it before and I repeat it now: when truth is buried underground, it grows and it builds up so much force that the day it explodes it blasts everything with it.[30]

Like Mandela after him, Zola causes the light to shine reflectively by appropriating the accusation. Dreyfus is no longer the accused. By way of Zola's performative '*J'accuse*' Dreyfus is exonerated and his accusers stand accused (regardless of, or at least *in opposition to*, what was being exacted by the historically determined law at the time). This accusation (reflection) is achieved entirely by way of a line of reflection, a reflection that opposes 'humanity' to the injustice of the French government: 'I have but one passion: *to enlighten those who have been kept in the dark*, in the name of humanity which has suffered so much and is entitled to happiness.'[31]

Zola realizes only too well that this accusation, this enlightenment, will in turn turn him into an accused. He thus accuses himself (but he never relinquishes his reliance on the light): 'Let them dare, then, to bring me before a court of law and let the enquiry take place *in broad daylight*!'[32] After the accusation, Zola stands accused as the accuser, and he is tried as such. From the point of view of form and effect, the position is no different from that of Mandela in the dock at the Rivonia trial.

And it is no coincidence that what comes to light at the point in Derrida's text where the accused holds up a mirror to the accuser, is at its most intense, is forceful, because it answers the question of the 'thing of the West': it turns out that Mandela's admiration for the law that he reflects onto his accusers has a presence in 'the interior of African society',[33] a presence that lies in the past, but a more immediate present for him as an African, nevertheless. The law is thus, not, or not exclusively, 'a thing of the West' – the West, parliamentary democracy, etc., is a weak force, is 'an example but not exemplarily'.[34] In early African society, Mandela finds the *seeds*[35] of a democracy that would not only be more forceful, 'revolutionary' as Derrida indicates, but also *exemplary*, because it would found a

---

30   Ibid.

31   Ibid. On the public effect of Zola's trial, Jacqueline Rose remarks that progressive intellectuals saw it 'as a moment of "conscience humaine"' (the French *conscience* is both 'consciousness' and 'conscience') that introduced into political life a new level of moral seriousness. Jacqueline Rose '"J'accuse": Dreyfus in our times' (2013) 32(11) *London Review of Books*, p. 3–9, available at http://www.lrb.co.uk/v32/n11/jacqueline-rose/jaccuse-dreyfus-in-our-times.

32   Zola, 'Letter to the President of the Republic: I accuse!'.

33   Derrida, 'The laws of reflection', p. 23.

34   Ibid., p. 25.

35   Derrida is at pains to emphasise that this is a 'virtually accomplished' democracy.

society without class and without private property – a democracy to be admired, a democracy to come, a democracy of which it cannot be said with any certainty that it will come from the future or from a past. And here we have then, already in 1985, the spectre of Derrida's 1993 *Specters of Marx*: 'there are several times of the specter. It is a proper characteristic of the specter, if there is any, that no one can be sure if by returning it testifies to a living past or to a living future, for the *revenant* may already mark the promised return of the specter of living being'.[36]

Mandela's opposition of the 'entire nation' to the white *coup de force*, is thus not, as Bernasconi[37] has noticed, merely an internal opposition or contradiction within the Western edifice or schema. The opposition enables, even leads, Mandela to reveal that the struggle of the black community against Apartheid is not simply an undertaking 'in the name of an imported law'.[38] The location of an already 'virtually accomplished' non-Western democracy within the interior of Africa is a dangerous supplementation from the outside that displaces the schema and causes it to tremble.[39] In the end, by way of this reflection of a revolutionary democratic existence in the heart of pre-colonial African society, it is not just that the interior law of Apartheid stands accused. Rather, it is the entire edifice of Western law and its imperialism as a 'civilizing mission' that stands, once more, accused.

V

This 'logic of supplementarity'[40] redoubles. The 'law' before which Mandela (and his people) appear is of two orders. The appearance before the law of the second, weaker order is symmetrically double: it is the law that he summons and the law that summons him (and his people). It is the law before which he appears and that appears before him/them, the law that will judge him and the law that he will judge. It is Apartheid.

But there is more. These reflections (redoubled in themselves) will be interrupted only by the appearance (supplementation) of another law, the law of the first order: the superior law which he admires, before which he also appears, which he also summons, but this time the Law to which he *appeals* and before which the constative 'I am the first accused' becomes an appeal, a plea: 'he addresses himself to the universal justice above his judges of one day only'[41] in a

---

36 Jacques Derrida (1994) *Specters of Marx: the State of the Debt, the Work of Mourning, and the New International.* Routledge: New York, p. 99.

37 Robert Bernasconi, 'Politics beyond humanism: Mandela and the struggle against Apartheid', in Gary B. Madison (2001) *Working through Derrida.* Northwestern University Press: Illinois, p. 94.

38 Derrida, 'The laws of reflection', p. 22.

39 Bernasconi, 'Politics beyond humanism', p. 115.

40 Ibid., p. 108.

41 Derrida, 'The laws of reflection', p. 27.

voice 'which never ceases to *appeal* to *the voice of conscience*, to the immediate and unfailing sentiment of justice, to this law of laws that speaks in us before us, because it is inscribed within our heart'.[42]

What is at stake here is the question of deontology. Derrida argues that Mandela, in confronting the question of his disobedience of the law as a lawyer, reflects the 'deontology of deontology', a 'law beyond legality'.[43] Mandela decides to adopt extraordinary measures in the name of deontology: he disrupts the law from within, by setting himself *'against the code in the code'*.[44] But this disruption triggers a 'supplementary inversion':[45] there is an 'increase of respect for the law', not a decrease. He practices his profession 'just where they wanted to keep him from doing so'. He literally occupies the law illegally, in defiance of the law. He disrupts professional deontology in the name of deontology. In doing this, he 'reflects the code' and produces (not reproduces) the visible by shedding light on that which 'the code in action rendered unreadable'. Rancière would say that this is politics: a disturbance of the totalizing account of the population, a disturbance of the police.[46] Derrida calls it the 'production of light' that is justice.[47] Mandela disrupts by way of holding up a mirror in which his adversaries 'should recognise and see their own contempt for the law being reflected'.[48]

Derrida would have us believe that Mandela 'does not accuse his judges, not immediately, at least not in the moment when he appears before them'.[49] Bernasconi has already worried (with reference to the part of Derrida's text that reads Rousseau in(to) Mandela) that Derrida imposes the logic of deconstruction onto Mandela's text and thereby 'domesticates Mandela, reduces him to an already established discourse and schema, and refuses to allow him to speak as an other'.[50] Is Derrida's refusal to see Mandela accusing his accusers at the very moment of his appearance ('I am the first accused') not further evidence of such a domestication?

If it was not for the fact that Derrida elsewhere denies the possibility of *simply* escaping the established schema of Western metaphysics,[51] and if it was not for

---

42 Ibid.
43 Ibid., p. 34.
44 Ibid.
45 Ibid., p. 36.
46 Jacques Rancière, *The Politics of Aesthetics*, p. 85.
47 Derrida, 'The laws of reflection', p. 34.
48 Ibid., p. 36.
49 Ibid.
50 Bernasconi, 'Politics beyond humanism', p. 115.
51 In an interview collected in *Positions* (Jacques Derrida (2004) *Positions*. Continuum: London, p. 9) the interviewer asks Derrida whether there can be a 'surpassing' of Western metaphysics, an 'effective transgression'. He responds that there 'is *not* a transgression, if one understands by that a pure and simple landing into the beyond of metaphysics' and goes on to speak about how, in transgressions, one is 'consorting with a code to which metaphysics is tied irreducibly, such that every transgressive gesture reencloses us', but that the 'work done on one side and the other of the limit' modifies the field. However,

the fact that Derrida sees in Mandela's appearance (and thus in his confirmation of the status of 'first accused') an appropriation of the occasion precisely 'in order to *speak*', I would have agreed. But Derrida himself shows how the occupation of the speech position, negotiated by virtue of such a confirmation of status before that court, allows Mandela to speak over the heads of his judges of that day, to 'the universal court' 'above them'.[52] And what is produced as visible, finally visible, is an alterity: 'the written text of his pleading, *which is also an indictment*'[53] and thus an accusation. It is precisely this conclusion that causes me to part ways with the Derrida writing about Mandela in his quick assumption that Mandela does not accuse from the outset. On Derrida's *own*[54] terms, 'I am the first accused' will always have been an accusation.

VI

And Mandela speaks as an other by appealing to the voice of conscience that is in conflict with the law.[55] This situation is not 'peculiar to this country. The conflict arises for men of conscience, for men who think and feel deeply in every country'.[56] An appeal then to the universality of conscience.

What is conscience? 'Conscience is not only memory but promise',[57] Derrida tells us towards the end of this extraordinary meditation on Mandela. Conscience, then, is both past and future which leaves us, of course, with the question of the present with the 'what is to be done?' Derrrida seems to argue that the answer to this question might well lie in an enlarged understanding of what it means to be a witness (which should be rigorously distinguished from the related, but, at least according to convention passive, spectator). First, we have to understand that Mandela is an 'exemplary witness' because he makes us think about the law that he reflects. Second, exemplary witnesses are exemplary because they represent a certain tear between conscience and the law. They are themselves 'torn' between

---

'[o]ne is never installed within transgression, one never lives elsewhere. Transgression implies that the limit is always at work' (Derrida 1981: 9–10). Those who think of deconstruction, then, as a simple escapism or as catering for a simple alterity, are, at least on Derrida's own terms, more than somewhat misguided.

52   Derrida, 'The laws of reflection', p. 36.
53   Ibid., p. 36 (emphasis added).
54   Of course, Derrida would be the first to insist that the very concept of what is 'own' and 'owned' is internally divided by the fact of alterity. The 'own' of Derrida's 'own' terms here takes the form of Derrida's *other* texts, those that do not address Mandela, but rather the thematics of internal division, autoimmunity, etc. – in short, the hors-texte which is nevertheless integrally a part of the text according to the famous 'il n'y a pas de hors-texte'.
55   Ibid., p. 39.
56   Ibid.
57   Ibid., p. 38.

the two. Sitze reminds us that Mandela's Xhosa name, Rolihlahla, means 'to pull a branch off a tree' or 'troublemaker' and he invokes Derrida's use of the word 'uprooting'[58] in his consideration of the exemplary witness, as another synonym for 'Rolihlahla'.[59] It is thus no stretch of the interpretation of Mandela's name to suggest that it also means 'to tear'. As an exemplary witness, Mandela tore the branch of conscience from the tree of Western law, in the sense that his conscience not only constantly rose above Apartheid law, but also in the sense that it radicalized the trouble that it found within Western law itself, namely that it was and is constitutively 'divided against itself, fighting itself'.[60] In his writing, Mandela himself invokes an exemplary witness from the West who exposed the very same issue: Bertrand Russell, whose protest against his democratic government's nuclear weapons policy earned him a conviction and a sentence.[61]

The exemplary witness shows himself, remembers, reflects in order to 'reinstitute the law for the future', the 'promise of what has not yet ever been seen or heard'.[62] The exemplary witness speaks out (against injustice), he is no passive spectator. Curkpatrick remarks that for Derrida, 'conscience' is not a sense of duty to ethical convention, but rather an 'absolute responsibility' to the other that surpasses public or general calculation. 'It is the call of the other, a secret, a self-sacrificial imperative, impossibly, to decide in the face of the undecidable.'[63] If there is to be talk of 'duty' in relation to this conscience, it is the duty of responding to/hearing a call of conscience (Heidegger literally calls the voice of conscience a 'higher court for Da-sein's existence'[64]) – a response to human dignity pushed to its limits under Apartheid. If there is to be talk of the 'voice' of conscience, it is not the private voice which addresses Mandela as a private individual, but rather, precisely, the voice of his people.[65] Conscience, says Heidegger,[66] is a 'summoning' of Da-sein to its 'ownmost potentiality-of-being-its-self', and as such, an accusation – a call to account as the etymology of the word indicates.[67] To respond to the call of conscience, is to affirm its accusation: 'I am the first accused.'

58   Ibid.
59   Adam Sitze, 'Mandela and the law', in Rita Barnard (ed.) (2014) *The Cambridge Companion to Nelson Mandela.* Cambridge University Press: Cambridge, p. 155.
60   Ibid., p. 156.
61   Derrida, 'The laws of reflection', p. 39.
62   Ibid., p. 38.
63   Curkpatrick, 'Mandela's "force of law"', p. 91.
64   Martin Heidegger (2010) *Being and Time.* State University of New York Press: Albany, p. 258.
65   Curkpatrick, 'Mandela's "force of law"', p. 93.
66   Heidegger, *Being and Time*, p. 259.
67   See *Online Etymology Dictionary* (http://www.etymonline.com/index.php?term=accuse).

VII

Why do we see at the address where our beloved Madiba has passed but indeed throughout the world such an outpouring of admiration? Admiration in the form of tributes expressed in thousands upon thousands of candles, prayers, wishes, attendances, texts in all the languages of the world? Why have people from every corner of the Earth taken the time and effort to express their admiration for Mandela once more, one more time, which will not be the last?

Without succumbing to a desire to oversimplify the motivation behind these performances of admiration, could it not be said that these homages are precisely beyond motivation, that they are compulsions to yield to a law of the Other, to pay tribute to Mandela as one who commands and always has commanded the laws of admiration? 'We will never cease to admire him: himself and his admiration.'[68] Is this not why we grieve and in this way? And is this not always the law of mourning, always the Other's law to which we subject ourselves without the sovereignty of a self-determined subjectivity, without choice, acting, in fact, beyond the reach of choice (if that was still possible), the law to which we yield without the slightest concern in the first place for ourselves?

Or is it more complicated than that? I recall here another text in which Derrida refuses absolutely the contention that mourning and by extension the *admiration* in or as mourning, can ever be without a concern for ourselves: 'Narcissism! There is not narcissism and non-narcissism; there are narcissisms that are more or less comprehensive, generous, open, extended ... I believe that without a movement of narcissistic reappropriation, the relation to the other would be absolutely destroyed, it would be destroyed in advance.'[69] Thus we mourn by way of the other also for ourselves, in our own interest, in order to overcome, to live on. We admire. And in Derrida's estimation there can be no mourning of and for the other without this simultaneous mourning for ourselves, without the 'narcissistic reappropriation' of the other to ourselves. No mourning without melancholia.

Admiration/mourning causes us to reflect: 'In this mourning work in process, in this interminable task, the ghost remains that which gives one most to think about – and to do. Let us insist and spell things out: to do and to make come about, as well as to let come (about).'[70] Nelson Mandela's admiration reflects – and it reflects absolutely. And he continues to reflect. To take an example, was there not precisely something of the reflection, the holding up of a mirror, at the Johannesburg memorial when the president rose to address the nation only to be addressed by it? Commentators raised a hue and cry about the 'appropriateness' of this incident. But since when has justice been 'appropriate'? Let us not forget that it was not 'appropriate' to appear in court dressed in traditional tribal attire as

---

    68   Derrida, 'The laws of reflection', p. 41.

    69   Jacques Derrida (1995) *Points ... Interviews, 1974–1994*. Stanford University Press: Stanford, p. 199.

    70   Derrida, *Specters of Marx*, p. 98.

Mandela did.[71] It was not 'appropriate' to address the Apartheid court politically on the history of the struggle. But who would deny today that it was justice? Politics is never 'appropriate'. It is inappropriate, it disrupts, it reflects, it disagrees, it is admired. It promises a law that is not yet, a democracy still to come.

The light of Nelson Mandela's reflection is the light of justice to come. It is a light that refuses to go out. As we reflect on this Light and in his light, a Leading Light, in mourning, which is to say in profound admiration, let us also take heart from the law, this Law, that is inscribed now within our heart as it always has been and always will be, this 'immediate and unfailing sentiment of justice', this 'law of laws that speaks in us before us'.[72]

Postscript: *Vaarwel*, Madiba

What does it mean to inherit Nelson Mandela and to inherit his extraordinary appearance at the Rivonia trial? Carrol Clarkson has argued that the Rivonia trial offered Mandela 'a legal site from which to issue a political appeal, and as a result, the relation between law and politics in South Africa became irrevocably troubled'.[73] She goes on to argue that 'Mandela's appearance *and audience* at the Rivonia trial amount to a rupture in the very logic of apartheid law'.[74] From the point of view of the logic of Apartheid *law*, the statement from the dock did not register *legally* and was regarded by the court as senseless. As Clarkson remarks, the statement was not a defence, nor a testimony that would be subjected to cross-examination, in fact it bore no positivist legal significance at all.[75] Anything Mandela said in the statement about his innocence would not be taken into consideration by the judge, it would not be legally functional and realistically, it might well have had the opposite effect. Yet, as Clarkson concludes: 'Rivonia had brought about a radical redistribution of the sensible: The political, antiapartheid protest had been voiced and heard in a court of law, making it possible for a self-designated nation to question and to reconsider its own delineations of what counted as legitimate and what did not.'[76]

What Clarkson means with her description of Rivonia as having brought about 'a radical redistribution of the sensible' is that the statement from the dock amounted

---

71   Clarkson, *Drawing the Line*, p. 52 eloquently argues that Mandela was well-attuned to the opportunity that the Rivonia trial offered him to perform his compelling moral force. She quotes Mandela as being fully aware of the fact that 'the authorities' would feel 'threatened' by the *kaross* he wore to court.

72   Derrida, 'The laws of reflection', p. 27.

73   Clarkson, *Drawing the Line*, p. 48.

74   Ibid., p. 49.

75   Ibid., p. 54.

76   Ibid., p. 55.

to a 'contingent suspension of the rules governing normal experience',[77] if we concede that the 'normal experience' of law under Apartheid hinged on a sustained suppression of politics. In Rancière's terms, the statement from the dock amounted to a form of 'dissensus'. Steven Corcoran argues that the logic of dissensus 'consists in the demonstration of a certain *impropriety*' to the order of consensus which is defined by the idea of what is proper and hence is the 'spontaneous logic underlying every hierarchy'.[78] Mandela's statement from the dock is a dissensus because it disturbed and subverted the 'spontaneous' hierarchical logic upon which the 'propriety' of the Apartheid legal order was based – a logic that turned, over and over again, on a rigid denial of any relation between law and politics. As such, it is a logic that was grounded in the compulsion to preclude, at all costs, the responsiveness of law to politics. Viewed from this angle, Rivonia constituted the seeds of a challenge to South African legal culture in ways that would become more explicit, more *pronounced*, only in the years to come.

In the aftermath of the Rivonia trial, in his celebrated inaugural lecture of 1971, John Dugard diagnosed the malaise in the logic of Apartheid law when he accused the South African judiciary of having adopted Austinian positivism as its predominant theory of law.[79] This theory of law is famous for the command thesis and the strict separation of law and morality that purportedly follows from it. Simply put, positivism, admittedly in its reduced and crude form, believes that it is possible (and necessary) to separate the law 'as it is' from the law 'as it ought to be' and sets for a court of law the sole – supposedly apolitical – task of 'discovering' the law as it is, while imploring it to refrain, at all cost, from enquiring about the law as it ought to be (which is supposedly the domain of politics). Positivism in this form views the judge purely as the 'phonographic' agent of supposedly value free mechanical application of legal rules to legal facts: '[t]he judge is denied any creative power in his mechanical search for the legislature's intention and desirable policy considerations, based upon traditional legal values, are viewed as irrelevant'.[80] In short, positivism is the jurisprudential watchword by way of which politics is checked at the entrance to the courtroom.

But in South Africa, Dugard argued, positivism was not simply the jurisprudential watchword by way of which politics and law were supposedly rigidly separated – it was also the watchword by way of which *conscience* could be kept outside the court of law. Referring to the positivist mindset that views itself as only interpreting the intention of the legislature, Dugard remarked: '[t]his enables the judiciary to apply the harshest of laws with an easy conscience'.[81]

---

77 Jacques Rancière (2010) *Dissensus: On Politics and Aesthetics.* Continuum: London, p. 1.

78 Ibid., p. 2.

79 John Dugard, 'The judicial process, positivism and civil liberty' (1971) 88 *The South African Law Journal*, p. 186.

80 Ibid., p. 182.

81 Ibid., p. 187.

He went on to blame the positivist bent of the South African judiciary for its 'quiescent attitude' towards Apartheid statutes that were invading individual liberty and, invoking the work of the American realists,[82] went on to show, quoting Jonathan Cohen, not only that legal positivism amounts to 'conservative politics in the guise of analytical jurisprudence',[83] but that, in South Africa, the 'major inarticulate premiss' of judges was – precisely because they were drawn from 'the privileged white élite' – loyalty to the Apartheid status quo.[84] In this way, Dugard exposed that, behind the positivist protestations of merely 'neutrally' mouthing the legislature's intention in the name of fidelity to law, lurked a dominant judicial politics of fidelity to Apartheid. To put the matter in terms reminiscent of Holmes: behind the positivist 'logic' of Apartheid law, was concealed its racist political experience or, to succumb to the temptation to this in Lacanian terms: behind the symbolic 'legal' lie of 'separate development' was concealed the real of the political lie of racial supremacy.

When Nelson Mandela's decision to read a statement from the dock in the Rivonia trial is read in the context of Dugard's observations, it becomes possible to draw the conclusion that Mandela as an 'exemplary witness' (and through the reading in a court of law of a statement that first and foremost resonated politically) refused to be complicit in the maintenance of this separationist logic of Apartheid law. In other words, he refused to participate in the farcical positivist game of the Apartheid court pretending that there was no politics in the courtroom. In this way, as I suggest in the epigraph to this text, Mandela illustrated not only his inability as a lawyer 'to live any longer in the domain of the rules',[85] but also that living in the domain of the rules was no longer 'enough' as a matter of conscience,

---

82   Joel Modiri and Karin van Marle, 'What does changing the world entail? Law, critique and legal education in the time of post-apartheid' (2012) 129 *The South African Law Journal*, p. 214, describe realism in language that resonates remarkably with Derrida's vocabulary in the Mandela essay: 'Instead, realist critiques see law as a reflection, indeed a mirror, of ideology.' Is this merely a coincidence? Or can it not be said that Mandela's reflections by way of the statement from the dock constituted precisely a veritable moment of realism in which the law was reflected as a mirror of racist ideology; a moment of realism, moreover, that attempted, through the call of conscience, finally to shake the law out of its ideological somnambulism? Is this what Derrida means when he writes: 'There is no law without a mirror'? (Derrida, 'The laws of reflection', p. 14). And is there an unintended convergence to be detected here between Derrida and Lacan, whose mirror stage is precisely the liminal subjective phase between the Real of the mother and the Law of the Father? In Lacan the mirror image / imago is precisely what separates and relates the Symbolic and the Real. It is also striking to note that in her contribution to the Derrida and Tlili tribute volume, Sontag writes that Mandela is exemplary because 'his version' of the cause for which he is fighting is 'the most realistic'. Susan Sontag 'This man, this country', in Derrida and Tlili, *For Nelson Mandela*, p. 49

83   Dugard, 'The judicial process, positivism and civil liberty', p. 189.

84   Ibid., pp. 190–91.

85   Houellebecq, *Whatever*, p. 11.

that living conscientiously within the Apartheid legal order demanded that one entered the 'domain of the struggle', the domain of politics. In this way, Mandela's dissensus disrupted the hierarchy that the Apartheid courts established between law and politics. It is the distribution of the sensible based on the superiority of the language of positivism as the determining force of what could be heard and seen by the law, which Mandela redistributes by speaking the political language of his dissensus.

Mark Sanders has remarked, with reference to Zola's *J'accuse*, that the compulsion to speak out emanates from a will or a desire not to be complicit.[86] The assumption of responsibility, then, stems from such a will to actively refuse complicity. As such, it knows that maintaining silence would allow a crime or an injustice to go undiscovered. Speaking out is a way of saying that one will not stand by as a passive spectator to the perpetration of injustice and thereby be complicit in it. Mandela, by breaking the silence about the politics of law in the courtroom, thus assumes responsibility not only for his political appearance before the law of Apartheid but also for the appearance of politics before this law. And for the exposure of the politics of the law. It is this assumption of responsibility for politics before the law that caused the relationship between law and politics to become forever troubled. Moreover, this responsibility, as Sanders notes, is assumed on behalf of another[87] and here Mandela assumes it of course on behalf of his people who are invisible in the time and space of the Apartheid court and rendered visible only by and through the recourse to politics. In this particular sense, Mandela's Rivionia trial speech is an 'aesthetic act' in Rancière's terms. Mandela exposes that the separationist logic of Apartheid adjudication is part and parcel of the racist logic of its structurization as a police order in Rancière's sense – it is part and parcel of making the people invisible before the law. It is in order to cause his people to appear not just before the law of the courtroom but before the law of conscience of humanity as a whole, that Mandela has recourse to a 'dissonant' political vocabulary that registers his dissensus in the law court. By no longer speaking the language of Apartheid's laws, but indeed speaking to the law in the language of the struggle of his people, Mandela reconfigures the sensible in such a way that he and 'his' people can no longer be simply and invisibly subjected to the law's exclusionary language and logic, even if the law before which he appears will still dare to judge, convict and sentence him.

And Clarkson is right that the Rivonia trial and Mandela's statement caused the relation between law and politics in South Africa to become *irrevocably* troubled, because it remains troubled to this very day. In this sense, the event that was Rivonia keeps returning, like a ghost, to haunt South African legal culture. In a lecture delivered at the University of Stellenbosch law faculty in October 2006, the late former Chief Justice, Pius Langa, still considered it necessary to set the

---

86   Mark Sanders (2002) *Complicities: The Intellectual and Apartheid.* Duke University Press: Durham, p. 4.

87   Ibid., p. 5.

judicial task under the new constitutional order explicitly against the 'delusional danger' of a technicist, literal and formal approach. He continued to remark that the transformative Constitution required judges to justify their decisions not with reference merely to authority, but with reference to 'ideas and values'.[88] He went on boldly to state: 'This approach to adjudication requires an acceptance of the politics of law. There is no longer place for assertions that the law can be kept isolated from politics. While they are not the same, they are inherently and necessarily linked.'[89] The suggestion or implication of the late former Chief Justice's statement is of course that there were (and are) still actors in South African legal culture who, despite the constitutional transformation, deny the politics of law.[90] This cannot be denied, nor that the contemporary manifestation of this denial takes the form of a classically liberal (and thus *political*) appeal to 'the rule of law'. To these actors the Chief Justice signified that, at least on the level of ideality (but most certainly as a matter of jurisprudence in the sense that I have invoked it here), the post-Apartheid distribution of the sensible displaced them, that is, 'no longer' provided them with a settled 'legal' 'place'.[91]

In the spirit of continuing the 'trouble' of the law/politics relation, Karin van Marle and Joel Modiri recently continued to ask 'to what extent a conservative legal education which negates the social, ethical and political significance of law links up with lawyers' and legal academics' complicity in the social ills that pervade post-apartheid society'.[92] In this respect, they echoed Dugard, who, at the end of his inaugural lecture, expressed a concern with positivist legal education and pleaded for a realist-cum-natural law approach in legal education – an approach

---

88   Pius Langa, 'Transformative constitutionalism' (2006) 3 *Stellenbosch Law Review*, pp. 353, 356–7.

89   Ibid., p. 353.

90   In a seminal article published in 1998, Karl Klare, 'Legal culture and transformative constitutionalism' (1998) 14 *South African Journal on Human Rights*, p. 146 argued that there was, from the point of view of the imperative of transformation through law, a potentially disastrous mismatch between conservative, positivist legal culture and a progressive Constitution in South Africa. In 2010, Dennis Davis and Karl Klare, 'Transformative constitutionalism and the common and customary law' (2010) 26 *South African Journal on Human Rights*, p. 509, concluded that the early years of transformative jurisprudence had indicated that concerns that the courts would be held back in their transformative task by traditional legal culture, were well taken.

91   In similar vein, Cathi Albertyn and Dennis Davis, 'Legal realism, transformation and the legacy of Dugard' (2010) 26 *South African Journal on Human Rights*, p. 190, taking their cue explicitly from Dugard, have argued for a critical legal realist approach to the judicial task under transformative constitutionalism and have emphasized that the assertion of the politics of law remains as important today as it was under Apartheid.

92   Modiri and Van Marle, 'What does changing the world entail?', p. 214.

that would instill in students an awareness of the values[93] upon which the legal system is based.[94]

If, as Derrida remarks, the postscript is 'for the future – for that part of the future most undecided today'[95] it seems to me that at least one of the important legacies of Mandela in the Rivonia trial calls lawyers and academics to continue the struggle against a distribution of the sensible that would ward off the politics of law, and, by implication, the call of ethico-political responsibility:[96] the call of conscience which moved the first accused to accusation, the posterity which proclaimed him innocent.

---

93   It should be pointed out that while both Dugard and Modiri and Van Marle call for a post-positivist transformation of legal education, Dugard's call is still for an awareness of the legal values upon which 'Western civilization' is based (Dugard, 'The judicial process, positivism and civil liberty', p. 200) whereas Van Marle and Modiri is concerned with 'a critical theoretical approach that is situated within and responds to the post-apartheid context' (Modiri and Van Marle, 'What does changing the world entail?', p. 218), i.e., an approach that is uniquely South African and that does not exclusively or even predominantly appeal to the West for its inspiration. Clearly, the question that still looms large here is the very same question that initially bothered Derrida about Mandela's admiration for the Western democratic institutions of law, namely whether these are, essentially, things of the West – a question of which the answer is, according to Derrida's reading of Mandela, in the negative and one to which, I venture to speculate, Modiri and Van Marle would answer 'no, but ...'.

94   Dugard, 'The judicial process, positivism and civil liberty', p. 200.

95   Derrida, 'The laws of reflection', p. 41.

96   I have, in the back of my mind, the conclusion of Slavoj Žižek's *Less than Nothing* (2012) Verso: London, p. 963: 'Politics is the very space in which, without any external guarantee, ethical decisions are made and negotiated.'

Chapter 9

'Black man in the white man's court': Performative Genealogies in the Courtroom

Awol Allo

"What are these trials about, eh? Who is it they are trying?" one of them asked. "The whole of South Africa is on trial", replied Professor Matthews, looking up darkly from his group. "You're on trial, we're all on trial. It's ideas that are being tried here, not people".[1]

Anthony Sampson's account of the above encounter is emblematic of both the substance and the tone of conversations taking shape on the streets of South Africa as the government stages a phenomenal spectacle in the courtroom. Describing the politics of repression at the heart of the treason indictment, counsel for defence captured the essence of the confrontation in terms of competing spectacles – a confrontation between spectacles of repression and resistance.[2] It was a cultural representation of a battle of ideas between those who 'seek equal opportunity for, and freedom of thought and expression by, all persons of all races and creeds' on the one hand, and 'those which deny to all but a few the riches of life, both material and spiritual, which the accused aver should be common to all'.[3] The first of the many high profile political trials, the spectacle backfired and generated what Sampson described as 'the oddest paradox': 'in the very court where they were being tried for treason, the Congress leaders were able to hold their biggest unbanned meetings for four years'.[4] In his memoir, *Long Walk to Freedom*, Mandela describes the trial's boomerang effect: 'Our communal cell became a kind of convention for far-flung freedom fighters. Many of us had been living under severe restrictions, making it illegal for us to meet and talk. Now, our enemy had gathered us all together under one roof for what became the largest and longest unbanned meeting of the Congress Alliance in years.'[5]

---

1   Anthony Sampson, *The Treason Cage: The Opposition on Trial in South Africa* (London: Heinemann, 1958), 28.

2   Michael Lobban, *White Man's Justice: South Africa's Political Trials in the Black Consciousness Era* (Oxford: Oxford University Press, 1996), 17.

3   Vernon Berrange, cited in Helen Joseph, *If this Be Treason* (London: Andre Deutsch, 1963), 37.

4   See Sampson, *The Treason Cage*, 203.

5   Nelson Mandela, *Long Walk to Freedom: The Autobiography of Nelson Mandela* (Boston: Little, Brown and Co., 1994), 201.

Apartheid's spectacles of oppression were overtaken by liberatory counter-spectacles. What was orchestrated to produce and generate images and concepts productive to the racist regime were redirected and used by the oppressed as a platform for visibility and hearing: to give account of themselves in their own terms, with their own discourse and dialect.[6] As he later noted, 'By representing myself I would enhance the symbolism of my role': 'I would use my trial as a showcase for the ANC's moral opposition to racism.'[7] Instead of defending themselves against the charges, they laid a charge against the system, accusing it of racism, violence, injustice, immorality and illegitimacy; transforming themselves into 'the subjects of history rather than … impersonal objects of official historical records'.[8] An event staged with the sole purpose of squashing resistance against the usurpation of the voice and visibility of the black subject, generated the opposite result: it created a defiant black subjectivity capable of detecting oppressive norms at sites never seen before, a subject that finally apprehended and named Apartheid's order of representation and its schematics of subjection.

This chapter will examine the significance of Mandela's courtroom performances of resistance in illuminating our understanding of the constitutive and regulative conditions that sustained Apartheid. Much of the emphasis will be on Mandela's appropriation of his speaking position and the conditions of possibility immanent in the trial. By identifying a few scenes from the Incitement Trial (1962), I will offer a historicist (genealogical and performative) reading of Mandela's understanding and approach to the law, focusing on the objections he raises and the moves he makes between different analytic registers.

---

6   See Joel Joffe, *The State vs. Nelson Mandela: The Trial That Changed South Africa* (Oxford: Oneworld, 2007), 28. Joffe recounts the defendant's jubilant mood in anticipation of the opportunity to speak and give account of themselves and their people: 'We had come on legal business to consult the accused. But it was clear that they were in no mood for consultation. They were rediscovering, it seemed to us, the joys of speech, not unlike people who had been dumb and had suddenly had the power of speech restored to them. They were miraculously wondering at the joy of it, turning it over on their tongues, feeling the savour of it on their lips; they were drunk with speech, with human communication, and contact, with being able to talk, to meet with and touch other people, too involved in all these new sensations, too intoxicated with them to be prepared to consider serious problems of the law.'

7   Mandela, *Long Walk to Freedom*, 201.

8   Dmitri Nikulin, 'The Names in History: Rancière's New Historical Poetics', in Jean-Phillip Deranty and Alison Ross (eds) *Jacques Rancière and the Contemporary Scene: The Philosophy of Radical Equality* (London: Continuum, 2012), 67.

Performative-Genealogies in the Old Synagogue Court

> *We would not defend ourselves in a legal sense so much as in a moral sense. We saw the trial as a continuation of the struggle by other means.*[9]

In 'Just Stories', Milner S. Ball conceives 'narrative' as a medium through which a political community is continuously and permanently constituted, renegotiated, and reconfigured.[10] He argues, 'Narrative is the primary medium for talking together about who we are – and would be – as people, and this is the talk in which conversation about justice chiefly subsists'.[11] It is in the telling and retelling of stories of people, in the continuities and ruptures, in the homogeneities and heterogeneities that the raw material for contestation, re-creation and renewal resides.[12] As Melvyn Hill tells us, 'Stories tell us how each one finds or loses his just place in relation to others in the world'.[13] In particular, some stories of law embody paradigmatic dilemmas that confront and expose the bottomless chasm between our professed values and actual practices.[14] They confront the body politic with fundamental questions of responsibility, representation, recognition, equality and justice. These are stories 'in which the community defines itself, not once and for all, but over and over, and in the process it educates itself about its own character and the nature of the world'.[15] Mandela's trials constitute those singular national occasions in which a resistant subject confronted South Africans with foundational questions – what kind of society they are and what kind of political community they want to have for the future. In recounting the story of exclusion and misrecognition of black identity and personhood, the defendant transformed the legal moment into what may be called a counter-constitutional moment that sought to redeem the voices of those excluded by the original act of founding.[16]

---

9   Nelson Mandela, Long Walk to Freedom, 360.

10   Milner S. Ball, 'Just Stories', 12 (1) *Cardozo Studies in Law and Literature* (2002), 37.

11   Ibid.

12   Erik Hobsbawm and Terence Ranger (eds) *The Invention of Tradition* (Cambridge: Cambridge University Press, 1983), 7.

13   Melvyn Hill, 'The Fictions of Mankind and the Stories of Men', in Hannah Arendt (ed.) *The Recovery of the Public World* (New York: St. Martin's Press, 1979), 290.

14   Ron Christenson, *Political Trials: Gordian Knots in the Law* (Oxford: Transaction Books, 1986), 8.

15   James Boyd White, 'Plato's Gargias: The Ethics of Argument', 50 *U. Chi. L. Rev.*, 849 (1983), 882.

16   I am here relying on Ackerman's formulation of constitutional moment. Mandela's transformation of the trial into a moment of constitutional politics from outside is a counter-constitutional moment that seeks to displace the original social contract. Since 'only people already enjoying democratic and constitutional rights have grounds for speaking of ... constitutional' moments, Mandela's intervention makes a counter-constitutional offer to displace the constituent principles of the present. For an account of 'constitutional moments',

'Recounting differently', the defendant composes a genealogical account not only of South African justice but also South Africa the nation.[17] In recounting stories of origin differently, i.e., in reconfiguring and retelling South Africa's violence of law-making and law-preserving, Mandela brings politico-historical inquiry into the orbit of law and legality.

In displacing the gathering effect of the 'we', he offers a genealogical and performative reading of the founding moment generally and the law specifically: he uses the moment of the trial to show the gap between law and mere law. In 'recounting differently', as Ricoeur observes, 'the inexhaustible richness of the event' of founding, he situates himself genealogically and performatively, in the spaces, interstices and speaking positions offered by the system, to expose the intense political and legal crisis haunting Apartheid.[18] Mandela's critique both uses and mocks the law, he upholds and defeats the law. In this double movement, he stages a genealogical and performative problematization that displaces and reinvents law. Without abandoning Enlightenment values of equality, freedom and liberty, Mandela's critique of Apartheid law and 'justice' takes a genealogical turn; launching a stinging demythologization of the mythical foundation of law - and the desacralization of sacred knowledge.

But what do genealogies do in the context of the political trial? First of all, genealogies are diagnostic tools: as a historical inquiry into the conditions of the present, genealogy reveals the coherence underlying sovereignty, the subject, institutions, discourses and identities as contingent and contested.[19] As a diagnostic or analytic tool into the conditions of the present, genealogy excavates submerged juridico-political crisis into an arena of visibility and shows the relationship between the practices of the present and the submerged crisis of the past.[20] The political trial is simply a surface manifestation of that submerged

---

see Bruce Ackerman, *We the People: Foundations* (Cambridge, MA: The Belknap Press of Harvard University, 1991). For a critique of Ackerman's position, see Michael J. Kilarman, 'Constitutional Fact/Constitutional Fiction: A Critique of Bruce Ackerman's Theory of Constitutional Moments', 44 (2) *Stanford Law Review*, 759 (1992).

17   Nelson Mandela, Transcript of the Incitement Trial, Nelson Mandela's First Court Statement, (hereafter The Incitement Trial Transcript), http://www.nelsonmandela.org/omalley/index.php/site/q/03lv01538/04lv01600/05lv01624/06lv01625.htm (last accessed 6 September 2013).

18   See Emilios Christodoulidis, 'Strategies of Rupture', 20 *Law and Critique*, 3 (2009), 22.

19   Michel Foucault, 'Nietzsche, Genealogy, History', in Donald F. Bouchard, *Language, Counter-Memory, and Practice: Selected Essays and Interviews* (Ithaca: Cornell University Press, 1977), 142–4; see also Colin Koopman, *Genealogy as Critique: Foucault and the Problems of Modernity* (Bloomington: Indiana University Press, 2013), 6–8. See also Wendy Brown, 'Politics Without Bannisters: Genealogical Politics in Nietzsche and Foucault', in *Politics Out of History* (Princeton: Princeton University Press, 2001).

20   See Vikki Bell, *Culture and Performance: The Challenge of Ethics, Politics, and Feminist Theory* (Oxford: Berg, 2007), 82; Koopman, *Genealogy as Critique*, 2.

crisis, a crisis of sovereignty that makes an appearance on the normative structures of the system once in a while. By tracing the conflict that rages beneath law's normative mainstays to the submerged crisis of the past, genealogy historicizes the juridical realm and exposes the contingency that lies beneath the coherence of the normative order. It brings that submerged problem into view 'so as to do something with them'.[21] Mandela conceived the trial not as 'a taste of the law' or as a site of 'truth-telling', but, in his own words, 'as a continuation of the struggle by other means'.[22] In all the three trials – from the Treason Trial to the Incitement Trial and the Rivonia Trial, Mandela brings historical inquiry into the orbit of law and legality, with the view to doing something with it, with the view to unlocking, if you like, juridically closed meanings.

Situating himself within, Mandela reconfigures the polyvalent material and spatial configuration of legal discourses to appropriate the tensions and contradictions that plague Apartheid's legal order. As Foucault writes in 'Nietzsche, Genealogy, History', 'the nature of these rules allows violence to be inflicted on violence and the resurgence of new forces that are sufficiently strong to dominate those in power'.[23] In a passage that encapsulates the kind of strategic move adopted by Mandela, Foucault writes:

> The success of history belongs to those who are capable of seizing these rules to replace those who had used them, to disguise themselves as to pervert them, invert their meaning and redirect them against those who had initially imposed them; controlling this complex mechanism, they will make it function so as to overcome the rulers through their own rules.[24]

Mandela's reconfiguration of South Africa's story of 'origin', his recounting of the story and history of its laws, his re-signification of the meanings of juridical concepts such as legality, criminality, equality, the rule of law, violence, communism, democracy, etc. is evidence of a certain genealogical logic at work in his defence.[25] He denounces the absurdities of Apartheid's legal order and the false legalism of his trials; he both invokes and protests rights, in a move that Foucault referred to as the 'simultaneous declaration of war and of rights.'[26] Mandela's deployment of Apartheid's own rules against those who own them, re-functioning

---

21 Koopman, *Genealogy as Critique*, 2.

22 Mandela, *Long Walk to Freedom*, 428–9.

23 See Foucault, 'Nietzsche, Genealogy, History', 151.

24 Ibid.

25 Ibid.

26 Michel Foucault, *Society Must be Defended: Lectures at the College De France, 1975–76*, edited by Mauro Bertani and Alessandro Fontana, translated by David Macey (London: Penguin Books, 2003), 73.

them (to use the Brechtian term), so as to expose the violent underside of legal rules is characteristic of a genealogical mobilization of 'effective history'.[27]

Consistent with this genealogical sensibility, Mandela conceives the struggles and confrontations within Apartheid laws, institutions and the social sphere in terms of a race-war that divides the South African *body politic* along a racial line.[28] More over, just as Foucault's genealogical analysis of power[29] draws on a reformulation of Carl Von Clausewitz's classic aphorism – 'war is a mere continuation of policy by other means' – Mandela viewed his trial as a continuation of the battle by a legal means. Indeed, Mandela makes this logic more explicit when he referred to 'the classic work of Clausewitz' in the Rivonia trial as one of the intellectual thoughts that shaped his political philosophies.[30] He said: 'The Court will see that I attempted to examine all types of authority on the subject – from the East and from the West, going back to the classic work of Clausewitz, and covering such a variety as Mao Tse Tung and Che Guevara.'[31]

I further argue that Mandela's strategy of resistance is clearly performative. By exposing the hidden violence that marks the moment of origin, by revealing the performative *coup de force* that unsettles the law from within, he counters the original performative with a new performative, a fiction with a fiction, to create an occasion for interruption. By referring to a higher law, what Derrida calls 'the law of laws', the law to come, that law which is responsive to the ethic of justice and responsibility, he performatively brings into being a new standard of justice that always interrupts the law and opens it up to 'the incalculable singular demand of justice beyond circumscription by the law'.[32] Since his intervention is aimed at creating conditions of possibility for change and transformation, his genealogies are not merely diagnostic. They are reconstructive and transformative. It is here, where genealogy engages in reconstruction and transformation that it takes a performative turn.

Although appeal to humanist ideals of reason, freedom, liberation, truth and democracy are pervasive in his defences and elsewhere in his writings, Mandela's mode of critique and struggle are both performative and genealogical.[33] In both the

---

27   Ibid.

28   Ibid., 47, 56.

29   Ibid., 16, 47.

30   Nelson Mandela, The Rivonia Trial, at http://law2.umkc.edu/faculty/projects/ftrials/mandela/mandelaspeech.html (last accessed 6 September 2013).

31   Ibid.

32   Stephen Curkpatrick, 'Ethical Discourse in an Age Cognizant of Perspective. Reflections on Derrida's "The Laws of Reflection: Nelson Mandela, In Admiration"', 40 (1) *Sofia*, 81 (2001), 100.

33   While Mandela's critique unravels the power relations law and the judicial apparatus reproduces and disseminates, he does not stop at unravelling. In order to support a programmatic solution, he imagines and outlines the shape and form of a future South Africa. It is this imagination of a higher law and appeal to moral codes such as justice and morality that makes him at once genealogical and performative.

Incitement and the Rivonia trials, we see forms of critique and political struggle that are genealogical and performative. Without abandoning Enlightenment values of rights and political liberty, Mandela's scrupulous excavation of the constitutive and regulative conditions of Apartheid law takes a genealogical and performative turn.

In 'The Other Heading: Reflections on Today's Europe', Derrida wrote:

> If the Enlightenment has given us human rights, political liberties and responsibilities, it would surely be out of the question to want to do away with the Enlightenment project. But it may also be necessary not simply to affirm but to question the values it has given us ... The imperative remains ... they have given us our language; our language of responsibility.[34]

While Foucault rejects the idea of resistance in the name of a new law or a moral code, and somehow appears to exaggerate the effectiveness of disciplinary normalizations, he nevertheless endorses the strategic appropriation of the organizing concepts and normalizing procedures of law as a counter-power and counter-discourse. As Timothy Mitchell put it, 'disciplines can breakdown, counteract one another, or overreach. They offer spaces for manoeuver and resistance, and can be turned to counter-hegemonic purposes.[35] In using and critiquing these values, Mandela is doing exactly this - using the spaces offered by enlightenment ideals 'for manoeuvre and resistance' to re-politicize the juridical realm and create conditions of possibility for intervention and critique. Through a productive coupling of performative genealogies with Enlightenment values, he slips under Apartheid's normative mainstays to expose the violence it neutralizes and renders inaccessible while critiquing the terms of its rationality.

Jurisdictional Objections: Opening up Space within Space

In *The Human Condition*, Hannah Arendt writes, 'Wherever the relevance of speech is at stake, matters become political by definition, for speech is what makes man a political being'.[36] Whereas one can still communicate without speech, Arendt maintains, 'No other human performance requires speech to the same extent as action'.[37] For Arendt, therefore, political action proper requires a form of speech that reveals the appearance of the acting subject 'in the human world'.

---

34 *The Other Heading: Reflections on Today's Europe*, translated by Pascale-Anne Brault and Michael Naas (Bloomington: Indiana University Press, 1992), xiii.

35 Tomothy Mitchell, *Colonizing Egypt* (Berkeley: University of California Press, 1991), xi.

36 Hannah Arendt, *The Human Condition* (Chicago: University of Chicago Press, 1998), 3–4.

37 Ibid., 179.

However, political action is not solely restricted to the domain of speech. In her book, *Just Silences*, Marianna Constable observes that 'silence is not always an absence of voice'.[38] It can be heard as voice of consent or dissent. Identifying a paradox often appropriated by regimes in silencing competing voices from being heard as intelligible voices, she writes, 'the empowerment that is to come with voice is a power that cannot be conjured without first being asserted; but the voice that asserts or demands power must in some sense be already empowered'.[39] This is precisely the paradox that animates the setting into motion of the judicial machine with the view to achieving repressive political goals.[40] The courts offer political defendants the very stuff they intend to deny them: hearing and visibility.

In political trials, 'jurisdiction' matters precisely because of the opportunity it offers for contestation.[41] The debate over whether the court is a competent court of jurisdiction to examine the matter and determine its merit, or whether the matter is justiciable in the first place, etc., provides the resistant subject with the opportunity to slip into the normative structure of the order – unravelling the dirty linen underneath its symbols of legitimation. If the Incitement Trial was aimed at eliminating resistant voices from being heard, in reality, it did exactly the opposite: instead of silencing Mandela and others, instead of suffocating black liberationist narratives and discourses, the trial offered them a space for hearing and visibility, allowing them to filter stories of injustice and indignation into the court of world opinion.[42] In his essay, 'Silence in the Courtroom', Andrew Green writes this about the trial of Socrates: 'Although the trial represented an attempt to silence the critic ... the speech survived for the next two and a half millennia – a solid refutation of the Athenian government's ability to quiet a voice of dissent.'[43] In this trial, a subject whose voice is usurped and whose discourse marginalized is given an opportunity to re-create himself as resistant and to negotiate his relation with the law. It enabled him to both resist and claim authority. Of course, the court would eventually silence foes of the state through incarceration or other measures, but the 'hearing' proper provides precisely that – a hearing and visibility through which they can offer an account of themselves, in their codes and dialects, through their discourse.[44]

---

38   Marianne Constable, *Just Silences: The Limits and Possibilities of Modern Law* (Princeton: Princeton University Press, 2005), 58.

39   Ibid.

40   The use of the courtroom as a technology of repression leaves behind a trace, a remnant that no one can predict how it might be recalled and deployed on the historical stage.

41   See Otto Kirchheimer, *Political Justice: The Use of Legal Procedure for Political Ends* (Princeton: Princeton University Press, 1961), 37; Christenson, *Political Trials*, 9.

42   Christenson, *Political Trials*, 9.

43   Andrew Green, 'Silence in the Courtroom', 24 (1) *Law and Literature* (2012), 81.

44   See James C. Scott, *Domination and the Arts of Resistance* (New Haven: Yale University Press, 1990), 109.

Mandela begins his politicization of the judicial space by establishing rapport with the court. He assures the judges of his highest respect for them and the law. In carving out space for action, a political space within the legal space, he mounts a generative objection that is at once legal and political. From the outset, he reminds the judge that the 'case is a trial of the aspirations of the African people' – one that is neither reducible to nor comprehensible within the confines of the trial's communicative offers. By respectfully submitting himself to the law, warning but not accusing, he defines what the trial is – the trial of the 'aspirations of the African people' – and delineates its domain of emphasis: 'on important questions that go beyond the scope of this present trial'.[45] Here we have a preliminary political injunction – the subject of the trial is not the tragic hero, Nelson Mandela, who at once claims and resists authority, but South Africa as a whole. It is the crisis of South African sovereignty, the moral degeneration of its institutions of justice, that is on trial. By inviting them out of the restraining domain of the juridical into the political, he deploys the communicative offer of the trial to communicate his experiences, and how Africans in South Africa lost their 'just place in relation' to whites.

Asked by the judge whether he pleads guilty, Mandela refused to answer the question directly. Instead, he raises jurisdictional objections: 'Your Worship, before I plead to the charge, there are one or two points I would like to raise.'[46] By objecting to the competence of the court to hear his case, Mandela carves out space for the possibility of acting, to enable politics at a site where politics is deactivated, and to turn the destabilizing impetus of the political trial against the very power that abuses the rituals of legality. Questioning the court's authority to sit in judgment and dispense justice, Mandela asked the judge to suspend the invitation for a plea and made a counter-invitation; inviting the judge into his turf – to take flight into the submerged crisis of sovereignty and its constituent point of South African politics. Speaking as a lawyer, a man of law who at once upholds and contests law, he makes an objection that cannot be ignored: 'I want to apply for Your Worship's recusal from this case. I challenge the right of this court to hear my case on two grounds.'[47]

This is how, at the earliest stage of the trial, he refuses to enter a guilty plea, to expand the responsive ranges of this space and this moment:

Firstly, I challenge it because I fear that I will not be given a fair and proper trial.

Secondly, I consider myself neither legally nor morally bound to obey laws made by a parliament in which I have no representation.

---

45   See The Incitement Trial, Transcript.
46   Ibid.
47   Ibid.

The first objection is an internal critique that does not remain internal but transcends. Departing from forms of critique that are possible within law's frameworks and analytic categories, he creates the conditions of possibility for a critique of law that is neither reducible to nor subsumable within law's categories. It is a critique that deploys the language of Enlightenment – equality, fairness, judicial impartiality, and the principle that one cannot be a judge in his own case. He says, 'It is improper and against the elementary principles of justice to entrust whites with cases involving the denial by them of basic human rights to the African people'.[48]

The second objection, however, is a meta-level objection that is both genealogical and performative. It is not a mere denunciation of the inaugural violence of exclusion, it is also a performative claim that seeks, to use Derrida's formulation, to 'justify, to legitimate or transform the relations to law, and so to present itself as having a right to law'.[49] It is an institutive act of intervention that seeks to legitimate itself as law while trying to displace state law. As Emilios Christodoulidis argues, these are meta-level considerations necessary to open up space for an 'act of resistance [that] registers without being absorbed, integrated or co-opted' by the system and the discourse it resists.[50] It is an objection that elevates itself beyond the legal-illegal distinctions into the meta-level critique of the just law and the unjust law, the moral law and the immoral law to 'resist injustices of assimilation and recognition'.[51] As James Tully argues, only at the meta-level can 'politics resist and redress the multiple forms of its co-option'.[52] By elevating the contestation from the level to the meta-level, i.e., from the legal-illegal to the just-unjust, moral-immoral, Mandela appropriates the interruptive force of justice and morality to import a spatiality 'that cannot be captured, and certainly is not exhausted, in any notion of the political constitution' to redeem the speaking position of 'the entire nation'.[53]

Conceiving his trial as a surface manifestation of a long submerged and much deeper crisis of sovereignty, he excavates the strange singularities that undergirds law's universality, and unravels the incoherence of the order. He identifies gaps, tensions, discursive dynamics and assemblages that reveal how the coherence of Apartheid's judicial order is contingently articulated.[54] To create a line of flight

---

48   Ibid.

49   Jacques Derrida, 'Force of Law: "The Mystical Foundation of Authority"', in Drucilla Cornell, Michel Rosenfeld and David Gray Carlson (eds) *Deconstruction and the Possibility of Justice* (London: Routledge, 1992), 2.

50   Christodoulidis, 'Strategies of Rupture', 5.

51   James Tully, cited in Emilios Christodoulidis, 'Against Substitution', in Martin Laughlin and Neil Walker, *The Paradox of Constitutionalism: Constituent Power and Constitutional Form* (Oxford: Oxford University Press, 2007), 206.

52   Christodoulidis, 'Strategies of Rupture', 17.

53   Ibid., 207; see also Anthony R. DeLuca, *Gandhi, Mao, Mandela, and Gorbachev: Studies in Personality, Power, and Politics* (Westport: Praeger, 2000), 73.

54   See Koopman, *Genealogy as Critique*, 6.

for forms of critique that go beyond the crisis that manifests itself as the surface effect of a much deeper problem, he begins from forms of critique that are possible within. But to transcend 'the multiple forms of its cooption', as Tully says, to resist the confines of the deliberative offer, he instigates a crisis that cuts the ties between the subject and the legal order and obliterates their reciprocal obligations.

From Epistemic Injustice to the Ethic of Coexistence

As a black defendant before Apartheid law, Mandela enters the deliberative framework of the trial with a speech impediment. In spite of procedural and substantive safeguards enshrined in Apartheid's juridical codes, Africans in South Africa, like the plebeians of the antiquity, are subject to injustices of misrecognition. The founding violence that institutes an exclusionary grid of intelligibility subjects the excluded to epistemic and hermeneutic marginalization that cannot be redressed in law. The political philosophy of white supremacy and racist discourses that have become normative and quotidian effectively socialized and racialized institutions of law and justice. Within that racialized and socialized institutional paradigm, the black body represents a problem and a danger. For Mandela, the concern here is what Fanon refers to as the dangerousness of being identified with a danger.[55] It is not the law as such that is a problem, but the dehumanized black being that is before the law which creates a problem for law. It is Mandela's explication of what W.E.B. Du Bois calls 'existence as a member of a racial group deemed problem people'[56] and the epistemological permutations of this dynamics that is the focus of this section.

Mandela's first objection – 'I fear that I will not be given a fair and proper trial' – is not merely an internal critique suggestive of biases and prejudices, it is not even a concern with the politicization of the administration of justice. It is an objection to the impossibility of justice under Apartheid, a claim expressive of the Fanonian 'anti-black racial gaze'[57] that, to use Foucault's expression, 'attached itself to the body', inscribed 'in the nervous system, in temperament, in the digestive apparatus' of the white man and the white court to which Mandela submits himself. Here is Mandela's trenchant articulation of that conundrum:

> Broadly speaking, Africans and whites in this country have no common standard of fairness, morality, and ethics, and it would be very difficult to determine on my part what standard of fairness and justice Your Worship has in mind. In their relationship with us, South African whites regard it as fair and just to pursue policies which have outraged the conscience of mankind and of honest

---

55   Franz Fanon, *Black Skin, White Masks*, translated by Richard Philcox (New York: Grove Press, 2008), 143.

56   W.E.B. Du Bois, *The Souls of Black Folk* (Boston: St. Martins, 1997), 34.

57   See Fanon, *Black Skin, White Masks*, 89–100.

and upright men throughout the civilized world. They suppress our aspirations, bar our way to freedom, and deny us opportunities to promote our moral and material progress, to secure ourselves from fear and want. All the good things of life are reserved for the white folk and we blacks are expected to be content to nourish our bodies with such pieces of food as drop from the tables of men with white skins. This is the white man's standard of justice and fairness. Herein lies his conceptions of ethics. Whatever he himself may say in his defense, the white man's moral standards in this country must be judged by the extent to which he has condemned the vast majority of its inhabitants to serfdom and inferiority.[58]

In this diagnosis into the political rationality and the moral and ethical standards of the white community, Mandela is accounting for a mode of knowing and acting that excludes the very possibility of communication and understanding between 'whites' and blacks in South Africa.

This is a conundrum that Miranda Fricker, writing almost half a century after Mandela's speech, identified as 'epistemic injustice'.[59] According to Fricker, epistemic injustice takes place 'when a speaker receives the wrong degree of credibility from his hearer owing to a certain sort of unintended prejudice on the hearer's part'.[60] In offering a theoretical exposition of this problematic, Fricker refers to this domain as a domain of 'rationality and the ethics of what must surely be our most basic and ubiquitous epistemic practice – the practice of gaining knowledge by being told'.[61] As an object of epistemic injustice excluded from participating in the production of truth bearing discourses, Mandela's genres of discourses, dialects, and truths are *a priori* excluded. As an agent that harbors what Fanon calls the look of a black male body, Mandela's image generates a prejudice that exposes his claim to what Nancy Fraser calls 'injustice of misrecognition'.[62]

This problematization of the cognitive and affective substrate of Apartheid's normative structures is both redemptive and resistant: redemptive because, by demanding the right to have equal access to knowledge production, Mandela claims epistemic agency. It is resistant because his intervention contests and resists the hermeneutic marginalization of blacks and recreates a rationality that resists in epistemic terms, as epistemic resistance. Here, Mandela offers a destabilizing critique of epistemic domains that *a priori* excludes the possibility of justice for a 'black man in white man's court'. Put in the Foucauldian paradigm, it is an

---

58   Mandela, The Rivonia Trial, Transcript.

59   Miranda Fricker, 'Epistemic Injustice and a Role for Virtue in the Politics of Knowing', 34 (1/2) *Metaphilosophy* (2003), 154.

60   Ibid. See also Miranda Fricker, *Epistemic Injustice: Power and the Ethics of Knowing* (Oxford: Oxford University Press, 2007), 18.

61   Fricker, 'Epistemic Injustice and a Role for Virtue in the Politics of Knowing', 61.

62   Nancy Fraser, 'Heterosexism, Misrecognition, and Capitalism: A Response to Judith Butler', *New Left Review*, I/228, March–April 1998, 141; Fanon, *Black Skin, White Masks*, 94.

intervention that subverts Apartheid's moral/juridical codes, dislocates its 'orders of knowledge', and decentres the domains and objects in which the system's true and false is inscribed.[63] When he claims that whites 'regard it as fair and just to pursue policies which have outraged the conscience of mankind ... suppress our aspirations, bar our way to freedom, and deny us opportunities to promote our moral and material progress, to secure ourselves from fear and want',[64] he is drawing a direct line between the submerged crisis of sovereignty to its surface manifestations – his trial. Using this moment as an opportunity, he is problematizing the instituted forms of law and justice to generate and present an alternative narrative of his period so that such discourses and practices can no longer go without saying.

As a subject whose identity 'can deprive [him] of the very resources [he] needs in order to attain the virtue[s]' necessary to 'preempt or [overcome] such injustice', Mandela deploys his knowledge of the law to navigate through law's gate-keeping discourses. Even then, he largely 'remain[s] hostage to the broader social structures in which [his] testimonial' is heard.[65] Recognizing the prejudice that is inscribed in the nervous system of his hearers and the consequent impossibility of justice in the court of a white man, Mandela declares that his point is neither the representation of the 'unrepresentable' nor the promise of the impossible. The decisive point, Mandela argues, is not one that is reducible to the question of whether this conflict can be represented in law and can be heard fairly and impartially. 'The court might reply to this part of my argument by assuring me that it will try my case fairly and without fear or favor', he argued, 'but such a reply would completely miss the point of my argument'.[66] Our central contention, Mandela argues, turns not so much on the juridical question of fair hearing but rather on meta-ethical questions of hearing itself. He is interested in apprehending and finally naming a domain that organize and structure Apartheid's unequal distribution of voice to speaking bodies. His is a concern with the ethic of reception; the conditions that needs to be there for a hearing of any kind to lead to understanding. It is a concern with the responsibility of hearing the 'Other', a plea for testimonial sensibility.[67]

This, then, is a kind of critique aimed at generating contradictions capable of captivating the imagination of white South Africans and the world ambivalent in the face of a moral crisis in which the law is deployed to safeguard illegality – preventing the majority from changing an illegal situation by a legal means. By desecrating 'white man's standard of justice' from the colourless, incalculable and singular demands of justice, by exposing the socialized nature of white justice, calling into question the '*ethicity* or the morality of [their] *ethics*' as Derrida

---

63   Michel Foucault, 'Questions of Method', in *Power: Essential Works of Michel Foucault, 1954–1984*, vol. 3, edited by James D. Faubian (London: Penguin, 1994), 230.

64   Mandela, The Rivonia Trial, Transcript.

65   Fricker, *Epistemic Injustice and a Role for Virtue in the Politics of Knowing'*, 172.

66   Mandela, Incitement Trial, Transcript.

67   Fricker, *'Epistemic Injustice and a Role for Virtue in the Politics of Knowing'*, 159.

would say, his intervention displaces the existing form of epistemic sensibility and compels the system to face up to the surprising emergence of this 'new subject in history' who contests and interrupts the continuity of practices, discourses and gestures that up until then go without saying.[68] By digging deep into the epistemic and ontological nature of violence and injustice in South Africa, he sought to clarify the ethical and moral decadence underlying a system in which three million whites totalize the 'we', usurping the speaking position of 13 million people and use the court system to preserve and conserve that founding violence.[69]

White Justice: 'Black Man in a White Man's Court'

Exploring the Nationalist Party's 'sanitizing rhetoric', Stephen Curkpatrick explores how the party formulated a discourse that conceals the race element from its racist project and sought to rationalize 'apartheid' in terms of 'separate development', 'multiracial' in terms of 'multinational', justifying the 'Bantustan policy' in terms of 'plural democracy', 'self-governing territories' and 'democratic-federalism'.[70] In coupling this self-serving rhetoric with existing power–knowledge constellation, it defends the 'homelands' policy as equivalent to 'European ethnic nationalities and statehood'.[71] Curkpatrick goes on to state that in the struggle for the preservation of white supremacy, 'Each period represents a shift in rhetoric for international appeasement, but no change in the fundamental characteristics of apartheid'.[72] Despite these efforts by the system to deploy the full range of concealing juridical resources to suppress its racist formation, Mandela's intervention decisively infiltrated its apparatus of truth generation and knowledge production to bring into view Apartheid's oppressive underside. Without a critical excavation of the racist subtext that animates the setting into motion of the justice system, the whole exercise will be meaningless and misleading.[73]

In one of his most disruptive self-assertions, Mandela asks: 'what is this rigid color-bar in the administration of justice? Why is it that in this courtroom I face a white magistrate, am confronted by a white prosecutor, and escorted into the dock by a white orderly? Can anyone honestly and seriously suggest that in this

---

68   Jacques Derrida, 'Passions', translated by David Wood, in *On The Name* (Stanford: Stanford University Press, 1995), 133. Derrida asks about the ethicity of ethics, the morality of morality, the legality of law, and what responsibility signifies by and of itself.

69   Mandela, The Rivonia Trial, Transcript.

70   See Curkpatrick, 'Ethical Discourse', 99.

71   Ellen Armour, *Deconstruction, Feminist Theology, and the Problem of Difference: Subverting the Race/Gender* (Chicago and London: University of Chicago Press, 1999), 228.

72   Ibid.

73   Mandela, Incitement Trial, Transcript. For an account of how the equality of persons before the law can be manipulated for partisan political goals, see Joel B. Grossman, 'Political Justice in the Democratic State', 8 (3) *Polity*, 358 (1973), 372.

type of atmosphere the scales of justice are evenly balanced?'[74] It is a form of critique that Christodoulidis identifies as immanent, in that it drives its standard from the 'material actuality' of life as lived under Apartheid and contrasts it to the normative inscriptions of equality and justice.[75] It is a critique that turns upside down the violent underside of Apartheid normativity, and makes manifest the violence produced and conserved by a whole series of juridical codes and institutions. Unable to co-opt and integrate within its economy of containment, the system concedes to the whiteness of its laws, its institutions and its justice at a site in which such admission is both legally and politically meaningful. The judge says: '*There Is Only One Court today and that is the White Man's Court. There is No Other Court.* What purpose does it serve you to make an application when there is only one court?'[76] This is perhaps an instance of what Christodoulidis, drawing on Verges, refers to as rupture. He writes: 'A rupture registers when an act appears incongruent to the logic of its representation, and with such intensity that it can neither be domesticated nor ignored.'[77] When the court of justice admits of its whiteness, clearly, this is a response that registers incongruently 'to the logic of its representation'.[78] Speaking of the strategy of rupture he practiced in the trial of Klaus Barbie, Verges writes, '[R]upture traverses the whole structure of the trial. Facts as well as circumstances of the action pass onto a secondary plane; in the forefront suddenly appears the brutal contestation with the order of the State'.[79] Because of the contradictions that pervade the entire structure of the justice system that uses the devices of justice to secure racial inequality, the confrontation between the defendant and the state discloses the brutality of the system in 'ways that excludes all compromise'.[80]

If 'rupture registers in terms of a response it triggers', the court's admission is a response that registers as rupture. The judge's admission that 'there is only one court today and that is the White Man's court', exposes the court, first and foremost, as something other than a house of justice; and the judge as an agent of oppression than a guarantor of justice. It authenticates and reinforces the defendant's claim that 'I am a black man in a white man's court': a truth Apartheid cannot contain, or, to use Christodoulidis' phrase, cannot 'seal-over'.[81] In fact, Mandela is certain, as he engages in a series of double movements that at once resists and claims authority, upholds and denounces the law, that he has already registered a disturbing surprise against the system's normative claims when he returned to the judge's admission of the colour of South African justice. Realizing

---

74 Mandela, Incitement Trial, Transcript.
75 Christodoulidis, 'Strategies of Rupture', 6.
76 Mandela, Incitement Trial, Transcript.
77 Christodoulidis, 'Against Substitution', 194.
78 Ibid.
79 See Jacques Verges, in Christodoulidis, 'Strategies of Rupture', 5.
80 Ibid.
81 Ibid., 7.

that there is nothing more politically disruptive for the system than to recite and reiterate its visible markers of injustice, Mandela pushes the judge further into far more colossal admissions about the fraudulent logic underlying the administration of justice: 'Your Worship has already raised the point that here in this country there is only a white court. What is the point of all this?' Replying to his own question, he said: 'the real purpose of this rigid color-bar is to ensure that the justice dispensed by courts conform to the policy of the country, however much that policy might be in conflict with norms of justice accepted in judiciaries throughout the civilized world'.[82]

Switching the plane of his critique to a meta-level, Mandela asks the judge: 'What sort of justice is this that enables the aggrieved to sit in judgment over those against whom they have laid charge?'[83] Here, Mandela speaks in the plural 'them'–'us' binary; draws on the ethic of difference to challenge the system to justify its oppression of the native people, to account for the racialization and socialization of the administration of justice. Questioning authority at a site where authority is ceremonially elevated from the realm of interrogation, Mandela speaks to white South Africans, in English and as a lawyer, affirming that resistance to white justice is not merely consistent with the European legal tradition; it is indeed its very expression.[84] What is the essence and ultimate purpose of this 'white' justice that 'enables' the oppressor 'to sit in judgment' over the oppressed? While seeming to ask an ethico-juridical question – 'what sort of justice enables them to sit in judgment over those they have laid charges' – Mandela has done nothing but to enable politics, to claim the right to politics, and engage the collective 'Other'. It is a question that transforms the personal moral struggle in Mandela into a collective political struggle between the subjugated black majority and the ruling white minority. It is a strategic intervention that seeks to capture in one immanent intervention the rupture that navigates across Apartheid's decadent structures. In addressing the question to the 'other' – the oppressor – Mandela is seeking to place the 'other' 'in contradiction to' its professed values and principles.[85] By choosing to demand the judge's recusal from the case, he opens up the space for a defiant intervention that allows him to project this fundamental wrong that is antithetical to any conception of justice. By emphasizing the rationality and system of meaning

---

82   Mandela, Incitement Trial, Transcript.

83   Mandela here deploys the inexhaustible and interruptive force of justice to expose the radically calculative and tactical nature of Apartheid law and legality. He asks, 'what kind of justice', to reveal what Derrida calls the aporia or impasse between the calculable laws of nations 'as a re-iterable register or mark of human relations' and the incalculable presence of justice. Using justice as interruption, Mandela redirects the trial to adjudicate the inaugural justice of Apartheid law, and expose the illegal foundation of Apartheid law.

84   See Jacques Derrida, 'The Laws of Reflection: For Nelson Mandela, In Admiration', in Jacques Derrida and Mustapha Talili, *For Nelson Mandela* (New York: Seaver Books, 1987), 33.

85   Christodoulidis, 'Strategies of Rupture', 5.

upon which truth and justice rested in Apartheid South Africa, Mandela exposes the fundamentally inhuman logic that frames and structures Apartheid and the radical disjuncture between Apartheid and the cardinal virtues of equality, dignity and justice.

In his speech, he is re-creating a new world of possibilities and a new identity that resists its identity as passive and obedient. By unearthing the contingency of what the judge sees as self-evident – 'What purpose does it serve you to make an application when there is only one court, as you know yourself? What court do you wish to be tried by?' – Mandela insists that that is perhaps 'my main point of contention'.[86] By problematizing the normalizing discourses of law that the court sees as self-evident, Mandela's performative resistance prevents closure, creates an opportunity for re-opening, and compels hegemonic discourses to enter the realm of visibility.[87] We have here a politics of resistance that deploys historical knowledge of colonization and subjugation to disrupt gate-keeping legal technologies of domination that include as excluded. Appropriating the amplifying potential of the courtroom, Mandela infiltrates this patronizing colonial logic, and its mode of thought to expose a singular logic that refuses to register and represent the unjust death, and grief of the excluded majority. Mandela's repertoire of resistance successfully overruns the state's spectacles of repression when the judge failed to contain, suppress or integrate those destabilizing critiques that established the colour of Apartheid justice.

Whatever the liberatory potential of this admission, regardless of the transformative potential attributed to the disclosure of the racist logic that animates the operation of the system, this intervention 'registers without being absorbed, integrated or co-opted into the system against which it stands'.[88] The question is not so much what happened to Apartheid in the immediate aftermath of this trial, but the unquantifiable truth-effects that circulated a true discourse about the legitimate aspirations of the native population that ultimately led to the demise of Apartheid. The system cannot admit to the whiteness of its justice in a black majority country and continue to pretend that Apartheid courts are sites of truth and justice. By admitting its true colour, the court can no longer invoke its European heritage. Convinced that this fundamental wrong is something much more profound than the failure of the judiciary, Mandela re-enacts life as lived in the space of the courtroom to consign and institute this story in the archive of the very state he denounces as racist and unjust. In his own words:

---

86 Mandela, Incitement Trial, Transcript.

87 On the revealing potential of performativity, see Judith Butler, *Excitable Speech: A Politics of the Performative* (New York: Routledge, 1997), 94; Bell, *Culture and Performance*, 25–7; Lois McNay, 'Subject, Psyche and Agency: The Work of Judith Butler', in Vikki Bell (ed.) *Performativity & Belonging* (London: SAGE Publications Inc., 1999), 177.

88 Christodoulidis, 'Strategies of Rupture', 5.

> The court cannot expect a respect for the process of representation and negotiation to grow amongst the African people, when the government shows everyday, by its conduct, that it despises such processes and frowns upon them and will not indulge in them. Nor will the court, I believe, say that, under the circumstances, my people are condemned forever to say nothing and to do nothing.[89]

Using his speaking position as defendant, he reveals to South Africans and the international community the fundamental inhumanity of Apartheid and therefore the constitutive impossibility of equality, dignity and justice within its 'grotesque system of justice'.[90]

Between Law and Justice: Law's Illegality and Immorality

> I consider myself neither morally nor legally obliged to obey laws made by a parliament in which I am not represented.[91]

In 'Mandela's "Force of Law"', Stephen Curkpatrick draws on Derrida's 'Force of Law' and 'The Laws of Reflection' to explore the Derridean performative that cuts through Mandela's speech.[92] Curkpatrick says, 'The law is fundamentally illegal at the point of its performative origin. In the mystical foundation of its authority, law is legal because of convention'.[93] For Derrida, this inaugural aporia is not unique to the performative institution of law but the very characteristic of law in general. Law is legal because of 'the mystical foundation of authority', those 'legitimate fictions on which [law] founds the truth of its authority'.[94] For both Montaigne and Derrida, there exists a fundamental rift between law and justice: 'justice as law is no justice'. Every decision entails unique interpretation 'which no existing, coded rule can or ought to guarantee': every decision 'must conserve the law and also destroy it or suspend it enough to have to reinvent it in each case and re-justify it'.[95]

Mandela's 'force of law' resides not only in his incisive articulation of law's divisibility and iterability, but also in his appropriation of its perpetual contestability. In this particular scene, Mandela switches the plane at which he was operating to a meta-level to deploy justice and morality as interruption – forces interruptive of the 'calculable economy' of 'law as convention'[96] – to reinvent a new and radically

---

89 Mandela, Incitement Trial, Transcript.
90 Ibid.
91 Mandela, Incitement Trial, Transcript.
92 Stephen Curkpatrick, 'Mandela's "Force of Law"', 41 (2) *Sophia*, 63 (2002).
93 Ibid.
94 Derrida, 'Force of Law', 12.
95 Ibid., 23.
96 Ibid., 12–15; see also Curkpatrick, 'Mandela's "Force of Law"', 75.

egalitarian regime of legality responsive to justice.[97] In order to fully appreciate the attack that reveals the law as a sort of coded and institutionalized violence against Africans, allow me to reproduce his intervention:

> The second ground of my objection is that I consider myself neither morally nor legally obliged to obey laws made by a parliament in which I am not represented. That the will of the people is the basis of the authority of government is a principle universally acknowledged as sacred throughout the civilized world, and constitutes the basic foundations of freedom and justice. It is understandable why citizens, who have the vote as well as the right to direct representation in the country's governing bodies, should be morally and legally bound by the laws governing the country. It should be equally understandable why we, as Africans, should adopt the attitude that we are neither morally nor legally bound to obey laws which we have not made, nor can we be expected to have confidence in courts which enforce such laws.[98]

This is one of the common threads that run through both the Incitement and the Rivonia Trials. As a lawyer aware of the performative illegality of law's origin, and a man with access to an alternative idiom of legality – the radically egalitarian African law that the state disqualified through its inaugural violence – Mandela presents himself as having the right to law and a claim to authority. Integrating Enlightenment rationality into his strategy, he uses the discourse of equality, representation, recognition and justice to make visible the gulf that opens up in the movement from 'European legal tradition, which seeks a universal symmetry of equality before the law' to Apartheid legality where the former is betrayed, adulterated and abused by the latter.[99]

By deploying such a performative strategy in a new site – the court of law – he was trying to 'reshape and expand the terms of political debate, enabling different

---

97 This is a classic genealogical object because instead of 'getting to the bottom of things', to discover an essential truth of the constitutive point of politics, it aims to bring it about that the actors and the spectators of the trial – 'prosecution, the jury, the bench, the authorities and the body politic – "no longer know what to do", so that acts, gestures, discourses which up until then had seemed to go without saying become problematic, difficult and dangerous'. The legal moment is appropriated as an opportunity to recount the political economy of exclusion and dispossession that secures and guarantees 'a grotesque system of justice'. It is performative too because it speaks of the idea of a law beyond Apartheid law, the law of laws, the law beyond a determinate legality.

98 Mandela, Incitement Trial, Transcript.

99 See Derrida, 'Laws of Reflection', 16. Reflecting on this question, Derrida notes, 'is this law, which gives orders to constitutions and declarations, essentially a thing of the West? Does its formal universality retain some irreducible link with European history'. He concludes: 'that its formal character would be as essential to the universality of the law as its presentation in a determined moment and place in history'. See also Curkpatrick, 'Ethical Discourse', 96.

questions to be asked, enlarging the space of legitimate contestation, modifying the relation of the different participants to the truths in the name of which' Apartheid governs.[100] He is both 'critical' and 'genealogical'. When he says that 'I consider myself neither legally nor morally bound to obey laws made by a parliament in which I have no representation', or 'It is improper and against the elementary principles of justice to entrust whites with cases involving the denial by them of basic human rights to the African people' or that 'The white man makes all the laws, he drags us before his courts and accuses us, and he sits in judgment over us', he is raising insoluble objections that Apartheid can neither integrate nor suppress within its economy of representation. In this, Mandela's performative intervention is disruptive and constitutive. It is disruptive because it destabilizes Apartheid's normative basis for claiming obedience to a law that is itself illegal; constitutive because this mode of critique calls into being a new subject that imagines the world of political universe differently and acts in ways that breaks from and displaces what the system recognizes as the normative.

As a 'man of law', a man that makes possible the disruptive force of law, Mandela traces the genesis of Apartheid law to its European root to use this genealogy against the enemy that distort it while pretending to be true to its unsettling force. Mandela does not merely conceive the struggles and confrontations that go on within Apartheid laws and institutions in terms of what Foucault calls a race-war.[101] He also adopts a strategic-historicist critique towards law. In reconfiguring and recounting this genealogy, rather differently, he makes visible the uncharted terrains of 'European legal tradition, which seeks a universal symmetry of equality before the law, but is unable to tolerate such difference as to effect this universality for radical difference'.[102]

The performative *coup de force* that inaugurated a legal order and concealed law's violent gesture of exclusion is here reconfigured and used by a resistant subject to recognize his own subjection and subjectification by the order and to negotiate and transform his subjecthood.[103] As Nancy Fraser says, 'The speaker speaks for the world, which means the speaker speaks to it, on behalf of it, in order to make it a "world"'.[104] When he says that I understand why white South Africans obey Apartheid legality and why, following the same logic, Africans 'should adopt the attitude that we are neither morally nor legally bound to obey laws which we have not made'; he is, particularly, though not exclusively, speaking to Africans, for Africans, with the view to bringing into being a new subject and a new idiom

---

100   Nikolas Rose, *Powers of Freedom: Reframing Political Thought* (New York: Cambridge University Press, 1999), P-277; see also Mitchell Dean, *Governmentality: Power and Rule in Modern Society* (London: SAGE Publications, 1999), 19, 25.

101   See Foucault, *Society Must be Defended*, 26.

102   See Curkpatrick, 'Ethical Discourse', 96.

103   See Judith Butler and Athena Athanasiou, *Dispossessions: The Performative in the Political* (Cambridge: Polity Press, 2013), 140.

104   See Nancy Fraser, in Christodoulidis, 'Against Substitution', 201.

of legality that radically breaks from and displaces the instituted model. In calling upon South Africans to defy and disobey Apartheid, he performatively calls into being a new defiant subjectivity, what Foucault calls a 'new speaking subject', who says 'I' and 'we' as he recounts 'history', a subject who 'tell[s] the story of his own history'; one that 'reorganize[s] the past, events, rights, injustices, defeats, and victories around himself and his own destiny'.[105] In other words, this speech act re-invents a 'subject' that is nameless, vote-less and invisible, into a defiant subject resistant to the invasive and productive complex of subjection.

In unmasking the deceptive logic at the heart of the constituted grid of legality, he not only dislodges the legal basis of legality itself but also prescribes his own standard of legality that promises to host the voices and aspirations of all South Africans regardless of race or colour. While he denounces Apartheid's infelicitous illegality, he uses the law and the speaking position it offers to contest and claim authority. So he speaks not only to describe prevailing epistemic standards that frame and determine the limit of what is possible and achievable, but also to propose an alternative epistemic standard that allows us to imagine and perceive a world of politics that breaks off from the instituted model. In short, he is speaking to the world, to use Fraser's words, 'to create another world' – a new South Africa.

By expressing his admiration to the Anglo-American law and African traditional law, he contrasts the equity of Apartheid law to these two legal traditions.[106] In this comparison that traces the genesis of Apartheid law to the Anglo-American tradition that he admires, an admiration that is cognizant of law's spectral haunting, Mandela shows his contempt for the law, the law that is the antithesis of justice, simply to declare his utmost respect for the law.[107] Here is Mandela:

> Perhaps the court will say that despite our human rights to protest, to object, to make ourselves heard, we should stay within the letter of the law. I would say, Sir, that it is the government, its administration of the law, which brings the law into such contempt and disrepute that one is no longer concerned in this country to stay within the letter of the law. I will illustrate this from my own experience. The government has used the process of law to handicap me, in my personal life, in my career, and in my political work, in a way which is calculated, in my opinion, to bring about contempt for the law.[108]

In identifying the law as a normative instrument Apartheid mobilizes to close all avenues of lawful protest, leaving social agents with the only options of accepting

---

105   Foucault, *Society Must be Defended*, 135.

106   See Derrida, 'Laws of Reflection', 16–17. Mandela expresses his admiration for both the English parliamentary tradition and the American separation of powers principle. He is fascinated by the Magna Carta, the Universal Declaration of Human Rights and the radically egalitarian structure of African law.

107   See ibid., 36.

108   Mandela, The Rivonia Trial, Transcript.

either 'a permanent state of inferiority', 'a perpetual subordination' or defying the government and its laws, Mandela taps a contradiction that 'inform[s] a crisis that is experienced by social agents in the materiality of their life'.[109] By using the law to eliminate all forms of dissent and opposition, by using the law to prevent him from practising law in sites where this practice is of paramount importance to his people, by using the law to outlaw a man of the law, the system shows the utmost contempt for the law.[110]

Mandela's contempt for Apartheid law is 'the symmetrical inverse of [his] respect for the moral law'.[111] Speaking as a man of law and 'with a confidence of one', he demonstrates not only that he belongs to a tradition respectful of law, but also one committed to the law of laws, the law responsible and answerable to its normative correctness. Taking himself as an example, he is reflecting the contempt of the white man for his own laws. More importantly, he is making the point that by scorning the law, i.e., by operating outside the framework of the law 'to handicap me, in my personal life, in my career, and in my political work', the argument goes, what goes on in Apartheid courts is not judgment but a certain coalescence of what Walter Benjamin identifies as lawmaking and law preserving violence.[112] Reflecting on this reflection, Derrida notes, 'those who, one day, made him an outlaw simply did not have the right: they had already placed themselves outside the law'.[113] If the system holds its own law in contempt, he argues, it cannot expect the subjugated to respect the very law the owners hold in great contempt. This voice that has become a mirror for the white man 'to recognize and see their own scorn for the law reflected',[114] as Derrida insists, does more than reflecting: it produces justice.

Conclusion

Mandela's strategy of resistance aims at infiltrating the system to expose its productive and repressive logic. It is a strategic engagement with law that seeks to expose while also seeking to transform the racial relations in South Africa on the basis of the principles articulated in the 'Freedom Charter'. Through critical and prophetic statements transformative of the moment, Mandela sought to expose the infelicitous performative planted at the heart of Apartheid legality and dismantle the fictions of law and justice that sustains an explicitly violent and racist order.

---

109   See Christodoulidis, 'Strategies of Rupture', 6.

110   Derrida, 'Laws of Reflection', 34–6. Derrida notes, as a man of law, Mandela 'is reflecting the deontology of deontology, the deep meaning and spirit of the deontological laws'.

111   Ibid., 32.

112   Mandela, The Rivonia Trial, Transcript.

113   Derrida, 'Laws of Reflection', 32.

114   Ibid.

Whatever framework of analysis one adopts in engaging his words, the appealing force of Mandela's critique of Apartheid and its epistemic regimes turns on its unique ability to reveal the preeminent role of law in perpetuating these relations, and its potential to reimagine a world of political action. His is a generative intervention that expands the horizons of the imaginable and discloses a political universe heretofore unfamiliar to the subject; that utopian universe he calls 'a democratic and free society in which all persons live together in harmony and with equal opportunities'. After all, one can counter a legitimate fiction only with a competing fiction, a spectacle of domination with a spectacle of liberation, 'creating an aporia in the law that is always' reflexive and open to new claims for dignity and justice but this time a fiction of justice that seek to supplement its inevitable originary violence with an ethic of care, justice and responsibility.

Chapter 10

Reading Choreographies of Black Resistance: Courtroom Performance as/and Critique

Joel M. Modiri

Law creates the space, the subjects, the choreography, the words, the incentives,
and the pleasures of the everyday practices of domination and submission.[1]

Introduction

This chapter joins the call to reflect on the courtroom as a space of resistance through an excursion into the history of the political trials of black radical revolutionaries in South Africa and the United States. I shall draw on Frank B. Wilderson's account of the trials of Black Liberation Army (BLA) soldiers in the United States in the late 1960s up until the early 1980s and extend his analysis further through an engagement with the 1976 trial of members and student leaders of the Black People's Convention and South African Students Organisation (known as the BPC/SASO Trial), and specifically Steve Biko's testimony in that trial.[2] True to Michel Foucault's insight that '[w]here there is power, there is resistance',[3] the courtroom in these trials is appropriated and transformed from a site representing the institutional reinforcement of unjust power and legal violence to a site of struggle, where black resistances to racial oppression are choreographed and performed. In recalling these trials, specific attention will be paid to the tactics by which the black radical activists resist and disrupt the logics, mechanisms and protocols of the court and by extension, of (the) law itself. Attention will be paid as well to those instances where they appropriate and reclaim the time and space of the courtroom for the articulation and enactment of their political ideology.

I shall then proceed to read those acts of resistance performed in the courtroom as forms of legal critique operating in the guise of a 'general jurisprudence' and

---

1   A.P. Farley, 'The Poetics of Colorlined Space', in F. Valdes, J.M. Culp and A. Harris (eds) *Crossroads, Directions and a New Critical Race Theory* (2002, Temple University Press: Philadelphia) 150.

2   See M. Arnold (ed.) *The Testimony of Steve Biko: Black Consciousness in South Africa* (1979, Granada Publishing: New York).

3   M. Foucault, *The History of Sexuality: An Introduction*, trans. R Hurley (1978, Pantheon Books: New York) 95.

standing in the tradition of critical race theory. This reading relies on Wendy Brown's argument on the timeliness of critique, and its indispensability in times of crisis and darkness, as well as Foucault's ruminations on critique, where he draws a connection between critique and transformation. Brown and Foucault's combined formulations of 'critique' will then also be extended into a brief exploration of the relation between theory and practice, specifically as this relation pertains to a left critique of law. Through this reading, and with reference to the notion of critique, I claim that traces of critical race theoretical critique can be discerned in the moments of resistance that transpire in the political trials of the BLA and in Biko's testimony, where the setting of power is suspended and inverted in such a way that the court, as the aesthetic and institutional representation of the Law, is itself put on trial. Put another way, I will suggest that the acts of resistance encountered in the political trials of the black radicals discussed below emerge from a decidedly critical legal standpoint (specifically exhibiting the core themes of critical race theory) in order to underscore the relation between resistance and critique as a historic feature of black struggles against white supremacy.

After establishing this important connection between resistance and critique, the chapter moves from a commemoration of past heroes and struggles to a contemplation of our legal and political future(s) through an examination of the contemporary problematic describable as the rise of legalism in social and political discourse or the juridification of politics and human relations that has taken hold in 'post'-1994 South Africa.[4] Here the aim will be to explore and problematize the ostensible shift from the black radicals' view of the court as a site of oppression, invested in the reiteration and legitimation of racial subordination against blacks to the liberal 'post'-apartheid[5] view of the court as a hallowed space exclusively bearing both the promise and capacity for racial justice and of the judiciary as the appropriate final arbiter of political and social conflict.

---

4   J. Comaroff and J. Comaroff, 'Preface', in J. Comaroff and J. Comaroff (eds) *Law and Disorder in the Postcolony* (2006, University of Chicago Press: Chicago) viii. See also Comaroff and Comaroff, 'Law and Disorder in the Postcolony: An Introduction', in *Law and Disorder in the Postcolony*, 1–56.

5   Where I do use the phrase 'post-apartheid' (which will mostly be for purposes of ironizing it), I shall enclose the 'post' in 'post-apartheid' in inverted commas to indicate my own discomfort, if not outright rejection, of the casting of apartheid as a historical period that has now definitively come to an end. I share the view that the present post-1994 legal and political regime in South Africa is an intensification and re-consolidation of white supremacy and that celebratory and triumphalist accounts of the post-1994 constitutional transition function ideologically to obscure the continuation of a manifestly anti-black reality in South Africa. Even at the level of historiography, the signifier 'post-apartheid' is also misleading since 'apartheid' itself was only one spectacular juridical instantiation or iteration (from 1948 to 1994) in the now almost four centuries of white supremacist colonial rule in South Africa that begins with arrival of the European colonialists in 1652 and is yet to meet its true end. See J.M. Modiri, 'Law's Poverty' (2015) 18 *Potchefstroom Electronic Law Journal* (forthcoming).

Although this chapter is a response to a conference invitation dedicated to the fiftieth anniversary of Nelson Mandela's famed testimony as an accused in the 1963–64 Rivonia Trial, the omission of Mandela and the Rivonia Trial from this analysis is, save only for one brief instance, not accidental. It is, first of all, political because this chapter is written from a black radical socialist political perspective that Mandela was known to be intensely hostile towards and dismissive of while he was on Robben Island.[6] Halfway through this chapter, I take issue with the fetishization of law and constitutionalism within the South African public imagination. To the extent that this fetishization is central to a conception of national patriotism and constitutional citizenship in South Africa of which Mandela is the most iconic ideological representative, the exclusion of his politics and testimony is crucial to the consistency and integrity of my text. Indeed, the canonization of Mandela and its association with the post-racial legal optimism and multicultural reformism embodied in the Constitution is a significant part of the rise of the culture of legalism that is being contested in this chapter. Echoing Foucault again, this chapter might then itself also be taken in the spirit of a certain resistance against dominant narratives of post-1994 South Africa and, specifically, the mythologization and idealization of Mandela within those narratives.

The broad concern provoking this enquiry, and specifically the reason for the juxtaposition of the critical acts of resistance in the courtroom with the turn to legalism and the juridification of politics, is what I sense as the loss of faith by certain parts of the left in the viability of a more radical political future in the face of the seeming givenness of the present and inescapability of the *status quo* of liberal democracy and neoliberal capitalism. Returning to this archive of struggle in the black radical tradition might revive or reinvigorate current political struggles, discourses and movements in South Africa to expand the width and depth of their projects to encompass deeper, more substantive, conceptions of freedom, equality, democracy, transformation and community. Also underlying this chapter is the continuing search for a critical race jurisprudence and for a future refiguring of racial justice, equality and freedom for a 'post'-apartheid South Africa that seemingly no longer recognizes blacks' historical claims for justice, reparations and redress. This chapter thus stands at the intersection between past and future, taking the opportunity not only to celebrate, but also to mourn.

---

6   See in his *The Long Walk to Freedom: The Autobiography of Nelson Mandela* (1994, Little Brown Company: Boston) 486 where he derisively describes the philosophy of Black Consciousness as immature, exclusionary and in need of guidance from the Congress Movement. See also his essay 'Whither the Black Consciousness Movement', in M. Maharaj (ed.) *Reflections in Prison* (2001, Zebra and Robben Island Prison: Cape Town) 40.

Blackness in the Courtroom: The Subversion of the 'Law of White Spaces'

Frank B. Wilderson argues that a defining feature of the political trials of the black insurgents of the BLA who had, from the 1960s to the 1980s, waged a guerrilla struggle, against the oppression of blacks in the United States, was the 'moment when it became *de riguer* for revolutionaries to refuse the role of defendant and assume (while still in custody and often handcuffed) the role of prosecutor and judge – with the public gallery as jury'.[7] This reversal in the ordering logic of the court for Wilderson constitutes an 'unparalleled inversion of jurisprudential casting in which the court itself (and by extension the US government) became defendants'.[8] It is particularly this aspect of putting (the) law itself on trial, of calling its claim to objectivity, reason and fairness into question, and of troubling its presumed legitimacy, that is crucial to the connection between acts of resistance and legal critique about which more will follow in the next section.

In order to sustain the theoretical reading that follows, we must briefly turn to an understanding of how the courtroom is conceived of within the black radical imagination. Due to the extent to which the law and legal rules themselves were (and still are) deployed for the purposes of institutionalizing racial hierarchies, the courtroom as the symbolic personification of law and legal culture and the institutional enforcer of legal rules, loses its disguise of apolitical innocence and takes on another, more insidious figure in the eyes of black revolutionaries. Rather than being seen as an isolated institution, autonomous of racial power and white hegemony, the courtroom is understood as a functionary of that power and that hegemony and as a powerful site for the legitimation and normalization of racist legal systems, such as in the case of Jim Crow USA and apartheid South Africa. Rather than being seen as outside of the social dynamics of racial stratification and Western imperialism, the court is understood as deeply imbricated by those dynamics, as a space for the centralization and affirmation of Western and white cultural norms and values, and indeed for the protection of actual white interests. Examples of this view of the courts abound, for example, in Bruce White's phrase 'black robes, white justice' in reference to the US criminal justice system and in Nelson Mandela's description of himself as a 'black man in a *white* man's court'.[9] Applications made in cases such as *S* v. *Collier*[10] requesting the recusal of a white judge based on the contention that his membership in a dominant racial group renders him incapable of producing a race-neutral and, thus, ideally fair outcome in racially contested disputes also emanate from this view.

---

7   F.B. Wilderson, 'The Vengeance of Vertigo: Aphasia and Abjection in the Political Trials of Black Insurgents' (2011) 5 *InTensions* 1.

8   Ibid., 2.

9   See Bruce Wright, *Black Robes, White Justice* (1987, Lyle Stuart Inc: New Jersey) and R. Finalyson, *Nelson Mandela* (1999, Twenty First Century Books: Minneapolis) 84.

10   1995 (8) BCLR 975 (C).

As highlighted in the epigraph above, the law and the legal system are conceived as primarily defined and structured by white social power. It follows then from this understanding that the courtroom is viewed as being part of the system against which the struggle for black liberation is being waged. Together with the police and the prison, it is traditionally seen as part of the institutional machinery of the racist state, not as a safe haven for the vindication of the rights of black citizens. The reasoning here is simple: if the law and other law-enforcement institutions are not neutral, nor is the court. Hence Sherene Razack's insistence that courts should be understood as situated spaces, spaces deeply imbued with a specific racial, cultural and gendered perspective. Razack argues therefore for a view of the courtroom as one key site where encounters between dominant groups and subordinated groups are repeatedly staged; that is for a view of the courtroom as chronically characterized by power imbalance.[11] This particular argument is, of course, applicable not only to historic political trials in authoritarian regimes, but also in respect of ordinary courtroom disputes dealing with, for example, contracts, evictions and divorces in liberal-democratic states.

In her later work, Razack speaks of a process by which a place or space 'becomes a race through the law'.[12] In contexts such as apartheid South Africa or Jim Crow USA, where law was organized expressly around white supremacist principles, the spaces (such as the courtroom) constituted by and for law, by default and design, inevitably functioned to reproduce and maintain racial hierarchies. When a space has become a race in this way, Raquel Montoya-Lewis tells us, not only are the effects of race and racism on law and legal reasoning either negated and ignored or perpetuated and enabled, but whiteness silently assumes normative superiority within that space.[13]

In the black radical imagination, therefore, the courtroom can be regarded as a 'white space' in at least the following three senses. First, in the aesthetic sense that the physical construction of the courtroom relies on a Western European architectural model. Second, in the formal sense of its operations and proceedings being co-ordinated by protocols, dress codes and rules that are patently colonial. And third, in the political sense that the ideal subject of law is cultured and positioned as 'white'.[14] Montoya-Lewis further argues that 'white spaces' such as the courtroom function by means of a law, which she names the 'law of

---

11   S. Razack, *Looking White People in the Eye: Gender, Race and Culture in Courtrooms and Classrooms* (1998, University of Toronto Press: Toronto).

12   'Introduction: When Place Becomes Race', in S. Razack (ed.) *Race, Space and the Law: Unmapping a White Settler Society* (2002, Between the Lines: Toronto) 1.

13   R. Montoya-Lewis, 'Whiteness in a Red Room: Telling Stories and Legal Discourse in the Tribal Courtroom', in J. Parker, R. Sumantri and M. Romero (eds) *Interdisciplinarity and Social Justice* (2010, SUNY Press: Albany) 92.

14   Montoya-Lewis, 'Whiteness in a Red Room', 92–4.

white spaces', that governs both the conditions for speech, appearance and legal subjectivity as well as the rules for entry and inclusion into the space.[15]

This view of the courtroom converges with Wilderson's account of the political trials of black insurgents if not because he explicitly charges the courts as being 'systematically implicated in the ongoing Black Holocaust'[16] but because of the extent to which the actions and words of the black insurgents who were on trial and their supporters stand in open defiance of this 'law of white spaces'. As we will see, through their acts of resistance, they derange the space of the courtroom and the laws it upholds, claiming it as a terrain of struggle and as a platform for both placing the atrocities and injustices suffered by blacks on the public record and for articulating their political ideology. In this way, they reclaim both the voice and visibility that is traditionally denied to them in legal institutions.

Wilderson captures many moments of resistance in the political trials that he explores. Among the most compelling, he cites one biographical account by BLA revolutionary Assata Shakur, who recalls how members of the black community attended her trial every day in order to 'watch the *circus*'.[17] The use of the word *circus* with its connection to performance, play and pretence, exposes law's complicity in racial injustice as well as its arbitrariness. In this vein, consider BLA member Kuwasi Balagoon's closing statement in the so-called Brink's Trial in which he declares openly that this 'place here [the trial courtroom] is an armed camp [even though it appears to have all] the *trappings and props* of a court' and then further goes on to label the judge in his trial as 'a state-issued clone in a black robe'.[18] Consider also Assata Shakur's own opening statement and specifically her justification for choosing to act as co-counsel in her own case:

> I have spent many days and nights behind bars thinking about this trial, this outrage. And in my own mind, only someone who has been so intimately a victim of this madness as I have can do justice to what I have to say.[19]

Shakur continues in her autobiography to note how deeply struck she was by the paradox that she observed while she was awaiting trial where a pregnant woman was sentenced to 90 days for stealing a box of nappies while the former US president Richard Nixon was pardoned for his criminal involvement in the Watergate scandal without even awaiting trial.[20] It is to this paradox that Shakur addresses the question:

---

15   Montoya-Lewis, 'Whiteness in a Red Room', 92–4.

16   Wilderson 'The Vengeance of Vertigo', 13.

17   Wilderson 'The Vengeance of Vertigo', 2, citing A. Shakur, *Assata: An Autobiography* (1987, Lawrence Hill Books: Chicago) 212.

18   K. Balagoon, 'Brink's Trial Closing Statement', *The Anarchist Library*, available at http://theanarchistlibrary.org/library/kuwasi-balagoon-brink-s-trial-closing-statement.

19   Shakur, *Assata: An Autobiography*, 166.

20   Ibid., 166–7.

What kind of justice is this?

Where the poor go to prison and the rich go free.

Where witnesses are rented, bought, or bribed.

Where evidence is made of manufactured.

Where people are tried not because of any criminal actions but because of their political beliefs.[21]

The candour and fortitude in both Shakur and Balagoon's statements reflects the sense of drama, of theatricality, of undressing the law, that Wilderson highlights as one key feature of the political trials of the BLA soldiers. As he writes of Shakur's account of her trial:

> [It] paints a vibrant picture of an intra-mural conversation between Black folks from all walks of life, for whom the court and the trials functioned much like backwoods churches did during slavery. A courtroom of people who joined the defendants in their refusal to rise when the judge came in; folks giving each other the Black Power salute in full view of the U.S. Marshals; Black Muslim men and women spreading their prayer rugs in the corridors of the court and praying to Allah; Black parents explaining the underlying racism of the American legal system.[22]

In another dramatic moment in Shakur's account of her trial, we are told that as the judge entered the courtroom, a child looked up at him and then turned to her mother and asked 'Mommy is that the fascist pig?'[23] Predictably, members of the gallery broke out in laughter and applause.

For Wilderson, these various acts of resistance performed in the courtroom need to be understood in the context of the counter-hegemonic politics of the Black Liberation Army and specifically the tacit consensus by the left at that time not to co-operate with legal institutions like the police, prosecutors and judges.[24] For him, the uproar caused by the child's question, the refusal of the defendants and their supporters to stand when the judge entered the courtroom as well as the Black Power salute exhibited a mode of resistance much deeper than merely upsetting court decorum. They also set up an epistemological and jurisprudential challenge, questioning as they do the very legitimacy and validity of the law and the courtroom.

---

21 Ibid., 167.
22 Wilderson, 'The Vengeance of Vertigo', 2.
23 Ibid.
24 Ibid., 7–8.

As evidence for this claim he cites the justification given by Balagoon's co-accused in the Brink's Trial, David Gilbert and Judy Clark, for why they sat out of most of that trial, appearing only 'to make statements condemning white supremacy and U.S imperialism'.[25] As they saw it, participation in the trial would be 'to recognise the legitimacy of the court to *criminalize* political acts'.[26] In their view, the US government lacked the legal basis to put them on trial both because their actions were of a political character, and thus had to be resolved politically, and more importantly because of that government's own illegitimacy on account of its blatant oppression of blacks.[27] For Wilderson, their actions registered a rejection of 'the terms of jurisprudential engagement by refusing the hermeneutics of individual guilt or innocence'.[28] As he writes:

> In short, they sought to short circuit the court's disciplinary logic by exploiting their trial ... as an opportunity to shift the terms of adjudication from moral questions of guilt and innocence to ethical questions of state power and political morality.[29]

The designation of these trials as 'political trials' is thus noteworthy. They are political because they concern more than the infringement of criminal law codes; instead they raise deeper questions about law's relation to political morality and structural injustice and showcase a broader crisis in the political organization of a society.[30] This is why many BLA revolutionaries put on trial consistently argued for their standing in the court to be recognized as 'political rather than juridical'.[31]

This refusal to be constrained by the rigid logic and conservative language of law in favour of a radical politics is repeated once more when the black insurgents who were on trial and the witnesses called to testify against them would begin their testimony by announcing to the judge and jury that they would not answer any questions put to them during the trial, knowing that they would receive an almost automatic prison sentence.[32] Here again Wilderson explains these acts of resistance as performing not simply a circumvention of evidentiary rules but also a rejection of the court's right to convene, to unilaterally determine the questions at issue and the terms of the dispute.[33] In his own words, Wilderson reads these

---

25　Ibid., 6.

26　Ibid., citing D. Berger, *Outlaws of America: The Weather Underground and the Politics of Solidarity* (2006, AK Press: Oakland) 252–3.

27　Wilderson, 'The Vengeance of Vertigo', 7, citing Berger, *Outlaws of America*, 252–3.

28　Wilderson, 'The Vengeance of Vertigo', 7.

29　Ibid.

30　See R. Christenson, *Political Trials: Gordian Knots in the Law* (1999, Transaction Publishers: New Brunswick) 1–14; 183–220; 221–2.

31　Wilderson, 'The Vengeance of Vertigo', 7; 16.

32　Ibid., 8.

33　Ibid.

acts of resistance in the courtroom as 'an ethical refusal of the legal system itself, as opposed to a moral objection to legal excesses'.[34]

Wilderson's analysis can be extended to Steve Biko's testimony in 1976 at the BPC/SASO Trial. In the BPC/SASO Trial, nine student leaders of the BPC and SASO were charged with violations of the Terrorism Act after they organized a rally to celebrate the installation of FRELIMO as the ruling party in the government of Mozambique despite an order by the police not to continue with such a rally. Arguably among the historic political trials of the apartheid era, it is often said that what was actually on trial in the BPC/SASO Trial was the Black Consciousness Movement (BCM) itself if one looks at the terms in which the indictment was framed and the type of questions posed by the prosecutor and the judge.[35]

Records from the trial suggest that it was equally dramatic, with the tone for a tense and antagonistic atmosphere already being set at the opening of the trial when one of the defendants in the trial, Saths Cooper, refused to plead, whereafter the judge refused to allow him to read a statement from the dock and entered a plea of not guilty on his behalf.[36] As one report of these trials further tells us:

> The accused Africans entered the courtroom singing freedom songs. They raised their fists in the black power salute and shouted, "*Amandla!*". Returning the salute the black spectators in the courtroom cried in response "*Ngawethu!*".[37]

It seems then that just as in the trials of the BLA revolutionaries taking place around the same time in the United States, the Black Consciousness revolutionaries in South Africa also choreographed a courtroom performance whereby they would disturb the court's sense of power by reorganizing its space in terms of the familiar.[38]

But let us turn to Steve Biko's testimony in the trial in order to uncover a different choreography, or gesture, of resistance – one that can be discerned only through a close conceptual reading of his testimony. Biko was the main witness for the defence in the BPC/SASO Trial and through his testimony delivered what has been described as the most classic statement of the philosophy and political praxis of Black Consciousness.[39] What is remarkable about Biko's entire testimony is the relentlessly political tenor of its articulation. Throughout the trial he maintains

---

34   Ibid.

35   'Editor's Note', in S. Biko, *I Write What I Like* (1978, Picador Africa: Johannesburg) 109.

36   R. Christenson (ed.) *Political Trials in History: From Antiquity to the Present* (1991, Transaction Publishers: New Brunswick) 84.

37   Study Commission on US Policy towards Southern Africa, *South Africa – Time is Running Out: The Report of the Study Commission* (1981, University of California Press: Berkeley) 180.

38   See M. Lobban, *White Man's Justice: South African Political Trials in the Black Consciousness Era* (1996, Clarendon Press: New York and Oxford).

39   Christenson, *Political Trials in History: From Antiquity to the Present*, 85.

a refusal to translate and thereby distort his claims into the language of law or rights – a refusal that lies at the heart of a counter-hegemonic legal consciousness.

Instead Biko chooses to assert the 'margins' not as a space of deprivation or lack but as a 'site of radical possibility [and] a space for resistance' in the sense argued for by bell hooks.[40] hooks has long called for the margins or marginality to be reconceived and reclaimed as a 'radical standpoint, perspective and position' that furthers the aim of 'oppositional political struggle'.[41] For her, the struggle against racial domination requires those struggling to self-consciously inhabit political and ideological spaces from which to best assert 'an aesthetic and critical presence'.[42] In this vein, she calls for a shift from the centre to the margins which she describes as a site of radical openness and as '[the] central location for the production of a counter-hegemonic discourse'.[43] But hooks ends her argument by cautioning that '[l]ocating oneself there is difficult yet necessary. It is not a "safe" place. One is always at risk'.[44]

This choice by Biko to locate himself at the margins in the courtroom, as part of the community of the oppressed, can be seen as an acceptance of the risk involved in entering a court presided over by a white judge during the apartheid era to defend comrades charged with terrorism while still offering a critique of white supremacy at the same time. Recall for example his exchange with Judge Boshoff on the question of the precise meaning of the term 'black' in Black Consciousness thought. After Biko offers a comprehensive explanation of the negative symbolic connotations attached to 'blackness' and the choice of the BCM, following the *Negritude* thinkers, to affirm and signify blackness as a political identity and mark of pride and resistance, the judge sarcastically asks him: 'But now why do you refer to you people as blacks? Why not brown people? I mean you people are more brown than black.'[45] Biko, seemingly unfazed by the ignorance and racism in that question, calmly replies: 'In the same way I think white people are more pink and yellow than pale and white.'[46] Biko's calmness and poise in the face of the judge's racist provocations (including his repeated reference to blacks as 'you people') shows him to be more cultured and rational than the judge, as possessing traits traditionally understood in the white colonial imaginary as precisely what blacks do not have; as that which whites must teach to blacks in their training to white civilization. Not to mention also that Biko's attentiveness to history and

---

40   b hooks, *Yearning: Race, Gender and Cultural Politics* (1990, South End Press: New York) 145.

41   hooks, *Yearning*, 152; 145.

42   Ibid., 148.

43   Ibid., 149. See also b hooks, *Feminist Theory: From Margin to Center* (1984, South End Press: New York).

44   hooks, *Yearning*, 149.

45   Biko, *I Write What I Like*, 115.

46   Ibid.

social context is unparalleled in contrast to the judge's unschooled opinions and simplistic assumptions.

We see this again, I think, when Biko exposes the superficiality of the judge's opinion on the influx control laws and his account of crime in the townships.[47] Where the judge is of the impression that influx control laws are useful in controlling the 'bad elements among the people' and brings order to chaotic and overcrowded townships ridden with crime, Biko suggests the opposite: that the racially discriminatory nature of the influx control laws (including the degradation of black men having to be strip-searched by doctors) is what aggravates the already existing problems of violence, crime, education inequality and unemployment. Biko here emphasizes the differential vulnerability and precarity of blacks and the imbalances produced by systemically entrenched, legally sanctioned racial hierarchies whereas the judge seems to view the overcrowding in the townships as a choice made by blacks and the crime in those townships as the inherent nature of the 'bad' blacks.[48]

But there is more. I want to suggest that Biko's most transgressive but also theoretically innovative moments in the trial can be found in the way in which he employs the courtroom as a platform from which to elaborate on the basic tenets of Black Consciousness. Through this elaboration, Biko performs the relation between law and politics differently, explicitly subordinating the former to the latter, defying the court's linear and rule-bound logic by being more expansive in terms of what is relevant as legal evidence. As a result one can discern in Biko's testimony, a jurisprudence that is both 'general' in Douzinas and Gearey's sense[49] – in its concern for not only the positive law but also the law of law, law's conscience, and questions of social being and existence – and also 'generous' in Patricia Williams'[50] and Karin van Marle's sense[51] – in its openness to subjectivity, lived experience, identity and its desire to stretch the law to its limits. Of specific relevance for our purposes are those aspects where he exposes both the racism of the apartheid legal system and the complicity of 'white society' in the maintenance of what he calls the 'total white power structure'.[52] To be sure, it is not so much what Biko is doing that is unique; it is where – that is, he is challenging from the inside, the very configurations of power that the courtroom in his time (and indeed even in ours) symbolized, namely the law and whiteness.

---

47 Ibid., 121–2.

48 Ibid., 121.

49 C. Douzinas and A. Gearey, 'From Restricted to General Jurisprudence', in *Critical Jurisprudence: The Political Philosophy of Justice* (2005, Hart Publishing: Oxford) 3–42.

50 P.J. Williams, *The Alchemy of Race and Rights: Diary of a Law Professor* (1991, Harvard University Press: Cambridge, MA) 8.

51 K. van Marle, 'Laughter, Refusal, Friendship: Thoughts on a Jurisprudence of Generosity', in K. van Marle (ed.) *Refusal, Transition and Post-Apartheid Law* (2009, SUN Press: Stellenbosch) 15–28.

52 Biko, *I Write What I Like*, 163.

Recall for example that in his lucid summation of what Black Consciousness entails, Biko recognizes the role of the law in the 'institutional machinery' of racial oppression that restricts, exploits and deprives blacks and his account of how this system generates an alienated black subjectivity (traditionally understood as self-hatred or a feeling of inferiority).[53] In that summation he also traces the complex ways in which this system of oppression and this process of subjection begins from childhood and continues well into adulthood, thereby painting a picture of how racism subsumes all facets of human life. But he goes further in his analysis, to show the mutual relation between the oppression of blacks and the privilege of whites. He speaks of white racism as being 'institutionalised, and also cushioned with the backing of whites'.[54] This is how he understands the social construction of whiteness and white racial power:

> [A] white child does not have to choose whether or not he wants to live with the white, he is born into it. He is brought up within white schools, institutions, and the whole process of racism somehow greets him at various levels ... so whites are together around the privileges they hold, and they monopolise this away from society.[55]

Black Consciousness is thus premised on a structural understanding of racism, one that maintains the historical unity between racism and white supremacy. Racism-as-white supremacy on this account is not merely a collection of prejudices and biases held by whites; it is a socio-political system and thus can exist beyond its overt legal supports.[56] During his testimony, Biko also shows how this understanding of racism is also linked to an anti-colonial African politics. His exploration of the effects of colonial racism also encompasses a concern for cultural imperialism. When asked about what the 'open society' he envisages would look like, Biko replies that all that they [the BCM] insist on is:

> [A] culture that accepts the humanity of the black man. A culture that is basically sufficiently accommodative of African concepts, to pass as African culture.

---

53   Ibid., 110–11.

54   Ibid., 149.

55   Ibid.

56   C. Mills, 'White Supremacy as a Socio-Political System', in A.W. Doane and E. Bonilla-Silva (eds) *White Out: The Continuing Significance of Racism* (2003, Routledge: New York) 35–48. See also C. Mills, *The Racial Contract* (1997, Cornell University Press: Ithaca, NY) where Mills describes white supremacy as the one political system that has, more than any other, foundationally shaped the modern world – and hence shares historically close epistemological, moral and political affinities with liberalism, capitalism, patriarchy and modernity.

What we are saying now is that at the present moment we have a culture here which is a European culture.[57]

In addition to these erudite elucidations of the political and social philosophy of Black Consciousness, Biko's testimony also contains a firm commitment to black solidarity and consciousness-raising. His entire testimony reads as a stinging condemnation of apartheid and the legal and political institutions that were complicit in its perpetuation.

Thus, what we can see in the political trials of the BLA insurgents and in Biko's testimony at the BPC/SASO Trial is an insistence on counter-narrative, on naming the political reality of the time with reference to the phenomenological experience of the racially oppressed.[58] Such a counter-narrative is delivered in a distinctly political register that exemplifies the joining of two unique modes of resistance that bell hooks has variously named 'talking back' (an epistemological challenge to the dominant discourse)[59] and 'loving blackness' (an affirmation of racial and cultural difference and black identity).[60]

What I am suggesting then is that that the acts of resistance that we witness in the trials discussed above involve more than a mere disruption of decorum or a refusal to comply with rules of evidence. They are animated by more than a desire to heckle, mock or annoy power, and they indicate more than the revolutionaries' predilection for rancour or mischief. Instead, they reveal deeply sophisticated conceptual insights about law, power and identity. Rather than being mere theatrical ploys, they issue instead from a searing challenge to law's epistemological and moral foundations. It is to this dimension of critique inherent in those acts of resistance that I now turn.

Reflections on Race and Critique

This effort to apprehend the acts of resistance performed in the courtroom by the US and South African black revolutionaries as gestures of legal-theoretical critique takes its cue from Foucault's definition of critique as the 'art of not being governed quite so much'.[61] In what follows I tentatively argue that those acts

---

57   Biko, *I Write What I Like*, 147–8.

58   See Part 2, 'Storytelling, Counter-Storytelling, and "Naming One's own Reality"', in R. Delgado and J. Stefancic (eds) *Critical Race Theory: The Cutting Edge* (2000, Temple University Press: Philadelphia) 41–91.

59   *Talking Back: Thinking Feminist, Thinking Black* (1989, South End Press: New York) 5–9.

60   'Loving Blackness as Political Resistance', in *Black Looks: Race and Representations* (1992, South End Press: New York) 9.

61   M. Foucault, 'What is Critique', in S. Lotringer and L. Hochroth (eds) *The Politics of Truth* (1997, Semiotext(e): New York) 29.

of resistance, by refusing to be governed by the logic of law, bear within them theoretical, political and jurisprudential exposures of the role of law and the courts in the subjugation of blacks. That is to say that their orientation in and towards the courtroom space reveals a corresponding idea, even theory, of law. For if law operates through commanding, silencing, regulating and governing, the work of critique is to upend and confound these operations, to question law's right to do these things.

A useful starting point then would be Wendy Brown's argument for critique 'as a hope rather than a luxury in dark times'.[62] She makes this argument centrally through a recollection of the etymological roots of the term 'critique'.[63] As she tells us, critique is an old term that derives from the Ancient Greek term *krisis*. Interestingly for our purposes, she indicates that *krisis* is actually a jurisprudential term identified with the art of making distinctions; an art, she writes, considered essential to judging and rectifying an alleged tear in the order of democracy. Even more so, in its Biblical terminology, *krisis* is also equated to justice and Right. Brown notes that 'in contrast to contemporary concerns with distinguishing the two, in its original usage *critique is an explicit project of judgement*'.[64] Useful in Brown's account is how she restores the traditional place of critique in our political time: critique does not abolish, condemn or destroy; rather it is explicitly connected to responding to a crisis (of justice), and to repairing a tear in the social fabric.

If we currently inhabit a political time in which left critique is denounced as a wholly negative practice, as ultraleftist or ultratheoretical, and as without purchase in the mythic place called 'The Real World', then linking critique to the acts of resistance performed in the courtroom at the height of two of the most insidious systems of white supremacist terror in the United States and South Africa, allows us to grasp critique as a practice of resistance in a way that clarifies critique's profound attentiveness to politics, to the realities and experiences of people, and to justice and reparation.[65] A brief detour from Brown to Foucault is necessary at this point. In his essay, 'So is it Important to Think', Foucault tells us that critique goes beyond mere criticism and rejection of current systems and practices. It also involves an exploration of 'what type assumptions, of familiar notions, of

---

62   W. Brown, 'Untimeliness and Punctuality: Critical Theory in Dark Times', in *Edgework: Critical Essays on Knowledge and Politics* (2005, Princeton University Press: Princeton) 5.

63   See also R. Bernasconi, 'The Crisis of Critique and the Awakening of Politicisation in Levinas and Derrida', in M. McQuillan (ed.) *The Politics of Deconstruction: Jacques Derrida and the Other of Philosophy* (2007, Pluto Press: London) 81–97.

64   Brown, 'Untimeliness and Punctuality' 5, my italics.

65   W. Brown and J. Halley, 'Introduction', in W. Brown and J. Halley (eds) *Left Legalism/Left Critique* (2001, Duke University Press: Durham, NC) 25.

established, unexamined ways of thinking accepted practices are based'.[66] He goes further to tell us that critique:

> [c]onsists in uncovering [hidden thought] and trying to change it: showing that things are not as obvious as people believe, making it so that what is taken for granted is no longer taken for granted. To do criticism is to make harder those acts which are now too easy.[67]

Foucault presents critique as an epistemological and political project of problematizing certainties and challenging the perceived naturalness of things (including law). But he does not stop there. For while it is not in dispute that critique is concerned with problematization, disruption and exposure, it is of equal importance to recognize that critique is also tethered to transformation, thoughtful reflection and change. In Foucault's own words, radical critique 'is utterly indispensable for any transformation ... [A] transformation that would remain within the same mode of thought, a transformation that would only be a certain way of better adjusting the same thought to the reality of things, would only be superficial'.[68]

Because of the restorative and transformative underpinnings of critique, disclosed both in its ancient lineage and in Foucault's rendition of it, there can therefore be no such thing as 'mere critique', 'critique for the sake of critique' or 'untimely critique'.[69] Critique cannot be nihilistic or destructive precisely because its project is to '[discern] and [repair] a tear in justice through practices that are themselves exemplary of the justice that has been rent' and it cannot be untimely or disinterested because it disrupts the fixity of a given sense of time precisely in order to reclaim the present from the conservative hold on it.[70] To be clear, critique – connected as it is to knowledge, deliberation and judgement – aims to render the crisis readable so as to orient us *through* and *out* of the dark.[71] Critique, then, is what prevents the darkness, and the times, from closing in on us, and as such it is a hope rather than a luxury. In fact, on this view of critique, the luxury lies not in the purported indulgences of theoretical critique, but rather in the distinctly unreasoned and anti-intellectual conceit that there is a stalemate between critical theory and activist politics that needs to be resolved through the subordination of the former by the latter; as if we could make such a choice between acting in the world and thinking about it.

---

66 M. Foucault, 'So is it Important to Think?', in J.D. Faubion (ed.) *The Essential Works of Foucault 1954–1984 Vol. 3: Power* (2000, New Press: New York) 456.

67 Foucault, 'So is it Important to Think?' 456.

68 Ibid., 457.

69 Brown, 'Untimeliness and Punctuality' 6.

70 Ibid., 4; 6.

71 Ibid., 15.

Read together, Brown and Foucault's respective formulations of critique provide a strong counterpoint to the traditional binary oppositions between theory and practice, which posit critique as theoretical, and therefore disconnected from reality and hostile to reconstruction, and resistance as practical and active (and therefore, somehow, a good in itself), and as having transcended the indulgent desire for theoretical critique.[72] From this standpoint, critique need not choose between deconstruction or reconstruction; it need not even seek to creatively inhabit the tension between them.[73] Critique's disruptive orientation is inherently reconstructive.

To take this point further, I want to also suggest that the practices of struggle and resistance launched by the black radical activists of the BLA and BCM were based on, and even dependent on, strong theoretical and intellectual foundations. More specifically, I want to place these acts of resistance in the framework of the genre of legal critique known as critical race theory (CRT), a genre that Douzinas and Gearey introduce as staging a constant tension between 'white law' and 'black power'.[74] As we saw, the choreographies of black resistance performed in the courtroom by the black revolutionaries were provoked by a frustration with 'law's complicity in the violent perpetuation of racially defined economic and social order',[75] and in so doing, they offer us an understanding of the relationship between law, power relations and racial ideology that is almost identical to the one proffered in critical race theory scholarship.

The black revolutionaries' acts of resistance in the courtroom stands in the tradition of first-generation critical race theory, exemplifying as they do the position that Derrick Bell called 'racial realism', where the social reality of racism and black suffering are made central to legal analysis.[76] Simply put, racial realism is the idea that law produces and is a production of racial domination, and is therefore incapable of racial neutrality. The black revolutionaries' non-reliance on law espoused through community self-reliance, armed self-defence and civil disobedience indicates traces of this. From the perspective of racial realism, the narrow project of legal reform founded on racial equality through the law is doomed to fail and should be widened in favour of a continued struggle for liberation. This racial realist perspective was later consolidated by critical race

---

72   For Brown's meditation on the theory–practice relation, see W. Brown, 'Democracy Against Itself: Nietzsche's Challenge', in *Politics Out of History* (2001, Princeton University Press: Princeton) 121–3. See also b hooks, 'Theory as Liberatory Practice' (1991) 4 *Yale J of Law and Feminism* 1–13.

73   As proposed by Angela Harris in 'The Jurisprudence of Reconstruction' (1994) 82 *California Law Review* 741–85.

74   'White Law, Black Power: Racism, Resistance and Critical Jurisprudence', in Douzinas and Gearey, *Critical Jurisprudence*, 259.

75   Douzinas and Gearey, 'White Law, Black Power', 259.

76   D. Bell, 'Racial Realism' (1992) 24 *Connecticut Law Review*, 363–79; *Faces at the Bottom of the Well: The Permanence of Racism* (1992, Basic Books: New York).

theorists into a *critique of (legal) liberalism* – a critique which now stands at the heart of CRT and critical legal theory in general.

The critique of liberalism in CRT has roughly two primary targets: first, liberalism's individualistic conception of equality, with its lack of proper focus on structural group oppression and, second, its emphasis on incremental reform undergirded by a notion of rights-based freedom.[77] Steve Biko's now-famed rebuff of white liberals was not simply an assertion of black independence; it also turned on stark ideological differences between Black Consciousness' revolutionary socialism on the one hand and liberalism on the other. A key bone of contention noted by him then was the broad BCM's desire to take the struggle beyond the law, which they saw incapable of implementing a total overhaul of 'the System' – in part because the law was a central part of that system.

The core theme of CRT that is also exemplified and performed by the black revolutionaries involves the insistence on a 'black point of view'.[78] This can be seen in their political trials from the way in which their statements are always framed by a critique of white supremacy and Western imperialism as well as a call for black liberation and solidarity. It is also obvious in the often calculated ways in which the black revolutionaries would often arrive in the courtroom dressed in African or Muslim regalia. This insistence on the normative legitimacy of blacks' experiences, realities and perspectives as forms of legal knowledge in the courtroom brings together CRT's employment of a writing technique named 'counter-storytelling' as well as its focus on structural determinism.[79] In using their opening and closing statements to amplify the voices of black women and men and bring them to the attention of the court, and thus of the law, the black revolutionaries explicitly challenge the dominant legal and cultural narratives of their time, exposing their failure to provide a language with which to protest against racism, suffering and oppression. Because law aspires to an 'aesthetic of uniformity' that negates racial and cultural difference, those dominant legal and cultural narratives were defective not only because they offered a limited and reductive vocabulary for the full expression of the legal and political claims of the black radical activists at the time but they also reflected a normalized and taken-for-granted white point of view.[80]

At the same time, the resistant speech and action of the black radical activists also served to make race a legitimate candidate for legal attention, by showing how legal constructions are also contoured by a racial subjectivity and also how

---

77　K. Crenshaw, N. Gotanda, G. Peller and K. Thomas (eds) *Critical Race Theory: The Key Writings that Formed the Movement* (1995, The New Press: New York) xxxii; J.M. Modiri, 'The Colour of Law, Power and Knowledge: Introducing Critical Race Theory to (Post)-Apartheid South Africa' (2012) 28 *South African Journal on Human Rights* 415–16.

78　Williams, *The Alchemy* 51; M. Matsuda, 'Looking to the Bottom: Critical Legal Studies and Reparations' (1987) 22 *Harvard Civil Rights-Civil Liberties Law Review* 324.

79　Modiri, 'The Colour of Law', 419–20; 421–3.

80　Williams, *The Alchemy*, 48.

race modifies one's relation to the tonalities and effects of law.[81] This exhibits the race-conscious approach to law advocated in critical race theory as an alternative to the race-neutral and colour-blind paradigm which structures legal liberalism's understanding of race and racism.[82] This race-conscious legal method was also consequent to CRT's emphasis on the concrete and particular in contrast to the abstract and universal. Under such a race-conscious legal method, law explicitly becomes another scene of racial exposure, where the contingent, socially fabricated and racialized nature of everyday social practices, legal concepts and institutional arrangements is exposed. Racial exposure involves making every person and institution aware of (their) race and of the material and symbolic, conscious and unconscious, direct and indirect, subjective and objective effects of (their) being raced.

CRT's discovery of the systemic and ingrained nature of racism closely mirrors the black revolutionaries' repeated protestations in the courtroom against legally sanctioned white supremacy in apartheid South Africa and Jim Crow USA. What these protestations indicated was a deep recognition of how race was the fundamental contradiction in their societies, and an awareness of their own blackness, of their 'Being Black in an anti-Black world'.[83] This is evident whether one is speaking of Balagoon's appellation of the trial court in the Brink's Trial as a 'racist court' or his description of police brutality as 'terrorist acts against Black people';[84] or of Shakur's explanation that '[The] idea of a Black Liberation Army emerged from conditions in Black communities ... [and] came about because Black people are not free or equal in this country';[85] or also of Biko's insistence that 'Black Consciousness refers itself to the black man and to his situation'.[86] In this way, they each embody Mari Matsuda's insistence that the history, culture and intellectual traditions of blacks should serve as an epistemological source for legal and social theorizing – an insistence which she put forward on the premise that '[t]he method of looking to the bottom can lead to concepts of law radically different to those generated at the top'.[87]

---

81 Ibid.

82 See G. Peller, 'Race Consciousness' (1990) *Duke Law Journal* 758–847 and the follow-up *Critical Race Consciousness: Reconsidering American Ideologies of Racial Justice* (2012, Paradigm Publishers: Boulder). See also G. Minda, *Postmodern Legal Movements: Law and Jurisprudence at Century's End* (1995, New York University Press: New York) 178–81 and J. Modiri, 'Towards a Post-Apartheid Critical Race Jurisprudence: "Diving our Racial Themes"' (2012) 27 *SA Public Law* 244–6.

83 See N.C. Mangayi, *Being-Black-in-an-Anti-Black-World* (1973, Raven Press: Johannesburg).

84 Balagoon, 'Brink's Trial Closing Statement'.

85 Shakur, *Assata: An Autobiography*, 169.

86 Biko, *I Write What I Like*, 110.

87 Matsuda, 'Looking to the Bottom', 325–6. On the related notion of the black subaltern subject as 'organic anthropologist', see b hooks, *Writing Beyond Race: Living Theory and Practice* (2013, Routledge: New York) 41, 42 and 69.

But there is one more reason that supports the claim that those acts of resistance in the courtroom were informed by a critical race idiom and praxis long before a legal philosophy or academic movement that would be called critical race theory came into being.[88] Matsuda contends that because the racially oppressed and marginalized not only had, but *had lived in*, the knowledge that law serves to legitimate existing hierarchies of power along racial lines, most black radical activists worked off an almost 'intuitive' critical jurisprudence with traces of legal realist, CLS, CRT and even Marxist theories of law.[89] At this point, the connection between critique as argued for above and critical race theory should be obvious. The black radical activists' version of critical race theory is 'critical' not only because it is sourced from an inherently counter-hegemonic legal consciousness but also because the black activists of the BLA and BCM also mirrored CRT's desire to attend to and address the lived experience and conditions of blacks, and they did this in part through acts of resistance that were informed by a racial reading of their times and a struggle to reclaim those times *against* the crises and brutalities of racism and *for* a more radical democratic socialist future.

It is through an appreciation of this meaning of critique that we are given CRT's most endearing lesson for race and law scholarship in South Africa and beyond: because racism is a core (constitutive, not incidental) feature of Western legal modernity, even the great ideals of law – truth, justice, equality, rule of law and liberty – ideals traditionally said to be safeguarded by the court, are open to interrogations that reveal their complicity with racial power and injustice.[90]

The Litigious Turn in 'Post'-Apartheid Jurisprudence

If the acts of resistance in the courtroom documented in this chapter reflect a broader attitude towards the law, namely an attitude of critique, race-consciousness and political suspicion, then yet one last line of enquiry is possible – one that will pull us from the Black Liberation and Black Consciousness past to the neo-apartheid present. I want to juxtapose the critical idea of law and the courts found in the acts of resistance and practices of critique identified in the political trials of the black revolutionaries against what I see as a thoroughly 'juridified' South African

---

88   Most of the trials documented in this chapter took place in the 1970s while CRT – as an organized movement – formally began in the late 1980s. See D. Bell, 'Who's Afraid of Critical Race Theory' (1995) *University of Illinois Law Review* 898 and A. Harris, 'Foreword', in R. Delgado and J. Stefancic, *Critical Race Theory: An Introduction* (2001, New York University Press: New York) xvii–xxi.

89   Matsuda, 'Looking to the Bottom', 327–8.

90   Harris, 'The Jurisprudence of Reconstruction', 741–85.

society, a society overtaken by an uncritical obsession with law and an unwavering devotion to legality and constitutionalism.[91]

I want to consider what could be called the "litigious turn" in the current public and political life of South Africa, a turn which signifies the juridification of not only politics but all spheres of life and human relations: sex, education, the government budget, the internal affairs of political parties, family disputes, medicine, sports, succession in traditional leadership, to name a few. What makes this turn even more acute is that the litigants and claimants approaching the courts and asserting their claims through exclusively legal means emanate from such varied sites as the left and the right of the political spectrum, from the ruling party to opposition parties, the propertied and the dispossessed, schoolchildren and principals, NGOs and social movements, as well as citizens, 'non-citizens' and corporations. I intend to enquire into the shift effected by this phenomenon of juridification, namely the shift from a position where the courtroom is seen as a repressive and silencing space, presided over by a judge who is deeply interpellated by the dominant powers of the age, to one where it is seen as a sacred space, one in which all social ills can be vanquished, in which judges are wise and profound sages with solutions to all the problems and complexities facing the nation.

But what conundrums and implications does the turn to juridification and litigiousness raise for democracy, social transformation and for the political future of South Africa? What happens when left progressive movements and causes are also submitted to the logic of law and law reform? What gets lost, reduced or forgotten in even the most well-intentioned attempts to instrumentalize law with the aim of litigating away historical injury and dispossession? What gets sacrificed in what Comaroff and Comaroff describe as the metamorphosis of class struggles into class actions,[92] and what Brown refers to as the transposition of political venue from the streets to the courtroom?[93] My argument is that juridification not only results in excessive litigation (or 'lawfare') that expands the 'power of law',[94] but that its ascendancy as a form of rationality or normative reason facilitates

---

91   See H. Corder, 'Lessons from (North) America (Beware the "Legalization of Politics" and the "Political Seduction of the Law")' (1992) 109 *SALJ* 204; Comaroff and Comaroff, 'Law and Disorder in the Postcolony: An Introduction' 24; J. Meierhenrich, *The Legacies of Law: Long-Run Consequences of Legal Development in South Africa, 1652–2000* (2008, Cambridge University Press: New York and Cambridge); S.L. Robins, *From Revolution to Rights in South Africa: Social Movements, NGOs and Popular Politics after Apartheid* (2008, James Currey: Woodbridge); D. Davis and M. Le Roux, *Precedent and Possibility: The (Ab)use of Law in South Africa* (2009, Double Storey Books: Cape Town) 185–6.

92   'Law and Disorder in the Postcolony: An Introduction', 27.

93   W. Brown, 'Suffering the Paradoxes of Rights', in Brown and Halley, *Left Legalism/Left Critique*, 420.

94   C. Smart, *Feminism and the Power of Law* (1989, Routledge: London) 4–25; 138–59, has also warned that the resort to law reform, policymaking and rights discourse preserves law's place in the hierarchy of discourses and accordingly prevents any de-centring

the usurpation of a democratic, political and public vocabulary and social consciousness with a legalist and constitutional one. When South African life is juridicalized in this way, a new relationship to law and the courtroom emerges, one that differs markedly from that encountered in the courtroom performances of the BLA and BCM.

Of specific relevance here is Wendy Brown and Janet Halley's assertion that juridification marks a shift from 'left critique' to 'left legalism'.[95] In this shift, Brown and Halley tell us, the left critical view of law as invested in sustaining social injury and maintaining subordination, that image of law as productive of and complicit in injustice, is suddenly replaced by a traditionally liberal understanding of law as a neutral arbiter of legal disputes and as a source of fair and just solutions to social problems.[96] Their interest lies in the political and practical effects of left political projects that rely on the liberal state's promise to deliver justice, equality and freedom through law.[97] Stuart Hall argued long ago that the crisis of the left, its lack of coverage and relative obscurity within public discourse and global politics, is due neither to internal divisions in the left (those, say, between the activist and academic left, between the orthodox Marxists and the poststructuralists, or caused by the upsurge of identity politics) nor to the triumph or inevitability of liberalism, capitalism or the right. Rather Hall's charge is that the failure of the left lies solely in its own failure to 'apprehend the character of the age and to develop a political critique and a moral-political vision appropriate to this character'.[98] If Hall is correct, then the immediate question arises of how the left intends to assert an alternative moral and political vision of society and of the world if it remains so preoccupied with and tightly attached to legal liberalist strategies and precepts.

This also raises the paradox of a left progressive critique which depicts the legal system as part of the political problem being combatted while simultaneously submitting its political claims to law and the courts. It would seem that this paradox has features of what Peter Goodrich aptly named the '[left] critic's love of law'[99] and also what Brown diagnosed as resembling the 'epistemological structure of the fetish as described by Freud: "I know, but still … "'.[100] But beyond the political

---

of law with the effect that more robust and radical political projects are overshadowed, ignored and, ultimately, invalidated.

95   Brown and Halley, 'Introduction', 1.

96   W. Brown, 'Introduction: Freedom and the Plastic Cage', in *States on Injury: Power and Freedom in Late Modernity* (1995, Princeton University Press: Princeton) 27.

97   Brown and Halley, 'Introduction', 7.

98   W. Brown, 'Resisting Left Melancholy' (1999) 26 *Boundary 2* 19, citing S. Hall, *The Hard Road to Renewal: Thatcherism and the Crisis of the Left* (1988, Verso: London). On the political and theoretical disorientation of the left and its failure to contend with the 'dictatorship of no alternatives' under which the world suffers, see R.M. Unger, *What Should the Left Propose?* (2005, Verso: London) 1–17.

99   P. Goodrich, 'The Critic's Love of Law: Intimate Observations on an Insular Jurisdiction' (1999) 10 *Law & Critique* 343–60.

100   Brown, 'Introduction', in *Politics Out of History* 4.

incoherence, unintended side effects and ideological contradictions of legalism's triumph over critique, and the absorption of parts of the left by a legalist logic, juridification in general also harbours deeply conservative and depoliticizing modalities which are harmful to any vision for substantive democracy, equality and freedom, and to the political aspiration to a socialist future. I want to repeat the words of Audre Lorde: 'the master's tools will never dismantle the master's house. They may allow us to temporarily beat him at his game, but they will never enable us to bring about genuine change'.[101]

Juridification marks a patently undemocratic and maybe even anti-democratic turn. It aids law's expansion by making it the central instrument of conflict-solving and thereby empowers the most unrepresentative branch of government.[102] It also provides an avenue for unelected civic and political organizations and opposition parties to circumvent the decisions of the democratically elected government through the courts to the point of ruling through them. With this, juridification also increases the professional power of the (mostly white-dominated and conservative) legal profession and the judiciary, by redefining and classifying social and political (public) issues as legal issues, and in this manner bringing them under the 'operational domain' and control of lawyers and judges.[103] This redefinition dissociates and detaches public matters from politics and places them in the sphere of law and human rights to be resolved not through deliberation, contestation and bids for power but through litigation, adjudication and exchanges of lawsuits. Undoubtedly, the very meaning and value of democracy is inverted completely when rule by the people (the *demos*) becomes rule by the courts and by legal experts.[104] The turn to the courts also effects a transferral of agency and voice that was simply never entertained by activists within the black radical tradition who, as we saw, often insisted even on representing themselves in their trials.

Co-extensive with juridification's erosion of democratic practice and action is that it marks law's colonization of all facets of public and political life. Consequently, alternative forms of critical political action and mobilization are negated; the margin is consumed by the centre. When law takes over everything, it empties out the spaces in which this action once took place or could take place and more importantly it renders the political outside of legalism a barren wilderness, denuded of all radical possibilities. This emptying out in turn sets the stage for the easy operation of biopolitical power, social surveillance and disciplinary

---

101   A. Lorde, *Sister Outsider: Essays and Speeches* (1984, Crossing Press: Freedom, CA) 112.

102   W. Brown, 'We are All Democrats Now ...', in G. Agamben, A. Badiou, D. Bensaid, et al., *Democracy in What State?* (2011, Columbia University Press: New York) 48.

103   See K. Malan, *Politocracy: An Assessment of the Coercive Logic of the Territorial State and Ideas Around a Response to it*, trans. J. Scott (2012, PULP: Pretoria) 228–9; 308.

104   Malan, *Politocracy*, 228–9.

regulation through law,[105] thereby steadily promoting what Jürgen Habermas called the 'disintegration of life relations'.[106]

When the possibility of imagining legalism's political outside is eviscerated, we are also denied the opportunity to claim the margins of law as a site for rich dialogue and deliberation, a space for the appearance of vibrant counterpublics, and a place where law's hegemony can be constantly questioned and challenged. But this is not the only effect. As Brown and Halley note, once legalism usurps its political outside, that is, once legalistic logic and language monopolizes political and social discourse, it becomes difficult to even imagine 'alternative ways of deliberating about and pursuing justice'.[107] It not only translates wide-ranging or expansive political questions into narrowly framed legal ones, it also places a further restriction that now requires that the definition of ideals such as equality and freedom take place exclusively within the rigid parameters of the law. And they also remind us that neither this translation nor this restriction is neutral, for legalism, and liberal legalism in particular, carries a very specific (liberal and moderate) politics, and more so, a politics that is hostile to 'discursively open-ended, multigenre, and polyvocal conversations about how we should live, what we should value and what we should prohibit, and what is possible in collective life'.[108]

Robin West has added to this by claiming that legalism, which she names 'ideological legalism', is inherently conservative. In its elevation of rule-abidance to a morally superior form of living, legalism also preserves institutions of the past that are produced by those rules; institutions – such as the Family, the Market and the State – which recent critical theoretical interventions have characterized as reservoirs of considerable economic and social power and hegemony, and sites of severe forms of injury, exclusion and subordination.[109] Legalism on this view partakes in its own 'distribution of the sensible',[110] and has its own rules of social, political and cultural grammar, establishing what is sayable or unsayable, visible or invisible, and indeed possible or impossible in any given field of meaning and representation. It also circumscribes what is permissible or plausible as legal reasoning or political argument.

Politically speaking, I am deeply sympathetic, even if not totally convinced, to arguments in defence of effective and strategic deployments of rights discourse

---

105 Brown and Halley, 'Introduction', 11–16.

106 J. Habermas, 'Law as Medium and Law as Institution', in G. Teubner (ed.) *Dilemmas of Law in the Welfare State* (1986, Walter de Gruyter: Berlin) 211. See also G. Teubner (ed.) *Juridification of Social Spheres* (1987, Walter de Gruyter: Berlin).

107 Brown and Halley, 'Introduction' 19.

108 Ibid.

109 R. West, 'Reconsidering Legalism' (2003) 88 *Minnesota Law Review* 120.

110 See J. Ranciere, *The Politics of Aesthetics: The Distribution of the Sensible* (2004, Continuum: London).

and legal mobilization by the left,[111] specifically those defended by Patricia J. Williams[112] and Kimberle Crenshaw[113] about both the pragmatic utility of legal rights strategies and their symbolic historical and psychic significance for black, and other marginalized communities.[114] As Brown reminds us, however, there is an interval between theory and political practice that requires a recognition of the 'persistently untheoretical quality of politics', a recognition, that is, of the many ways in which the exigencies, immediate needs and hard choices of actual political life resist theoretical capture.[115] There is no doubt that theory and politics frequently contain different, and even conflicting, premises, aims, impulses and logics. But the recognition of this interval should provoke more critical reflection, rather than to help erect defensive and moralistic shields against critiques of the upsurge of rights discourse and legalism among left academics and activists and the implicit installation of litigiousness as a way of political, private and public life.[116]

My worry is that once legalism and constitutional optimism have so profoundly disoriented our politics, there is the danger, more so in the case of left law reform projects that seek emancipation though law, that we will (or maybe we already have) confuse legal protection, welfare grants and state regulation for political freedom, agency and substantive democracy and equality. Put another way, I am concerned about the containment, distortion or dilution of radical democratic

---

111   See the various contributions in J. Handmaker and R. Berkhout (eds) *Mobilising Social Justice in South Africa: Perspectives from Researchers and Practitioners* (2010, PULP: Pretoria) and M. Langford, B. Cousins, J. Dugard and T. Madlingozi (eds) *Symbols or Substance: The Role and Impact of Socio-Economic Rights Strategies in South Africa* (2013, Cambridge University Press: London).

112   Williams, *The Alchemy*.

113   K.W. Crenshaw, 'Race, Reform and Retrenchment: Transformation and Legitimation in Antidiscrimination Law' (1988) 101 *Harvard Law Review* 101.

114   It has become a scholarly cliché in such debates to rely on the response by critical race theorists to the CLS critique of rights as justification for the use of legal mobilization strategies by the left. Apart from the possibility that the context to which the CRT response to the rights critique had addressed itself might no longer be relevant or persuasive, it should be mentioned that the affirmation of rights for either pragmatic (Crenshaw) or historical (Williams) reasons is not a position representative of all of critical race theory. The work of Derrick Bell, for example, including his notion of racial realism and his thesis on the permanence of racism in liberal legal orders, evidences a deep concern for the incapacity of rights to deliver on their promise and his worry that any court victories and rights gains achieved though legal mobilization tend to fade away as unequal power relations adapt and progress. It is noteworthy that Patricia Williams has also distanced herself from a reading of *The Alchemy* as a 'flat defence of rights as many seem to think'. She goes on to state: 'I really was criticising CLS's faith that the so-called discourse of needs was going to provide something that the language of rights hadn't … or had effectively blocked. So my faith isn't in rights *per se*' (Q. Mirza, 'Patricia Williams: Inflecting Critical Race Theory' (1999) 7 *Feminist Legal Studies* 117).

115   Brown, 'Democracy Against Itself: Nietzsche's Challenge' 122.

116   Brown, 'Preface', in *States of Injury* xii.

politics within what Herbert Marcuse called the 'comfortable, smooth, reasonable, democratic unfreedom' that prevails under the regime of liberal legalism and neoliberal governance.[117] Even if strategic social reform through constitutional litigation is all that is possible in the current order, and even if such reform produces some short-lived gains in the way of material benefits and inspirational outcomes, what happens when the left progressives constantly trade in their claims to the fundamental restructuring of society, economy and political organization for such law-based reform; when they constantly delay the full elaboration and actualization of a radical democratic alternative in the name of more realistic and expedient legal solutions? In any case, to be 'practical', 'realistic' and 'strategic' – as many law reformers claim to be – to my mind is simply to operate on, and thereby *accede to*, the terms of the dominant symbolic order – the order which a revolutionary politics should precisely aim to overthrow. None of this is to say however that human rights should be flatly rejected, nor that they are incapable of a left critical theoretical and political expansion and reconstruction but rather that more ambitious justice projects should not be eclipsed by rights discourse; that we should, while pursuing legal and rights-based strategies, also pursue justice, equality, democracy and freedom in other vocabularies, through other social, political and economic institutions and by means of other mechanisms and practices that are not legalist and rights-centred.[118]

Compare here the black revolutionaries' recognition of (apartheid) law's affiliation with, and legitimation of, racially subordinating powers and their ensuing refusal to co-operate with apartheid legal institutions and to categorize/ organize their struggle against racial oppression in legal terms with what Comaroff and Comaroff observe to be the fetishization of law and constitutionality that pervades social, moral and political being in post-1994 South Africa.[119] Let us revisit a passage from Biko's testimony:

> [W]hat we want is a total accommodation of our interests in the total country, not in some portion of it. So we don't have a side programme, we don't have any alternative. We believe ultimately in the righteousness of our strength, that we are going to get to the eventual accommodation of our interests within the country.[120]

---

117 H. Marcuse, *The One Dimensional Man: Studies in the Ideology of Advanced Industrial Society* (1964, Beacon Press: Boston).

118 I.R. Wall, 'Rights, Tolerance and Critique: An Interview with Wendy Brown' available at http://humanrights.i.e./civil-liberties/rights-tolerance-waning-sovereignty-inter view-with-wendy-brown/ (accessed 2 January 2014).

119 Comaroff and Comaroff, 'Law and Disorder in the Postcolony: An Introduction', 24.

120 Biko, *I Write What I Like*, 152.

These words, I think, express the kind of urgency that should animate critical scholars whose intellectual and political work is dedicated to a critique of post-1994 law and society, and to uncovering the many continuations of inequality, social misery and injustice and the ongoing subordination and exclusion experienced by blacks in spite of (or perhaps, because of) the establishment of a liberal constitutional democracy based on human rights and the elaboration of a substantive equality jurisprudence. In my view, the tenacious persistence of racial inequalities and hierarchies and their normalization within the present South African context, reflects how deeply racism remains definitive of the current political and social landscape, and conversely, also how any attempts to enlist law to the task of addressing and eradicating the substantive material conditions of racism, poverty and suffering are doomed to fail. Freedom and equality cannot be legislated into being just as historical injury cannot be litigated away. It is this revelation of the falsity of legal liberalism's promise that should inform our approach to race, law and critique. And so, what makes the legacy of the black radical tradition and its orientation towards law so appealing to this exploration and also so enduring even in the present is that they offer one historical example of a movement of insurrectionary subjects pursuing a radical, emancipatory and egalitarian politics without totally grounding its identity or its political goals in law. Incited in large part by law's own patent endorsement of anti-black racism and white supremacy, the black radicals had to seek and affirm an alternative normative source, other than and against law, on which to base their struggle. Would that the left would be more attentive to such historical lessons, we might find ourselves in a different time and place.

Conclusion: Critical Futures

In this chapter, I have suggested that the acts of resistance in the courtroom explored above should be understood as modes of critique reiterative of the core jurisprudential themes of critical race theory. With reference to the central tenets of critical race theory and the work of Michel Foucault and Wendy Brown, I linked this to a reconstructive and transformative notion of 'critique', showing it to be central to left political and legal theory and practice. I did this also to displace unnecessary anxieties regarding the tension between theory and practice that has been a common debate in the academic and activist left in South Africa. My aim was to show that it is critique's inseparability from restoration and judgement (including practical judgements about what must done, when and how) that belies the contemporary anti-intellectual conceit that posits the tension between theory and practice as damaging rather than as productive. I then moved on to contemplate the disappearance of the culture of resistance and critique found in the political trials that were discussed in the chapter, and expressed worry over its replacement in the post-1994 context with a culture of legality and devotion to constitutionalism.

This reflection on the courtroom as a space of resistance through a memorial recollection of the political trials of activists in the black radical tradition provided an apt occasion for a simultaneous reflection on our past, present and future; a reflection on both the future of critique and the future's critical condition. It is this temporal concern for the power of the past over future that informed the three core elements of this chapter, namely the extension of Wilderson's theoretical reading of the political trials of BLA insurgents to Biko's testimony in the BPC/SASO Trial; the connection drawn between political resistance and theoretical critique; and the argument against juridification and legalism as forms of action and mobilization in post-1994 South Africa.

To the extent that the radical vision of freedom, anti-subordination, equality and democracy that was espoused by thinkers and activists in the black radical traditions in South Africa and the United States remains painfully unfulfilled in our time, we would do well to consider not only the binding effect of law on emancipatory political projects but also the consequences of the eclipse of a revolutionary horizon signalled by an identification with law reform.

From this view, the problems of the rise of a legalist rationality and register go beyond its subversion of critique, and of a more critical sense of time, truth, reality, power and knowledge. In addition to this, the turn to legalism and juridification of political projects is symptomatic of the loss of a sense of futurity by the left and a certain anxiety and hesitation towards the viability of a radical socialist democratic alternative. Given that rights-based freedom and protection can only serve to mitigate and attenuate, rather than eradicate and resolve, the powers and conditions that produce powerlessness, alienation, suffering, violence and marginalization, the contemporary resort to law conveys, too, a left politics so deeply immersed in desperation, complacency and fatalism that it can conceive of no other choice but to capitulate to the givenness and necessity of present juridical, economic and social arrangements. This loss of faith, of course, has attributes of what Biko, during his testimony, lamented as the loss of hope and sense of defeat that had set in into the black community in the 1970s. But as Biko said further:

> Now this sense of defeat is basically what we are fighting against; people must not just give in to the hardship of life, people must develop a hope, people must develop some form of security to be together to look at their problems, and people must in this way build up their humanity. This is the point about conscientisation and Black Consciousness.[121]

The theme of hope is echoed again in Shakur's opening statement at her trial when she speaks of her aspiration to 'make this a better world'.[122] That both Biko and Shakur as black revolutionaries uttered these words in the courtrooms of powerful white supremacist nations serves as evidence that it is possible to fashion a new

121   Ibid., 127.
122   Shakur, *Assata: An Autobiography*, 170.

form of politics, and of social being and being-together, that is not dependent on law for its coherence or recognition. Theoretically, it also illustrates that a critique of law, and a call for a constant resistance of law's language, power and violence, need not be seen as threatening to particular objects and practices, as it can carry a potentially richer utopian vision of a restored and transformed social order. I find the linking together or alchemies of resistance and hope, critique and reconstruction suggestive for the development of a South African critical race jurisprudence, and for a radical socialist refiguring of racial justice.

In conclusion then, and against the backdrop sketched here, how can those of us who still believe in left critique (and even those who have begun to lose faith in it) harness the energy of resistance of the black revolutionaries? How do we reclaim their deep intolerance for injustice and their refusal to concede anything to inequality and oppression in order to reaffirm once more that revolutionary possibility that the world can be remade, again and again, in the pursuit of authentic justice? It is in the spirit of this as-yet-unrealized revolutionary possibility that this chapter was written and offered here in tribute to the ongoing global struggle for black liberation and decolonization.

Chapter 11

What is Revealed by the Absence of a Reply? Courtesy, Pedagogy and the Spectre of Unanswered Letters in Mandela's Trial

Alison Phipps

... that is a letter raising vital issues affecting the vast majority of this country ...
(Mandela: Incitement Trial)

I am not a legal scholar. My approach to the text and performative power of both the Incitement Trial and the Rivonia Trial are not trained by the conventions of law or administrative justice, but by dramaturgy, languages and anthropology. I also bring a strong sensitivity schooled in liberation theology and through advocacy work over many years in the context of the struggles of refugees. And I am a poet and liturgist. I say this at the outset to mark out a space for a different set of disciplinary and tonal conventions which for many with legal training will seem strange, perhaps ill-disciplined, perhaps imprecise, displacing. I would ask for your gentleness in academic hospitality and that you also accept my gratitude for the generosity of your reading. I say this, this way, because it echoes the formal conventions of speech in the trials we are considering, the necessity of eloquent respect of those we address with our words and the possibilities such spaces afford when such conventions are respected, the possibility of being largely and expansively *heard*.

In this chapter I will consider the import of letters both in Mandela's trial but also in protest movements worldwide today. I will juxtapose the account given of the letters not favoured with a reply in Mandela's trial and the unopened, unanswered letters of protesters and the kinds of language and evocation required for a letter to be received and heard. I will then consider the languages of justice, the forms of speech and languages admitted in the Rivonia Trial and those struggling for admittance today. To accomplish these moves I will: (1) attend theoretically to the questions posed by drawing on the work of feminist and postcolonial scholars, notably Judith Butler, Anne Carson, Luce Irigary and Elaine Scarry as well as scholars of languages; (2) Offer comparison with letters sent in protests pertaining today, with particular attention to two situations. First, letters sent by internationals in the struggles for justice in Israel and Palestine reflecting on the rhetorical comparisons to Apartheid South Africa. Second, in the more intimate contexts of anti-deportation campaigns in the UK, and in particular letters of my own which are not 'favoured with a reply'; (3) I will suggest poetic and linguistic resources which fuse the rhetorical power of Mandela's defence and the ethical preference for hope into fresh expressions in times when language and 'vital issues' are under duress today. I do so in order to highlight the effectiveness and necessity of social rituals of courtesy in personal and international relations, and within the context of the operations of law.

Looking for a Reply

The central drama in the *text* of Mandela's defence at his incitement trial in his first court statement of 28 October 1962 revolves around a catalytic moment: the absence of a reply to the letter sent by Mandela to the prime minister and to the letter sent by Chief Lutuli to the prime minister. This opening moment repeats itself through the text and performs an important function as a pivot for the rhetorical imagination of law, land, language and letters.

Let me begin with what I perceive to be a central drama in the Incitement Trial and let me repeat the dramatic action:

> Among the witnesses was Mr. Barnard, the private secretary to the then Prime Minister, Dr H F Verwoerd, whom Mandela cross-examined on the subject of a letter sent by Mandela to the Prime Minister demanding a National Convention in May 1961. In cross-examining the witness, Mandela first read the contents of the letter:
>
> > *I am directed by the All-in African National Action Council to address your government in the following terms: The All-in African National Action Council was established in terms of a resolution adopted at a conference held at Pietermaritzburg on 25 and 26 March 1961. This conference was attended by 1,500 delegates from town and country, representing 145 religious, social, cultural, sporting, and political bodies. Conference noted that your government, after receiving a mandate from a section of the European population, decided to proclaim a republic on 31 May. It was the firm view of delegates that your government, which represents only a minority of the population in this country, is not entitled to take such a decision without first seeking the views and obtaining the express consent of the African people. Conference feared that under this proposed republic your government, which is already notorious the world over for its obnoxious policies, would continue to make even more savage attacks on the rights and living conditions of the African people.*
> >
> > *Conference carefully considered the grave political situation facing the African people today. Delegate after delegate drew attention to the vicious manner in which your government forced the people of Zeerust, Sekhukhuniland, Pondoland, Nongoma, Tembuland and other areas*

to accept the unpopular system of Bantu Authorities, and pointed to numerous facts and incidents which indicate the rapid manner in which race relations are deteriorating in this country. It was the earnest opinion of Conference that this dangerous situation could be averted only by the calling of a sovereign national convention representative of all South Africans, to draw up a new non-racial and democratic Constitution. Such a convention would discuss our national problems in a sane and sober manner, and would work out solutions which sought to preserve and safeguard the interests of all sections of the population. Conference unanimously decided to call upon your government to summon such a convention before 31 May. Conference further decided that unless your government calls the convention before the above-mentioned date, countrywide demonstrations would be held on the eve of the republic in protest. Conference also resolved that in addition to the demonstrations, the African people would be called upon to refuse to cooperate with the proposed republic. We attach the Resolutions of the Conference for your attention and necessary action. We now demand that your government call the convention before 31 May, failing which we propose to adopt the steps indicated in paragraphs 8 and 9 of this letter. These demonstrations will be conducted in a disciplined and peaceful manner. We are fully aware of the implications of this decision, and the action we propose taking. We have no illusions about the counter-measures your government might take in this matter. After all, South Africa and the world know that during the last thirteen years your government has subjected us to merciless and arbitrary rule. Hundreds of our people have been banned and confined to certain areas. Scores have been banished to remote parts of the country, and many arrested and jailed for a multitude of offences. It has become extremely difficult to hold meetings, and freedom of speech has been drastically curtailed. During the last twelve months we have gone through a period of grim dictatorship, during which seventy-five people were killed and hundreds injured while peacefully demonstrating against passes. Political organisations were declared unlawful, and thousands flung into jail without trial. Your government can only take these measures to suppress the forthcoming demonstrations, and these measures have failed to stop opposition to the policies of your government. We are not deterred by threats of force and violence made by you and your government, and will carry out our duty without flinching.

MANDELA: You remember the contents of this letter?

WITNESS: I do.

MANDELA: Did you place this letter before your Prime Minister?

WITNESS: Yes.

MANDELA: On what date? Can you remember?

WITNESS: It is difficult to remember, but I gather from the date specified on the date stamp, the Prime Minister's Office date stamp.

MANDELA: That is 24 April. Now was any reply given to this letter by the Prime Minister? Did he reply to this letter?

WITNESS: He did not reply to the writer.

MANDELA: He did not reply to the letter. Now, will you agree that this letter raises matters of vital concern to the vast majority of the citizens of this country?

WITNESS: I do not agree.

MANDELA: You don't agree? You don't agree that the question of human rights, of civil liberties, is a matter of vital importance to the African people?

WITNESS: Yes, that is so, indeed.

Theoretically, the ground here is ground worked over by Lacan, Derrida and Zizek in their consideration of the deconstructive amateur detective story of Edgar Allan Poe, *The Purloined Letter*. These theorists address the possibilities of what might happen when letters do not arrive at their destination or when they are not acknowledged as having done so. As such these theorists are concerned to illuminate the question that concerns me here: of a failure in social conventions and communications concerning an important letter. In Poe's story a letter has gone missing and is then found again by cleverness and by the possibility, celebrated in Foucauldian readings of this text, of surveillance systems being fallible to an amateur's wit. To summarise quite simply what are complex and important arguments, Lacan (1988) asks why it is that a letter always arrives at its destination, and Derrida typically then asks the converse; 'Why, indeed? Why could it not – sometimes, at least – also *fail* to reach it?' (Derrida, 1987). Zizek (2013) then considers the nature of both the turn of events and the presenting absence, 'the fact that *events took precisely this turn* could not but appear as uncanny, concealing some fateful meaning – as if some mysterious hand took care that *the letter arrived at its destination*'. Much of the analysis of these three writers lingers over the terrain and discourse of psychoanalysis and rightly so. The absence of a text, and a letter all the more so, has a tantalising hold on the human imagination. By raising the spectre of the letter which was not acknowledged but which raised 'matters of vital concern to the majority of the citizens' of South Africa, Mandela is working in the trial with the same material as detains Lacan, Derrida and Zizek. Analysis of this element also adds to the debates concerning the exposure of wider structures of power, even of fate, which these theorists also excavate, namely, the absence of an important and much anticipated text, in the form of a reply.

The absence of important texts lingers over scholarly imagination and drives much interpretative and conjectural work. Socrates left no text, that we know of, but philosophy is haunted by the possibility. Aristotle's *Poetics* possess the text on tragedy but the text on comedy is missing. New Testament hermeneutics is haunted by the absent 'Q Text' – the text upon which the synoptic Gospels of Matthew, Mark and Luke are purported to be based – but which is nowhere present. We do not believe we have all of the Epistles of Paul or know that they all did indeed arrive, and upon these is built one of the three religions of the book. By drawing attention to a letter which is absent from a record where convention would demand a reply, Mandela feeds the imagination and seeds the question – what if a reply had been sent? What might it have said? How might things have turned out differently? What would have constituted a just reply as opposed to a silencing discourtesy? The ragged record with its gaping absences in philosophy and hermeneutics, demonstrates how much work can come from absence of text as well as presence, and how the fates are summoned to act as witnesses within this work.

It isn't just in the arena of philosophy and Biblical hermeneutics that the absence of text and lack of epistles captures the imagination. It is also a trope in popular culture. The examples below show that within the complex story of the missing text or letter is an element of the drama of the letter which either did not arrive or did not receive a reply:

> Completing a journey started over half a century ago: Man who received lost postcard 55 YEARS after it was sent by his parents will now visit aquarium pictured on the back. By Snejana Farberov, 26 April 2012 (*Daily Mail*).

> **1967 Postcard Arrives 46 Years Late, Mystifying Family** "Bert Jacobson was just 13 when he took a trip with his father and cousins to the East Coast and wrote his mother a postcard to describe the fun he was having. At that time, in 1967, Lyndon B. Johnson was president, the Beatles were groovy and postage home cost 4 cents. That postcard never reached Jacobson's mother – not until this week, that is, when the letter, dirtied and tattered, arrived at his family's concrete business P.O. Box."[1]

The discovery of lost letters continues to tantalise scholars. In June 2013 a Professor of Scottish History at my own university found a lost letter from Robert the Bruce, 1310, to King Edward II sent less than four years before Robert Bruce won a famous victory at the Battle of Bannockburn against the English king which

---

1   The Huffington Post, http://www.huffingtonpost.com/2013/02/11/postcard-arrives-46-years-later-bert-jaconson_n_2665106.html.

paved the way for Scottish independence. This discovery of such a lost letter is, in the context of a country that was at the time preparing for a referendum on independence, a significant symbolic find. The question, which brings us back to the drama of the Incitement Trial, is why such absences and missing or failed replies – the intervening dramas in the politics and possibilities of receiving a reply – have such a performative hold on the imagination?

Anne Carson, Classics scholar and poet, perhaps provides an answer to the tantalising hold an absent response has for human dramas. In her work *Eros the Bittersweet* (1998) she dissects the geometrically opposed elements in the erotic desire and the way the force of Eros behaves when thwarted, scorned, dishonoured or simply disappointed:

> The Greek word *eros* denotes "want", "lack", "desire for that which is missing". The lover wants what he does not have. It is impossible for him to have what he wants if, as soon as it is had, it is no longer wanting ... All human desire is poised on an axis of paradox, absence and presence its poles, love and hate its motive energies. (Carson, 1998: 10–11)

Under this definition of Eros the reply to the letter would signify to Mandela that relations are following conventions and that there is hope of pursuing diplomatic and political means in the struggle for justice in South Africa. The absence of a reply signifies the absence of the very thing most desired – the affordance by the South African government of respect towards the opposition. Where this is absent, as symbolised in the absence of a reply to a letter, then the impossibility of normal, political conventions is, paradoxically, made evident. In the context of the letter brought centre stage in the trial the absent letter, the reply never written, constitutes an uncivilised and scandalous action for Mandela, it dishonours his love of his people and country. In the exchange between Mandela and the Witness a reversal occurs which exposes as 'uncivilised' the power the government has assumed of naming actions uncivilised or scandalous, on the basis of colour. What it means to be civilised and who is able to demonstrate civilised actions becomes the central drama:

> **MANDELA:** Would you agree with me that in any civilised country in the world it would be at least most scandalous for a Prime Minister to fail to reply to a letter raising vital issues affecting the majority of the citizens of that country. Would you agree with that?
>
> **WITNESS:** I don't agree with that.
>
> **MANDELA:** You don't agree that it would be irregular for a Prime Minister to ignore a letter raising vital issues affecting the vast majority of the citizens of that country?

WITNESS: This letter has not been ignored by the Prime Minister.

It is not the savagery or barbaric enactment of Apartheid laws which is named as uncivilised and scandalous, but rather the failure of the prime minister to reply to a letter. Derrida notes this in 'The Laws of Reflection', his piece written in admiration of Mandela:

> Mandela thus accuses white governments of never *answering*, while at the same time demanding that blacks be quiet and make written representations: resign yourself to correspondence and to corresponding all alone. The sinister irony of counterpoint: after his conviction, Mandela is kept in solitary confinement for 23 hours a day in Pretoria Central Prison. He is employed in sewing mailbags (Derrida, 2008: 78–9).

This raises questions relating to the Incitement Trial's performative power as to the nature of the breach involved in the refusal to dignify a letter with a reply.

In writing on the nature of the social bond, without which societies slide quickly into violence and chaos, the theologian Rowan Williams (2000) speaks of 'the civilities of fraternity' as the core elements ensuring that energy is directed away from competition or confrontation and towards the 'maintenance of friendly exchange'. The ability to keep an exchange going, to commit to a conversation, at the most basic level to participate in the known social rituals of meeting and greeting, allows for the space to be maintained for those exchanges which surround the conflicts of interest and desire. Williams maintains that because we are not transparent to each other the maintenance of a common language and common opportunities to learn of one another is fundamental to politics, and therefore to the possibilities of justice. In short, the maintenance of appropriate rituals of social exchange – from the chat over the garden wall about the weather, to the reply to a letter – is the continuing symbolic and practised acknowledgement that 'my interest *involves* yours and yours mine' (Williams, 2000: 101).

Eros – what is desired and absent, here, is justice, for a country, for the law and human dignity, and, in this trial, for the accused man's life. It is invoked in the social ritual of civil forms of relationship between political leaders: the letter. Eros here is thwarted through the contempt, the denial of a reply, the refusal to respond with respect to another. It is staged on the drama of the missing reply, the failed reply, and all that this represents. What was a personal exchange between party leaders becomes a matter of wild forces unleashed as the drama of the snub, the discourtesy, slighted lover of citizens and country, is laid out. Meticulously, or as Carson may suggest, *geometrically*, Eros is activated here publicly and with stakes as high as treason and death. The structural components in the drama are the lover (Mandela), beloved (the question 'of human rights, of civil liberties, as a matter of vital importance to the African people') and that which comes between them ('vital issues affecting the vast majority of the citizens of that country', the neglect of which is manifest in the absence of a reply to the letter). They are three points of transformation on 'a circuit of possible relationship, electrified by desire so that they touch not touching. Conjoined they are held apart' (Carson, 1998: 16). Quoting the tradition that the entrance to Plato's academy bore the words 'Let no one enter here who is ignorant of geometry', Carson suggests that:

> When the circuit-points connect, perception leaps. And something becomes visible, on the triangular path where volts are moving, that would not be visible without the three-part structure ... The man sits like a god, the poet almost dies: two poles of response within the same desiring mind. Triangulation makes both present at once by a shift of distance, replacing erotic action with a ruse of heart and language. For in this dance the people do not move. Desire moves. Eros is a verb. (Carson, 1998: 17)

This verb is active in these opening segments of the Incitement Trial, piling up examples of letters which have not been dignified with a reply. The sleight, yes, to the signatory authors, but now wildly and widely to the African people. Derrida speaks in admiration of Mandela's ability to represent: '"My people and I", he always says, without speaking like a king' (Derrida, 2008: 63). The letter now stands for dignity, civilisation, common conversation, the possibility of negotiating difficult things. White power is exposed in the examples from the ANC history of letters which have not received a reply, as entirely lacking in these characteristics:

MANDELA: Now this letter, Exhibit 18, is dated 26 June 1961, and it is also addressed to the Prime Minister, and it reads as follows:

> *I refer you to my letter of 20 April 1961, to which you do not have the courtesy to reply or acknowledge receipt. In the letter referred to above I informed you of the resolutions passed by the All-in African National Conference in Pietermaritzburg on 26 March 1961, demanding the calling by your government before 31 May 1961 of a multi-racial and sovereign National Convention to draw up a new non-racial and democratic Constitution for South Africa ... .*

Working back in time, just as with Zizek's description of the power of the events concealed in Poe's *The Purloined Letter*, Mandela performs an archaeology of the indignity symbolised by the letters which have not received a reply. The accusation 'you do not have the courtesy to reply or acknowledge receipt', lies atop the earlier statement, 'to fail to reply to a letter raising vital issues', atop 'that it would be irregular for a Prime Minister to ignore a letter', atop 'He did not reply to the letter', which is a correction of the witness's claim that it was the writer who did not receive a reply. The matter in hand, the site of the drama, is the letter, not the writer and accused. All of this lies atop the first action in the trial as it begins, after the plea of not guilty has been made, where the letter is read out and is therefore performatively demonstrated, beyond all doubt, to have been received, and a space opens up for the possibility of a reply. The whole action of the trial, when considered in reverse, unfolds from this context. Reading the layers in this way reveals through the device of a simple lack of courtesy in dignifying a letter with a reply, the whole operation and injustice of the Apartheid system of government. Mandela does not need to give a disquisition on Apartheid and its operation, he simply shows that in the failure to reply to a letter, is a failure of statehood, a failure of civilised behaviour, a failure of that very system of Apartheid government and its legitimacy. This indignity is central to the matter of this trial, which occurs within this very system of government which is deconstructed here, through the device of the letter.

Mandela produces another example of such a lack of reply, heightening the suspense of the drama, and the matter of definition of what constitutes courtesy and civilised actions becomes the point of contest:

> **MANDELA:** This is the letter which you received on 28 June 1961? Again there was no acknowledgement or reply by the Prime Minister to this letter?
>
> **WITNESS:** I don't think it is – I think it shouldn't be called a letter in the first instance, but an accumulation of threats.
>
> **MANDELA:** Whatever it is, there was no reply to it?
>
> **WITNESS:** No.

The ground moves again, the issue is not a question of when a letter is not a letter, or an accumulation of threats, but that there was no reply. The matter is charged, moving, erotic. Layers of evidence in the form of letters ignored put the Apartheid government itself on trial and turn the tables. This government is not fit to govern:

> **MANDELA:** Throughout its fifty years of existence the African National Congress, for instance, has done everything possible to bring its demands to the attention of successive South African governments. It has sought at all times peaceful solutions for all the country's ills and problems. The history of the ANC is filled with instances where deputations were sent to South African governments either on specific issues or on the general political demands of our people. I do not wish to burden Your Worship by enunciating the occasions when such deputations were sent; all that I wish to indicate at this stage is that, in addition to the efforts made by former presidents of the ANC, when Mr. Strijdom became Prime Minister of this country, my leader, Chief A J Lutuli, then President of our organisation, made yet another effort to persuade this government to consider and to heed our point of view. In his letter to the Prime Minister at the time, Chief Lutuli exhaustively reviewed the country's relations and its dangers, and expressed the view that a meeting between the government and African leaders had become necessary and urgent.

This statesmanlike and correct behaviour on the part of the leader of the majority of the South African population did not find an appropriate answer from the leader of the South African government. The standard of behaviour of the South African government towards my people and its aspirations has not always been what it should have been, and is not always the standard which is to be expected in serious high-level dealings between civilised peoples. Chief Lutuli's letter was not even favoured with the courtesy of an acknowledgement from the Prime Minister's office.

Once again, government standards in dealing with my people fell below what the civilised world would expect. No reply, no response whatsoever, was received to our letter, no indication was even given that it had received any consideration whatsoever.

The matter culminates. The indignity is now not only towards 'My people and I' but also 'My leader, Chief Lutuli'. The possessive pronouns personalise the insult to the accused, but at the same time the longing is writ large across the living and the ancestral dead. James C. Scott describes the effects of such indignities as providing fuel to the imaginary speeches rehearsed by the dominated to the oppressor. In the rhetorical shape and form of Mandela's statements to the court we can sense the hidden transcript, long gestating in 'subordinations that impose indignities of one kind or another on the weak. These indignities are the seedbed of the anger, indignation, frustration, and swallowed bile that nurture the hidden transcript' (Scott, 1990: 111).

Meticulous legal and political rhetoric and evidence is juxtaposed with the silence which is given public interpretation as contempt. Courtesy herself is on trial. Eros the motive energy turning the audience into the judge, impelling them with its desire, showing clearly what has been scorned, and how.

The publication of the letter at the start of the Incitement Trial, the performative power of its positioning in the precision and integrity of Mandela's language, as he conducts his defence, and the release into the world of the evidence of a fundamental indignity was one element in the exposure of multiple injustices which eventually brought the end of the Apartheid regime. This is not to say that the lack of reply was any kind of originary cause – though this could perhaps be excavated – but it is to say that in such triangulations of desire, such unjustifiably frustrated longing, have profound social and political consequences.

James C. Scott (1990) also makes an important distinction between dignity and the uncontainable energy of indignation which moves us to act, to register resistance. In the last book before his death Paulo Freire discusses pedagogies of indignation (Freire, 2005). In this work Freire speaks to the necessity of making and remaking one's self throughout a lifetime. The role of education is connected intimately to personal development, and the daily life tensions between freedom and authority. Through Freire's ideas we may read Mandela in these trials, and in the face of this indignity as a teacher, drawing upon his own depth as a person, and teaching the court, and the wider watching world what it means to speak from a position of authority, as an act of resistance. Freire's book begins with a letter, sent to Paulo, by Balduino Andreaola, and it sets out in the first sentence the social rituals of courtesy which a letter received from friends requires.

> I have received your *Pedagogical Letters*, kindly sent to me by Nita ... Personally speaking Paulo, I feel that letters received from friends must also be replied to in letter form. (Freire, 2005: xxxiii)

The personal belief that letters received from friends must be replied to, becomes political in the context of letters received at the level of government and its operations. Letters received from constituents compel a response under the operations of elected democracy, letters received from members of opposing parties or from elected representatives of pressure groups or civic organisations must also be replied to in letter form. The use of the modal – 'must' – indicates the highest level of imperative. The public traffic in courtesy suggesting that a society is indeed able to maintain internal and external civilised relations is evidenced in its replies to letters. The purchase and publication and archiving of letters of state is, for this reason alone, an important indicator of the high symbolic content of letters of state. For Freire, additional to this symbolic value, letters expressing of indignation and hope, are pedagogical in force. Mandela's example, cited alongside others from liberation movements, in Freire's understanding, becomes an exemplary didactic form, creating the need for the dignified, courteous replies in any struggle for justice worldwide. The letters themselves reveal pedagogies of indignation at work. To examine this in action I shall now turn to examples from protest movements where the absence of a reply to a letter features in the dramatic action of the struggle in ways which echo those of Mandela's trial.

Idle No More: The State and the Land

Theresa Spence is the Chief of the Attawapiskat First Nation in Canada. On 11 December 2012 Chief Theresa Spence began a hunger strike or 'sacred fast' in protest at the housing crisis of the Attawapiskat and declared that the hunger strike 'won't end until Prime Minister Stephen Harper and Gov. Gen. David Johnston agree to sit down and talk about Canada's treaty relationship with First Nations leadership'.

I choose this example to highlight the resonance and space that the matter of a right of reply exemplifies in wider protest movements. Here again we have an ongoing, centuries old struggle for justice, played out in a postcolonial context. Here again we have a prime minister refusing to acknowledge a leader of an indigenous people's group. The lack of response brings a public, embodied, protest in the form of a hunger strike and sacred fast of an indigenous woman and chief. The court becomes public opinion and the protest movement 'Idle No More' comes into being. On 28 December 2012, writing on behalf of Chief Theresa Spence and 'Idle No More' Amnesty International sent an Open Letter to Rt Hon Stephen Harper, prime minister of Canada. The important point to note is in the following quotation:

> The government must always deal "honourably" with the established and asserted rights of Indigenous peoples. And in every case, in order to uphold the "honour of the Crown", there must be good faith consultations to ensure that Indigenous peoples' concerns are "substantially addressed".
>
> International human rights standards, such as the United Nations Declaration on the Rights of Indigenous Peoples, require that decisions affecting the rights of Indigenous peoples be made only with their full and effective participation. And when the decisions concern the lands and resources of Indigenous peoples, the appropriate standard is that of free, prior and informed consent.
>
> Prime Minister, we call on you to acknowledge Canada's responsibility to fully respect and uphold the rights of Indigenous peoples and to ensure their full and effective participation in any and all decisions that could affect these rights. We urge you to meet with Chief Spence as an immediate demonstration of your commitment to building a collaborative partnership with Indigenous peoples.

The matter presented in the letter is based on the request to deal 'honourably' and to 'fully respect and uphold the rights'. Courtesy is again at stake, in a field charged with desire for justice, and the mode of address is, as with Mandela, courteous and evidenced. The call for a meeting again plays out on the terrain identified by Williams as crucial for social relations and the maintenance of a common conversation. Stephen Harper, in the eyes of Idle No More, Amnestie Internationale/Amnesty International and Chief Theresa Spence, is dishonourable in not favouring her request with a meeting.

In her work on advocacy and the letters written by Amnesty International supporters on behalf of victims of torture, Elaine Scarry (1985) identifies resistance to 'tonal instability' as a key element in the organisation's ability to bring about its aims, namely the cessation of torture:

> The language of the letter must also resist and overcome the inherent pressures toward tonal instability: that language must at once be characterized by the greatest possible tact (for the most intimate realm of another human being's body is the implicitly or explicitly subject) and by the greatest possible immediacy (for the most crucial fact about pain is *its presentness* and the most crucial fact about torture is that it *is happening*). Tact and immediacy ordinarily work against one another; thus the difficulty of sustaining either tone is compounded by the necessity of sustaining both simultaneously.

Diane Orentlicher (1990), claims that 'tone is substance'. Both Scarry and Orentlicher point to an important aspect of the tone of such letters. It will not do for the tone to miss the mark. There is a careful level of tonal control to be enacted in the letters, a level of courtesy in address, of reason in the argument, or care in the choice of words that must be present for the letter to be one that can make claims. In the cases of Chief Teresa Spence's sacred fast, and Nelson Mandela's trial and his expectation of a death sentence and his subsequent imprisonment, these aspects of 'torture' are concerns for the intimate bodies of both leaders, but equally and urgently for the body politic of the peoples both leaders' bodies represent. Tact and immediacy as the tonal features of the letters point directly to the substantive matters and when combined, urge the reply, the meeting. Without this tonal stability the substance would be lost. The writing of such letters as may be effective in this way is an art, learned through years of practice in the pedagogies of indignation. In the case of Amnesty International's intervention with the Harper government in Canada it is the 'honour of the Crown' that is at stake in the dishonour done to Chief Theresa Spence and her people. This stands in parallel to the claims of 'civilised/ uncivilised' made by Mandela in his trial relating to the Apartheid government and further traces the line of courtesy in letters of protest. Furthermore, Eros is present and released in this example, through thwarted attempts at a meeting and the dishonouring of the chief. Again, in the presence of Eros and her subjective energies tact and tonal stability are paradoxical qualities, which, when harnessed artfully, enable a widening of the case from the specifics of a letter unanswered, to the history of injustice and indignation. More than this, however, I would venture to argue that the tonal expressions of the plaintive substantively reproduce for a wider audience, that which is absent – civilised behaviour, honour, a sense of proportion. In other words, we glimpse the actualisation of what it is that Eros, in each instance, desires, and what is suddenly tantalisingly close, and substantive.

This element of 'tone as substance' may be further exemplified in the context of Israel and Palestine at the level of personal correspondence in international relations.

Israel and Palestine: The Continuation of Apartheid

I do not need to rehearse here the many arguments of activism groups and scholars who have pointed to the similarity between Apartheid in South Africa and the oppression of the Palestinian people by the State of Israel today. Knowledge is no more lacking of what is occurring here than in the context of Apartheid South Africa. The debates relating to action – whether or not non-violence reaches a limit as a principle; of the necessity or otherwise of sanctions and boycotts – have produced pages of debate. It is here too that principles present in the trial and practised as embodied actions have been writ large across campaigns, protest and initiatives, from the personal to the legal contexts, and with many hundreds of public letters being written.

I am presently involved in a project to introduce the concepts of Lifelong Learning to Palestine, concepts that enable a meeting of the principles embodied in Freirean pedagogy with the strong spirit of resistance learned over 64 years by the Palestinian people throughout their Nakba, their experience of disaster.

In early November 2012 I finalised my interim report with my colleagues in Gaza on the extraordinary practices of learning and leadership, dignity and hope we had found during our fieldwork in Gaza. The coda to the report took simple, tonally stable words, gifted to us in our fieldwork by those we worked alongside, which described the qualities that enabled the resistance to continue. These qualities are also present, in one form or another, in the deportment of Mr Mandela, during his trial: Leadership qualities in Gaza as a Learning Society: Dignity; pride; tenacity; hope; generosity of spirit; faith; confidence; determination to build peace through justice; competence; excitement; delight; joy; smart tactics; professionalism. Strength comes from: Allah/God; the Justice of our cause; suffering; feeling of kinship; giving light; patience.

A day after submitting this report the following report reached me by email from my colleagues and friends:

> *We just have witnessed an all out war in Gaza. Israel is hitting everywhere. The sky is full of drones.*
>
> *This evening I was in Gaza City and my 6 years old wanted to buy toys. Then, after listening to the news and watching what's going on outside the car told me "let's go home to safety, there will be toys tomorrow".*
>
> *Hopefully, Gaza will survive the next 12 hours with minimum damage.*
>
> *A.*

> Dear A,
>
> Just sending you prayers for peace and that you and your lovely family will be protected and held under the mercy and grace that is peace. That the bombing will cease and war will be no more. We are feeling for you so very much and I will be holding a vigil for you all at home tonight.
>
> Peace to you – Salem.
>
> May we soon meet again and in good times – Insh'allah.
>
> Alison

Dear Alison,

Thank you very much for your prompt, warm and friendly email. It is very kind of you to send me such considerate and thoughtful message in these difficult days and nights in the terrorized and bleeding Gaza.

Thanks to God, we are all safe. For the time being all schools and universities in the Gaza Strip are closed and life is almost paralysed.

We all do hope that this intensive wave of aggression ceases and peaceful life prevails to all humans.

Once again, your kindness and thoughtfulness are highly appreciated, wishing you and your family the best health, wealth and peace of mind.

And so the dance of dignified, courteous, tonally stable exchanges, in the personal, the familial and the international sphere continues. The report and its findings bombed to pieces, the projects shattered, but the words of courtesy continuing, and the deeper truth of our findings, intact. I say this cautiously, for such grand narratives have been discredited through poststructuralism and rightful scepticisms over the last decades of careful thought. And yet, yet, as the political writes itself into the personal and as the personally political loving example of a 'black man in the white man's court' demonstrates, when love and justice meet, 'volts move'. In these exchanges, each one compelling a reply in the full knowledge that it may be the last to be written, such is the intensity of the shelling, we cling to courtesy. There is no swearing, no break in tonal stability, no angry incredulity, though we feel this. Instead, and following this thread from Mandela's trial, the ability of my correspondents in Gaza to be civilised, courteous, proportionate in tone as all is destroyed around them, exposes the actions of the State of Israel as entirely 'disproportionate'. The Apartheid South African government, the Canadian government under Stephen Harper, the State of Israel, are shown, respectively, to be 'uncivilised', 'dishonourable', 'disproportionate' through the tone of the letters of those advocating a different path, by using the language with which they would wish to be addressed themselves.

My final example is personal.

UKBA: The Personal

In November 2012 the Chief Inspector of Immigration, John Vine, published a report detailing a backlog of unanswered letters and lost papers in asylum and immigration claims totalling over 100,000 and some going back over 10 years. For those of us whose daily struggle for justice focuses on the rights of asylum seekers and refugees and the pernicious toxicity of the present UK public discourse on immigration and race relations, this came as absolutely no surprise. Rather it was a moment in which what we have experienced was recognised officially, at last. In 2009 my foster daughter, an unaccompanied minor seeking asylum from Eritrea, was put on notice of her imminent deportation. We had found her in Glasgow destitute and given her a home after she had fallen through all the supposed safety nets, following a highly traumatic journey to reach the UK. In the UK she encountered a culture of disbelief in the agents tasked with assessing her claim for asylum, and a system of justice that simply failed.

Over the course of the next two years, through her detention, release, police signings, the raids on our home and threats, we ran a large campaign aimed at both securing our daughter's future safety but at the same time campaigning against the structural injustices which we knew pertained to many. We know that well over 1,000 letters were sent and over 2,000 postcards, few of which were ever answered by UKBA. We learned what it meant for your letter 'not to be dignified with a reply'. For white middle-class professionals this was a good lesson in solidarity and the development of an allied sharing with those for whom this is the regular experience of discrimination. Despite having advocated and campaigned and protested for as long as I can remember, it was only when campaigning for asylum seekers and refugees, and becoming mother to an asylum-seeking daughter, that I came to know in the ways you know when, quite literally, 'you have skin in the game'. It was estimated that, at the time, around 400 children a year were being wrongly age-assessed to assist their deportation from the UK to third countries and thus 'ease the burden on the welfare state'. Dublin II is the convention governing the movement of asylum seekers around the European Union.

After three years of struggle and protest our daughter was granted refugee status, four years after the letters were sent which were never dignified with a reply. Some politicians did reply. Writing as 'Professor Alison Phipps' may have helped. Sadly, I suspect so. It certainly aided my passage into media coverage and BBC documentaries. None of the latter helped or received any response from those with power, however, and became part of the wallpaper of awareness-raising, which is the fallback of effective campaigning. In a previous paper I have discussed the difficulty of advocating and the writing of the letters that begged for her life (Phipps, 2012). Through my own lessons in the pedagogies of indignation I too found the need for more than a balancing act between tone (that of indignation and incredulity and anger) and substance (that of clear, deliberate, wilful misrecognition by the UKBA). Tone in our campaigning became the substance of the campaigning, woven through the with authority which comes from the personal experience of suffering. In this, I realise, there is common experience with Mandela, with the Gazan people, with 'Idle No More' in that the suffering I was experiencing was not at one step removed. My own subjective experience provided the knowledge necessary to reveal 'truth'. Subjectivity is a further element in the performative power of the knowledge of discourtesy, dishonour, disproportionality, which the cases under discussion here demonstrate:

What would I advise women to do? ... Never abandon subjective experience as an element of knowledge. The most transcendental theory is also rooted in subjective experience. The truth is always produced by someone. That does not mean that it contains no objectivity. (Irigaray 2007: 47)

Desperation does not create good conditions for tact and immediacy or for tonal stability. Desperation is also associated with Eros – the desire for the object which is just out of reach, the desire to hold in safety that which is beloved and in peril – a people, land, a daughter. It took me time to settle and to learn, be steady, prepared, to harness the motive energies of Eros, which threaten always to be all-consuming, into tact, immediacy, stability. Once prepared, I too, as others have done before, wrote a letter. Mine was to UK Border Police.

An Open Letter to UK Border Police

Dear Sirs,

I'm not sure when you will come. Others I know who you have come for say I should expect you between 4 and 5 O' Clock in the morning. That's very early. You will be weary, I expect. It may have been a long night and you probably don't relish the visit you have been ordered to make to our house.

We may be asleep when you come. You will wake us. First with the door bell. Then with the banging. Just give me a moment to find my dressing gowns and slippers and run down the stairs to let you in. We know you are coming. We expect you now. Every time the door bell rings we think it might be you.

It is possible there will be other guests in the house. We often have folk staying with us, They come with like the ebb and flow of the tide. Always welcome.

You too will be welcome, though it will be harder for us, it is what we do and what our home is for. I've been baking, so there will be fresh bread and homemade jam or marmalade. Its hungry work, this work you do, taking children away from their parents, putting them in prisons. 'Removal' is what you call it. It's the law. 'A future fair for all'. 'Every Child Matters'.

I'll make sure there is milk in the fridge. You will probably need a cup of tea or coffee.

Our child, the precious one given into our care for a while, has already been separated from her parents once. The police have already taken away her father, she has already seen inside Dungavel and Yarl's Wood. Apparently last time you told her that she doesn't need to worry about Dungavel; that it is just like a big cinema or a big disco. That wasn't how she described it when she was released to us, so she will take some persuading this time, I expect. And she may not understand, you say strange things about laws and rights and you do it in an English, and even I will struggle to recognize it as a mother tongue.

I'd like to ask you not to be rough. I've seen the bruises on others. You may say it is necessary to use force. I was on the Ethiopian Airlines plane that recently landed at Heathrow airport and I saw how you took the young girl off the plane there. Please, I know you are 'only doing your job' but please, don't do that to our lovely daughter.

Yours in expectation,

Alison[2]

Where did I learn this? How did these words replace the first ones I wrote in anger, the ones which closed all space for dialogue and common language, where my enemy was closer to me than breath itself, and as indifferent. The answer, from Mandela; and from the history of careful arguments for justice and for non-violence which pertains 'as far as [it] is able' (Romans 12). In a forthcoming book on Mandela this tonal stability and tight emotional grounding is described as follows:

> It was his quick-thinking, calm authority, almost serenity in the face of danger, that impressed me most on that occasion. His speeches were rarely emotional and were never scintillating. In a deep, resonant voice, speaking slowly and deliberately, choosing his words carefully, in a stiff style, he would appeal to reason from a deep sense of conviction of the justice of his cause. (Hepple 2013)

This, like the letters of Amnesty International and the many creative examples of struggles for justice, rests, theoretically, practically and, for me, theologically, in the work of the late Walter Wink (Wink, 1984, 1986, 1992) . Wink wrote persuasively and analytically following the Civil Rights Movement and his own role in the Apartheid struggles, of the need for tactics in struggles for justice which are a kind of spiritual activism (McIntosh, 2008). In 'On not becoming what we hate' Wink too inhabits the terrain of Eros, demonstrating through multiple examples from the peace, justice and protest movements around the world, how easily when what is desired is attained the result is that the liberated becomes the oppressor, and how easily within those very struggles the protestor becomes precisely what the protestor hates, and no justice is done. Judith Butler speaks of this strange moment when that which is distant becomes proximate, when we are consumed by the need to act on behalf of others. She does not speak of the way

---

2   Phipps 2012.

Eros is at work here, between the energies of love and hate, presence and absence, as Carson does, but rather of the way 'ethical obligations emerge not only in the contexts of established communities that gathered within borders, speak the same language, and constitute a notation' (Butler, 2011: 4). The Incitement Trial and the Rivonia Trial instantiate and exemplify the performative power and claim justice and ethical obligations may have. The unsettling effects of courtesy in the face of discourtesy, in the trial and in the more recent examples of protest here, show that in each context a new tonal stability has to be found, a different path needs to be taken for what has been dishonoured to be revealed in actions that are themselves in resistance, honourable.

Conclusion

Fifty years on, Mandela's conduct in the Rivonia Trial continues to inspire and provide workable templates for the struggles against oppression and for justice. Yet it is too simplistic to regard the transcripts of the trials as mere scripts or templates. If a template were designed which suggested 'Insert courteous phrase of address here' such as we find in the templates for writing, say, a business letter, then the personal integrity necessary to the performative element in each distinctive situation of struggle, would be lost and revealed to be a sham. Rather it is necessary to understand and respect the performative force, without ever forgetting the 27 years of imprisonment, confinement and hard labour, or the very many lives lost and lost continually, in the human quests for liberation from oppression throughout the world. During these 27 years, as documented in *Conversations with Myself*, Mandela turns several times to letters, and his letters are published through the project of the Mandela Archives. These letters trace the demands for a reply to previous letters, or document letters which have 'disappeared in transit' (Mandela, 2010: 199). The failure for his letters to be dignified with a reply runs like an open wound through the text of *Conversations with Myself* as it does in the Incitement Trial. It again shows up as an erotic force, a longing to be treated as a human being worthy of courtesy and a civilised tone. Always out of reach in the absence of responses to letters which must receive a reply Eros keeps her charge and energy and year after year demands a reply to the love which longs for such a freedom. In his opening plenary to the conference *The Rivonia Trial: 50 Years on* George Bizos said of Mandela that the one thing he would not tolerate was discourtesy.

In Apartheid South Africa, through the Incitement Trial and in the examples I have given from other sites of struggle, dignity is deliberately and actively withheld, and courtesy fails to be accorded to another human being or to a people. Exposing this reveals a peculiar face to injustice and barbarity. Eros is thwarted with violence and the discourtesy appears to be a fundamental element in rendering barbarity possible, in dehumanising another human being. But despite this Mandela demonstrates that Freire's lessons of love can indeed be learned, that it is possible to leave a long, crushing imprisonment with forgiveness and seeking reconciliation. 'If I do not love the world – if I do not love life – if I do not love people – I cannot enter into dialogue.' The trial, as a political event, becomes a liminal force, capable of marshalling through the performative power of language at the height of its powers, the possibilities of newness, hope and the space for justice to do her own work, not that of those who think she is theirs to command. Mandela, the defendant not the judge, is able to create the conditions in which he passes judgement on the spirit of another human being: 'Well, Mr. Moolla' says Mandela, carefully addressing his witness with the courtesy of his title, 'I want to leave it at that, but just to say that you have lost your soul'. In saying this, and with such economy, Mandela as defendant, continues, it would seem, to be in possession of his own. In Old Testament theology Walter Brueggemann points to the structuring of moments of profound transformation as requiring the public expression of pain, the ridicule of established power and the song and dance of women (Brueggemann, 2000). All are present and with integrity in these trials and the dramatic events surrounding them:

> At the close of the trial the crowd ignored a special prohibition on all demonstrations relating to trials and marched through the streets singing a freedom song, "Tshotsholoza Tshotsholoza Mandela", a call to Mandela to continue the struggle. (Nelson Mandela Centre of Memory: Incitement Trial Transcript).

The liminal power of Eros in the demand and regret for the reply that never comes, places a creative, performative force into the body politic which is like yeast, live, active, biding its time until the conditions for its large life are possible, then rising. And this yeast, I hope I have shown through these examples, is alive in the large-scale political protests across the world of today, in what is most intimate and personal, and in what is political; in the demand for a dignified response.

This chapter has taken as its focus the absence of a reply to a particular letter, in order to demonstrate the way Mandela uses the symbolism of such an absence to reveal the barbarity of the Apartheid government. In the tonal stability and subjective integrity of Mandela's own defence the element of Eros appears and, resonating in the body of the plaintive, is shared collectively and made present for all to see. In insisting on courtesy, on civilised values, by harnessing indignity into stable, tonal expression Mandela holds paradoxical elements together through which the hope for a future that is equally courteous, civilised, and humane is made present and real. That absent letters and the absence of replies to letters are a common and popular trope in fiction as well as in scholarship points to the symbolic role played by the absence of reply to a letter. The desire for a reply brings Eros into play in different situations of struggle and creates a space in which Eros may speak of that which was desired, that which was scorned, that which is thwarted. To do so in such a way as to betray the usual tonal instability associated with Eros in full cry, equally paradoxically produces that which is desired yet thwarted. In the case of Idle No More the dishonour is named through the commonly agreed language of international treaty; in the case of Gaza the disproportionate violence is present in the greetings and salutations of peace; in the case of UKBA in the steadying of anger into sad yet hopeful prose.

As an educator active in the field of languages and intercultural education it is perhaps the lessons of the Mandela's being, tone as substance, and erotic stance in the face of the indignity that provides a generative theme for future struggles. There is something important to be learned from this stance for the communication of justice and, indeed, love, in contexts of oppression. bell hooks, in her book *Teaching to Transgress*, states that 'When Eros is present in the classroom, love is bound to flourish'. In the light of Mandela's example might we also state: 'When Eros is present in the courtroom, love is bound to flourish.' Indeed, in several socially ritualised contexts of communication it becomes clear that love may indeed flourish despite oppression when complex and paradoxical elements are brought together with such tonal subjectivity and substance as to reveal the oppression and perform its opposite. To get to such a place of flourishing, into and through a movement of solidarity and protest which can be respected and sustained, requires attention to such detail as is necessitated by courteous replies to letters, to the tonal substance of demands. For in social movements which embody the kinds of worlds that are desired, there is already present something of the kind of erotic energy which delights in glimpses of the kinds of social realities for which change is sought. At such times there is also present an evidence of the flourishing of a different kind of social relation, evidence of a strange joy despite all the oppression and the sentencing, released across a people and across continents; a joy which Andrade calls 'counter-proof'.

References

Brueggemann, W. (2000). *Texts that Linger, Words that Explode: Listening to Prophetic Voices*. Minneapolis: Fortress Press.

Butler, J. (2011). 'Precarious Life and the Obligations of the State', Nobel Lecture. http://www.nobelmuseum.se/sites/nobelmuseet.se/files/page_file/Judith_But ler_NWW2011.pdf.

Carson, A. (1998). *Eros the Bittersweet*. London: Dalkey Archive.

Derrida, J. (1987). *The Post Card: From Socrates to Freud and Beyond*. Chicago: University of Chicago Press.

Derrida, J. (2008). 'The Laws of Reflection: Nelson Mandela in Admiration'. In *Psyche: Inventions of the Other*, Volume II. Stanford: Stanford University Press.

Freire, P. (2005). *Pedagogy of Indignation*. Herndon, Virginia: Paradigm.

Hepple, B. (2013) *Young Man with a Red Tie: A Memoir of Mandela and the Failed Revolution 1960–1963*. Jacana Media.

Lacan, J. (1988). *The Purloined Poe*. Baltimore: The Johns Hopkins University Press.

Mandela, N. (2010). *Conversations with Myself*. London: Macmillan.

McIntosh, A. (2008). *Rekindling Community: Connecting People, Environment and Spirituality*. Bristol: Green Books.

Orentlicher, D. (1990). 'Bearing Witness: The Art and Science of Human Rights Reporting/Fact Finding', in *Harvard Human Rights Journal*, Vol. 3, 83–135.

Phipps, A. (2012). 'Voicing Solidarity: Linguistic Hospitality and Poststructuralism in the Real World'. *Applied Linguistics*, 33, 582–602.

Scarry, E. (1985). *The Body in Pain: The Making and Unmaking of the World*. Oxford: Oxford University Press.

Scott, J.C. (1990). *Domination and the Arts of Resistance: Hidden Transcripts*. New Haven: Yale University Press.

Williams, R. (2000). *Lost Icons: Reflections on Cultural Bereavement*. London and New York: T&T Clark.

Wink, W. (1984). *Naming the Powers: The Language of Power in the New Testament*. Minneapolis: Fortress Press.

Wink, W. (1986). *Unmasking the Powers: The Invisible Forces that Determine Human Existence*. Philadelphia: Fortress Press.

Wink, W. (1992). *Engaging the Powers: Discernment and Resistance in a World of Domination*. Minneapolis: Fortress Press.

Zizek, S. (2013). *Enjoy your Symptom! Jacques Lacan in Hollywood*. London and New York: Taylor & Francis.

Archival Sources

Nelson Mandela Centre of Memory: Incitement Trial Transcript. http://www.nelson mandela.org/omalley/index.php/site/q/03lv01538/04lv01600/05lv01624/06lv 01625.htm

Chapter 12

Lawscapes: The Rivonia Trial and Pretoria

Isolde de Villiers

Introduction

The Rivonia trial represents a watershed moment in South Africa's struggle for freedom and democracy. Named after a Johannesburg suburb that once served as 'the nerve centre of the liberation movement' where leading members of Umkhonto we Sizwe were arrested, Rivonia entered the South African popular consciousness as a significant moment that laid the foundation for a 'free and democratic society'. In the words of Lord Joel Joffe, it is 'the trial that changed South Africa'.

Even though the accused were arrested on Liliesleaf farm in Johannesburg, currently an award-winning state-of-the-art heritage site dedicated to the commemoration of South Africa's long march to freedom,[1] the trial did not take place in Johannesburg. Both the Treason trial and the Rivonia trial took place in Pretoria,[2] as did several other important Apartheid era political trials. As Apartheid's capital city, the city of both executions and civil servants, Pretoria represents a palimpsest that carries the traces of its complex relationship with the political trials of that period. Drawing on Philippopoulos-Mihalopoulos's recent formulation of the notion of 'lawscape', I want to investigate the uncanny relationship between the Rivonia trial and the lawscape of Pretoria.[3] According to Philippopoulos-Mihalopoulos, the city is law's greatest testing ground, 'its loudspeaker and its gaming table' – the biopolitical relationship between law and the city illustrates a uniquely spatial dimension of juridical power.[4] Following this spatial reading of law and the legal domain, this chapter explores the simultaneously repressive and productive relationship between the Rivonia trial and the lawscape of Pretoria.[5]

---

1 http://www.liliesleaf.co.za/.

2 Subsequent use of the term 'Treason trial' refers to this trial from 1956 to 1961. The trial is formally reported as *Regina* v. *Farid Adams and Others*. Because of the length of the trial and a re-indictment in 1959, many of the initially accused were acquitted during the course of the trial.

3 See the section on the lawscape and the legal imagination, below.

4 A. Philippopoulos-Mihalopoulos (ed.) *Law and the City* (2007, Routledge Cavendish: Oxon and New York) at 9.

5 Ibid.

My central argument is that the lawscape of Pretoria shaped the outcome of the Rivonia trial and that the Rivonia trial, along with other political trials, influenced the lawscape of the administrative capital. The notion of the city as palimpsest presents one way of capturing the tautology of the term lawscape. Through the palimpsestic layers of the past and the uncanny I will explore how the city of Pretoria was (as it still is) haunted by other political trials which contributed to a certain legal culture and influenced the Rivonia trial in a certain way, while the Rivonia trial also haunts the subsequent cases decided in the city and therefore forms part of Pretoria's lawscape.

The lawscape presents many different points of view from which to consider the law and the city, both separately and collectively. I will focus on two aspects of the lawscape: its interaction with aesthetics and its insistence on the city and the law as palimpsests. Though the overarching theme here is the spatial dimension of the political trial and its relationship with the city, the chapter also considers the geometric space of the courtroom and the architectural designs and external settings of Pretoria's lawscape: the Old Synagogue, the Palace of Justice, the Church Square and other scenes of significance. Central to these considerations is the question of the political trial as place, as opposed to space, of resistance. I expand on this distinction and its importance below.

In using the lawscape as an explanatory framework for understanding the relationship between Pretoria as city, as Pitoli,[6] and as Tshwane,[7] and the Rivonia trial, the chapter moves beyond the physical space of the courtroom to the meta-level political space produced and enabled by the strategic encounter between the city and its political trials: how did Pretoria and Rivonia reciprocally shape and inform each other? In other words, what did these trials contribute to the lawscape of Pretoria and what role did Pretoria's cityscape play in our understanding of these trials?

The chapter proceeds in the following order: the first section introduces the concept of the lawscape as framework for looking at law and city. The second section considers the space of Pretoria and of the political trial. The third section situates the lawscape in relation to utopia, aesthetics and the legal imagination

---

6   Siyaya I Pitoli is an important struggle slogan meaning 'We are marching to Pretoria' and signifying all the petitioning marches to the Union Buildings in Pretoria. See *State of the Capital City Address* by the executive mayor of Tshwane, councillor Kgosientso Ramokgopa, on 3 April 2014 at 1:1. 'At the height of our peoples' final march to freedom, they sang a song that rallied all behind a call to go to Pretoria – they sang "Siyaya ePitoli" – "We are going to Pretoria". Theirs was not only an announcement of an eminent arrival in Pretoria – it was also a declaration of their path to power and their state of readiness to govern, and it had to start in Pretoria – the capital of Apartheid South Africa.'

7   The name of the city is the subject of ongoing debates. As things currently stand, the broader metropolitan area is called 'Tshwane', while the central business district is (still) referred to as 'Pretoria'. Throughout this chapter I use the name Pretoria because most of the references relate to the city before 1994 (and before the process of the name-change). Usually the term 'City of Tshwane/Pretoria' is preferred.

to explore the relationship between Rivonia and Pretoria, and the final section addresses the palimpsestic nature of law and city in considering notions of haunting and the uncanny presented by political trials in the city of Pretoria.

The Lawscape

The facetious question, therefore, whether the law dictates the city or the city dictates the law is to be answered with a stentorious circularity.[8]

The significance of the concept lawscape, as opposed to law and space, is the tautological nature thereof. In *Law and the City*, Philippopoulos-Mihalopoulos explains that the 'and' of the title *Law and the City* does not institute a continuum between the law and the city, but it rather opens the law up to the city.[9] He continues that the 'and' is an indication of how 'the two have always-already been co-extensive' while on the other hand the 'and' also bears the responsibility of inscribing difference between the law and the city.[10] This is the lawscape, he writes: 'neither a tautology, nor a simple disciplinary coincidence, lawscape is the ever-receding horizon of prior invitation by the one to be conditioned by the other'.[11]

The lawscape initiates a discussion on how the city appropriates law and the law the city. This relationship between the law and the city builds on the intellectual heritages of Law and Geography, Law and Space and Law and Architecture.[12] The edited collection of essays around the interaction between law and the city brings together various 'vantage points', most notably feminism,[13] biopolitics and aesthetics.[14]

Pretoria is the administrative capital of South Africa and because of a high concentration of government officials, state functionaries and bureaucratic bodies,

---

8   Philippopoulos-Mihalopoulos, 2007 at 9. He refers to a similar question posed by David Harvey in D. Harvey, *Spaces of Hope* (2000, Edinburgh University Press: Edinburgh). Harvey formulates the question with society instead of law, i.e., whether society dictates the city or the city society.

9   Ibid., 8.

10   Ibid., 7–8: 'In the receding circularity of the lawscape' we find both the 'performativity of the legal meaning of space' and the 'spatial meaning of the law'.

11   Ibid., 8.

12   In the context of South Africa it resonates with what Wessel Le Roux has described as the aesthetic turn in post-Apartheid jurisprudence. See W. Le Roux, 'The aesthetic turn in the post-apartheid constitutional rights discourse' 2006 *Journal for South African Law* 101–20.

13   The concept draws on feminists' explorations of the body, the female, space and the imaginary in a way that questions the 'prioritisation of the male, the mind the public domain, time and reality' in an attempt to bring forward their relation with 'the female, the body, the private, space and the imaginary'. See Philippopoulos-Mihalopoulos, 2007 at 7.

14   Philippopoulos-Mihalopoulos, 2007 at 5.

a biopolitical understanding of the lawscape suitably frames Pretoria's lawscape. For Philippopoulos-Mihalopoulos, an understanding of the law–city relationship from a biopolitical vantage point presents the opportunity of understanding it through 'a phenomenology of urban movement ... a sensualisation of the quotidianity of law ... a legal mapping of sexuality ... a criminological analysis of space, or an exploration of the "cognitive unconscious"'.[15]

Pretoria is the capital of administration and bureaucratic functioning of government as well as the capital of executions. Both of these attributes are represented in a biopolitical perspective and therefore also present in the lawscape. Foucault illustrates the ways in which architecture and law are intertwined and the ways in which the city's construction, its buildings, monuments and layout constructs both the nature and the behaviour of the subject.[16] As examples of this control over the nature and behaviour of the subject, Philippopoulos-Mihalopoulos directs our attention to law's obsession with naming, categorizing, organizing and tidying. These activities are revealed in the city's social and spatial working order. On the other hand, the city's 'multi-polarity and social differentiation' assist in highlighting law's material side: its relation to violence in the sense of its force of application.[17]

The Political Trial as Space

This volume asks the question of the courtroom as a place of resistance. However, the courtroom as space, as opposed to place, refers not only to the architectural building of the court itself, but also to the event of the trial, to the surroundings, the publications in the trial's aftermath and, cumulatively speaking, the 'world' created around and by the trial. The world that produces and is produced by the political trial is the 'lawscape'. It is an interaction between the city and the law. In the case of the Rivonia trial, it is the interaction between Pretoria, Apartheid's capital city and city of executions, and the law. The possibility of resistance in the courtroom as space lies in the way in which the trial resists the lawscape by changing it and contributing to it. The political trial finds itself within the lawscape and, yet, it has the ability to change the lawscape. Many refer to the Rivonia trial as the trial that changed the course of South Africa. Even though legal culture is often expressed in terms of continuation or inertia, the political trial can in some ways break with the lawscape in resisting the dominant legal culture or at least presenting a challenge to the lawscape by having a lasting impact on it.

From the vantage of the lawscape, the courtroom as place becomes space. The distinction between space and place may seem self-explanatory and the

---

15   Ibid., 5.

16   M. Foucault, *Discipline and Punish: The Birth of the Prison*, trans. A. Sheridan (1991, Penguin: London).

17   Philippopoulos-Mihalopoulos, 2007 at 8.

terms are sometimes used interchangeably. Sometimes both space and place are used synonymously with concepts such as location or region. A common way of capturing the difference between space and place is to characterize space as abstract and devoid of meaning. Space, therefore, within this understanding of the distinction, becomes place when meaning is invested in it.[18] Christian Norberg-Schulz, whom I later rely on in the context of spirit of place and its interaction with the uncanny, distinguishes between space, place and character and the whole of the experience of place can be analysed through the aspects of space and character.[19] In his terms space is what is described and experienced in the context of pronouns (under, above, beside) while character can be placed within that which is described with adjectives (quiet, calm, busy, etc.). Place is the coming together of space and character in nouns (river, home, forest).[20] Phil Hubbard attributes the distinction to the difference between humanistic and materialistic accounts of geography.[21] The former, based on existentialism and phenomenology, acknowledges the 'sense of place' implicit in all settings and focuses on lived-in place in an attempt to replace the people-less geographies brought about by positivist spatial sciences.[22] The latter, drawing on Marxist theories of space, was also a response to the empirico-physical conception of spatiality that viewed the world as a tabula rasa and accounted for colonial conceptions of *terra nullius*. Materialist accounts of geography focus on space and the power relationships produced by and in space.[23] Doreen Massey's idea of a 'progressive sense of place' challenges the distinction between space and place altogether. She suggests that place is the coming together of flows and therefore not bound spaces.[24] Because this contribution is not primarily focused on the intricate geographical distinctions between space and place, my aim is not to explore this rich theoretical heritage in full, but rather to ask how this (in) distinction features in the concept of the lawscape.

The city can be seen as law's measure and, vice versa, the law is the '(in)flexible (un)reliable metallic ruler that makes its presence felt through inches and centimetres of propinquity and distance' in the city.[25] The Rivonia trial, and other political trials, were held in Pretoria for the sake of control, order and security. Hilda Bernstein explains that bringing leading members of the African National Congress to court in Johannesburg would have caused 'tremendous crowds

---

18   For one example of this distinction, see T. Cresswell, *Place: A Short Introduction* (2004, Blackwell Publishing: Oxford) at 8–10.

19   C. Norberg-Schulz, *Towards a Phenomenology of Architecture* (1980, Rizzoli International Publications: New York) at 18.

20   Ibid.

21   P. Hubbard, 'Space/place', in D. Atkinson et al., *Cultural Geography: A Critical Dictionary of Key Concepts* (2005, IB Taurus: New York).

22   Hubbard 2004 at 42.

23   Ibid. One key proponent of this approach is self-proclaimed philosopher of the everyday Henri Lefebvre.

24   D. Massey, *Space, Place and Gender* (1994, Polity Press: Cambridge).

25   Philippopoulos-Mihalopoulos, 2007 at 9.

to gather at the courtroom'.[26] This was the case with the Treason trial, which commenced in Johannesburg, but was later moved to Pretoria. All the accused in the Treason trial were acquitted on 29 March 1961. The court found that the prosecution did not discharge its onus to prove satisfactorily that the policy of the African National Congress was violent. Because of this, all the accused were acquitted and it was unnecessary for the defence to answer to the prosecution's case. Since the prosecution failed in the Treason trial because of a lack of evidence of violence, the arrests at Liliesleaf and the documents on operation Mayibuye that were seized during the arrests were key, because the prosecution now had evidence of violent operations planned by Umkhonto. In a way, and this is evident from the narratives and recorded interviews at the Liliesleaf museum, the Rivonia arrests and documents seized during the arrest were exactly what the Apartheid state was waiting for. This is ironic in light of the fact that operation Mayibuye was rejected at the meeting that was underway when the accused in the Rivonia trial were interrupted and arrested by the police. In many ways the Rivonia trial was the prosecution's reaction to the failures of the treason trial. The Rivonia trial was held in Pretoria from the start, unlike the treason trial that first started in the Drill Hall in Johannesburg at the beginning of 1957. Both the Drill Hall and the synagogue in Pretoria were prepared specifically for purposes of this and other political trials. The creation of these special courts for the 1956 Treason trial could have been on account of the sheer numbers of the accused and the volumes of evidence used, but the response of the prosecutor and the judges in the synagogue to the application by the defence for the Treason trial to be held in Johannesburg is indicative of a deeper political agenda and another form of spatial engineering by the state. The attack on the venue of the Treason trial came in January 1959 after the remaining group of 91 were re-indicted in two separate groups. The defence applied for the trial to be conducted in Johannesburg instead, where all the accused (and the defence counsel) resided. Writing in the third year of the Treason trial, Freda Troup sets out the conditions of the Treason trial and also explains the arguments surrounding the moving of the venue.[27] The defence argued that the venue prejudiced the accused on the grounds that the hours spent on travelling was a hardship, they also argued that this affected the time for consultation between the accused and their counsel, and the time spent on commuting reduced the hours available for employment.[28] The prosecution supported its opposition to the application to move the trial by referring to 'disturbances which occurred in

---

26   H. Bernstein, *The World that was Ours* (2007, Persephone Books: London) at 169: 'Even with the ban on gatherings, even with police dogs and the display of military might, people will come – this is the experience of previous political trials'. See a further discussion of her novel in the section on aesthetics in the lawscape.

27   F. Troup, 'The treason trial – forever?', in *Africa South* vol. 4, no. 1, 1959, 57–63.

28   Troup, 1959 at 62.

Johannesburg in the early days of the preparatory examination' and arguing that 'large cities are "nothing short of dynamite"'.[29]

This argument indicates that the city of Johannesburg seemed larger than Pretoria in a more figurative way, which points to the lack of control, surveillance and power to regulate crowds and attendees of the trial in Johannesburg as opposed to Pretoria. It could also allude to the fact that there were more supporters (larger groups) of the African National Congress in the surroundings of Johannesburg than in the much more conservative area of Pretoria.[30] According to population statistics in 1960, Johannesburg's population was already more than a million, with Pretoria's population just below half a million. Still, it is interesting that the prosecution did not regard Pretoria as a 'large city' for purposes of this argument.

Hilda Bernstein's novel *The World that Was Ours* captures the difference between Johannesburg and Pretoria (and the resistance of the lawscape) by referring to the geography of the two cities. Pretoria, she explains, is like its climate. Whereas the trial would become intrinsically involved with Johannesburg and would not be easily separated from the city, Pretoria would just 'smother' the trial instead of reacting to it.[31] Pretoria's setting in a ring of hills protects it, closes it in and accounts for the warmer climate: 'When Johannesburg is warm, Pretoria is hot. When Johannesburg is hot, Pretoria swelters.'[32]

> From now on for nearly a year I will travel to Pretoria and back at least once a week, usually more, sometimes every day, and come to know every inch of it; outwards from Johannesburg with intense anticipation; back again with flat resignation. It will seem sometimes that a great portion of my life is consumed with the petrol along those forty miles of the road to Pretoria.[33]

Despite the defence's application to move the treason trial (back) to Johannesburg, it ran and ended in the Old Synagogue that was converted into a special criminal court in Pretoria. Apart from the Treason trial and Rivonia trial the synagogue also hosted Nelson Mandela's incitement trial in 1962 and the inquest into Steve Biko's death in 1977. The performativity associated with these courtroom

---

29   Ibid.

30   Wessel Le Roux captures the (current) difference between the two cities in the symbolism of the Union Buildings versus that of the Constitutional Court. The Union Buildings were designed by Herbert Baker and are situated on Meintjies Kop in Pretoria. These buildings are still the home of the executive branch of the government of South Africa. Le Roux writes: 'The [Constitutional Court] complex is not a grand singular object to be appreciated at a distance, as was the dream of the acropolitan Union Building complex, but an urban environment encouraging participation in a street-life.' Wessel Le Roux, 'From acropolis to metropolis: the new Constitutional Court building and South African street democracy' 2001 16 *South African Public Law* 139–168 at 161.

31   Bernstein, 2007 at 169.

32   Ibid.

33   Ibid., 122.

spaces echoes in the 'performativity of the legal meaning of space and the spatial meaning of law'.[34] Philippopoulos-Mihalopoulos calls the performativity of the lawscape 'a process of receding collaborative performativity'.[35] This means that the act of naming in the city includes acts of exclusion, categorizing, the institution of boundaries and, in the context of the political trial, the act of naming someone guilty or not guilty. All of these acts, seen as part of the lawscape, instantaneously 'name[s], perform[s] and imbue[s] the urban with a universe of legal mythology'.[36] On the other hand, where the lived spatiality of the city relies on these legal mythologies it similarly 'names, performs and imbues law with a universe of urban narrative'.[37] The political trial as space therefore constitutes and becomes the city as space and the resistance of the political trial is both curtailed and made possible by the courtroom/city. The lawscape as *ou-topos*, a place of no place, is the collective imagination of the law and the city.[38] In the next section I explore the imagination of the lawscape through different aesthetic engagements with political trials.

Utopia, Aesthetics and the Legal Imagination

The lawscape explores the law's spatiality in which the city is seen as a multiple locality where the law is incorporated in its making and existence while at the same time presenting a 'phenomenon that escapes the dimensionality of geography' and expands to a 'utopian no-place' where law and city are inextricably bound:[39]

> As the blind spot of urban reality, utopia offers an interesting vantage point, paradoxically both in (as destination) and out (as critique) of the lawscape, rendering the emplaced observer both aware of the utopian probability and unaware of the utopian impossibility.[40]

If a city can be described as a just city, it means that it is a city that no longer requires law. Similarly, if justice is the utopia of law, then it means that justice no longer needs law and the loss of law signifies law's utopia.[41] In his own contribution to *Law and the City*, Philippopoulos-Mihalopoulos uses the perspective from an

---

34   Philippopoulos-Mihalopoulos, 2007 at 10.

35   Ibid.

36   Ibid.

37   Ibid.

38   In providing an overview of the different chapter contributions, Philippopoulos-Mihalopoulos explains that 'the lawscape is observed from a position of utopia'. See Philippopoulos-Mihalopoulos, 2007 at 10–13.

39   Ibid., 1.

40   Ibid., 11.

41   Ibid., 246–7.

aeroplane and the metaphor of landing to capture the title of the chapter 'Brasília: utopia postponed'. He argues that where society suspends itself in the form of self-criticism the result is a reaction against itself. This reaction against 'its very self' can manifest as utopia.[42] Looking at the lawscape from the position of utopia reveals some of the blind spots of the city and of law and connects to the lawscape as aesthetic.

The lawscape, as aesthetic engagement, offers the possibilities brought about by the Situationist International in that this approach highlights the relation between 'the urban, the legal and the political'.[43] The city presents a visual representation of the materiality of law and illustrates, through its physical and discursive environment, the signifying power of law and its entanglement with violence and strategies of control.[44] The violence, power and control of the city is made visible in the political trial where these displays are an integral part of the proceedings. James Boyd White writes, in the preface to *The Legal Imagination*, that 'law makes a world'.[45] In its insistence on law's spatiality, the legal imagination here converges with the lawscape. Boyd White refers to different works of literature to illustrate similarities and differences between lawyers, poets and historians and argues that law's greatest power lies in the coercive aspect of its rhetoric. Language, like law, creates worlds and, with reference to Bernstein's novel, I look at this world created by the law and at the world that created the law, i.e., the lawscape.

The account of the Treason trial by Troup traces the proceedings by drawing various analogies between the evidence of the Treason trial, forms of literature, theatrical imagery.[46] The large cage, Troup writes, which enclosed the accused on the first day of the trial in the Drill Hall gave it elements of fantasy and farcical qualities.[47] The cage was removed after the vehement objections raised by the defence, but the 'theatrical vaudevillian' atmosphere remained.[48] There was a 'clubby cosiness', according to Troup, brought about by the various activities and the strange décor of the Hall: 'deck chairs, correspondence course lectures, cross-words, and knitting through the sessions; and in adjournments: darts, fraternising across the court room and colour bar, choir practice and poker.'[49] The seriousness of the offence and the fact that it carried capital punishment as a sentence cast these close-to carnival components of the trial in a dark shadow that was the injustice of the hearing. The artistic comparisons were continued by 'zealous reporters', who showed that the evidence for the trial from the 10,000 documents

---

42   Ibid., 247.
43   Ibid., 7.
44   Ibid., 8.
45   J. Boyd White, *The Legal Imagination* (1973, University of Chicago Press: Chicago) at xiii.
46   Troup, 1959 at 57–63.
47   Ibid., 59.
48   Ibid.
49   Ibid., 59–61.

submitted and the 2.5 million words delivered during evidence given filled 8,000 pages, 'or as much as would be required by 33 novels'.[50] Troup writes that the recorded evidence would have taken 35 hours to listen to – or the length of 15 full-length films.

These comparisons to literature and films are striking, but not surprising. The magnitude of the hearing captured the imaginations of those who endeavoured to describe the scale of it. It was unprecedented in size and because of this, Troup argues, writers had to revert to the realm of fiction and art to capture it.[51] From the records and responses it appears, however, that the judges, prosecutors and witnesses for the state remained unmoved by the theatrical elements and that it illustrated something of the inability of the law to imagine, and exposes the politics of law in political trials.

Bernstein highlights the link between politics and law and the relationship between the law and space as she describes their house and its features. Within the context of the raid that took place after the arrests on Liliesleaf farm, she points out how the aspects of the house that they had initially changed in order to make the house liveable were the same aspects that made them vulnerable during the raid and surveillance of the house. The change in political circumstances and the presence of the law required a change in the spatial features of the house:

> Our house in Regent street, Observatory, Johannesburg had been altered to suit our needs fourteen years before when we moved in … The front door and sidelights were glazed with ribbed glass through which forms could be seen and even identified; it opened directly into our living room without the intervention of a passage or hall – we had removed the wall between … before the Nationalists had come to power when circumstances had not yet made us aware that political conditions could dictate architectural needs. What the house really needed now was a high surrounding wall and a locked and solid gate; windows with sills above head level, none overlooking the entrance area; an entrance hall completely detached from the house; and an incinerator.[52]

Bernstein's description of their house in the quotation above effectively explains how the law seeped into and shaped private spaces during Apartheid. The flip side is also important: the manner in which space, spatial codes and spatial configurations shaped (and still shape) the law. The photographs, stage productions and books that followed in the wake of the Rivonia trial aesthetically represent the Pretoria lawscape. In 2010 a four-hour production of the Rivonia trial was staged in the state theatre, a few blocks from the Palace of Justice where the trial took place. In 2011 the play ran again, but this time it was cut to two and a half hours to, in the

---

50   Ibid., 59.
51   Ibid.
52   Bernstein, 2007 at 21–2.

words of the director, 'allow for the drama to unravel itself only through the eyes of the witnesses and that of Winnie Mandela, Albertina Sisulu and Hilda Bernstein'.[53]

The road to Pretoria was the road to political trials and executions. Most executions were carried out in Pretoria Central Prison. The city had to serve as a symbol of the exercise of state power. How much of this image has remained in the administrative capital? In 'The Pretoria Road', Bernstein captures the symbolic value of the fact that the Rivonia trial took place in Pretoria. The road between Johannesburg and Pretoria embodied for her the gradual introduction to a different spatiality. She describes this journey from the city that she considers to be home, to the city that is a threat to her home, through carefully describing the landmarks she passes on the road. Meticulously she records the suburban houses she passes from her house to Louis Botha, the main road to Pretoria at that time. She lists the small industries along the road, tells about the traffic, notes the roadhouses and garages along the way and makes reference to Alexandra Township. The township she sees is one where the population has been reduced by half on account of forced removals, 'the families destroyed, the backyards emptied, the smoke so much thinner, as though even the haze that obscures Alexandra morning and evening has also been "endorsed out"'.[54] Bernstein renders visible the force of the law and the pervasiveness of the destruction along the journey. Her account of Alexandra stands in stark contrast to the country estates of Kelvin and Buccleugh 'where tired Johannesburg businessmen build their luxury homes in acres of grounds'.[55] Later in the book Bernstein describes a different journey on the road to Palapye, a village with a landing strip, as Hilda, Rusty and their children flee out of South Africa.[56] Spaces remember and are sluggish to change and, due to spatial inertia, much of Bernstein's description can still be identified on the present Pretoria road.

The Rivonia trial commenced in the Palace of Justice and continued in the Old Synagogue. The synagogue was appropriated by the state and converted into a court for purposes of the treason trial of the 1950s. Judgment was again handed down in the Palace of Justice. The High Court in Pretoria consists of two buildings: the Palace of Justice constructed in 1893 and the 'new' High Court building across the road built in 1990. The High Court building was constructed to accommodate jurisdictional changes in the 1990s. The pilasters and windows on the outside of the building is of a neo-classical style reminiscent of the buildings in Washington, DC. The Palace of Justice, on the other hand, is of modernist typology, like many of the buildings in Pretoria.

Wessel Le Roux, who has produced a rich body of work on architecture and law in South Africa, demonstrates how the Palace of Justice captures a complicated political history and represents the attempts by both President Paul Kruger and Chief Justice John Kotzé to exploit the design and construction of the Palace of

---

53 Programme of *Rivonia Trial Back by Popular Demand*, 2011.
54 Bernstein, 2007 at 122.
55 Ibid., 123.
56 Ibid., chapter 23, 364.

Justice to further their own standing in the Republic.[57] The Palace serves as a monument to the Roman Dutch law origin of South African law and so does the 'new' building across the street, inscribing a very specific sense of place which can be detected in the order of the High Court. Le Roux draws attention to the work of Martin Chanock, who refuses to found South Africa's legal history in Rome and Renaissance Europe.[58] This possibility to resist the monumental sense of place of law's sites is captured in the architecture of the Constitutional Court, which Le Roux, following the work of Lourens Du Plessis, characterized as memorial rather than monumental.[59]

The Palace of Justice is still used as a court, but the Old Synagogue stands empty and desolate as a heritage site awaiting its fate in the project of gentrification of the administrative capital. Fran and Barbara Buntman argue that an inclusive heritage vision for the synagogue can bring together and shape 'new publics'.[60] They consider how traces of the past inform the history and memory of South Africa. For the synagogue these traces include its Jewish origins, its use as a court for political trials during Apartheid, its bureaucratic decline and finally its abandonment. These traces, according to the authors, require conscious effort to remain embedded in a site where history and memory need to be interpreted. The article sets out a thorough history of the building and dramatic architecture of the court. They argue convincingly with reference to Nelson Mandela's autobiography, various newspaper reports on the Steve Biko inquest, and Mogane Serote's novel *To Every Birth in Blood*, that the name of the Old Synagogue stuck even though it was no longer used as synagogue, but as a court.[61]

This is also evident in another aesthetic element of the Rivonia trial, in the form of Alan Paton's testimony in mitigation of sentence. Paton claimed during his testimony that he was there 'because [he] felt it was [his] duty to come' and also 'because [he was] a lover of [his] country'.[62] During Paton's cross-examination by prosecutor Percy Yutar, Yutar confronted his support of the convicted by asking:

---

57   Wessel Le Roux, 'Studying legal history through court architecture: scattered comments on the Palace of Justice, Church Square, Pretoria' 2003 54 *Codicillus* at 54–5.

58   Le Roux 2003 at 55 referring to Martin Chanock, *The Making of South African Legal Culture 1902–1936: Fear, Favour and Prejudice* (2001, Cambridge University Press: Cambridge).

59   Wessel Le Roux, 'War memorials, the architecture of the Constitutional Court and counter-monumentalism', in Van Marle and Le Roux (eds) *Law, Memory and the Legacy of Apartheid: Ten Years after AZAPO v President of South Africa* (2007, Pretoria University Law Press: Pretoria) at 65.

60   Fran Buntman and Barbara Buntman, '"Old Synagogue" and Apartheid Court: constructing a South African heritage site' 2010 *South African Historical Journal* 62:1 183–201 at 183.

61   Ibid., 191.

62   Testimony of Alan Paton, Liberal Party member and author of bestseller *Cry, the Beloved Country*, in mitigation of sentence. Available at http://law2.umkc.edu/faculty/projects/ftrials/mandela/patonltestimony.html (accessed 20 September 2013).

'Did you approve of the bombing of the Old Synagogue, just because it was used as a special criminal court?'[63] To this Paton replied that he did not approve of any bombing whatsoever. The core of his testimony in mitigation was that he associated none of the accused with violent behaviour. The death penalty was the expected penalty in the Rivonia trial and all testimony in mitigation of sentence was therefore of extreme importance. The manner in which the past is invoked when referring to the synagogue by its old name suggests the layered nature of the city: new names are given, new buildings are built, but the old remains in ways that bring to the surface the uncanny and reveal the spirit of place that lingers in the lawscape.

Ghosts in the Lawscape

The city reveals, palimpsestically (i.e., by burying the old under new layers) its fractured, conflictual and piecemeal nature. The practical question, ultimately, is how to see through these layers and acquire a sense of spatialised history of the manifestations of the law.[64]

The lawscape calls for recognition of the layered nature of law and city. These layers capture the ostensible breaks and underlying continuities and engage the ghosts in the lawscape. In a literal sense it is haunted by the memories of those sentenced to death and executed in the Pretoria prison. In the lexicon of the lawscape it is haunted by the old buried under new layers in a palimpsestic manner. The layers are not necessarily visible at first glance, but are revealed in references and representations. Many other political trials form the layers in the lawscape of Pretoria, leaving behind traces that will be re-called, re-membered and re-deployed in ways that neither the law nor city has anticipated. Reflecting on the legacies of these remainders, Helen Cixous writes:

And before June 12, 1964, there was November 7, 1962. And before November 7, 1962, there was March 21 1960, and before the day in Sharpeville and before and before there was December 1952, and before the trial for treason there was 1948, and before the infamous apartheid laws there were so many befores. And Nelson was born July 1919. And afterward there was Wednesday June 16 1976.

In her contribution to this volume, Catherine Cole argues that the Truth and Reconciliation Commission was a 'continuation of performance traditions

---

63   Even though Yutar refers to the court as the Old Synagogue here, Justice De Wet, on page 33 of the judgment, refers to the same bombing incident, but in the following terms: 'bombing by the Umkonto organization and that one in Pretoria relating to the special criminal court building also complied with the directions of the Umkonto organization'.

64   Philippopoulos-Mihalopoulos, 2007 at 10.

associated with South African law as it emerged around moments of state transition' in the broad sense of the word. Most of these dates can be mapped out on the lawscape of Pretoria. A recent example of this mapping of history can be found in the Afrikaans film *Verraaiers* (*Traitors*) released in 2013 and coinciding with the 50-year commemoration of the Rivonia trial. It tells the story of a father, his son and two sons-in-law accused of high treason during the Anglo Boer war. The film is based on the book *Boereveraaier* by Albert Blake, a lawyer in Roodepoort.[65] The opening scene presents the delivery of judgment in a 1953 treason trial in the Palace of Justice in Pretoria and the film closes with a scene in Church Square, opposite the court. In between it tells the story of the trials and executions of so-called traitors during the Anglo Boer war in temporary makeshift military courts during the first years of the 1900s. A commander convinces his sons to lay down their weapons in the face of the scorched earth strategy. Despite the fact that Blake clearly argues that retrospective arguments claiming that the conduct of the traitors was justifiable, are speculative and historically incorrect, the film succeeds in getting the viewer to sympathize and side with the traitors against the legal and court systems of the time.[66] It manages to convey the complexity of the decision to withdraw from a war that (apparently) had been lost already and the ambivalence of the term traitor.

Although the film raises interesting questions on the theme of war, for the purposes of this piece I am interested in the opening and closing scenes of the film and the way in which these scenes invoke the Pretoria lawscape. Both these scenes are filmed in Church Square. The fact that this film was released to coincide with the fiftieth year after the Rivonia trial is uncanny in itself specifically because the film explicitly avoids and accordingly denies this coincidence. It engages with themes of resistance to power, treason and sabotage, but as a period film escapes any inter-textual references to the Rivonia trial. One is tempted to follow the references in the film and see how they relate to the lawscape of Pretoria and more broadly South Africa. However, what is troubling about the film is the attempt to present its theme in a vacuum, as if to avoid political trials subsequent to those during the Anglo Boer war. In respect of the amnesia of the Anglo Boer war trials, Blake asserts that even though the detail of the treason killings during this time have been forgotten, the legacy of the treason is still deeply engrained

---

65   Albert Blake, *Boereverraaier: Teregstellings tydens die Anglo-Boereoorlog* (2010, Tafelberg).

66   Blake, 2010 at 11. In this respect both the book and the film can be seen as nostalgic renditions of the executions of Boer war traitors. Blake rekindles the Afrikaner sentiment that was set on fighting for Republics they believed were theirs, and the film romanticizes the circumstances under which these executions took place. Nonetheless, both sources present valuable accounts of the Pretoria lawscape and the haunting effect that these hearings and executions had on the South African legal system.

in the psyche of the Afrikaner, and definitely was during the years of Apartheid.[67] He aims to counter this ostensible blankness of the treason hearings during the Anglo Boer war and gives an account from the point of view of law by elaborating on the legal principles, based on Roman Dutch law, that were used to prosecute the traitors during the Anglo Boer war.[68] These principles were subtly woven into the South African lawscape and remains. The indictment in the Rivonia trial was mainly based on contravention of specific acts in legislation,[69] but Justice De Wet made several references to common law in the final judgment.[70] The judge also relied on the case of *Mouton and Others* v. *Beket*, 1918 A.D. 181 and specifically the common law principle on page 192 of this judgment, which concerned a Vecht-Generaal during a rebellion. He relied on this case to reach the conclusion that Nelson Mandela, since he 'was one of the leaders of the Umkonto' and because he 'had set certain machinery in motion' he was found guilty even though he was serving jail time when some of the alleged offences were committed.[71] Justice De Wet acknowledged Mandela's presence in spirit. The notion of haunting should not be seen as merely temporal, but rather the uncanny and ghostly appearances should be situated within space as well as time. Bernstein and Troup invoke the ease of exercising control in Pretoria as one of the reasons that political trials were held in Pretoria and not Johannesburg, and the sheer proximity of the gallows to the courtroom added to the Pretoria panopticon, haunting the trial as a presence and a constant unspoken threat.

---

67   Ibid., 8.

68   Ibid., chapter 16, 231–46.

69   The Act allowing 90 days' detention without trial was passed just before the commencement of the Rivonia trial. Count 1 and 2 were sabotage in contravention of Section 21(1) of Act No. 76 of 1962, count 3 was the Contravention of section 11(a), read with sections 1 and 12, of Act No. 44 of 1950, and count 4 the contravention of section 3(1) (b), read with section 2, of Act No. 8 of 1953.

70   The basis of liability of a socius criminis in our law is laid down in *Rex* v. *Peerkhan and Lalloo*, 1906 T.S. 798 at p. 802 as follows: 'The true rule seems … to be that the common law principles which regulate the criminal liability of persons other than acts of perpetrators should apply in the case of statutory as well as of common law offences.' In *Rex* v. *Longone*, 1938 A.D. 532 at page 537: 'The requirement of knowledge is important because it supplies the *mens rea* – the guilty mind – required for criminal responsibility … when [the accused] is charged as a *socius* in a crime the extent of his criminal responsibility must be judged by his own *mens rea*. This is clear from the case of *Rex* v. *Parry* 1924 A.D. 402 [at] page 406; "The true position is that though such a socius is equally guilty his guilt results from his own act and his own state of mind. It is the existence of criminal intent in each of those who jointly committed a crime which entails on each a criminal responsibility".' *The State* v. *Nelson Mandela* Judgement at 67. Available from the electronic Rivonia Trial Collection, number AD1844, item number A31.2.

71   Judgement at 37–8.

The edited collection *Popular Ghosts* aims to re-establish the balance between space and time in everyday hauntology.[72] The editors remind us of the specificity of ghosts, meaning that they appear in a particular place at a particular time. Arno Meteling's chapter, '*Genius loci*: memory, media, and the neo-gothic in Georg Klein and Elfreide Jelenik' explores the value of the concept of *genius loci*, or spirit of place, for conceptualizing ideas on haunting that places haunting in space and time. Meteling connects *genius loci*, theatre and the uncanny through the medieval technique of 'mnemonics'. The most important feature or image of mnemonics is the 'method of loci' also called 'memory palace' or 'theatre of memory'. These theatres, Meteling explains, organize and help to remember things by putting the images of memories in certain imaginary storage rooms, thus giving mental spaces discrete addresses (*loci*).[73] In order to retrieve the facts, the memory artist only has to walk through the imaginary palace or theatre and look where the different objects, persons or events are deposited. Ideally, everything remembered is unified in a single, complex memory building. Semiotically these mental memory spaces can be read as haunted spaces, inhabited by the ghosts or imaginary representations of the referential objects, persons or events.[74] *Genius loci* is an ancient Roman belief that entailed that every independent being had its guardian spirit, or *genius*. It is a life-giving spirit that determines the essence or identity of things. Even the gods were believed to possess a *genius*. It determined both the being and the becoming of things.[75] During these times, survival depended on a good physical and psychic relationship to the place. The notion *genius loci* is also known as 'spirit of place'.

In his work, Norberg-Schulz argues against a mere scientific or purely functional approach to art and architecture and insists on an existentialist approach. Modernity has created the illusion of freedom from place and brought about the belief that science and technology have made us independent from places. The complex qualitative totalities of place cannot, according to Norberg-Schulz, be described in terms of analytical or scientific concepts. Rather, he argues, this identity of place can only be captured through the method of phenomenology.[76] The 'return to things' conceived by phenomenology enables a return to the everyday life-world as opposed to abstract analytical scientific constructions.[77] Anthony Vidler gives

---

72   See in general the introduction to Maria Del Pilar Blanco and Esther Peeren, *Popular Ghosts: The Haunted Spaces of Everyday Culture* (2010, Continuum: New York), specifically at xi where the editors argue that Derrida's *Spectres of Marx* acknowledges only the temporal aspect of ghosts.

73   Arno Meteling, '*"Genius loci"*: Memory, media, and the neo-gothic in Georg Klein and Elfreide Jelenik', in Del Pilar Blanco and Peeren, 2010 and at 188.

74   Meteling, 2010 at 188.

75   Norberg-Schulz, 1980 at 11.

76   Ibid., 8.

77   The concept 'everyday life-world' was introduced by Husserl in *The Crisis of European Sciences and Transcendental Phenomenology* (1936).

an account of the notion of haunted spaces in his book *The Architectural Uncanny* and links the possibility of the uncanny to theatre.[78] Apart from the theatrical role of architecture, the uncanny is also present in a more analogical way that demonstrates a 'disquieting slippage between what seems homely and what is definitively unhomely'.[79] He explains how the uncanny found its first home in the short stories of Hoffman and Poe and that Walter Benjamin later noted that the uncanny was also born out of the rise of great cities. Part of the *genius loci* or spirit of place is the fact that it was used as a military hospital for British troops during the Anglo Boer war at the beginning of the twentieth century. The façade of the palace is well-known for photographs of high-profile political trials, such as the Rivonia trial. One of the first architects in South Africa, Dutch-born Sytzke Wierda, designed the Palace of Justice and characterized the style as modern monumental, the style of the Italian Renaissance.[80]

The opening scene of the film *Verraaiers* shows a clerk of the court stomping through the columns of the Palace of Justice. The date is apparently 1953. The court orderly knocks on the door of a judge, who is busy preparing for the delivery of judgment in a high treason case. The judgment he reads out loud is actually an excerpt from the case of *R* v. *Leibbrandt & Others* 1944 A.D. 253 where the court had to establish what constituted treason. Leibbrandt was a boer rebel who endeavoured to assist the German war effort during the Second World War and was accused of committing acts of sabotage during wartime that were intended to weaken the resistance of the state. In the *Leibbrandt* case the Appellate Division quoted with approval the words of Judge Schreiner of the court a quo who remarked as follows:

> The typical act of treason, historically, may be the adherence to or the furnishing of aid to a foreign foe, so that in war time it may be stated more directly that any act which is designed to assist the enemy either positively, by giving him help of any kind, or negatively, by obstructing or weakening the forces arrayed against him, is an act of high treason.

The judge in the film, after quoting the above section, continues in Afrikaans:

> The honourable motives that persuade an accused to commit a negative act of treason are irrelevant to the determination of guilt, but takes prominence when

---

78   Anthony Vidler, *The Architectural Uncanny: Essays in the Modern Unhomely* (1992, MIT Press: Cambridge, MA).

79   Ibid., 6.

80   Available at http://www.artefacts.co.za/main/Buildings/archframes.php?archid= 1892 (accessed 16 November 2012).

an appropriate sentence is to be imposed. This makes it difficult to establish an appropriate sentence. Because war is insanity and treason is a broken word.[81]

It is uncertain what the date of 1953 refers to in the film: whether it refers to the treason trials during the 1950s in general or whether it, by deliberately not stating which specific trial it has in mind, recalls all the treason trials during Apartheid in order to bring it in relation with the Anglo Boer war treason trials. The same quote from the *Leibbrandt* case features prominently in the Delmas treason trial that took place from 1985 to 1989.[82] The film therefore enters into an inter-textual conversation with this later trial, which took place during the height of the state of emergency. The trial was an attempt to silence the United Democratic Front. The state applied security laws to prosecute more than 20 activists, including the three most senior leaders of the United Democratic Front, namely Popo Molefe, Frank Chikane and Mosiuoa Lekota. The trial, like the Rivonia trial, took place in the Palace of Justice in Church Square. What marked this trial in history is the tragic and disturbing killing spree of Barend Strydom – a former policeman – on the day that judgment was handed down in the Delmas Treason trial. Later known in the media as 'die wit wolf', Strydom testified how he was waiting outside of the Palace of Justice where he expected various church leaders, ambassadors, members of the press and the legal representatives and family members to gather for the verdict. Strydom testified that he was looking for 'someone black to kill'.[83] During his cold-blooded overtly racist quest, he killed 8 people and injured another 16. Some writers claim that there are parallels between Leibbrandt's trial and Strydom's trial. Strydom acknowledged Leibbrandt as one of his heroes.[84]

The film, through the imagery of the Palace of Justice and the quote from the Leibbrandt case, connects the political trials in the Pretoria lawscape: early Anglo Boer war trials, treason trials under the Union, trials in the new republic and political trials during the last period of the Apartheid regime.[85] The film ends with a scene at the base of the statue of Paul Kruger (which is still in Church Square). In the sanitized representation Pretoria resembles the familiar, but the clean and empty Church Square is so detached from its real image that it becomes an uncanny space that invokes the political images of the Rivonia trial despite the sentimental book-ending. Bernstein assigns the *genius loci* of Pretoria in those days to the administrative function of the city, the seat of civil service as a 'preserve of

---

81   Own translation. The last sentence 'Because war is insanity and treason is a broken word' forms the leitmotif of the film and displays some of the sentimentality alluded to earlier.

82   A transcript of this trial can be found at http://www.historicalpapers.wits.ac.za/inventories/inv_pdfo/AK2117/AK2117-L05-01-jpeg.pdf (accessed 14 June 2013).

83   His trial commenced on 15 May 1989.

84   Rob Marsh, *Famous South African Crimes* (1991, AA Struik: Cape Town) at 106–9.

85   Of which the Delmas trial was one. The bail application of the Delmas trial was reported as *S* v. *Baleka and Others* 1986 (1) SA 361 (T).

Afrikaans speaking whites'. She also mentions the University of Pretoria and the statue of Paul Kruger as factors contributing to the culture of Pretoria. Of Kruger she says: 'In his long-tailed frock-coat and high top-hat, stern and unrelenting, he *is* Pretoria.'[86] If this unrelenting spirit of place is what the lawscape of Pretoria represents and if this is the significance of the fact that the Rivonia trial was held in Pretoria and not in Johannesburg, the question remains: how is the Pretoria lawscape to be a space of resistance?

Conclusion

The courtroom as space is not an empty receptacle within which trials merely take place, it is not a vacuum for the characters involved in the trial to simply perform their roles within the trial. Instead, the trial is a space with a character itself and this character shapes and is shaped by the broader lawscape, in turn formed by the character of the city within which the court is placed. In the case of the Rivonia trial it is the character of Pretoria. The characteristics of cities are marked by spatial inertia, and Pretoria is no exception as the descriptions of the Pretoria lawscape above show. Therefore, resistance in the lawscape more often takes the shape of resistance to change than resistance understood as an opposition to the status quo. The lawscape is not only the influence of the city on the law, but also the impact of the law on the city. Alternative truths witnessed in the city during political trials form part of the lawscape, and these truths hauntingly reciprocate the city's resistance to change creating a lawscape within which competing lines of resistance co-exist.

The function of the Rivonia trial court, according to Justice Quartus de Wet, was to 'enforce law and order and to enforce the laws of the state within which it function[ed]'.[87] Upon reflection, the role of the Rivonia trial was, as is the case of most political trials, much broader than what Justice De Wet expressed in his judgment 50 years ago. In the case of political trials the role of the trial court is particularly complex. As Martti Koskenniemi points out, political trials are caught up in a paradox: in order to convey an undisputed truth, the accused should not be allowed the opportunity to speak, since allowing the accused to deliver his version of events will inevitably present a challenge to the truth that the trial started out to present.[88] This is a paradox because silencing the revolutionary truth

---

86   Bernstein, 2007 at 170.

87   'Remarks in Passing Sentence' In the Supreme Court of South Africa (Transvaal Provincial Division) Before: The Honourable Mr. Justice De Wet, Judge President. In the matter of: The State vs. Nelson Mandela and Others. 12th June 1964. Transcript sourced from Rivonia Trial Collection, Historical Papers, University of the Witwatersrand, Johannesburg.

88   M. Koskenniemi, 'Between impunity and show trial', in J.A. Frowein and R. Wolfrum (eds) *Max Planck Yearbook of United Nations Law* (2002 Kluwer Law International: Netherlands) at 35. With reference to the context of the Milosevic trial in

of the accused, which will necessarily relativize the prosecutor's version and the accused's guilt, will turn the trial into a show trial.[89] This tension of the political trial opens up a possibility of the courtroom as space of resistance.

The Hague, that international criminal law switches between the aim to punish individuals who are responsible for large-scale harms against humanity and the 'danger of becoming a show trial' at 1.

89   Koskenniemi, 2002 at 35.

Chapter 13

Literary Autonomy on Trial: The 1974 Cape Trial of André Brink's *Kennis van die Aand*[1]

Ted Laros

In January 1974, a decade after the Rivonia trial, André Brink's novel *Kennis van die Aand* (a novel that was translated by himself as *Looking on Darkness*) was banned in South Africa by the Publications Control Board, the administrative censorship body that was instigated by the Verwoerd government through the Publications and Entertainments Act of 1963.[2] *Kennis* represented Brink's first "*roman engagé*." One of the main threads of the narrative describes the tragic relationship of a "Coloured" man with a white girl of English descent, a relationship that was illegal under apartheid law. From various pieces that Brink had published in the course of the late 1960s and early 1970s,[3] it had become obvious that he was aiming at contesting the apartheid system. In rather unmistakable terms he had stated in an article that appeared in the anti-apartheid newspaper *Rand Daily Mail* of June 20, 1970:

> If it is true that Afrikaans writers do have greater freedom vis-à-vis censorship than others ... what have they done with this freedom? How have they used it? The depressing answer is: no Afrikaans writer has yet tried to offer a serious political challenge to the system ... We have no one with enough guts to say: NO ... [I]f Afrikaans writing is to achieve any true significance within the context of the revolution of Africa (of which we form part) and within the crucible in which this country finds itself, it seems to me it will come from these few who are prepared to sling the 'NO!' of Antigone into the violent face of the System. (Brink qtd. in Pienaar, "Histories-Juridiese Aspekte" 243)

---

1   This chapter represents a reworked and condensed version of the fifth chapter of my dissertation "Long Walk to Artistic Freedom: Law and the Literary Field in South Africa, 1910–2010" (Carl von Ossietzky University of Oldenburg, 2013). The dissertation was written within the framework of the German Research Foundation funded project "The Judicial Treatment of Literature in Belgium and South Africa" of Prof. Ralf Grüttemeier (University of Oldenburg). I would like to thank the anonymous reviewer and the editor for their comments on an earlier version of this chapter.

2   Hereafter: PEA.

3   E.g., Brink, "Antwoord aan Smit"; Brink, "Op soek na Afrika"; Brink, "Tussen Sestig en Sewentig."

Quite clearly, *Kennis van die Aand* constituted Brink's own Antigonian "NO!" The apartheid censors responded by ensuring that the novel became the first literary work in Afrikaans to be banned under the PEA (cf. Brink, Preface 10; Davis, *Voices of Justice and Reason* 116).

The censors banned the novel on political, moral, and religious grounds. Brink and his publisher Buren appealed against the censors' decision to the Cape Provincial Division of the Supreme Court, and on August 5 to 7 of 1974, the Cape Court dealt with the case. Brink and Buren's appeal did not just represent an effort to have the book released; it was just as much a struggle for literary autonomy, an attempt to resist the state's grasp over the literary field. With Brink's newly undertaken shift from a rather autonomist to a full-blown engaged conception of literature, that is, with his new politicized, subversive conception of literature, this also meant a struggle to maintain, or rather *create*, a platform from which to launch (discursive) attacks against the apartheid system. Unmistakenly, Brink and Buren laid claim to a far-reaching degree of institutional autonomy for literature in their appeal. If their claim would be acknowledged by the Court, they would succeed in opening up a space for the kind of dissident discourse that *Kennis van die Aand* presented.

On October 1, 1974, the Cape Court handed down its judgment, which declared that the appeal should be rejected and the ban, thus, upheld. Yet, although Brink and Buren's appeal thus evidently did not succeed as far as its *individual* dimension was concerned, a closer look at the judgment reveals that on the *institutional* level, Buren and Brink—and, hence, South African literature as a whole—scored some significant triumphs in the trial. It is the purpose of this chapter to describe these latter triumphs. By subjecting the trial to a cultural sociological analysis,[4] it aims to reconstruct how the Cape Court positioned itself vis-à-vis the South African literary field. The analysis of the case will be guided by the following question: How can the institutional and literary conceptual treatment of Brink's case by the Cape Court be described and explained? In attempting to answer this overall question, this chapter will proceed as follows. The next section will discuss the position that the Publications Control Board[5] took in Court. The following section will describe the position that Brink and his publisher took. The next section will present an analysis of the unanimous judgment that the Court came to—a judgment that was, however, underpinned with three seperate motivations. The final section will formulate an answer to the main question of this chapter.

---

4   For an exposition on the method of combined (Bourdieuian) institutional and literary conceptual analysis which lies at the basis of the present chapter and the theoretical and methodological rationale behind it, see Grüttemeier, "Law and the Autonomy of Literature"; Grüttemeier and Laros, "Literature in Law"; van Rees and Dorleijn, "The Eighteenth-Century Literary Field in Western Europe."

5   Hereafter: PCB.

The Position of the Publications Control Board

Let us first examine the objections that the PCB raised against the book in Court, so as to see what issues were at stake. As neither the initial censorship report on Brink's novel, nor a record of the argument delivered in Court on behalf of the PCB are available today (cf. McDonald, *Literature Police* 54; cf. also *Buren* v. *RBP* 381), and as newspaper reports of the trial do not offer much data regarding its argument either (cf. Peters, *Op. zoek naar Afrika* 67, 69, *passim*), the position of the Board has to be reconstructed on the basis of references made to its standpoint in the three opinions that the Cape Bench delivered.

The PCB's objections can be subsumed under three main categories: moral, religious, and political ones (cf. *Buren* v. *RBP* 411). The three categories of objections did not receive an even amount of attention in the argument that the Deputy State Attorney for Cape Town delivered on behalf of the PCB: the "political" and "religious" objections formed the core of the argument (cf. *Buren* v. *RBP* 404, 408). As to the former category: it was contended that both parts of the book and the book as a whole were undesirable on political grounds (cf. 408). The argument of the Deputy State Attorney seems to have concentrated on the objection that the book was harmful to the relations between sections of the nation's population because it demonized whites (cf. 397, 408–9, 421). In order to make the Board's case regarding the "religious" objections, two theologians were called upon to deliver testimony. Both considered the book blasphemous and felt that it would offend the religious convictions or feelings of Afrikaner Christians (cf. *Buren* v. *RBP* 406, 418, 421). Judging from the decisions delivered by the Cape Court, it appears most likely that the ground for these contentions lay in the fact that the work was considered, first, to be employing the Lord's name idly; second, to be ridiculing traditional religion; and, most of all, third, to be coupling sex with religion in an affronting manner (cf. 400–401, 406–8, 418–421, *passim*).

One of the issues that the debate in Court was principally concerned with was the question whether the concept of the likely reader should be read into "religious" and "political" articles 5 (2) (*b*) to (*e*) of the Act. The South African legislature had derived this concept from the English Obscene Publications Act of 1959 and had incorporated it into its Publications and Entertainments Act of 1963 so as to provide the judiciary with an instrument to distinguish between different types of audiences, who would be less or more prone to be corrupted by certain types of texts.[6] In contrast to the "moral" article 5 (2) (*a*), no mention of the concept was being made in the "religious" and "political" articles 5 (2) (*b*) to (*e*). The issue was important, because the concept of the likely reader might be employed to invalidate charges made against a book and grant literature a higher degree of autonomy. The suggestion that the likely-reader concept should be read into the mentioned articles had been made by the attorney of Buren Publishers and

---

6   The concept had been introduced in the English Act for the same reason.

Brink. In reaction hereto, counsel for the PCB argued that it should not be read into them (cf. 403).

When it came to determining the likely readership of *Kennis*—for the purpose of assessing the novel in terms of "moral" article 5 (2) (*a*)—the attorney of the PCB argued that the work would have attracted "a wide reading circle from the general audience" (404; cf. also 411). This contention was based on the expert testimonies that were delivered in Court on behalf of the Board. A considerable part of the experts that the PCB had called in to deliver testimony were chosen from its own ranks, as the panel of expert witnesses that appeared on its behalf consisted of PCB member and Afrikaans literature professor T.T. Cloete, PCB Chairman J.J. Kruger, PCB member and Afrikaans literature professor A.P. Grové and, finally, a certain Mr J.J. van Rooyen, managing director of C.F. Albertyn Publishers. The PCB's strategy seemed aimed at convincing the Court that the novel's likely readership should not be perceived to be made up entirely of a select circle of "strong"—i.e., intellectual, literary socialized—readers, but that its readership was likely to be broad and heterogeneous and that it would by implication also be comprised of "weak" readers. It might also have been, however, that its strategy was (also) aimed at convincing the Bench that the novel lacked the kind of aesthetic value of which the judges might have felt that it warranted special legal protection.

The argument delivered on behalf of the Board did not revolve solely around these more institutional matters though: literary conceptual issues also played a part in it. The latter issues were taken up in response to a long testimony that had been given by Brink. In this testimony he had laid out the literary theory underlying the novel, i.e., the literary theoretical precepts that, according to him, had guided the conception of the novel and that generally would, and certainly should, guide the reader's interpretation of the work (cf. 390–93; Brink, "*Kennis* Verbode" 90). Moreover, the expert witnesses called in by the appellants had also made statements regarding literary conceptual matters in their testimonies. In the argument that Grové delivered, he discussed the then highly current bipolar framework which situated "aesthetic novels" (*Buren* v. *RBP* 391), the novel as "hermetically sealed universe" (cf. 391), on the one extreme pole, and "'engaged' novels" (391), the novel as a form of "littérature engageé,"[7] on the other. He argued that Brink was feigning to have written a non-corresponding, "aesthetic" novel, while in reality he had purposely written a corresponding, "engaged" novel (cf. 391–2). To put it in M.H. Abrams' terms: he was pretending to have written an "objective," or *autonomous*, work of literature while having expressly written a mimetic-pragmatic work (cf. Abrams, *The Mirror and the Lamp* 3ff.)—one that, moreover, contained elements that were not adequate for good literature in the eyes of the Board. Cloete made an almost identical argument as Grové with the only difference between the two being basically that the former categorized

---

7   Grové explicitly used this Sartrean concept to explain the concept of "*betrokke*" *romans* and to characterize Brink's novel, which in his eyes represented a full-blown "roman engagé" (cf. 391).

Brink as an "engaged" writer in more implicit terms (cf. 392–3, 422). The issue at stake in all this appeared to be the fictionality/transformation principle, i.e., the (judicial) question to what degree Brink's work, i.e., the sensitive parts of it, effectively distanced itself from/managed to transcend reality.[8] The point of the PCB was that *Kennis* did not succeed in transcending reality: it failed to transform reality into a work of art.

The Position of Brink and His Publisher

The argument that was delivered in Court on behalf of Brink and his publisher Buren was primarily focused on the concept of the likely reader (cf. 403), i.e., both on the more principal and the more practical issues concerning the concept. The more principal part of the argument was constituted by the already mentioned contention that the concept of the likely reader should be read into the "religious" and "political" articles—5 (2) (*b*) to (*e*)—of the Act. On the more practical side it was contended that the novel would (normally) have had a limited reading circle, which, moreover, would have been made up of literarily socialized individuals (cf. 387–9, 404, 411)—the kind of readers that were not likely to be negatively affected by the book. The contention that the readership of the novel would (under normal circumstances) be comprised of literati was underpinned by the testimonies of expert witnesses D.J. Opperman, Ernst Lindenberg, I.D. du Plessis, Daantjie Saayman, Leon Rousseau, J.J. van Schaik, and G.J. Coetzee (cf. 405, 411–13). The former three were prominent figures within the Afrikaans part of the South African literary field and also linked to Afrikaans departments of South African universities; the latter four were all high-ranking individuals from within the Afrikaans literary book trade. In the testimonies delivered by these individuals, both intra- and extra-textual arguments were brought to the fore so as to make clear that Brink's book was not a book that would appeal to a mass audience but to a limited group of literati only. The intra-textual arguments all came down to the contention that because of the book's "literariness" (cf. 405) it would have made an appeal to the latter public only. The extra-textual arguments comprised a number of observations that mostly concerned the material side of the product *Kennis*.

Apart from the topic of likely readership, the argument delivered on behalf of Buren and Brink also focused on the question whether parliament had meant for the Act to have a more prescriptivist or descriptivist character when it came to moral issues, i.e., whether it had designed the Act first and foremost as an

---

8 For discussions of the idealist aesthetic roots that this principle appears to have in certain Western European jurisdictions, see Grüttemeier, "Law and the Autonomy of Literature" 182–3; Huber, *Deutsche Verfassungsgeschichte* 275; Huber, *Zur Problematik des Kulturstaats* 8ff.; Knies, *Schranken der Kunstfreiheit als verfassungsrechtliches Problem* 148ff.; 207ff.; Petersen, *Zensur in der Weimarer Republik* 191.

instrument for decisive paternalistic intervention, or whether it rather, apart from providing a tool to enable certain kinds of interventions, would have wanted for certain freedoms to be respected also. Buren's attorney argued that it was meant to have the descriptivist meaning, and that a judge thus first had to establish who the likely readers of a certain work were before he could decide whether it would have a detrimental effect on these readers (cf. 384–5).

Literary theoretical issues were drawn into the debate as well. They were drawn in both through the long testimony delivered by Brink himself and by the expert witnesses that were called in by the Buren party to testify in Court. Brink took a decisive autonomist position in his testimony. "*Kennis van die Aand*," he declared:

> was conceived of as fiction from the very start, and in this respect it is vital to point out that all forms of fiction—and the novel more than any other—during the couple of decades since World War II more than ever before have been studied by Literary Studies across the globe (but most of all in Germany and the United States, with a strong following in Britain and South Africa) as art forms in their own right, to be distinguished from 'reality representation.' The essential point of departure from standard works such as Booth's *Rhetoric of Fiction*, Stanzel's *Narrative Situations in the Novel* and literally hundreds of others, is that the literary work establishes a world of words in its own right, in which correspondences with the world outside are completely irrelevant. The approach, judgment, and test of such a work lies solely in the establishment of the meaningful relation between all elements within the work itself and the essential elements are usually summarized as: characters, action, space, and time. (Brink, "*Kennis* Verbode" 90).[9]

In his offensive, Brink thus also chose to rely on the fictionality/tranformation principle. Indeed, he employed it as the main argument to underpin an apparently absolute autonomist conception of literature, a conception which, in turn, was meant to underpin a claim to a far-reaching degree of institutional autonomy—for literature in general, but, indeed, especially for the kind of subversive literature that he felt the contemporary situation in South Africa called for. After having emphasized the hegemonic status of the conception of literature he allegedly adhered to, he drove home his argument as follows:

> In writing *Kennis van die Aand* I could thus *a priori* trust that the work, conceived as a novel, would be judged exactly in this context and in this manner, and not in any other. For the purpose of still more insurance that the work would only be *judged* as fiction because it only *exists* as fiction, this standpoint was printed in a foreword to the book: there it is categorically stated that everything 'within the new context of the novel … (is) fictive'; and further, that 'the demonstrable

---

9   All translations appearing in this chapter are mine.

surface of the current affairs (is) not relevant as such anywhere, only the patterns and relations under it are'. (Brink, "*Kennis* Verbode" 90; Brink's emphasis)

Brink was backed in his literary theoretical positioning by the expert witnesses that were called in by his party to deliver testimony.

The Judgment of the Court

The judgment of the Court was unanimous: on the basis of the PEA, the book was "undesirable." However, the three judges had quite different reasons for coming to this conclusion, and so each of them formulated an individual motivation. Not only did the judges have distinct opinions as to the question on which grounds Brink's work ought to be considered "undesirable"—Judge President van Wyk found it to be undesirable on religious, moral and political grounds; Judges Diemont and Steyn considered it undesirable on religious grounds only. More importantly, the positions they adopted vis-à-vis the literary field and the literary conceptual stances they took were also markedly different. Therefore, I will discuss the individual motivations of the three judges separately.

Judge President van Wyk

The position that Judge President van Wyk took both regarding literature in general and Brink's novel in particular had many heteronomist traits. This goes both for the institutional and the literary conceptual dimension of his point of view. As far as questions concerning the institutional status of literature were concerned, van Wyk was very clear: he held that the law had a decidedly interventionist aim—which, thus, also implied that it was aimed at keeping the institutional autonomy of literature in check, too. In response to a remark made by Buren's attorney that all that the Legislator had meant to accomplish with article 6 (1) of the PEA had been to prevent public morals from being corrupted and that a Court could only decide whether certain matter would be corruptive if it knew who would see or read the matter in question, van Wyk replied:

> It is indeed true that the aim of the Legislator is to protect public morals, but it does not follow from this that the Legislator compels the Court because of this to establish who will see or read certain matter for the purposes of art. 6 (1) (*c*). *On the contrary, the Legislator wanted to protect public morals on a broader basis, namely by declaring matter undesirable if it to the opinion of the Court deals with certain subjects in an improper manner.* (*Buren* v. *RBP* 384–5; my emphasis)

That van Wyk indeed employed the Act as an interventionist tool became evident when he came to the concept of likely readership, a concept that could in practice be employed as a means to both promote and curb the autonomy of the reader and, by implication, literature. Van Wyk quite obviously used it as a tool for doing the latter. He conceptualized likely readership very broadly: he argued that "persons whose thoughts could be exposed indirectly to the influence of the book" (383) also constituted the likely readership of the novel. "One could easily think of examples of such indirect influence," he stated, "like for example where the contents of parts of a book are being read or passed on to others" (383). Not only did van Wyk conceptualize likely readership broadly, he also emphasized that it did not have to be the case that a publication would actually corrupt the minds of readers, but that it was enough when the publication had a *tendency* to do so (cf. *Buren* v. *RBP* 383). Finally, van Wyk resolutely dismissed the argument of Buren's attorney that the concept of the likely reader should also be read into the paragraphs of the Act in which it was not being mentioned (cf. 384–6). It was the opinion of the Court that mattered in these articles, he declared (cf. 383–4; 386–7). Thus, especially when it came to alleged offenses on the basis of the "religious" and "political" articles of the Act, but also where "moral" issues were concerned, van Wyk was not willing to grant the literary field much autonomy. When van Wyk came to actually establish the identity of the likely reader of *Kennis*, he, not very surprisingly, did indeed postulate a broad readership. So despite the efforts of the expert witnesses appearing on behalf of the Buren party, van Wyk did not quite envision a limited audience consisting of literary socialized readers for Brink's novel.

Yet even though the cumulative evidence presented above makes it justified to say that van Wyk was not willing to allow the literary field much legal autonomy, there was a side to his position that evidenced that this field had in fact already attained, and could not be denied, a certain degree of institutional autonomy. Van Wyk namely evidenced to be realizing that the opinions of the expert witnesses that had been called in by both parties carried a certain weight, for he quite extensively employed the literary conceptual arguments delivered by some of the expert witnesses of the PCB to make his own argument. Effectively, this recognition of the expert status of the mentioned actors from within the literary field also meant granting the literary field a certain amount of institutional autonomy vis-à-vis the law—however modest this granted autonomy might have been, both in absolute terms and in comparison to the heteronomist side of his position.

In fact, van Wyk took a decisive literary conceptual stance in his judgment. Evidently, he read novels, or that of Brink's anyway, on the basis of a mixture of mimetic and pragmatic (*sensu* Abrams) literary conceptual premises. What is more is that he held that many likely readers of Brink's novel would share his conception of literature, and that they as a consequence would read Brink's novel in the same manner as he had. Referring to a remark made by Buren's witness Opperman that "[t]he function of the artwork as mirror is no longer being accepted" and that "your likely reader sees a novel as a soap bubble which gives a spherical vision, a bent reflection of reality," van Wyk declared:

> Of the soap-bubble-technique, of which Prof. Opperman speaks, in a novel which purports to be a novel which is based on reality, I was completely unaware until now. I am not a man of letters, but this also counts for most likely readers. I therefore have no reason to think that there would not be thousands of likely readers of the book who would share my 'ignorance' in this respect. My impression was still that such a novel, although the narrative itself is fictive, still to a great extent represented a reflection of reality as it is or was at a certain time. (393)

Indeed, van Wyk unambiguously declared that "[t]here [wa]s enough evidence that the book was purposely written in such a manner that the reader would get the impression that especially the more important incidents, although fictive, [we]re a mirror image of reality" (391). With great consent, he cited the analysis of PCB witness Grové, who had declared in so many words that Brink had explicitly taken a pragmatic stance in programmatic literary conceptual texts, but that, now that he was up for trial, he sought to pass for an autonomous author: "[T]he difficulty with second appellant [i.e., Brink]," Grové had stated:

> [is] precisely that he wants to sit on two chairs. With *Kennis van die Aand* he writes a *roman engagé*, a novel that breaks through the walls surrounding the world of the novel in a hundred ways, for example by mentioning situations, places, persons, localities, a novel that wants to 'write open' the S. A. situation, that wants to reform, that wants to expose injustices. But now that its one-sided representations and agitation are being pointed out, now he wants to hide behind the theory that regards the novel as a 'hermetically sealed universe'. As an assailant he wants to be a reformer; as a defender he wants to be an aesthetic. When he charges, the novel is a literary weapon to him; when he defends, the novel suddenly becomes a distinct world that has nothing to do with current events. He wants, thus, to have the best of both worlds. (391)

For van Wyk, this remark of Grové's hit the nail on the head (cf. 391). And as a consequense of this, or at least partly because of this, he tested the novel *inter alia* on the basis of mimetic criteria—in other words, the novel had failed van Wyk's transformation test, and was now being tested on its truthfulness. *Kennis* clearly did not pass this test. As van Wyk stated in reference to the way in which whites were being portrayed in Brink's novel:

> [i]t is improper to throw together such isolated crimes committed by Whites in such a manner that they are being held up as a reflection of the broad reality. By doing this a false image of Whites is being created, an image which brings Whites as a group into contempt. (394; cf. also 397)

Apart from the fact that *Kennis*, because of the way in which Brink had "thrown together" his episodes of racist crimes, constituted a "political" offense, it also represented an offense in terms of some of the "moral" sections of the law, according to van Wyk. In his eyes, Brink's "distorted fiction that was being held up as a mirror image of reality" was, *inter alia*, "also undesirable on the basis of sec. 6 (1) (*b*), because it was likely to be outrageous and disgustful to a significant number of the likely readers" (394).

What would also offend the likely readers of the novel according to van Wyk, were the coupling of sex with religion and the "idle usage of the Lord's name" (cf. 400–401). Yet, whereas van Wyk's objections to the untruthful representation of white cruelty against "Coloureds" was a direct result of the mimetic requirements he had postulated as a crucial test for judging the book, this latter objection seemed rather to have been a consequence of his conviction that the PEA had a decidedly interventionist purpose.

Judge Diemont

The second judge that formulated a motivation for the Court's decision in the case was Justice Diemont. This judge adopted a much more tolerant position than van Wyk had, a position that allowed the literary field considerable autonomy.

Although Diemont appeared quite categorically to be upholding the principle of parliamentary sovereignty,[10] he did declare that a judge always had to try to guarantee the fundamental freedoms that he perceived to be lying at the basis of the South African state for as much as he could, i.e., for as much as was possible within the boundaries of positive law. Approvingly, he quoted a celebrated passage regarding the freedom of speech and the freedom to publish a story that judge Rumpff had incorporated in his minority judgment in the 1965 Appellate Division case of Wilbur Smith's novel *When the Lion Feeds* (cf. 402–3; *PCB* v. *Heinemann* 160). In the name of freedom of speech, Diemont thus propagated a tolerant approach toward literature.

That Diemont was willing to allow the (literary socialized) reader—and hence literature—considerable autonomy seems to be evidenced by the fact that he, unlike van Wyk, did effectively hold that the concept of the likely reader ought to be read into the sections of the Act that did not mention the concept, as Buren's attorney had advanced. Indeed, Diemont argued that he "found it difficult to understand how the Court would be able to decide whether a book would be undesirable without asking the question – for whom is it undesirable? Who are going to read the book? This question is of vital importance" (*Buren* v. *RBP* 403). Surely, the question was "of vital importance" for the literary field, because when the criterion by which to measure the undesirability or otherwise of a publication was to be the likely reader in the application of every section stipulating the kinds

---

10 It appears that a "tradition of parliamentary sovereignty with a concomitant emphasis upon literalism in the interpretation of statutes" was dominant amongst the South African judiciary all throughout apartheid (Davis, "Judicial Appointments in South Africa" 40).

of offenses that would make a text undesirable, the field could potentially reach a considerable amount of autonomy. For at least since the 1932 case of *Rex* v. *Meinert*, the literary socialized, or "intellectual" reader, appears to have generally been conceptualized by the South African judiciary as a reader that was not as easily affected negatively as his non-intellectual counterpart was (Laros, "Long Walk to Artistic Freedom" 194).

When Diemont subsequently came to actually determine the identity of the likely reader, he argued that two factors should be taken into consideration first and foremost: (1) the contents of the book; and (2) the reputation of the author. As to the former aspect, Diemont emphatically declared that the book was not easy to read (cf. 404). To underpin his argument, he extensively quoted Buren's witnesses Opperman, Lindenberg, and du Plessis, who all had argued that the book was difficult to read for non-literati and that it would thus normally have had a select reading circle consisting of men of letters (cf. 405). Apparently he thus also recognized the value of literary expert opinion. After having discussed the expert evidence with which he concurred, Diemont came to the conclusion regarding his first point. He declared that he was of the opinion that if he took into consideration "the literary content of the book and the complicated style" (405), he had to conclude that its readers would largely be limited to people "with a serious interest in the art of the novel" (405). "Shallow people or those who seek titillating reading matter would quickly be discouraged" (405), he added. *A priori* Diemont thus posited that the kind of literature that Brink wrote was normally being read by literary socialized individuals only.

As far as the second point, the author's reputation, was concerned, Diemont declared that Brink was indeed known within literary circles, but that he was also renowned amongst the general audience. However, Diemont argued that Brink's renown amongst the broad public would not result in it being potentially interested in his novel. On the contrary, he contended, the author's reputation would scare off the "ordinary reader, the man who seeks light reading matter" (406), read: the not, or only poorly, literary socialized reader. Having established his position regarding the two determining factors he had posited, Diemont came to his overall conclusion regarding the likely readership of the novel. His conclusion was that the book would have a limited circle of readers consisting for the largest part of literary socialized readers, i.e., "men of letters, persons with an education and a serious interest in matters" (406), "people with an interest in literature, philosophy, and sociological problems" (408).

After he had determined the identity of the likely reader, Diemont set forth what effects the book would probably have on this reader. As far as the "religious" component of the book was concerned, he stated that the likely reader would probably not consider the book blasphemous (cf. *Buren* v. *RBP* 406). However, he argued that the book would in all likelihood offend the religious feelings of many a likely reader. The reason he gave for this was that:

[t]he reading circle might be relatively small and it might be ... that it consists of men of letters and educated people for the largest part, but it must also be remembered that many of them, perhaps the majority, would also be Afrikaans-speaking Calvinists, or members of the Dutch Reformed Church or one of its sister churches. Most of these persons have had an orthodox Christian upbringing and although they may be sophisticated worldly-wise readers today, many of them would consider parts of this book as offensive nonetheless. (406–7)

With the indefinite "parts of the book," Diemont was thinking first and foremost of "incidents and descriptions in which sex was being coupled with religion" (407). As to the argument that the passages in which sex was being connected to religion made a contribution to the narrative, that they were "functional," Diemont declared:

This may be so, but I do not think this is relevant. I have to apply the provisions of the Act. I have to decide, regardless of the part that these incidents of sex-religion play in the story, whether the provisions of sec. 5 (2) (*b*) of the Act are being transgressed. The answer is affirmative, in my opinion. (407–8)

Again, for Diemont, the law was the law, and neither his eventual own preferences (literary or moral or otherwise) nor literary conceptual issues like these could therefore be of any relevance: whatever amount of autonomy could be granted to literature, there was a point where the autonomy of the literary field had to succumb to the sovereignty of the field of power, and in Diemont's view, Brink had surpassed that point with his "incidents of sex-religion."

When it came to the "political" component of the book, Diemont was quite straightforward. As to the first "political" objection that was raised against the book, i.e., the objection that it would harm relations between certain sections of the South African population, Diemont declared that the likely reader, being the sensible person that he was (cf. 408–9), would not react to the book, and particularly to the way in which whites were being portrayed (cf. 408–9), in such a way that it would trouble or harm "race relations" (409). As to the second objection, which was that the book would be prejudicial to the safety of the state, the general welfare, or the peace and good order, Diemont came to the same conclusion: he could not imagine that the kind of people that would read Brink's novel would react to it in such a way that any of these might become endangered (cf. 408).

As the way in which Diemont dealt with institutional matters might be termed quite autonomist-oriented, the manner in which he handled the key literary conceptual question that the case posed could also be characterized thus. Diemont namely accepted Brink's claim that it has been his intention to write a non-mimetic work of literature and that he might *a priori* assume that its readers would interpret it accordingly. Approvingly, he quoted a passage from Brink's foreword to the book in which the fictive character of his novel was being emphasized (see 409; also Brink, "*Kennis* Verbode" 90). If the likely readers of the book "had enough sense to read and understand this type of book," the judge concluded, "they ought to realize that this is all fiction" (*Buren* v. *RBP* 408). Unlike van Wyk, Diemont thus not only thought Brink's non-mimetic literary conceptual position-taking to be relevant, he also endorsed it. Indeed, he held that the novel should not be judged on the basis of mimetic criteria, or the criteria of non-fiction, as van Wyk had done: whatever elements of reality Brink had used in his novel, the way in which he had used them had transformed them into artistic elements per se.

Judge Steyn

The last judge that formulated a separate motivation in the case was Judge Steyn. The position that Steyn adopted in his judgment was rather autonomist-oriented too, even more so than that of Diemont's.

Steyn began his judgment by delivering a rather fierce critique of the PEA and approvingly quoting the same words on the freedom of speech that Rumpff had uttered in the Smith trial as Diemont had in his judgment (cf. *Buren* v. *RBP* 409–11). Nonetheless, he also emphasized—again, just as his colleague Diemont had—that the law was the law, and that a judge could not use his own discretion instead of the directives laid down by the Legislature (cf. 411). If parliament decreed that the autonomy of creative expression should be restricted, a judge had to act accordingly, regardless of his own thoughts on the matter.

After having set forth his principled position vis-à-vis the PEA, he came to the more practical matters that the case posed, and the first issue he took up was the issue of the likely readership of Brink's novel. Steyn reached his conclusion regarding this matter after having made "a careful consideration of the various statements under oath" (415). Indeed, he quite elaborately discussed the remarks concerning the identity of the likely reader that the witnesses had made in their respective testimonies. As this fact already presents us with implicit evidence that Steyn found literary expert evidence to be a potential asset in cases like these, more explicit evidence that he valued such evidence—and in fact even seemed to find it indispensable in some cases—can be found a little further on in his argument. Taking up the question whether expert evidence should be allowed when applying sections 5 (2) (*b*) to (*e*) of the PEA—sections in which no mention was being made of either "the opinion of the Court" or the likely reader—he stated that a judge "should not rule out evidence – and indeed sometimes can hardly fulfill his duties properly without it – when he has to decide whether a particular publication is affected by the prohibitions concerned" (416). Steyn was predominantly thinking of the religious and political sections with his remark, yet he also felt that for the application of the moral sections, "factual" evidence as to the likely readership of a publication should be welcomed (cf. 417). As Diemont did, he also felt that one should always take into account who was going to read a particular publication, for he too found it absurd to ban a publication because it would offend people who were not going to read it (cf. 417).

Still more evidence that Steyn attached considerable judicial weight to literary expertise, was evidenced by the fact that he took all the testimonies of the witnesses that had good literary credentials—i.e., were important actors within the literary field—seriously, but more or less disqualified the testimonies of the witnesses that in his view lacked, precisely, expertise in the field of literature. One can sense from his discussion of J.J. Kruger's testimony, that he did not take much of the argument of the PCB's Chairman—who indeed did not have the literary credibility that most of the other witnesses had (cf. McDonald, *Literature Police* 52–3; Peters, *Op. zoek naar Afrika* 37; Kannemeyer, *Geskiedenis van die Afrikaanse Literatuur* 233)—very seriously. Yet even more clearly, he invalidated the testimony of J.J. van Rooyen, director of publishing house C.F. Albertyn. Expressly he brought to the attention that van Rooyen was really not a literary expert: he was "really a newspaper man" (*Buren* v. *RBP* 414), who, despite the fact that he was now employed in a publishing house, seemed to have no experience with publishing literature. After having stated that he believed the testimonies of Buren's witnesses to be more objective than those of the witnesses testifying on behalf of the PCB, he quite unambiguously stated: "As far as [van Rooyen] is concerned, one needs only refer to his comparison between the back page of a Sunday paper and a serious novel of 500 pages[11] to realize that we perhaps should not overestimate his opinion. His experience in the field on which he delivers testimony indeed seems rather limited to me" (415). Having weighed the expert evidence, Steyn reached his conclusion regarding the likely readership of the novel. His conclusion was that the book would have had a select reading circle.

However, even though Steyn felt that the "ordinary" reader would not have been very interested in the novel, he did not think that its readership would have solely consisted of literati either. Amongst the non-literati that would also have been interested in the novel, Steyn counted "informed citizens, who have an interest in national affairs and in politics" (416). "There are many concerned South Africans," he explained, "who have a strong sense of alleged injustice in the administration of their country and who would gladly want to see how an author of the stature of second appellant deals with this matter in an engaged novel" (416).

Having established the identity of the likely reader, Steyn could carry on with determining what effect Brink's work would have on him. In doing so, he proceeded by successively discussing each of the three categories of objections that had been raised against the book—religious, moral, and political objections. In his discussion of the first kind, Steyn first set out to determine whether or not the book should be deemed to be blasphemous. He thereby focused both on the meaning that had been given to the concept in South African law and on the theological debate as it had been held in Court through the testimonies of three theology professors. As far as the latter debate was concerned, he approvingly quoted Prof. Lombard, an apparently unorthodox theologian who had testified on

---

11   Steyn was referring to van Rooyen's remark that "the book c[ould] count on a rather wide reading circle in the same way as the popular back pages of certain Sunday papers f[ound] such a reading circle" (415).

behalf of the Buren party. Lombard, unlike the other two theology professors, had argued that the book should not be considered to be blasphemous (cf. 406, 418–19, 421).

When it came to the novel's alleged offensiveness to religious convictions or feelings, however, Steyn had to reach a conclusion that was not so favorable for the Buren–Brink party. Steyn did start his discussion by emphasizing that the Court ought to be liberal whenever this matter was at issue. Yet even though he took a tolerant position regarding "religious" matters, and indeed had found it "incredibly difficult" (420) to assess the impact on religious convictions and feelings that Brink's work would have, he still had to conclude that it should be considered undesirable in terms of the PEA. The reason for this was that he felt that the "unnecessary, crude and unfunctional coupling of sex and religion" (420) that was to be found in it would be offensive to a significant number of likely readers (cf. 420–21). There were, thus, limits to the amount of autonomy that Steyn was willing to grant literature too.

As to the "moral" objections to the book, Steyn was short. He declared that it was unnecessary for him to deal with the objections that the book was indecent or obscene or harmful to public morals. He did, however, want to note that although "the author on occasion sketche[d] sexual scenes in a sensitive manner," he on the other hand, "add[ed] explicit sex on several occasions where this d[id] not seem functional to [him, i.e., to Steyn himself] at all" (421).

As far as the "political" grounds were concerned, finally, Steyn, remarkably enough, did not settle the matter in a markedly judicial manner; instead, he decided it on the basis of full-fledged literary conceptual arguments. In fact, his discussion of the "political" objections, which formed the peroration of his entire judgment, was more a defense of literature than anything else. That is to say, it dealt only in so far with the "political" dimension of the case that it was aimed at invalidating the central premises of van Wyk's argument, these being that it had been the aim of Brink to write a mimetic novel and that the majority of its likely readers would interpret it thus. Steyn countered these contentions by postulating, first, that one had to distinguish between books that were "directed towards reality" (422) and those that were "faithful to reality" (422). In taking position in what he termed the "polemic" that had been held in Court through the testimonies of the expert witnesses "on how the novel [of Brink] should be approached" (421), he namely declared:

> Engaged literature is certainly as old as man's ability to write. When an author, fired up by his worries about for instance injustices or undesirabilities in his own community wants to employ the novel as a means for reformation, there can, as far as I am concerned, be no objection against the fact that his book, although directed towards reality, is not faithful to reality. To then always judge an engaged novel on the 'truth' or to condemn it because it is 'false' or 'exaggerated' or conveys 'a distorted image' is completely and utterly unconvincingly to me. (422)

Quite obviously, Steyn was engaging in a polemic himself, for he quite harshly deconstructed van Wyk's characterization of Brink's novel here. As Steyn went on with his argument, he came to defend a conception of literature that differed from the one van Wyk adhered to. "In this respect," he namely continued his argument:

> Henry James's well-known statement is appropriate for me when he says: 'The only reason for the existence of a novel is that it does attempt to represent life ... and the analogy between the art of the painter and the art of the novelist is so far as I am able to see, complete'. As photographic art is not the only convincing art form, just as little is truthful engaged literature the only convincing literary art form. (422)

The reference to Henry James might be taken as an indication that Steyn was well acquainted with the contemporary Anglophone part of the South African literary field. For one of the most influential critics within that subfield at the time was F.R. Leavis (McDonald, "Old Phrases" 294; Johnson, "Literary and Cultural Criticism" 828–9, 831–2), and the latter had notoriously proclaimed Henry James to be one of the only four "great English" novelists that history had produced (Leavis, *The Great Tradition* 9). In any case, Steyn effectively underpinned his defense of non-mimetic pragmatic literature against van Wyk's criterion of truthfulness with James's conception of literature. The fact that Steyn relied on a literary actor in a judicial polemic also goes some way toward indicating that the South African literary field had reached a considerable degree of institutional autonomy at the time.

The second counterargument of Steyn was aimed at falsifying van Wyk's presupposition that the likely reader would read Brink's novel as a mimetic work of literature. Steyn argued that the completely opposite was the case. Yet, as said, Steyn's peroration did not solely seek to disqualify van Wyk's central premises, and, thus, his entire argument. Even more than it was aimed at serving this latter purpose, it was directed at presenting a defense of literature. Steyn held that upholding the right to free speech also entailed granting literature a fairly high degree of autonomy. For, as he declared, even novels that were written by "sneaky authors" with the aim to "offend," such as *Kennis*, should be protected—indeed, when necessary, at the expense of the "sensitivity of the intolerant and immature."

Yet apart from defending literature on the ground of free speech, he also defended it in a much more straightforward manner: he namely also quite clearly defended it on the basis of a "public good" argument, as known from contemporaneous British and US law, i.e., on the basis of it being worthy of defense in its own right, as it made a valuable contribution to the (cultural) life of a nation. To begin with, after having declared that as far as he was concerned, there could be no objection to an engaged novel not being faithful to reality, he went on by stressing, indeed, the *importance* of engaged literature (422).

Not only did Steyn break a lance for engaged literature, he also took the occasion to debunk "conforming" literature: "Conforming men of letters," he stated:

faithful to the needs of the administration of their time, seldom succeed in making contributions that enrich their language and culture. Sure, Alfred Austin was poet laureate of England.[12] He is, however, not remembered for his contributions to English literature, but for his servile doggerel verses which amongst other things praised the imperialism of his time by, for instance, elevating the Jameson raiders to heroes.[13] (422–3)

As both the content of the point that Steyn is advancing here—there appears to be a clear Afrikaner nationalistic undertone in this passage—and the rhetoric in which he presents it seem to give away: Steyn's views regarding literature appear not only to have been premised on the idea that it formed a "public good"; they also appeared to have been quite close to the conception of literature of the *Dertigers* ("Writers of the Thirties"), more particularly to that of preeminent *Dertiger* N.P. van Wyk Louw. Indeed, as Steyn's polemic against "conformism" indicates, his position might have been rather close to the Louwian concept of "loyal resistance" ("lojale verset"), which was very influential not only amongst the *Dertigers*, but also—still—amongst certain *Sestigers*, the "Writers of the Sixties" of which Brink was one of the foremost representatives (cf. McDonald, *Literature Police* 28).[14]

The final remarks of Steyn's judgment seem to provide further evidence for the hypotheses that he defended literature on the basis of it being a "public good" and that he adhered to a Louwian conception of literature—perhaps the former position was indeed underpinned by the latter. In these remarks he emphasized the importance of non-conformist literature anew—and again, particularly the content and the rhetoric appear to confirm the hypotheses: "I am aware of the fact that in our community with its diversity of peoples, languages and cultures, the freedom of speech has been curtailed to some extent so as to eliminate friction and conflict" he declared. "I am, however, not prepared," he continued:

> to accept that our Legislature would have wanted to enforce a conforming literature upon the Afrikaner, which would make him utter, like Napoleon did with regard to the decline of French literature: 'People complain that we do not have literature. This is the fault of the Minister of the Interior ... he should make sure that decent ware is being written' ...

> For these reasons I have come to the conclusion that respondent on account of the provisions of the Publications and Entertainments Act, 26 of 1963, was right

---

12 Alfred Austin (1835–1913) was an English poet who was appointed Poet Laureate in 1896.

13 The so-called Jameson Raid was an ineffective attempt by the British to overthrow President Paul Kruger of the Transvaal Republic in December 1895.

14 For a lucid discussion of the Louwian conception of literature, see McDonald, *Literature Police* 27ff.

in judging the book *Kennis van die Aand* undesirable. This is a decision that I have taken reluctantly for various reasons; most of all, however, firstly, because of the need for a virile literature in the Afrikaans language which would indeed write fearlessly about the current affairs of the South African situation. Secondly, because I now realize the insufficiency of my own Afrikaans; reading this book with its rich language has brought this home to me so clearly. In the light of the statutory provisions, the author's malice has left me no choice, however. (423)

Even more clear than in the other comments concerning literature that comprised the major part of Steyn's peroration, these remarks seem to evidence that he held literature to be a "public good," worthy of protection in the form of a significant amount of autonomy vis-à-vis the law. For unambiguously he declared here that there was a "need for a virile literature in the Afrikaans language," a literature that unlike "conformist" literature à la Austin *would* "succeed in making contributions that enrich[ed] [in this case: Afrikaans] language and culture." The fact that the "virile" literature that he envisioned "would indeed write fearlessly about the current affairs of the South African situation," would surely only increase the need for a guaranteed amount of autonomy vis-à-vis the law.

Conclusion

Although the trial of Brink's *Kennis* resulted in a confirmation of the ban that had been instigated by the PCB, the three opinions delivered in the case revealed that the literary field had effectively reached a considerable degree of (internal) autonomy already. Van Wyk, despite his emphasis on the interventionist spirit of the Act and his resultant unwillingness to allow the literary field a significant degree of legal autonomy, revealed to be realizing the value of (literary) expert evidence. In fact, he determinedly underpinned his opinion with the literary conceptual analyses delivered by the literary experts that had been called in to give testimony on behalf of the PCB. The amount of legal autonomy that van Wyk actually granted literature through the validation and employment of expert evidence was relatively insignificant though, when viewed in the light of the most fundamental aspect of his position: for van Wyk, the sovereignty that the field of power enjoyed over the literary field was namely far-reaching. Van Wyk's position represented the minority position, however. Diemont and Steyn were both much more autonomy-oriented.

The latter two both allowed the literary field a significant degree of autonomy within the law. This autonomy was created first of all because both categorically favored a freedom-oriented approach to publications regulation. Moreover, it came about because of the way in which the two judges conceptualized the likely reader, both on the more theoretical and on the more practical level: through their conceptualization of the likely reader, the two effectively recognized that the intellectual or literary socialized reader could lay claim to minority rights.

First and foremost, however, the significant degree of institutional autonomy was effectuated through their stance vis-à-vis literary expertise: whereas such expertise was only allowed to play a minimal role in the literary trials that had preceded the *Kennis* trial—i.e., the 1965 trials regarding Wilbur Smith's *When the Lion Feeds* and Can Themba's short story "The Fugitives" (see Laros, "Long Walk to Artistic Freedom" 53ff.)—it played a crucial role in the judicial deliberations of both Diemont and Steyn. Indeed, it not only played a fundamental role in their position-takings regarding institutional matters: conceptions of literature of contemporary South African actors appeared also to have penetrated into the judicial reasoning of at least one of the two, i.e., Steyn. Clearly, the recognition of the (judicial) value of literary expertise, the application of arguments advanced by these experts, and the legal recognition and, indeed, judicial employment of literary conceptual arguments adhered to by contemporary literary actors contributed to the creation of an institutional autonomy of literature vis-à-vis the law. In fact, a significant degree of structural and conceptual homology (*sensu* Bourdieu) between the juridical and the literary field appeared thus to have emerged by 1975. Yet, although both Diemont and Steyn adopted a position that established a considerable autonomy for literature, this autonomy clearly remained but relative. In the end, both namely declared that Brink's novel was undesirable in terms of the PEA, because they found that it had transgressed the boundaries of the permissible by its thematization of religion, i.e., Christianity—not with its thematizations of "political" or "moral" issues. It appears thus that the amount of autonomy that the two were willing to grant literature was smallest when it came to religion.

So, even though the defense of Buren and Brink brought a number of victories for the literary field both on the institutional and literary conceptual front, Afrikaner Nationalist forces—the architects and administrators of the Publications and Entertainments Act under which Brink's novel had been banned and under which the ban was upheld—came out victorious in the end. Just as with the much more famous—and much more consequential—Rivonia trial,[15] however, the *Kennis* trial would go on to play an essential role in the eventual triumph of freedom-oriented forces over apartheid politics—in this case apartheid politics with respect to literature regulation. In the 1980s, namely, the more autonomy-oriented opinions of Diemont and Steyn were employed by J.C.W. van Rooyen's Publications Appeal Board[16] so as to underpin its relatively freedom-oriented approach toward publications regulation, an approach that would prove to form the prelude to the artistic freedom that was instigated in South Africa on the constitutional level on April 27, 1994.

---

15 Cf. Catherine Albertyn's contribution to this volume.

16 The highest body in the censorship apparatus that was set up shortly after the *Kennis* trial through the Publications Act of 1974.

References

Abrams, M.H. *The Mirror and the Lamp: Romantic Theory and the Critical Tradition.* Oxford: Oxford University Press, 1975 [1953].

Brink, André P. "Antwoord aan Smit." *Kol* 1.3 (1968): 4–6.

Brink, André P. *Kennis van die Aand.* 2nd edn. Cape Town/Pretoria: Human & Rousseau, 1983.

Brink, André P. "*Kennis* Verbode." In André P. Brink, *Waarom Literatuur?* Cape Town/Pretoria: Human & Rousseau, 1985: 90–96.

Brink, André P. "Op soek na Afrika." *Standpunte* 28.8 (1973): 1–9.

Brink, André P. Preface. In Kobus van Rooyen, *A South African Censor's Tale.* Pretoria: Protea, 2011.

Brink, André P. "Tussen Sestig en Sewentig." *Kol* 1.1 (1968): 2–5.

Buren Uitgewers (Edms) Bpk en 'n Ander v. *Raad van Beheer oor Publikasies* 1975 (1) SA 379 (C). Western Cape Provincial Division of the Supreme Court of South Africa. 1975. The South African Law Reports (1947 to date). Juta Law, n.d. Web. February 17, 2011.

Davis, D.M. "Judicial Appointments in South Africa." *advocate* 23.3 (2010): 40–43.

Davis, Geoffrey V. *Voices of Justice and Reason: Apartheid and Beyond in South African Literature.* Amsterdam/New York: Rodopi, 2003.

Grüttemeier, Ralf. "Law and the Autonomy of Literature." In Gillis J. Dorleijn, Ralf Grüttemeier, and Liesbeth Korthals Altes (eds) *The Autonomy of Literature at the Fins de Siècles (1900 and 2000): A Critical Assessment.* Leuven/Paris/Dudley, MA: Peeters, 2007: 175–92.

Grüttemeier, Ralf, and Ted Laros. "Literature in Law: Exceptio Artis and the Emergence of Literary Fields." *Law and Humanities* 7.2 (2013): 204–17.

Huber, Ernst Rudolf. *Deutsche Verfassungsgeschichte seit 1789.* Vol. 1. Stuttgart: Kohlhammer, 1957.

Huber, Ernst Rudolf. *Zur Problematik des Kulturstaats.* Tübingen: Mohr, 1958.

Johnson, David. "Literary and Cultural Criticism in South Africa." In David Attwell and Derek Attridge (eds) *The Cambridge History of South African Literature.* Cambridge: Cambridge University Press, 2012: 818–37.

Kannemeyer, J.C. *Geskiedenis van die Afrikaanse Literatuur.* 2nd edn. 2 vols. Pretoria/Cape Town: Academica, 1984.

Knies, Wolfgang. *Schranken der Kunstfreiheit als verfassungsrechtliches Problem.* Munich: C.H. Beck, 1967.

Laros, Ted. "Long Walk to Artistic Freedom: Law and the Literary Field in South Africa, 1910–2010." Diss. Carl von Ossietzky University of Oldenburg, 2013.

Leavis, F.R. *The Great Tradition: George Eliot, Henry James, Joseph Conrad.* Harmondsworth: Penguin, 1972 [1948].

McDonald, Peter D. *The Literature Police: Apartheid Censorship and its Cultural Consequences.* Oxford: Oxford University Press, 2009.

McDonald, Peter D. "Old Phrases and Great Obscenities: The Strange Afterlife of Two Victorian Anxieties." *Journal of Victorian Culture* 13.2 (2008): 294–302.

Peters, Bas. *Op. zoek naar Afrika: Over het verbod op Kennis van die Aand van André P. Brink*. Leiden: SNL, 1996.

Petersen, Klaus. *Zensur in der Weimarer Republik*. Stuttgart: Metzler, 1995.

Pienaar, G.J. "Histories-Juridiese Aspekte van Sensuur in Suid-Afrika." *Suid-Afrikaanse Biblioteke/South African Libraries* 38.4 (1971): 238–49.

Publications Control Board v. *William Heinemann, Ltd and Others* 1965 (4) SA 137 (A). Appellate Division of the Supreme Court of South Africa. 1965. South African Appellate Division Reports (1910 to date). Juta Law, n.d. Web. February 17, 2011.

van Rees, K., and G.J. Dorleijn. "The Eighteenth-Century Literary Field in Western Europe: The Interdependence of Material and Symbolic Production and Consumption." *Poetics* 28 (2001): 331–48.

Chapter 14

"The Unkindest Cut of All": Coloniality, Performance and Gender in the Courtroom and Beyond[1]

Chloé S. Georas

Introduction: "The Unkindest Cut of All"[2]

On June 23, 1993, in Manassas, Virginia, after years of physical and verbal abuse that, according to testimony, culminated in another episode of marital rape, Lorena Bobbitt took an eight-inch red-handled steak knife from her kitchen and cut off the penis of her husband and ex-Marine, John Wayne Bobbitt.[3] She drove off with the penis and later discarded it on a grassy lot, where it was recovered by a police rescue mission and successfully reattached to her husband. John Wayne was tried and acquitted of marital rape charges. Facing a possible sentence of up to 20 years for "malicious wounding," Lorena claimed not to remember the act and deployed the insanity and battered wife syndrome defenses in response to the prosecution's argument that she had done it for revenge. Lorena was found not guilty by reason of insanity and spent only a few days in a mental hospital before being released.[4] Through her transgressive "cut felt around the world,"[5] Lorena Bobbitt not only amputated the organ that symbolized her misery but achieved instant fame. The globalized media machineries disseminated the infamous Bobbitt saga, variously appropriated along the lines of entrenched cultural anxieties.

Readers may wonder at the rationale for the inclusion of an article on the Lorena Bobbitt trial in this volume that addresses the Rivonia trial

---

1   In order to adapt to the space requirements for this initial submission, several sections of the original work upon which this derivative article is based have been completely omitted and others are a synthesis of a broader discussion.

2   "The Unkindest Cut of All: Enough Already," *U.S. News & World Rep.*, January 31, 1994, at 14.

3   Hereinafter Lorena Bobbitt will be referred to as "Lorena" and John Wayne Bobbitt as "John Wayne."

4   The excerpts from the trial in this article were published by Peter Kane, *The Bobbitt Case: Transcripts of the Sex Trial that Shocked the World* (Pinnacle Books, 1994). Hereinafter it will be referenced as "Transcript."

5   Rush Limbaugh, "No Tears for Lorena," *Newsweek*, December 24, 1994, at 56.

and the figure of Nelson Mandela. What could the Rivonia trial and Nelson Mandela, as one of the most consecrated historical icons of "post-colonial" struggles for equality, have in common with the trial of Lorena Bobbitt, an unskilled immigrant worker with no history of political activism that garnered lukewarm support, and usually condemnation, from intellectual elites in the United States? In fact, these disparate trials provide a unique opportunity to explore the courtroom as a space of domination and resistance. On the one hand, the Rivonia trial takes us to the contended heart of a nation-building project beyond the institutionalized forms of Apartheid racisms and, on the other hand, the Lorena Bobbitt trial takes us on a (mis)guided tour through the ethno-racial and sexual imaginary of the United States in relation to Latin America and the constitution of Latino identities.

In this chapter on the Lorena Bobbitt trial I explore how different theoretical approaches to the narrative, performative and cultural aspects of trials, particularly show trials, can illuminate the sexual and racial politics that underpinned the public's fascination with this case. The first section briefly sets the stage by addressing the location of Latinos in the trans-American social imaginary profoundly marked by the coloniality of power. The second section addresses how narrative and performative analyses can fruitfully recast the study of show trials to better appreciate their cultural and political implications. The third and final section analyzes the stories put forward by both the defense and the prosecution and how they reenacted highly problematic racial and sexual tropes characteristic of the coloniality of power.

Coloniality of Power and the Trans-American Imaginary

Quijano's notion of "coloniality of power" shows how despite the success of the nineteenth-century struggles for independence in Latin America, the forms of colonial domination (ethnic, racial and economic) continued to be reenacted within the frames of the newly formed nation-states. While classic imperial colonization normally refers to a wide-ranging, direct domination of territories by a central power, coloniality of power signals the more subtle domination deployed by the neo-colonial cultural hegemonists.[6] The ethno-racial hierarchies of colonialism are still reenacted despite the formal eradication of colonialism. Thus, coloniality can exist without a colonial administration or independence without decolonization (Latin America).[7] The importance Quijano places on

---

6 Aníbal Quijano, "'Raza', 'etnia' y 'nación' en Mariétegui: Cuestiones abiertas," in *Encuentro Internacional: José Carlos Mariátegui y Europa. El Otro Aspecto Del Descubrimiento* 167 (Empresa Editora Amauta S.A., 1992); "Colonialidad y modernidad/racionalidad," 13 *Perú Indígena* (no. 29) 11 (1993); "Modernity, Identity and Utopia in Latin America," 2 *Boundary* 140 (1992).

7 Quijano, *supra* note 6, "'Raza', 'etnia' y 'nación' en Mariétegui."

the cultural constructs of colonial history such as race and ethnicity show the impossibility of conceptualizing the material relations of domination alone; that is, without seeing their inscription in the social imaginary of domination: the images and words power deploys in the contested terrains of inequality. Coloniality is an axis of domination that is inscripted in, but distinct from, capitalist axes of exploitation. Coloniality and modernity are brainchildren of European expansion and colonization, leading to the invention of the Americas, Europe and Africa in a new geography of the world that privileges the West as the hegemonic social imaginary and trumpets the capitalist world system.[8]

The United States, as a site of settler colonization that achieved independence without decolonization, is deeply implicated in the histories of coloniality through the deployment of ethno-racial-sexual hierarchies that keep the others in their place despite the inclusive language of US liberalism. Latin America is one of the spaces of unfathomable otherness against which the United States reifies its own modernity and civilizatory progress. Thus, Latino identities in the United States are inscripted in long and complex histories of conquest and domination, dating to the invention of the Americas, and cannot be understood outside of historically situated social imaginaries of coloniality.[9]

Latinos are different from other waves of European immigrants to the United States. For one, Chicanos and Puerto Ricans have been directly "colonized, discriminated against and torn between a discourse of assimilation and citizenship and the realities of racial discrimination and poverty."[10] Second, the resentment of those affected by US interventions in Latin America has led to resistance to assimilation. Rather than moving inexorably toward assimilation, the Latino diaspora in this time of globalization exists in:

> a contrapuntual dwelling in/of modernity, where the homeland is not simply left behind but enters into multidirectional processes and configurations ... [Latinos are] inhabiting simultaneously and/or alternatively many cultural and political spaces of political and cultural articulation. This plurality of identification (as opposed to stable identities) moves back and forth between the national and the transnational.[11]

---

8 Quijano, *supra* note 6, "Modernity, Identity and Utopia in Latin America"; Walter Mignolo, *Local Histories, Global Designs: Coloniality, Subaltern Knowledges and Border Thinking* (Princeton University Press, 2000).

9 Agustín Laó-Montes, "Mambo Montage: The Latinization of New York City," in *Mambo Montage: The Latinization of New York City* 1, 5–6 (edited by Agustín Laó Montes and Arlene Dávila, Columbia University Press, 2001).

10 Juan Poblete, "Introduction," in *Critical Latin American and Latino Studies* ix, xviii (edited by Juan Poblete, University of Minnesota Press, 2003) (citing Suzanne Oboler).

11 Ibid., at xx (following James Clifford and Edward Said).

In this sense, it can be said that Latinos are part of a trans-American imaginary, a cultural geography or chronotope inhabited by transnational people "whose lives intersect in complex ways with the heterogeneous meanings of the symbols of 'Americanness'."[12]

Lorena Bobbitt became an important figure in the contact zone of the trans-American imaginary that made visible the coloniality of the discourses and representations of Latinos in the United States. She simultaneously destabilized and reified the highly racialized/gendered political and cultural borders that articulate the modern colonial American imaginary.

Show Trials as Sites of Critique and Resistance

In litigation parties contest their competing stories "before a public tribunal whose decision is rooted in law, has the potential of being the final word on the parties' dispute, and serves as a binding or persuasive authority for future similar cases or controversies."[13] Despite the years of debate over the influence of politics, economics and ideology on judicial decision-making, the dominant and traditional view of law is that it is a value-neutral enterprise. Critical legal scholars, in contrast, embed the legal domain in an analysis of relations of domination and see the very appearance of legal neutrality as an effect of power. The law is no longer seen as a reflection of an objective truth divorced from cultural specificity, but rather is inscribed interactively in cultural processes.[14] In viewing a trial's cultural inscriptions, narrative analysis, performance studies and anthropology have proven to be germinal spaces to look at the forms and strategies of power articulated through legal proceedings.

Contextual legal studies move away from positivist and objective interpretations of the law in favor of a post-structural re-examining of how the law constitutes the social through the enactment of legal categories and premises that organize particular configurations of discourse to power. Post-structuralist debates on the discursive strategies that inscribe the interpretation of a text, irrespective of the intentions of its author, have made visible the ideological underpinnings of discourse and opened legal texts to narrative analyses. Language no longer is understood to represent reality, but rather language becomes constitutive of that very reality. The privileging of certain discourses at the expense of others and the

---

12   Paula Moya and Ramón Saldívar, "Fictions of the Trans-American Imaginary," 49 *MFS Modern Fiction Studies* 1, 16 (2003).

13   Anthony Amsterdam, Peggy Cooper Davis and Aderson Francois, *Nyu Lawyering Program Readings* 210–11 (2003).

14   Peggy Cooper Davis, "Contextual Legal Criticism: A Demonstration Exploring Hierarchy and 'Feminine' Style," 66 *NYU L. Rev.* 1635, 1640–43 (1991).

selective deployment of terms and solutions becomes relevant as parties contest "facts" by mobilizing competing interpretive frameworks.[15]

Performance theory goes beyond the common assumption that reality is a social construction by recognizing that "our lives are structured according to repeated and socially sanctioned modes of behavior" and thus raising "the possibility that all human activity could potentially be considered as 'performance', or at least all activity carried out with a consciousness of itself."[16] Despite the "vantage of cultural practice" where "some actions will be deemed performances and others not," the performance principle can be applied "to all aspects of social and artistic life. Performance is no longer confined to the stage, to the arts, and to ritual. Performance is everywhere linked to the interdependence of power and knowledge."[17] Trials are particularly amenable to an analysis from the perspective of performance studies given their inherent dramatic structure.[18]

The structures of storytelling have been successfully applied to the analysis of legal spaces. Feigensen emphasizes the melodramatic conception of tort liability trials as narratives where: (1) individual agency is seen to cause an accident; (2) the individual's intrinsic character traits are the locus of causality for the accident; (3) the characters of the trial are divided between good and bad guys; (4) the focus of the trial is the suffering of the victim; and (5) good wins over evil at the trial.[19] Storytelling both shapes how we think and is a primary means through which breaches and violations become articulated legally. A narrative structure has emerged by looking at trials, namely, a steady state where norms prevail is destabilized by a breach that calls for some sort of action to either restore or transform the status quo.[20]

These forms of processual analysis clearly have a great debt with how anthropologist Victor Turner theorizes human experience as generally organized around "social dramas" or "processual units." Social dramas, trials included, represent sequences of publicly enacted events that are typically structured in four phases:

1. Breach phase as the violation of norms within a field of social relations.

---

15 Elisa Deener, *A Mediation Tale* 1, 2–3 (2004) (manuscript); Sara Cobb and Janet Rifkin, "Practice and Paradox: Deconstructing Neutrality in Mediation," 16 *Law & Soc. Inquiry* 35, 37–8 (1991).

16 Marvin Carlson, *Performance: A Critical Introduction* 4–5 (Routledge, 1996).

17 Richard Schechner, *Performance Studies – An Introduction* 30, 114 (Routledge, 2002).

18 Ibid., at 177.

19 Neal Feigenson, "Legal Meaning in the Age of Images: Accidents as Melodrama," 43 *N.Y.L. Sch. L. Rev.* 741, 745 (1999–2000).

20 Anthony Amsterdam and Jerome Bruner, *Minding the Law* 113–14 (Harvard University Press, 2000).

2. Crisis as the phase of mourning and escalation that can extend to become coextensive with a dominant cleavage unless it can be contained. This phase is when the real state of affairs is revealed.
3. Redressive phase as the attempt to limit the spread of the crisis through adjustive and redressive mechanisms by representative members of the social system.
4. Phase of reintegration or recognition of the schism.[21]

Trials as social dramas evince the narrative aspects of social expression and ritual moments of liminal transitions where norms are both suspended and revealed, opening a space for their re-entrenchment or transformation.

In her application of psychoanalytic literary theory to the analysis of trials, Shoshanna Felman deploys the concept of a cultural "abyss." An abyss inhabits us like an "internal hollowness" which resists awareness and cannot be seen. Trauma as abyss becomes an "accidented" space through which culture reveals itself as an unknowable gap.[22] The abyss cannot be totalized and thus cannot be contained in the closing argument of a trial. Law tries to bridge the bottomless abyss through legal rationalizations and codifications in an attempt to guard against the implacable irregularity and irrationality of the abyss. Although law tries to build a conscious foundation for the quintessentially unconscious and groundless abyss, the story of law and trauma is that of ships in the night doomed to the repetitive reenactment of the trauma, defying the closure sought by law. Thus, law is pre-destined to fail in its attempt to transform the traumatic abyss into undoubted facts.[23] In this way, the Nuremberg trial, *The Kreutzer Sonata* and the O.J. Simpson case become compulsive repetitions of the traumatic experiences of the Holocaust, sexism and/or racism.

Both Turner and Felman offer theoretical structures to understand conflict, but the first is informed by anthropological/cultural analysis and the second by the application of psychoanalysis to a collective societal unconscious. Since history for Felman becomes animated by an immanent unconscious that is unknowable and inaccessible, she can deny the interpretive agency of different actors within the social field and put the emphasis upon their incapacity to see rather than on the multiple interpretations, visibilities and representations surrounding any traumatic conflict. For instance, lawyers are not necessarily condemned to deny the existence of an underlying trauma through legal codifications, but can wield a certain amount of interpretive agency in how they maneuver within the rules and present the "facts."[24]

---

21   Victor Turner, "Social Dramas and Ritual Metaphors," in *Dramas, Fields and Metaphors* 23, 38–42 (Cornell University Press, 1974).

22   Shoshana Felman, *The Juridical Unconscious* 91 (Harvard University Press, 2002).

23   Ibid., at 95, 162.

24   Anthony Amsterdam and Randy Hertz, "An Analysis of Closing Arguments to a Jury," 37 *N.Y.L. Sch. L. Rev.* 55, 58 (1992).

Felman negates the multiple appropriations and struggles over meaning that are not reducible to modalities of blindness, instead of seeing them as creative engagements within broader fields of social conflict both within the legal arena and outside. In contrast, for Turner, visibility of the conflict is not precluded for social actors. The moment of crisis can actually be a moment of unmasking of the status quo (which if not as ultimate truth neither must it be as Felman's ultimate "unknowability"). In Turner there can also be resolution in certain scenarios of crisis whereas in Felman a traumatic abyss is inevitably condemned to repetitive legal reenactments. However, the Turner model can sacrifice the complexity of events that are compressed too strictly into the four-phase structure, and like Felman's it does not accommodate easily the problem of multiple appropriations and subject positionalities within a conflict, namely, how one person's breach can be another's redressive action. Turner has a pragmatic and teleologically linear approach to the abysmal moments of crisis, breaking it down into operational parts that enable social systems to function whereas Felman points to the larger-than-life unresolvable philosophical disfunctionalities and repetitive circularities of social traumas in social formations that, nevertheless, require decisions to be made. Both Felman and Turner offer theories to navigate the traumatic wounds of historical social imaginaries that can reemerge in different scenarios and often cannot be fathomed within the language and proportions of the law, on the one hand, or to conceptualize the structural moments of liminal shifts in, or reification of, the status quo, on the other.

The multiple rings of audiences invoked by a trial are crucial to understanding its engagement with the constitution of social imaginaries and the body politic. Criminal trials in particular are mandatory insofar they arise from a violation against a community and, as such, invoke the body politic at large that needs to be repaired by way of the law.[25] Criminal proceedings necessarily implicate "the people" as spectators of the historical process of establishing hegemonic interpretations of events perpetrated against a system.[26]

Although all trials are for show in that their function is to announce and enforce norms and show that the system is working, some trials are showier than others either because they involve, for instance, momentous historical events (Holocaust) or celebrities (O.J. Simpson and Michael Jackson). According to Felman, "[i]t would be safe to say that every major trial essentially involves 'something larger than law'. In every major trial, and certainly in every trial of political or of historical significance, something other than law is addressed in legal terms and is submitted to the narrowness of legal definitions."[27]

Contrary to ordinary trials where it is more difficult to make an indictment of historical traumas that lie under the surface of racial, sexual, class and colonial conflicts, show trials offer, despite Felman's cynicism toward legal procedures

---

25   Hannah Arendt, *Eichman in Jerusalem* 261 (Penguin Books, 1992).

26   Felman, *supra* note 23 at 81.

27   Ibid., at 65.

and codifications, the unique opportunity for political critique and struggle on broader social and political concerns. The openness and indeterminacy so crucial for the operations of the juridical discourse creates the conditions of possibility for the trial to become a site of critique and resistance. The challenge is to turn the trial into a critique of societal norms that generally remain unquestioned and invisible. The successful show trial legal strategy does not let the search for facts in the form of the literal gun in the face occlude the structural gun in the face. The lawyers can broaden the sphere of the "factual" by stretching its interpretive limits to metaphorically invoke society and normative "truths" as in the O.J. Simpson case where racism became a fact of the case rather than an opinion. A show trial can move the accusatory gaze from the usual suspects to society and law as the structural acts of violence, relocating the site of criminal monstrosity to a more complex scenario where criminal acts become symptoms rather than deviations from a state of order and harmony. The questions become whose order and for whom and who must pay the price for the harmony of some at the expense of others. Show trials are thus not necessarily doomed to be repetitive enactments of historical traumas, but can also be indictments of normality at a societal level, signaling, for instance, the immanence of racism or the bystander nation that becomes complicit with the legally sanctioned criminal acts of fascism as in the extraordinary show trial of Eichmann had revealed.[28]

Ordinary trials are premised upon the existence of a legitimate status quo that is then transgressed by an illegal act and the trial is a search for a legal remedy to re-establish the status quo. In a show trial it is the very status quo that is being tried and normality itself becomes (potentially) criminal. History and its specific normative values become the uncomfortable mirror where societal norms look unnatural and the seams of power are no longer hidden under a veil of universality and instead make a spectacle of themselves as contingent and historically entrenched. The successful show trial escapes the constraints of procedure and evidence to unravel the social imaginaries that underlie the everyday violences that articulate hegemonic forms of domination as social harmony.

Even an ordinary trial conducted under the rule of law such as the Lorena Bobbitt trial can be a show trial despite the lack of a deliberate political deployment of the trial by the parties or the government, marking a difference from the Rivonia trial or other trials discussed in this volume. Thus, even under democratic systems that operate under the rule of law, the trial can have a significant political dimension.[29]

Trials are skillfully enacted performances that hold an audience captive through stimulating highly emotive reactions, which in turn can chart "intensely fraught

---

28   "From the viewpoint of our legal institutions and of our moral standards of judgment this normality was much more terrifying than all the atrocities put together, for it implied ... that this new type of criminal, who is in fact hostis generis humani, commits his crimes under circumstances that make it well-nigh impossible for him to know or feel that he is doing wrong." Arendt, *supra* note 25 at 276.

29   I would like to thank Awol Kassim Allo for this observation.

dynamics of symbolic communication"[30] between lawyers, trial audiences and the contended spaces of societal imaginaries in moments of crisis marked by the transgression of norms. The lawyers of a show trial are in a multiple and conflicted bind of attempting to serve the interests of the client, manage the interpretive horizon of the courtroom proceedings and grapple with the political national and transnational arenas of resemantization of the events. Lawyers' narrative and strategic performative decisions can either entrench or undermine the dominant ideologies by how they engage with the pertinent cultural configurations that underlie the act as a violation of the social order.[31] The legal arena can thus be a stage for the reification of a truth whose historical contingency must be hidden under a mantle of neutrality and universality or for the unraveling of those norms via direct forms of confrontation or subversive complicities that can parody the dominant tropes from within.

Barbarity versus Catholicism: The Stories Lawyers Told

John Wayne Bobbitt, as the epitome of manhood with his iconic name evocative of American expansionism, and Lorena Bobbitt, as the "delicate" 95-pound Latina manicurist on a quest gone sour to achieve her American Dream were fertile grounds for varied appropriations by popular culture and the media. The secret materials and intimate details of the couple's lives revealed during the trial would be up for interpretive grabs both in the courtroom and in broader spectatorial circles surrounding the trial. This posed a challenge for the lawyers of the parties because inevitably they would have to privilege one narrative line at the expense of others according to their strategic legal decisions and within the procedural and substantive constraints of the law.

The prosecutors of Lorena portrayed John Wayne as the victim of his wife's "calculated and malicious act of revenge," claiming that "there is no justification … or excuse for taking the law into her own hands, for maiming her husband."[32] The prosecution stated that John Wayne did not remember having (forcible) sex with Lorena the night of the injury. In any event, in his view their marriage was a failure; he was planning to get divorced. The prosecution tried to keep the focus on the injury suffered by John Wayne as a result of the criminal act committed by Lorena.

After the testimony of several defense witnesses attesting to John Wayne's abuse of Lorena, the prosecution was forced to admit by the closing argument that there had been mutual violence in the relationship.[33] However, the prosecution used this recognition to reaffirm its narrative of a woman fully in charge of her

---

30   Sam Schrager, *The Trial Lawyer's Art* 13 (Temple University Press, 1999).

31   Ibid., at 14.

32   Transcript, *supra* note 4 at 432, 21.

33   Ibid., at 433.

own actions taking preposterously grievous steps of anger and revenge. The prosecution argued that Lorena full well knew what she was doing and was not temporarily insane or acting in the heat of passion. The prosecution framed its case as a conflict between civilization and barbarity, between law and chaos.[34]

In sharp contrast, the defense portrayed Lorena as a "young, petite, delicate and naive woman ... who for years, the evidence will show, suffered extreme brutality and violence perpetrated against her by the very person who, when she and he took their wedding vows, promised to protect and honor her."[35] The defense told a syncopated story of frequent "rape, beatings, kickings, punching, shoving, slapping, dragging, choking, and threats of more violence."[36] Lorena was said to come from a "very close-knit, traditional, strict Catholic household" from Ecuador (later Venezuela) and focused on "the cultural mores that Lorena grew up with, which place an emphasis on the woman's role in the family. [A] woman is considered the backbone of the family. And it is the woman, who is blamed if the marriage fails."[37]

The defense presented Lorena's story as a version of the American Dream. At the age of 18 Lorena came to America and lived with the Castro family, met John Wayne, and fell head over heels in love, and dated him for months. He showed no signs of violence. Lorena testified that she was "in love with him. To me he represented everything. That was the beginning of starting a family here in the U.S. And I feel that I wanted to have kids later on like a regular family. It was just like the beginning of my dream."[38] But the American Dream went sour during the first month when the "reign of terror in the marital home" begins, escalating in severity and frequency, both physical and verbal, over time.

The defense claimed that Lorena suffered from Battered Woman's Syndrome insofar as she "develop[ed] feelings of hopelessness and helplessness to the point where she believed that the situation she was in was such that she had nowhere to go; nowhere that she could be safe."[39] In addition, Lorena gives in to John Wayne's demands for her to have an abortion against her religious beliefs. She starts to

---

34 "This is a case about anger, it's a case about revenge, and it's a case about retribution. Her husband came home, he was drunk ... he wanted to have sex, she didn't, that's her right. He forced her to have sex, she was angry and retaliated against him. But, you know, folks, we don't live in a society that is governed by revenge. We don't live in a society in which whoever has the biggest knife wins. We live in a society of law and that's why you're here today.

And I will tell you this. This is not someone who was lost and adrift, innocent and naive in a foreign country. She had options and she knew about those options. She had a support system that was emotional, that was mental, that was physical, that was legal, that was religious." Ibid., at 444.

35 Ibid., at 21.
36 Ibid., at 22.
37 Ibid.
38 Ibid., at 154.
39 See ibid., at 24–8.

experience other medical problems and is diagnosed by expert witnesses as having major depression, Post Traumatic Stress Disorder and Panic Disorder at the time of the severance of John Wayne's penis, resulting from the years of marital abuse that led to an acute psychotic break. The defense portrayed Lorena as temporarily insane, so impaired by marital abuse that she had no capacity to control her (irresistible) impulse by emphasizing her terror of John Wayne's abusive behavior.

The opening statement of the defense culminates with the defense proposing that Lorena's life was "more valuable" than John Wayne's penis.[40] The question to be decided by the jury boils down to whether the jury would buy the prosecution's story of anger and calculated retaliation or the defense's story of insanity, self-defense, and irresistible impulse.

The defense's strategy was to reify Lorena, proving that she belonged to a timeless and unchanging culture locked in the mores of tradition, Catholicism, and family values. Lorena buttressed the defense's story by testifying that "mom and dad are like little kids, holding hands. There are a lot of love in my family. My brother and sister, we all, I would say together, like a regular, loving, Catholic family."[41] As part of her reification within this tradition-bound space, the defense portrays abortion as an act that goes against Lorena's nature, implying that John Wayne put her in the untenable position of having to choose between her husband and her child—between his selfish wish to get rid of a baby he did not want and her whole upbringing in a traditional Catholic family.[42]

Abortion becomes an unnatural imposition rather than a decision.[43] Given the feminist trope of "choice," this position of Lorena's is profoundly ironic. Deprived of her choice to not have an abortion, Lorena is forced to act against her own better "nature." This is a blow to her self-esteem that she never recovers from—at least not as long as she is married to John Wayne. In this vein, Lorena's testimony and defense make her into a poster child of conservative causes against divorce, abortion, non-traditional sex (anal), non-traditional families (wife as provider).[44] Lorena is the supplicant immigrant whose only desire is for a complete integration to the white dreams of a conservative assimilation.

The Battered Woman Syndrome defense is equally problematic. Years of abuse are said to lead to an entrenched sense of helplessness and psychiatric disorders

---

40   "And ladies and gentlemen, what we have is Lorena Bobbitt's life juxtaposed against John Wayne Bobbitt's penis. The evidence will show that in her mind it was his penis from which she could not escape, that caused her the most pain, the most fear and the most humiliation. And I submit to you, that at the end of this case you will come to one conclusion, and that is that a life is more valuable than a penis. Thank you." Ibid.

41   Ibid., at 150.

42   Ibid., at 24–5.

43   This explains why the pro-life movement appropriated Lorena's accounts as examples for their struggle. For instance, the website Lifenews.com states that Lorena's violence was not simply a result of domestic violence, but also of "post-traumatic stress from a forced abortion" (available at http://www.lifenews.com/nat277.html).

44   Transcript, *supra* note 4 at 88, 136–9, 151, 182.

such as major depression, Post Traumatic Stress Disorder and Panic Disorder. Although the purpose of the Battered Woman Syndrome defense is to bring social and structural considerations into the analysis of the plight of battered women, it relies heavily on the pathologization of women by linking their behavior to internal dispositional traits.[45] The Battered Woman Syndrome argument has an untenable explanatory tension between the structural social argument of abuse and the individualization of responsibility on the basis of internal traits. On the one hand, the Battered Woman Syndrome wants to signal the systemic causes of the plight of battered women and, on the other hand, it obscures the very systemic analysis it puts forward by personalizing causality based on the intrinsic weaknesses of the battered woman. A problematic and pathologizing individualism seeps into the analysis of structural and systemic problems of violence in intimate relationships.

The limitations of the Battered Woman Syndrome defense are compounded with cultural and racial reifications in the cases of non-white women. Lorena's culture, where women are the "backbone of the family" and bear the burden of its success, is the real backbone of the defense's argument of Lorena's implacable helplessness. As Lorena states, divorce is "a humiliation situation; it is a shame. I would feel embarrassed."[46] The most disturbing moment of the defense is when Dr. Susan Feister, as the expert psychiatrist for the defense, states that due to the uniqueness of Lorena's act, she felt the need to do an additional psychological profile test.[47]

The clear implication of Dr. Feister's statements is that only a "dumb"' and culturally rigid person would resort to cutting off a penis after years of abuse and rape. The attempt was made by the defense to show that Lorena's act was not the typical action taken by women suffering the effects of the Battered Woman

---

45   Jean Filetti, "From Lizzie Borden to Lorena Bobbitt: Violent Women and Gendered Justice," *Journal of American Studies*, 35, 3, 471, 476 (2001). "[B]y causally linking the violence perpetrated by the women to 'internal, dispositional traits rather than to situational factors', 'Battered Woman Syndrome' defenses ensure that the environmental factors that effect violence go unexamined." Ibid., at 480.

46   Transcript, *supra* note 4 at 151.

47   "Because this was such an unusual situation – cutting off a penis – I felt that in addition to the extensive clinical interview I felt that it was important to obtain some psychological testing to see if there were other psychological factors that might be present that would confirm my view or disconfirm my views. [...] The psychological testing showed that Lorena had a borderline normal intelligence level – on the low end of normal. And that was even after the score was recalculated to take into consideration the fact that because of her Spanish background, she might have difficulty with some of the language parts of the intelligence test. [The] test showed that Lorena was a person who used very rigid kinds of defenses and rigid ways of coping and that under situations of extreme emotion or extreme stress that her normal reasoning process would break down and the kind of rational thinking changed. At those times, she actually had what would be considered psychotic-like aspects to her thinking or aspects to her thinking that would almost suggest a break with reality." Ibid., at 344–5.

Syndrome. Despite the efforts to take "into consideration the fact … of her Spanish background," the defense ultimately reifies and racializes Lorena by inscribing her in a cultural space of stupidity, backwardness and psychotic irrationality. Lorena's infantilization as a "woman who was young, almost child-like in terms of her lack of life experiences"[48] invites a paternalistic gaze to protect her pathologized vulnerability and completely obscures the complex agency of her actions.

In contrast to the defense's overarching portrayal of Lorena's culture as Catholic and traditional, the prosecution reifies Lorena as belonging to a culture of lawlessness, barbarity and chaos where the "biggest knife wins."[49] Lorena's sexual drive and seductive powers are emphasized. John Wayne claims not only to never have raped Lorena, but also to have been a victim of her sexual drive when he was too exhausted to perform. Lorena, who "customarily" dressed in "silk lingerie," was purportedly making demands that John Wayne, exhausted as he was, still had to "perform" for her on that infamous night.[50]

According to the prosecution, Lorena is a woman with a mission: pleasure me or pay the price. It's not merely revenge because he is a wayward husband that spends nights out on the town, but revenge for his incapacity to perform sexually. Lorena becomes a woman of sexual excess and deviancy that knows no bounds in the search to quench her primitive needs.[51] Whereas the prosecution reifies Lorena as belonging to a culture of lawlessness and barbarity, the defense portrays Lorena as belonging to a timeless and unchanging culture locked in the mores of tradition, Catholicism and family values. Whether Lorena belongs either to a cultural monolith of stagnation or a cultural monolith of chaos, the fact remains that for both she is embedded in a space of backwardness and fixity that drives her toward symptomatic acts of violence, according to the prosecution, or from which she can only break away by psychotic ruptures of excess and irrationality, according to the defense. Both the prosecution and the defense reenact tropes of the modern colonial social imaginary in their representation of Lorena's pathological cultural inscriptions.

The breach for the prosecution was the "fatal" cut while for the defense it was the relationship of marital abuse; the crisis for the prosecution was the social lawlessness left in the wake of Lorena's actions while for the defense the crisis was the pathologized emotional state of Lorena at the hands of her abusive husband. By finding Lorena not guilty by reason of insanity, the redressive action of the trial vindicates Lorena legally. Perversely, however, despite the legal success of

---

48   Ibid., at 345.

49   Ibid., at 444.

50   Ibid., at 88–90.

51   Moreover, since Lorena embezzled money from her employer and shoplifted dresses from department stores, ibid., at 249–50, crime is purported to be within the purview of her calculated decision-making processes. In contrast, the defense portrays Lorena's embezzlement of her employer and stealing as acts of desperation to pay the mortgage on the household without the financial support of her husband. Ibid.

her team, Lorena's defense was also a betrayal in its complicity with the racist assumptions of the prosecution and the racist society at large.

In the battle between life and penis, life may have won the legal battle, but the imperial gaze won the symbolic battle that keeps its others in its phallic-dominant, pathologized and racialized space. There is an indictment of gender violence, but it is an ambivalent indictment insofar as it is at the expense of pathologizing Lorena and reifying a modern colonial imaginary that recolonizes Lorena. In this sense, the trial marks a moment of hegemonic ideological reintegration given the problematic (neo)colonial reinscriptions of the Battered Woman Syndrome argument. The defense effectively keeps Lorena out of prison but at the expense of reifying entrenched cultural tropes of racism and sexism.

Irrespective of the agency of the defendant and whether the defense team as a whole understood the broader social, cultural and political implications beyond the narrow interest of legality in a criminal trial, namely, the determination of guilt or innocence, the question and crux of the matter remains: Could the defense have won its case without relying on said racist and sexist stereotypes? Lorena as an unskilled immigrant worker with no history of political activism, who expressed guilt and regret for her actions, garnered lukewarm support, and usually condemnation, from intellectual (feminist) elites in the United States. The ranks of her supporters who acquired media visibility did not include many legitimate figures, but rather stayed within the confines of popular reactions that often seemed seedy and beyond the pale.[52] Given the absence of legitimate outside pressure, could Lorena's lawyers have articulated a story that did not pathologize her within the constraints of the law and been as effective in setting her free? Maybe not, but I think it is important to note how the legal choices of the defense's narrative participate or not in the ideological prejudices that underpin a trial.

I do not mean to underestimate the importance of Lorena's walking out of the courtroom a free woman, but rather to signal how the strategies, categories and narratives deployed by the defense and prosecution replicated legally the abuse she had withstood from her husband.

Many popular appropriations of the Lorena saga also reinforced entrenched assumptions regarding race and Latinas. An analysis of the humor and jokes that emerged around the Lorena saga reveals that John Wayne's race was never mentioned, thus reinforcing whiteness as the unstated norm of American society. Commentary on Lorena, however, did make reference to her Latin heritage. "In some jokes Lorena, and by inference all Latinas, was portrayed as emotional, irrational, unpredictable, inept, or stupid. Camille Paglia, an influential dissident

---

52   Linda Pershing, "'His Wife Seized His Prize and Cut it to Size': Folk and Popular Commentary on Lorena Bobbitt," 8 *NWSA Journal* 1, 16 (1996). Moreover, when there was support, it tended to be along the lines of victimization. Ehrenreich saw Lorena as "one more martyr in women's long weepy history of rape and abuse." Melissa Deem, "From Bobbitt to SCUM: Re-memberment, Scatological Rhetorics, and Feminist Strategies in the Contemporary U.S.," 8 *Public Culture* 511, 517 (1996).

feminist at the time, called her 'a Latin fire-cracker', while members of the general public satirized her linguistic heritage."[53] The media focused on the couple, first, in terms of gender and, second, in terms of ethnicity and race at the expense of class commentary because it is so "often avoided, naturalized, or otherwise rendered invisible in US culture. The media ... had little to say about the pressures that Lorena and John faced as working-class people who fought with one another about their limited financial resources, rather than questioning the larger economic system."[54]

The resemantizations of Lorena as either a woman with an insatiable sexual appetite or as a devout Catholic mark what Aparicio and Chavez-Silverman call hegemonic "tropicalizations" whereby Latino symbols or cultural productions are mainstreamed within "more normative and dominant values that make them attractive to a dominant American public whose reception reaffirms its dominance over minority cultures ... This whole gamut of themes suggests cultural integration yet also transforms them into objects of consumption rather than social and cultural practices."[55]

Media representations of Latina women are inscribed in hegemonic interests that gather full force when they are furthest from complex and nuanced cultural representations, that is, when they are rehashing overused and stereotypical performances of oversexualization that are distinct from that of Native and African Americans.[56] A case in point is the film *Colors* where the Latina character sways between the familiar stereotypes of the sexually modest good girl and the promiscuous slut in perpetual heat.[57] The prosecution's position in the Bobbitt trial tried to preclude the possibility of rape through the deployment of precisely the trope of the Latina in perpetual heat for white men as implicitly opposed to the

---

53   Pershing, *supra* note 52 at 5.

54   Ibid., at 7–8.

55   Frances Aparicio (interviewed by Juan Zevallos Aguilar), "Latino Cultural Studies," in *Critical Latin American and Latino Studies* 3, 25 (edited by Juan Poblete, University of Minnesota Press, 2003). "Many oppositional cultural practices are tropicalized in this way. Hegemonic tropicalization gives way to a discourse that delineates the Latino as an exotic and primitive other, the dominant society's object of desire. These discourses continue unabated in tourism, education, cinema, music and literature." Ibid., at 29.

56   Catherine Benamou, "Those Earrings, That Accent, That Hair: A Dialogue with Maria Hinojosa on Latinos/as and the Media," in *Talking Visions: Multicultural Feminism in a Transnational Age* 325, 326 (edited by Ella Shohat, New Museum of Contemporary Art & MIT, 1998).

57   Kimberly Crenshaw, "Beyond Racism and Misogyny: Black Feminism and 2 Live Crew," in *Feminist Social Thought: A Reader* 245, 251 (edited by Diana Tietjens Meyers, Routledge, 1997).

trope of the virginal white woman.[58] Latinas represent a cultural threat and invoke a sense of criminality through erotic suggestion and sexual aggressiveness.[59]

Lorena's sexuality and desire are dangerously polyvalent cultural expressions that had to be resemanticized in a way that domesticated their implications, maintaining hegemonic control over the potential excesses of the meanings of Lorena's cut and obscuring its questioning of racial and colonial histories of domination. Lorena's body became a gendered colonial metaphor in need of hegemonic regulation of her desires. Lorena thus evokes the relation between contemporary body politics and the history of the imperial gaze. The "tropicalization" of Lorena during the trial becomes a play on the "authenticity" of the indigenous. It opened the Pandora's box of America's colonial obsessions, becoming more about America's cultural projections regarding its Latina others than a "realist" document of the other. The trial thus inadvertently mirrored America's own racisms without being aware of it.

The Kindest Cut of All

One of the more disturbing "tropicalizations" of Lorena after the trial was reported in the *Washington Post*. Five months after restarting her work as a manicurist at a salon in Virginia she has been swamped with clients – many of them men.

> Her employer, who has seen business increase since Lorena Bobbitt came aboard, was happy to oblige [with being interviewed]. 'When people come in, they specifically say they want Lorena to do their nails … The poor thing doesn't get a break.'
>
> Since Bobbitt joined Illusions, Wheeler [the owner] said, curiosity about her has attracted many new clients, particularly men, who buy each other gift certificates for a session with the local celebrity.[60]

This was the ultimate sexual fantasy of racial and sexual submission. From the "unkindest cut of all,"[61] as reported after Lorena cut John Wayne's penis, to the kindest cut of all, from the sharp knife that severs to the careful scissors that groom, from bite to bark, Lorena's cutting utensils were honed to pleasure men who exchanged gift certificates to be polished by the most "dangerous"

---

58   Ella Shohat, "Introduction," in *Talking Visions: Multicultural Feminism in a Transnational Age* 1, 23 (edited by Ella Shohat, New Museum of Contemporary Art & MIT, 1998).

59   María Hinojosa in Benamou, *supra* note 56 at 339.

60   Leef Smith, "Lorena Bobbitt: A Favorite Among Men in Salon Set," *The Washington Post*, May 15, 1995, at D03.

61   *Supra* note 2.

woman on the planet. Lorena's cut was no longer with a knife that severed male authority, but with grooming scissors that reinstated male supremacy in a fantasy of gratified submission.

Chapter 15

Spectacular Justice: Aesthetics and Power in the Gandhi Murder Trial

Kanika Sharma

On 30 January 1948, as Mohandas Karamchand Gandhi walked towards his daily public prayer meeting in New Delhi a man suddenly blocked his path. Facing Gandhi, Nathuram Vinayak Godse bowed with folded hands, said 'Namaste, Bapu [Greetings, Father]', and then fired three shots at point blank range.

The conspiracy to kill Gandhi had begun to take shape in December 1947. At its core were Nathuram Godse and Narayan Dattatreya Apte. These two, close friends and colleagues, had started a newspaper titled *Agrani* to further the cause of two right-wing Hindu organisations – the Hindu Mahababha and the Hindu Rashtra Dal, of which they were members. The men firmly believed in a united India and were vociferously against the partition of the country, the blame for which they attributed to the Indian state in general and to Gandhi in particular. What began as a series of half-baked conspiracies ranging from destroying the Indian Parliament, to firing mortars at Pakistani Cabinet meetings, to attacking Gandhi, Jawaharlal Nehru, and H.S. Suhrawardy,[1] finally concretised into the plan to assassinate Gandhi.

Godse was caught on the spot, and nine of the other 12 accused were rounded up within the next month. The last three accused were never apprehended, and one of the accused turned King's evidence. The trial *R* v. *Nathuram V. Godse and the other accused* became the first spectacular trial to be held in independent India and unfolded at the suitably grand location of the Red Fort in Delhi. In the words of Tapan Ghosh, in 1948 this trial was 'the longest and costliest murder trial this ancient subcontinent ha[d] ever known, the trial for the murder of its First Citizen was itself a historical event'.[2]

The trial began on 27 May 1948; it was a Special Court held under the aegis of a single judge, Judge Atmacharan. The case was made against the 12 accused under 11 different categories of charges of the Indian Penal Code and the Indian Arms Act 1878. After almost 10 months – during which 149 prosecution witnesses testified, and reams of evidence were collected – the judge delivered his sentence on 10 February 1949. Godse and Apte were sentenced to death. V.D. Savarkar,

---

1 A popular Muslim political leader from Bengal, and later the fifth prime minister of Pakistan.

2 Tapan Ghosh, *The Gandhi Murder Trial* (Bombay: Asia Publishing House, 1974), vii.

Accused No. 7, a prominent Hindu nationalist leader, was acquitted and the rest of the conspirators got life imprisonment.

Under the rules of the Special Court, the accused had the right to appeal to the High Court within three weeks. The appeal was heard at the Punjab High Court held in Shimla. If the first trial was held at a national monument in Delhi, for the second, an iconographic building in Shimla was pressed into action. The appeal court was held at Peterhoff, the Viceregal Residence in Shimla, and was presided over by three judges, Justices Achchruram, A.N. Bhandari and G.D. Khosla. This trial largely upheld the verdict of the Special Court, but they acquitted two of the defendants, Shankar Kistayya and Dr D.S. Parchure.

Before beginning an analysis of the trial, it is important to briefly explore the categories of the political trial and the spectacular trial. This chapter is premised on the belief that the oft posited binary between law and politics reduces the term 'political trial' to a pejorative marker of the trial; and thus acts an obstacle against using the term as an analytical tool that helps us to understand the intersection between law and politics. The Gandhi Murder Trial can only be understood if we keep in mind the politics of the time. As Judith Shklar asserts, 'A trial, the supreme legalistic act, like all political acts, does not take place in a vacuum. It is part of a whole complex of other institutions, habits, and beliefs'.[3]

In an attempt to reclaim the term, I define political trials as trials that are orchestrated by the state against those who not only challenge a particular law of the state, but rather seek to undermine its very existence. In his seminal work on political trials, Otto Kircheimer identified three different types of political trials, and we find that the Gandhi Murder Trial fits firmly in the first category. This category focuses on the type of political trials that result from a common crime committed for political purposes. At first glance this looks like a trial whose political nature is determined by the defendant and not the prosecution; however Kircheimer qualifies this definition by including that such trials 'are conducted with a view to the political benefits which might ultimately accrue from successful prosecution'.[4] Such trials are usually given their political overtones by the state which seeks to use trials of corruption, murder or other criminal offences for the purposes of mud-raking and discrediting its political foes. Often in these cases the state resorts to the use of conspiracy theories, where the crime committed is sought to be linked to a larger conspiracy that is portrayed as a threat to the state.

An important dimension of every political trial is its spectacular nature, how it impresses upon the audience the authority of the state, even at the moment when this authority is at its lowest. Mark Findlay argues that political trials are an example of the 'use of legal institutions to bolster state authority, where that very authority which normally legitimises such legal institutions is itself widely

---

3   Judith Shklar, *Legalism: Law, Morals and Political Trials* (Cambridge, MA: Harvard University Press, 1986), 144.

4   Otto Kirchheimer, *Political Justice: The Use of Legal Procedure for Political Ends* (Princeton: Princeton University Press, 1961), 46.

condemned'.[5] The authority of these legal institutions is bolstered through trials that take the form of spectacular events – they are always created with the spectator in mind. Thus, I will employ the category of the spectacular trial to analyse the Gandhi Murder Trial.

This chapter will focus on the spectacular dimension of the political trial, and seeks to examine the visual tropes of power utilised during such trials. I begin by discussing the importance of spectacular events and images to law, arguing that they do not obscure law, rather they are an integral component of establishing law. I then seek to analyse the aesthetics of the building used to hold the trials and the way rituals were employed to visualise authority within the courtroom during the Gandhi Murder Trial.

Lastly, I argue that while the trial spectacle may be orchestrated by the state it always has some room for subversion. Political defendants are aware of the publicity that the spectacular trial may provide for them and their cause, and thus actively seek to use the trial process to undermine the legitimacy that the state seeks to create for itself. In the Gandhi Murder Trial we discuss how Godse and Savarkar attempted to subvert the spectacular trial.

Importance of the Visual within the Trial

Law has always enjoyed a peculiar relation with the ornamental and with spectacular images. During the colonial period, proponents of a codified positive law in India, such as T.B. Macaulay and William Bentinck, sought to replace the 'corrupt and barbaric native system' with the Western style rule of law, 'which would be efficient rather than ornamental'.[6] Here, we find an attempt to posit law in opposition to the ornamental; the latter is believed to distract the subject from law and hence reduce law's power and efficiency. In contrast to this, I argue that the spectacular is an inextricable part of the law – it is evident in the everyday process of law and is especially magnified in spectacular trials.

As Peter Goodrich asserts, the ceremonial is not merely ornamental or hedonistic; ceremonies of law do not merely accentuate law, they create and help to establish it. The ceremonial gives 'credence to law, and effect to rule',[7] it marks out a prior space of social approbation within which law can be displayed and enacted. The spectacular trial, then, becomes a tool that is established by law and yet in turn establishes law itself.

---

5   Mark Findlay, 'Show Trials in China: After Tiananmen Square', *Journal of Law and Society* 16 (1989): 353.

6   David Cannadine, Ornamentalism: *How the British Saw Their Empire* (London: Penguin Books, 2002), 22.

7   Peter Goodrich, 'A Theory of the Nomogram', in *Law, Text, Terror: Essays for Pierre Legendre*, edited by Peter Goodrich, Lior Barshack and Anton Schütz (London: Glass House Press, 2006), 17–18.

While discussing the Gandhi Murder Trial as a spectacular trial, three dimensions of the word spectacle are of importance for us: it is a specially prepared or arranged public display; it presents something of a striking or unusual character; and it acts as an illustrative instance or example. Therefore, the visualness of an event is key to designating it a spectacle. What then is the relationship between the spectacle and the images it employs?

Lawrence Bryant asserts that:

> As [a] historical object, a spectacle must be twice constructed: first as a series of performances, and then as a historical event. We cannot disassociate the performances from the 'historical event' of which they are a component part; spectacles cannot be taken as transparent and unproblematic descriptions of historical events.[8]

This becomes crucial to the understanding of the political trial as spectacle. The images deployed by law, the location of the court and all that occurs within the courtroom is part of the performance of the spectacle; this performance cannot be separated from the larger trial event. The decision to try the defendants, the charges laid against them, the judgment made, and how all of these are affected by and, in turn, affect the outside world are part of the 'historical event' of the trial. These two aspects come together to form the spectacle that seeks to influence the minds of the public.

The spectacle is designed to imprint an event on public memory, to assert legitimacy and therefore reinforce authority, and most importantly function as a propaganda exercise; while the form of the spectacle may have changed with the modern state, the essence of the spectacle has not. However, the relation between spectacle, state and power is not fixed or constant; at different times states can make use of the spectacle for various purposes. The role of the spectacle can range from magnifying the appearance of power – and thus increasing it – to merely reaffirming the presence of a particular form of power in society.

Thus, we see that law enjoys a close relation with spectacular events and images. They help law to establish itself and to create 'historic events'. Importantly, such images do not simply display the power that the state has; they also help to actuate it. In the case of the Gandhi Murder Trial, the creation of the spectacle is based upon earlier image-creating exercises of the state by the use of the Red Fort.

---

8   Lawrence Bryant, 'Configurations of the Community in Late Medieval Spectacles: Paris and London during the Dual Monarchy', in *City and Spectacle in Medieval Europe*, edited by Barbara Hanawalt and Kathryn Reyerson (Minneapolis and London: University of Minnesota Press, 1994), 8.

The Use of the Red Fort

As the political trial attempts to impress upon its audience the power and legitimacy of the state, it utilises various symbols of power available to it. Large imposing spaces or monuments, such as grand palaces, court buildings and public squares, are often utilised for such displays because they speak to 'law's architectural ambitions'.[9] The use of such impressive edifices marks out a ceremonial space for the trial, the grand display awes the subject with the power that the state has at its disposal, and may also provide the state with a link to the previous historical event that had taken place at the location.

Holding the Gandhi Murder Trial at the historic Red Fort allowed the Indian state to establish two important ideological constructs: first, it sought to stress the continuity between the various states that had ruled over India in the recent past – the Mughal Empire and the British Raj – by using the same architectural symbol of power that had been used by these states. In doing so, the newly independent Indian state also sought to underscore the legitimacy of its succession. Second, the use of the Red Fort helped to highlight the secular credentials of the state, as it sought to posit Gandhi's assassin as a communalist. The palace built by a Muslim King, and later utilised by the Christian ruling class, stood as a symbol of syncretic India, devoid of any religious overtones.

Guaranteeing the Continuity of the State

The Red Fort has witnessed three of the most spectacular trials in India. The first trial held at the Red Fort was staged by the colonial state in India in 1858. The Qila-i-Mubarak (The Blessed Fort) was built by Shah Jahan (also known for the Taj Mahal) in 1648, its red sandstone walls lending themselves to its name as the Lal Qila or the Red Fort. The Fort served as the Mughal Palace until the last Mughal king, Bahadur Shah Zafar, was captured in Delhi during the first large-scale armed revolt against the British Forces, i.e., the Indian Mutiny of 1857. Despite the presence of British courthouses in Delhi and the presence of large government houses in Calcutta (now Kolkata) and Madras (now Chennai) – both towns unaffected by the Mutiny – the British state chose to hold the trial of the last Mughal King in his own palace situated in rebellion ravaged Delhi.

Pramod Nayar refers to this trial as 'a carefully plotted spatial "event"', where there was a re-appropriation and transformation of space itself.[10] One such attempted transformation was the bid to uncouple the image of the Fort from the idea of the Mughal Empire, and instead make it serve as an image of the Indian state. This uncoupling was in keeping with the wider British policy of portraying

---

9   Linda Mulcahy, *Legal Architecture: Justice, Due Process and the Place of Law* (Abingdon: Routledge, 2011), 5.

10   Pramod Nayar, introduction to *The Trial of Bahadur Shah Zafar*, edited by Pramod Nayar (Hyderabad: Orient Longman, 2007), xxi, xxxiv.

themselves as natural successors to the Mughals.[11] The Red Fort provided the colonial empire with a link to the Indian past and a tool to legitimise their presence in the subcontinent. In addition to this, the trial was able to portray the dominance of the new Empire. Clifford Geertz argues that rulers take possession of their realms through ceremonial forms, 'In particular, royal progresses locate the society's centre and affirm its connection with transcendent things by stamping a territory with ritual signs of dominance'.[12] This is precisely what the British sought to achieve by trying the king in his own palace: they established in the eyes of the Indian population that they now ruled the country and made its laws. After the trial of Bahadur Shah Zafar, the British Forces systemically reduced the power of the Fort until it remained a shadow of its former self; the Fort itself had been designated the Military Police Headquarters.

The British faced the second significant armed threat against their authority in India from the Indian National Army (INA). This army mostly consisted of the Indian soldiers taken hostage by the Axis powers in Malaya during the Second World War. Helped by the Japanese, the INA fought against the British Army on the eastern frontiers of India in 1944–5, but eventually lost and most of its members were captured. The Red Fort featured heavily in the INA imagination; its slogan was 'On to Delhi', and its monthly propaganda magazine published under the same name carried above the masthead the picture of the Indian flag in the foreground and the Red Fort in the background. The aim of the INA was to capture the Red Fort and rid it of the British Forces. On 5 July 1943, the leader of the INA Subhas Chandra Bose announced in Singapore, '[O]ur task will not end until our surviving heroes hold the victory parade on another graveyard of the British Empire – the Lal Qila, or "Red Fortress", of ancient Delhi'.[13]

The only reason why the senior INA leaders were able to reach the Red Fort was because, in their desire to mock the INA for its ambitions towards the Fort, the British decided to try the INA leaders on its premises. Jawaharlal Nehru, who was later to become the first prime minister of India, was a part of the Defence Counsel during the INA trial. He wrote:

> Every stone in that historic setting tells a story and revives a memory of long ago. Ghosts of the past, ghosts of the Moghuls [*sic*], of Shah Jahan, of Bahadur Shah, proud cavaliers pass by on prancing horses, processions wend their way.

---

11   Thomas Metcalf, *An Imperial Vision: Indian Architecture and Britain's Raj* (Berkeley and London: University of California Press, 1992), 56.

12   Clifford Geertz, 'Centers, Kings, and Charisma: Reflections on the Symbolics of Power', in *Rites of Power: Symbolism, Ritual, and Politics Since the Middle Ages*, edited by Sean Wilentz (Philadelphia: University of Philadelphia Press, 1985), 16.

13   Quoted by Sugata Bose, *His Majesty's Opponent: Subhas Chandra Bose and India's Struggle Against Empire* (Cambridge, MA and London: Harvard University Press, 2011), 4.

You hear the tramp of armed men, and the tinkling of silver bells on women's feet ... There was a hum of life and activity, for this was the hub of a vast and rich empire.[14]

As is evident by this statement, the participants at the INA trial, who soon became leaders of independent India, were clearly aware of the previous trial held at the same arena. Once again, we find a stress on the continuity of the state through the trope of the Red Fort.

This symbolism of the Red Fort was carried forward, and even strengthened, in independent India. On the day after Independence, and on every Independence Day since then, the prime minister of India has addressed the nation from the ramparts of the Fort. As Bernard Cohn notes:

The end of the empire was marked where it might be said to have begun, in 1857, with the desacrilization [*sic*] of the Mughal's palace, with English officers drinking wine and eating pork. The moment of transfer of authority from the viceroy to the new prime minister of an independent India was marked at the Red Fort by the lowering of the Union Jack at midnight, 14 August 1947, before a huge crowd of jubilant Indians.[15]

By the mid-twentieth century, the Red Fort had been accepted as a symbol not only of Delhi, but of India at large. The new prime minister, Nehru, was very aware of the power that the Red Fort had as an icon for all Indians, and he sought to transform the Red Fort from a national icon to an icon of a particular brand of civic nationalism. In a circular to all governors in March 1948, Nehru urged them to direct all cinema houses to put up a picture of the Indian flag at the end of the performance rather than to play what they considered the national anthem.[16] However, not just any picture of the Indian flag could be used; Nehru had specifically arranged to supply them with a 'good picture of the National Flag on the Red Fort in Delhi'.[17] According to Partha Chatterjee, this particular image elevates the Red Fort to abstract ideality by keeping the illustration clear of any

---

14   Jawaharlal Nehru, foreword to *Two Historic Trials in Red Fort*, edited by Moti Ram (New Delhi: Moti Ram, 1946), iii–iv.

15   Bernard Cohn, 'Representing Authority in Victorian India', in *The Invention of Tradition*, edited by Eric Hobsbawm and Terence Ranger (Cambridge: Cambridge University Press, 2003), 209.

16   The Jana Gana Mana was adopted as the provisional national anthem only in August 1948, and was declared the National Anthem of India in January 1950.

17   Circular to all Governors, 7 March 1948, *Selected Works of Jawaharlal Nehru* (hereafter *SWJN*), 2nd Series, Vol. 5 (New Delhi: Jawaharlal Nehru Memorial Fund, 1984), 456.

elements except the bare façade of the Fort and the national flag flying from an impossibly high flagstaff, thereby producing a 'sacred iconicity of the monument'.[18]

The iconicity of the Red Fort was such that there was a belief that to raise your flag over the Red Fort was to raise your flag over all of India. In fact the Hindu nationalist organisations frequently accused supporters of Pakistan of attempting to capture the Red Fort and thus proclaim their domination over India. Press reports of the time claimed that the Rashtriya Swayamsevak Sangh (RSS) was able to prevent the Muslim Leaguers' intended coup to kill government officials and thousands of Hindus and 'plant the flag of Pakistan on the Red Fort and then seize all Hind'.[19] Though Nehru rubbished these claims, the incident proves the iconic reverence that the Red Fort demanded not just in Delhi, but all over India. In the national imagination, to control the Fort and to have your flag fly atop its ramparts was a symbol of control over the entire nation.

During the Gandhi Murder Trial the courtroom was a 100' × 23' room, situated on the first floor of a newly constructed building within the Fort. The building, erected as a military barrack by the British, reflected the symbolic nature of the laws; an inherently British structure contained within an outwardly Indian façade. The timing of the Gandhi Murder Trial placed it firmly at the juncture of colonial and post-colonial law. The trial was held by the Indian state, yet it was held in the name of the king of England, 'the Rex' who finds mention in the very title of the case itself. Thus the case remained an ostensibly Indian case, and yet at its core were British laws and the king of England.

Unlike the first two trials where the Red Fort was in fact in some way linked to the history of the case, in the Gandhi Murder Trial the Palace held no apparent symbolism for the case itself. Indeed, the symbolism of the Fort was established by the actions of the state. Here, the Fort stood as a symbol of the Indian state, and was used to highlight the legitimacy of the new state's succession to power, and to underscore its authority during its first period of crisis.

Not just the Indian government, the Indian media too was very aware of the symbolism of the building and highlighted it in its coverage of the trial. For instance *The Tribune* wrote: 'Fate had destined Delhi's historic Red Fort to be the venue of a trial of Indians charged with the assassination or conspiracy to assassinate the Father of the Nation soon after India attained independence.'[20] In fact, we find that the Red Fort became inseparable from the identity of the trial itself. In daily news reports the trial was alternately referred to as the Gandhi Murder Trial or the Red Fort Trial and headlines such as these were common: 'Examination of Shankar

---

18   Partha Chatterjee, 'The Sacred Circulation of National Images', in *Traces of India: Photography, Architecture, and the Politics of Representation, 1850–1900*, edited by Maria Pelizzari (Montreal: Canadian Centre for Architecture, 2003), 287.

19   Quoted in Nehru's letter to Bhagavan Das, 10 November 1948, *SWJN*, 2nd Series, Vol. 8, 121.

20   'Gandhi Murder Trial Opens in Red Fort', *The Tribune*, 28 May 1948.

in Red Fort Trial',[21] 'Arguments in Red Fort Trial Begin'.[22] By stressing on the importance of the Red Fort, these headlines reveal the prevailing view of the time; that this assassination was not simply an attack on a citizen of the state, rather it was an attack on the state itself.

The Question of Secularism

Gandhi had been assassinated by men who had all met each other through various Hindu nationalist organisations. During the trial, they always maintained that they were secular individuals who believed that each Indian should have equal rights, with no concessions for caste or religion. On the other hand, the Indian state accused them of being Hindu nationalists, who sought to establish a Hindu majoritarian state in the garb of democracy. In the wake of the partition of the country, and the subsequent communal riots, the Indian state sought to establish itself as a secular entity and not a Hindu state. This need to be perceived as a secular state was especially important in keeping with the Indian National Congress's (INC) belief that a secular state could exist in the subcontinent and that there was no need to divide the country on a religious basis, or create Pakistan. According to Ramachandra Guha, the new Indian state viewed its commitment to secularism as an 'affirmation of it being, if it was anything at all, the Other of a theologically dogmatic and insular Pakistan'.[23]

In the aftermath of the assassination, Hindu communal organisations came under great political pressure from the state. The Hindu Mahasabha succumbed to the pressure and defined itself as a cultural organisation. The RSS was banned for more than a year, until it too submitted to the demands of the state. This conflict between the state and the Hindu communal organisations came to a head and was explicitly articulated during the Gandhi Murder Trial.

Jawaharlal Nehru sought to portray Hindu nationalism as an ideology equally dangerous to the country as Muslim nationalism. He blamed communalism[24] for the creation of Pakistan and the murder of Gandhi, and moved to discredit communalism within India. A few months after the murder of Gandhi he opined: 'Communalism resulted not only in the division of the country, which inflicted a deep wound in the heart of the people which will take a long time to heal if it ever heals but also the assassination of the Father of the Nation, Mahatma Gandhi.'[25]

---

21 *The Hindustan Times*, 19 November 1948.

22 *The Hindustan Times*, 2 December 1948.

23 Ramachandra Guha, *India after Gandhi: The History of the World's Largest Democracy* (London: Picador, 2008), 80.

24 Communalism is a term popularly used in South Asia to denote political ideologies based on communal (usually religious) interests, similar to sectarianism.

25 Speech made by Nehru in Coimbatore, 3 June 1948, quoted in Sucheta Mahajan, *Independence and Partition: The Erosion of Colonial Power in India* (New Delhi: Sage Publication, 2000), 316.

As the Indian state sought to establish its secular credentials, it took recourse to the iconic symbol of the Red Fort. Monuments play a key role in the creation of national history; they come to symbolise different rulers, empires and even civilisations. Maria Pelizzari argues that historic buildings play an important role 'in the imaginative process of nation formation', and in fact monuments may be 'reappropriated in the post colonial period to function as symbols of a new national identity'.[26] The secular state in India could not take recourse to religious symbols, and yet had to create a sacred iconography that represented the 'transcendental efficacy' of the state. Pelizzari applies Kajri Jain's work on the circulation of images that reified the state in calendar and bazaar art. Thus, she argues, '[T]he secular state in postcolonial India has constituted itself on the basis of a nationalist imaginary wherein power, including state power, partakes of a certain notion of sacred or transcendental efficacy'.[27]

Unlike religions and religious symbols which could easily denote both a past and a desired future, the 'secular state' was less rooted – it needed icons that could link it to the past and thus help create a transcendental efficacy. The Red Fort in Delhi – steeped in national history and yet devoid of explicit religious connotations – became the chosen monument to represent allegiance to a particular brand of Indian nationalism. 'Here the Mughal fort is just an attribute of this secular "god" – no longer a temporal indication of battles and colonial durbars but rather a sacred appendix for a national tale.'[28] This carefully cultivated icon of secularism was chosen by the Indian state to establish its secular credentials and to nip in the bud the communal ideology of the Hindu nationalists, including those who had murdered the 'father of the nation'.

Thus, we see that the Red Fort was deliberately chosen as the sight of the Gandhi Murder Trial because of the various symbolisms attached to it. All these different exemplifications of the Fort – as an emblem of state power and continuity, and an icon of secular nationalism – were very carefully utilised by the Indian state during the Gandhi Murder Trial.

Inside the Courtroom: Setting the Stage

Having analysed the building in which the courtroom was located, we move within the courtroom itself. I argue that the courtroom acts as a theatre, where in order to ensure an orderly display, the courtroom may privilege the eye of the spectator over most other considerations, including the witnesses' or defendants' ability to

---

26   Maria Pelizzari, 'From Stone to Paper: Photographs of Architecture and Traces of History', in *Traces of India: Photography, Architecture, and the Politics of Representation, 1850–1900*, edited by Maria Pelizzari (Montreal: Canadian Centre for Architecture, 2003), 24.

27   Kajri Jain quoted by Pelizzari, 'From Stone to Paper', 55–6.

28   Pelizzari, 'From Stone to Paper', 56.

participate in the trial. I then analyse the architecture of the courtroom, and the rituals employed within, to argue that each element of the trial process seeks to highlight the power of the judge and through her the power of the state.

Privileging the Ocular

In *To Kill a Mockingbird* Harper Lee describes the first day of Tom Robinson's trial as a 'gala occasion', where the courthouse square was filled with picnicking families, and a 'holiday mood' seemed to prevail.[29] This fictional account reflects the reality of the trial procedure, and as Sadakat Kadri explains, from the eighteenth century onwards courts were becoming more packed than ever, because 'trials simply offered a lot to see'.[30] The Gandhi Murder Trial was no exception; often the courtroom would be packed, and drinking water servers, with earthen pots balanced on their heads, and metal glasses in their hands, constantly moved around the courtroom serving the thirsty.[31] Perhaps nothing captures the idea of the courtroom as a theatre more than the fact that on the day that Godse started giving his testimony at the High Court in Shimla, 'house full'[32] signs were placed outside, so that other visitors would not enter the premises.

Any courtroom has two publics; the first is constituted by those who are physically present at the trial, and the second is the world outside. The visibility of justice is always aimed at these audiences rather than the defendants, and can sometimes even be at the cost of the defendant. As Otto Kirchheimer noted: '[C]arefully chosen segments of deviant political activity are submitted to court scrutiny, less for direct repressive effect than for dramatizing the struggle with the foe and rallying public support.'[33] During the Gandhi Murder Trial too, every attempt was made to expose the defendants to the eyes of the public, despite the fact that it may have jeopardised the trial process by compromising the identification procedures. The opening day proceedings of the Gandhi Murder Trial had been filmed and photographed not only by independent media organisations, but also the Films Division crew of All India Radio.[34] These images were then flashed across newspapers and were made part of the newsreels supplied by the government to cinema houses. Many of the accused questioned the decision to photograph and film them, and believed that it was detrimental to their case. For instance, in his Written Statement, Gopal Godse, Accused No. 6 and Nathuram's younger brother,

---

29   Harper Lee, *To Kill a Mockingbird* (London: Penguin Books, 1970), 163–4.

30   Sadakat Kadri, *The Trial: A History from Socrates to O.J. Simpson* (London: Harper Perennial, 2006), 95.

31   Tushar Gandhi, *'Let's Kill Gandhi!': A Chronicle of his Last Days, the Conspiracy, Murder, Investigation and Trial* (New Delhi: Rupa & Co., 2007), 538.

32   P.L. Inamdar, *The Story of the Red Fort Trial 1948–49* (Bombay: Popular Prakashan, 1979), 170.

33   Kirchheimer, *Political Justice*, 17.

34   Inamdar, *The Story of the Red Fort Trial 1948–49*, 23.

complained that the publicity provided to these images had 'greatly prejudiced the case of the accused ... on the point of identification'.[35] The accused and their counsel insisted that the prosecution witnesses had been able to identify them in the courtroom, not because they were eyewitnesses to the various actions of the accused, but because they had been shown the defendants' photographs and had been coached by the prosecution. This had led P.L. Inamdar, one of the defence lawyers, to conclude his cross-examination rather sarcastically, 'Maybe this special trial will be remembered for the incredible capacity for identification that hotel staff and railway staff possess!'[36]

This privileging of the eye of the audience is carried forward into other aspects of the trial as well. The axiom that justice needs to be seen to be done is taken quite literally within the courtroom setting. The visual spectacle takes precedence over other aspects including the audibility of the procedures. The public may not be able to hear what is happening, but they must be able to see it. On the first day of the Red Fort trial, the loud speaker installed in the courtroom was not functioning properly, as a result of which the visitors and the reporters were 'reduced to mere spectators; no one could hear what was being said either by the judge or by the lawyers'.[37] Inamdar constantly complained about Judge Atmacharan's habit of always pushing aside his microphone, and thus, being inaudible in the courtroom: 'Atma Charan's [sic] avoidance of the microphone often annoyed us. We could not hear what he dictated to the typist'.[38] The more sinister implication of this was that by choosing not to use the microphone, the Judge ensured his total control over the trial record. Which in turn gave the state even more control over this spectacular trial.

Power within the Courtroom

The courtroom is supposed to be an essentially public space. Its accessibility plays a large role in determining its legitimacy. However, the seemingly 'public' space of the courtroom is divided into a series of impenetrable private spheres; each actor has her place and is not allowed to enter the space of the other. The settings articulate the social and legal relations of each of the actors. Linda Mulcahy argues that the many divisions in the courtroom reveal 'an ongoing fear of the public as volatile and a need to stage manage the spectacle of the trial in a way which contains emotion, noise and movement'.[39] All of this is done with the view to maximise the power of the state within the courtroom.

---

35   National Archives of India: Private Papers; 27, Mahatma Gandhi Papers (1880–1948); 12.D, Gandhi Murder Trial Papers; File 26, Printed Records of Mahatma Gandhi Murder Case, Vol. II; Written Statement of Gopal Godse, Accused No. 6, Para 30.

36   Inamdar, *The Story of the Red Fort Trial 1948–49*, 71.

37   Gandhi, *'Let's Kill Gandhi!'*, 538.

38   Inamdar, *The Story of the Red Fort Trial 1948–49*, 159.

39   Mulcahy, *Legal Architecture*, 56.

The inside of the courtroom is as demonstrative of the power that it contains as the outside façade of the court structure. The idea that 'justice needs to be seen to be done' takes on a new dimension within the courtroom. According to Peter Goodrich, this axiom 'captures the paramount symbolic presence of law as a façade, a drama played out before the eyes of those subject to it'.[40] The drama of the courtroom is not a mere by-product of the legal process; rather it is integral to the belief that justice has been served. The conceptualisation of the courtroom or the trial setting as a depoliticised and neutral space not only limits our understanding of how law operates, it also acts as an obstacle to the proper understanding of the legal process. As Mulcahy explains, 'The shape of the courtroom, the configuration of walls and barriers, the heights of partitions within it, the positioning of tables, and even the choice of materials are crucial to a broader and more nuanced understanding of judgecraft'.[41] For instance, the position of each chair, the height of the floor, the placement of barriers, each and every element can be used as a physical manifestation of hierarchy and power.

In the courtroom of the Gandhi Murder Trial, Judge Atmacharan was seated on a platform, on one side was a witness box and opposite it was the dock within which the accused sat. On the side of the witness box sat the lawyers for the prosecution, while the defence counsel sat next to the accused.[42] The courtroom was neatly divided with the help of partitions into spaces that had to be occupied by particular actors. The accused were to sit in the docks, surrounded by bars – a very explicit representation of the bars of prison. This 'incarceration' within the courtroom also acts as a visual marker of the danger that the defendants present to others in the courtroom, and undermines the accused's ability to engage in the trial process.[43]

The Judge occupied an elevated space, from where he faced the rest of the room. Hannah Arendt's description of the judges' position within the courtroom during the Eichmann Trial in Israel finds an apt example in the Gandhi Murder Trial, as indeed it would for most criminal trials: '[N]o matter how consistently the judges shunned the limelight, there they were, seated at the top of the raised platform, facing the audience as from the stage in a play.'[44] In the Gandhi Murder Trial, the judge was the only person who had an uninterrupted view of all the participants including the public; this ability to survey all people at all times embodied in many ways Foucault's idea of the panoptic. The architecture of the

---

40 Peter Goodrich, *Languages of Law: From Logics of Memory to Nomadic Masks* (London: Weidenfeld & Nicolson, 1990), 188.

41 Linda Mulcahy, 'Architects of Justice: the Politics of Courtroom Design', *Social and Legal Studies* 16 (2007): 384.

42 Jagdishchandra Jain, *I Could Not Save Bapu* (Benares: Jagran Sahitya Mandir, 1949), 61.

43 Mulcahy, *Legal Architecture*, 10.

44 Hannah Arendt, *Eichmann in Jerusalem: A Report on the Banality of Evil* (London: Penguin Books, 2006), 6.

courtroom enables the segregation and surveillance of the actors in such a way that 'the exercise of power is not added from the outside but is subtly present in ways which increase its efficiency'.[45]

Not only do the different actors access different and discrete spaces within the courtroom, they also use different entrances into the arena. As Mulcahy writes, 'By controlling movements the judiciary and court staff can contain exchanges, restrict the potential for spontaneous outbursts or meetings and increase the dramatic impact of arrival within the courtroom'.[46] The courtroom provides the stage upon which the theatre of the trial unfolds. The separate entrances ensure that the tension within the participants can only be vented within the courtroom, thus adding a greater element of drama to each of their meetings.

There are separate and cued entrances, and on the trial stage each actor has a predetermined spot and all actions are choreographed. As Arendt notes: 'The proceedings happen on a stage before an audience, with the usher's marvellous shout at the beginning of each session producing the effect of the rising curtain.'[47] However, it is not just the physical appearance of the courtroom that lends itself to theatricality, rather this theatricality is built into the process of the trial itself. There is a 'performativity of the courtroom',[48] a structural imperative that at each moment reminds the speakers – the judge, the defendant, lawyers and witnesses – that they are in fact talking in front of an audience.

As we saw in the section above, law seeks to underscore its magnificence by employing grandiose buildings. But what happens if the building itself lacks the necessary stature? In those cases we see that law relies on its other important visual component, i.e., the courtroom ritual. The pomp and power of the court is highlighted by the rituals employed within the courtroom. The court organises its operations in a highly spectacular and visual manner. Costas Douzinas argues that the 'power of spiritual, edifying icons' is present in each courtroom. It is manifested in the robes, the wigs, the staffs and other 'theatrical paraphernalia of legal performance'.[49] Justice G.D. Khosla, one of the judges who presided over the appeal against the Special Court judgment at Shimla, describes the pomp of the High Court trial. The partition of India had left the state of Punjab in deep turmoil, and many of the judges of the Punjab High Court had also been victims of partition. As they had moved from Lahore to the Indian part of Punjab, the judges had not necessarily carried their fineries with them. As a result of this, for over 18 months, the court had been held at the ex-Viceregal Residence, known as

---

45   Mulcahy, 'Architects of Justice', 399.

46   Ibid., 389.

47   Arendt, *Eichmann in Jerusalem*, 4.

48   Martha Umphrey, 'Fragile Performances: The Dialogics of Judgement in "A Theory of the Trial"', *Law and Social Enquiry* 28 (2003): 530.

49   Costas Douzinas, 'The Legality of the Image', *The Modern Law Review* 63 (2000): 815.

Peterhoff[50] in Shimla, with relaxed dress regulations. However, as Justice Khosla states, the elaborate costumes were brought back in full force for the appeal trial. 'We decided that as a special measure we should resume the old practice of wearing wigs, and that on our entry into the court-room we should, as in the olden days, be preceded by our liveried ushers carrying silver mounted staffs.'[51] The ballroom, which had been hastily converted into a courtroom, also enhanced the spectacle. Khosla's account reveals how the judges were aware of the intimidating and spectacular qualities of the rituals employed, and how they went out of their way to use such rituals in the Gandhi Murder Trial in order to impress upon the public the gravity of the situation.

This blatant show of power can be more than a little intimidating for the defendant, who has the most to gain or lose from the trial process. In her study of a magistrate's court in London, Pat Carlen found that the staging of such rituals '*in itself* infuses the proceedings with a surreality which atrophies defendants' abilities to participate in them'.[52] Thus, the spatial dynamics of the courtroom are of concern to us, because they have a considerable effect on the level of comfort that an actor experiences in the courtroom, and thus also exert an influence on the kind of evidence that she provides. Since, this evidence in turn becomes 'the basis on which judgments are made and the confidence that the public have in the process of adjudication',[53] it is key to ensure that the defendant is not unduly intimidated by the courtroom and its rituals.

Thus, we have seen that the theatre of the court can privilege the eye of the spectator over the defendant's ability to give evidence. In addition to this, the architecture of the courtroom lends itself to a surveillance and control of all visitors. All these factors may intimidate a witness/defendant, which in turn may affect the trust the court places in their testimony. However, all these conditions must not lead us to assume the complete domination of the trial process by the state; despite the power imbalance, there is room for subversion within the trial. As we shall see in the next section, political defendants are often aware of this, and seek to take advantage of it.

---

50   Peterhoff continued to serve as the Punjab High Court until 1955. Later, after the creation of Himachal Pradesh it was designated as the Raj Bhawan or the Residence of the Chief Minister. In 1998, the Himachal Pradesh Tourism Development Corporation turned it into a heritage hotel. Today, the Himachal Pradesh government is contemplating turning the hotel into a museum, and to recreate the trial within its premises. 'Himachal Pradesh Government Mulls Turning Nathuram Godse Trial Venue into Tourist Attraction', *DNA*, 31 January 2010.

51   G.D. Khosla, *The Murder of the Mahatma: And Other Cases from a Judge's Notebook* (London: Chatto & Windus, 1963), 211.

52   Pat Carlen, *Magistrates' Justice* (London: Martin Robertson, 1976), 19. Emphasis in original.

53   Mulcahy, 'Architects of Justice', 384.

Subversion of Power

Despite the inbuilt theatricality of the court and the power hierarchies that are at play inside the trial arena, the actual trial – in a democratic state – can never be entirely predetermined, and thus there is always room for subversion of power within the courtroom. The state may initially instigate the spectacular trial, but sometimes the turn that the trial takes may surprise the state itself. These are the trials in which the defendant takes the opportunity to make a political point. In contrast to the state-oriented view of political trials which claims that such trials are entirely orchestrated by the state, some theorists argue that political trials can be defined as political only if the defendant chooses to make a political point in the trial. For instance, Richard Uviller defines a political trial not by the role of the state, but the actions of the defendants. He argues, 'defendants and their counsel are using the trial for political ends; and are attempting to make the trial a political event'.[54]

Ronald Sokol reiterates the view that defendants in political trials are not just aware of the power potential of the trial, they actively try and manipulate it: 'The political defendant, far more than the usual accused, wants to be tried, wants to use the courtroom as a stage to dramatize his views and, perhaps ultimately, his execution as a final invocation to disciples and would-be disciples.' By appearing in court the political defendant gains '[a] stage, attention, care, an immediate physical audience, a larger audience not present, notoriety, perhaps fame, perhaps immortality. Today his potential audience is global'.[55] Thus the spectacular nature of the political trial is sought both by the state and the defendant, and thus, can never entirely be orchestrated by the former.

As famous assassins, such as Soghomon Tehlirian and Shalom Schwartzbard, had done before him, Godse made no attempt to run away after the shooting. In all these cases, the defendant was aware that while the act of killing expresses disagreement, it does not explain the reasons behind it. The killers want to be tried in court where they could debate with the state's opinion and prove that their stance was better, thus justifying their actions. In his statement before the police, Vishnu Karkare, Accused No. 3, explained why Nathuram Godse chose to kill Gandhi alone. The most important reason was the fact that Godse believed that 'he was an orator and writer and he would be in a position to impress upon the Government and the Court as to why he had killed Ganhiji [*sic*]'.[56]

---

54 Uviller's statement to Special Committee on Courtroom Conduct (1970–73), quoted in Norman Dorsen and Leon Friedman, *Disorder in the Court: Report of the Association of the Bar of the City of New York, Special Committee on Courtroom Conduct* (New York: Pantheon Books, 1973), 78.

55 Ronald Sokol, 'The Political Trial: Courtroom as Stage, History as Critic', *New Literary History* 2 (1971): 502.

56 National Archives of India: Private Papers; 27, Mahatma Gandhi Papers

Godse himself acknowledged this fact when, during the trial, he explained his actions immediately following the assassination, and the rationale behind them. 'I did not make any attempt to run away; in fact I never entertained any idea of running away. I did not try to shoot myself. It was never my intention to do so, for, it was my ardent desire to give vent to my thoughts in an open Court.'[57]

Even before he began speaking the prosecution objected to the reading of the entire statement of Godse, because they believed that large parts of it were irrelevant to the case. In fact, almost two-thirds of Godse's 93-page Written Statement dealt exclusively with Gandhi's ideology and his participation in Indian politics, and about Godse's relations (or lack thereof) with the rest of the accused, and only a minor portion focused on the murder itself. For these reasons, after Godse finished reading his statement the Chief Prosecutor, C.K. Daphtary, once again raised objections to the statement, and requested that since parts of it were inconsequential they should not be incorporated into the court's records. However, Atmacharan declared that parts of a Written Statement could not be deleted.

This rule, which promised the sanctity of the Written Statement, was successfully used by the defence to their advantage. The defendants had chosen to not bring any witnesses to the stand, and all the accused (except for Kistayya[58]) chose to read aloud their Written Statements. This allowed the defence counsel to minutely construct these Written Statements; for instance the use of terms such as 'the Prosecution is *ab initio* void'[59] in Karkare's statement show the clear influence of the defence counsel on the Written Statements of the accused. These carefully constructed Written Statements were then placed in their entirety on the court records for posterity.

During the appeal in the High Court, Godse had made a plea of poverty and based on this he requested that he be allowed to appear in person during the appeal trial. As a result of this, Godse was the only accused who was present during the trial at Shimla. As Justice G.D. Khosla, one of the three judges of the Appeal Court says, this request was only an excuse; in reality, Godse wanted to be present at the trial because he wanted 'to exhibit himself as a fearless patriot and a passionate protagonist of Hindu ideology'.[60] This becomes even more evident when we factor in the detail that Godse was not even challenging his death sentence during

---

(1880–1948); 12.D, Gandhi Murder Trial Papers; File 23, Statement of Accused in Original; Statement of Vishnu R. Karkare, p. 58.

57 National Archives of India: Private Papers; 27, Mahatma Gandhi Papers (1880–1948); 12.D, Gandhi Murder Trial Papers; File 26, Printed Records of Mahatma Gandhi Murder Case, Vol. II; Written Statement of Nathuram Godse, Accused No. 1, Para 149.

58 Kistayya could neither read nor write.

59 National Archives of India: Private Papers; 27, Mahatma Gandhi Papers (1880–1948); 12.D, Gandhi Murder Trial Papers; File 26, Printed Records of Mahatma Gandhi Murder Case, Vol. II; Written Statement of V.R. Karkare, Accused No. 3, Para 5. Italics in original.

60 Khosla, *The Murder of the Mahatma*, 214.

the appeal, all that he was challenging was the accusation of the existence of a conspiracy which involved all the other accused.

Godse's estimations of his own skills as an orator were not entirely exaggerated. According to Justice Khosla's account of the appeal trial, during Godse's speech:

> The audience was visibly and audibly moved. There was a deep silence when he ceased speaking. Many women were in tears and men were coughing and searching for their handkerchiefs. The silence was accentuated and made deeper by the sound of a[n] occasional subdued sniff or a muffled cough. It seemed to me that I was taking part in some kind of melodrama or in a scene out of a Hollywood feature film.

He goes on to say, 'the audience most certainly thought that Godse's performance was the only worth-while part of the lengthy proceedings'.[61] Khosla concludes by saying that he had 'no doubt that had the audience of that day been constituted into a jury and entrusted with the task of deciding Godse's appeal, they would have brought in a verdict of "not guilty" by an overwhelming majority'.[62]

Gopal Godse too vouched for the power of this speech, he added that after Nathuram had finished speaking and 'as soon as the judges returned to their chamber, the police pounced on the correspondents and snatched their notebooks. They did not stop at that. They tore down the note books into pieces and warned the pressmen on severe consequences if they published the true account of Nathuram's speech'.[63] The speech sought to undermine the legitimacy of the Indian state, and was so powerful that in a knee-jerk reaction the government of India banned the publication of Nathuram Godse's statement in an attempt to limit its spread.[64]

Another defendant who attempted to subvert the power structures in the courtroom was Accused No. 7, V.D. Savarkar. As a trained lawyer, Savarkar was aware of the iconology of the court and the trial syntax, and he deliberately sought to undermine the court's control on the visual displays within the courtroom; his subsequent acquittal proves his success to some extent. On the first day of the trial, the press was allowed to take pictures of the accused sitting in the docks. Savarkar complained against this act, and he insisted that he had not given permission to be photographed along with the others. Through his lawyer, L.B. Bhopatkar, he requested that because of his ill health he should be allowed to sit in a chair, and not on the benches occupied by the rest of the accused. The court accepted this

---

61 Khosla, *The Murder of the Mahatma*, 243.

62 Ibid.

63 Gopal Godse, 'Events and Accused', in Nathuram Godse, *May it Please Your Honour*, edited by Gopal Godse (New Delhi: Surya Bharti Prakashan, 2007), 26.

64 Dissemination of the speech in any form was banned until the 1960s; the ban only fuelled its popularity and the speech enjoyed wide underground circulation. After Gopal Godse was released from prison, he challenged the ban in the Bombay High Court in 1968, and the ban was finally revoked in 1970.

request. For the duration of the case, Savarkar sat outside the dock. This served to visibly separate him from the rest of the accused. In an arena where the physical space occupied by the actor is a signifier of their position within the courtroom, Savarkar's presence outside the dock spoke volumes. Robert Payne attributes this differential seating to Savarkar's attempt to portray that not only was he different from the other accused, but also that as a respectable man of the society he was in danger from their uncouth presence. 'He sat alone ... as though he felt the need to be protected by a body guard'.[65] The description of the courtroom provided by P.L. Inamdar, of the defence counsel, adds another element to this incident. According to him, Savarkar sat on a 'Law Chair' which he positioned in such a way that it was not only outside the dock but was also 'nearest to the Court'.[66] Thus, not only had Savarkar distanced himself from the accused, he had also attempted to infringe on the space that was traditionally occupied by the defence lawyers, thereby attempting to portray his superiority over the other accused.

Thus, we see that both Godse and Savarkar were – to different degrees – able to subvert the power structures of the Gandhi murder trial. Godse made use of the spectacular trial to further his own ideology, and even before the assassination, he was banking on the opportunity to present his case in the trial. Savarkar was more aware of the visual symbolisms of the court, and was able to visibly distinguish himself from the other defendants. In this process, he was able to successfully challenge the image that the state sought to create of him through the trial process.

This attempted subversion of the trial process raises important questions for the political trial. What happens if the participants refuse to follow the script set by the state? In his study of power and propaganda in seventeenth-century Spain, J.H. Elliott highlights the fact that the state's propaganda can only be successful as long as it is believed to be rooted in reality. When an insurmountable and obvious gulf opens between reality and the rhetoric, it gives rise to a credibility gap;[67] this is exactly the gap within which defendants of modern spectacular trials seek to place themselves. The defendants attempt to reconfigure the rituals within the courtroom, by refusing to accept the visual practices of the state – such as Savarkar's attempt to distance himself from the rest of the accused, or by ensuring that their statements are recorded in their entirety within the trial records – as Godse did with his Written Statement. Such practices allow the defendants to leave their imprint on the trial stage, and make the audience doubt the state's version of reality, thus partially subverting the spectacular trial.

---

65   Robert Payne, *The Life and Death of Mahatma Gandhi* (London: The Bodley Head, 1969), 615.

66   Inamdar, *The Story of the Red Fort Trial 1948–49*, 141.

67   J.H. Elliott, 'Power and Propaganda in the Spain of Philip IV', in *Rites of Power: Symbolism, Ritual, and Politics Since the Middle Ages*, edited by Sean Wilentz (Philadelphia: University of Philadelphia Press, 1985), 171.

Conclusion

Law enjoys a closely intertwined relation with the visual; this relation becomes very apparent in political trials, which tend to highlight the spectacular dimensions of law and the state. During the Gandhi Murder Trial, we saw that the state carefully selected each visual marker of the trial – from the building where the court was located, to the organisation of the courtroom itself. Since such trials are organised with the audience in mind, each icon used is replete with symbolism. For instance the Red Fort symbolised a continuity and legitimacy of the Indian state, and thus underscored the authority of the new post-colonial government. In addition, the Fort acted as a symbol of India's syncretic culture and the new state's secular ambitions, and this symbolism was used to counteract the threat posed by Hindu nationalist ideology within the country.

Within the courtroom, every attempt was made to ensure that the proceedings were aimed towards the external audience of the trial and not those within the courtroom. Courtroom architecture and the pomp of the rituals used were carefully selected to impress upon the viewers the importance of the trial and the power of the state. Yet, despite its meticulously planned symbolism, the political trial remains vulnerable to attempted subversions by the defendants. A spectacular trial is only worth the credibility that its audience is willing to lend to it. It is exactly this credibility that the political defendant seeks to attack, and by widening the gap between reality and the state's rhetoric, they attempt to usurp the power of the spectacular event. Thus, we find that Godse was able to air his views against the Indian state within the courtroom; his speech was so persuasive that the government felt compelled to ban it, and in the process managed to harm the legitimacy it has so painstakingly tried to create through the spectacular trial.

Index